Television Production

Fourteenth Edition

GERALD MILLERSON

JIM OWENS
Asbury College

ELSEVIER

AMSTERDAM • BOSTON • HEIDELBERG • LONDON
NEW YORK • OXFORD • PARIS • SAN DIEGO
SAN FRANCISCO • SINGAPORE • SYDNEY • TOKYO

Focal Press is an imprint of Elsevier.

Focal
Press

Focal Press is an imprint of Elsevier
30 Corporate Drive, Suite 400, Burlington, MA 01803, USA
Linacre House, Jordan Hill, Oxford OX2 8DP, UK

Library of Congress Cataloging-in-Publication Data
Millerson, Gerald.
   Television production / Gerald Millerson, Jim Owens.—14th ed.
      p. cm.
Includes index.
ISBN 978-0-240-52078-0 (pbk. : alk. paper)
 1. Television—Production and direction. I. Owens, Jim, 1957 – II. Title.
PN1992.75.M5 2009
791.4502'32—dc22

                      2009014147

British Library Cataloguing-in-Publication Data

A catalogue record for this book is available from the British Library.

ISBN: 978-0-240-52078-0

For information on all Focal Press publications
visit our website at www.books.elsevier.com

09 10 11 12 5 4 3 2 1

Printed in Canada

Typeset by: diacriTech, Chennai, India

Television Production

Dedicated to my wife, Lynn, and my daughter, Sarah

CONTENTS

vii

PART 2 • The Process, Script, and Production Plan

ix

CONTENTS

x

xi

PART 5 • Recording and Editing the Production

PART 7 • Engineering

An incredible number of people and organizations contributed to this project. I have tried to list most of them below. I am especially grateful to Asbury College, my school, which has allowed me the flexibility as well as encouraged me to stay involved in professional television production around the world.

The editors at Focal Press have been a constant encouragement, guiding me through the writing process: Elinor Actipis and Michele Cronin.

I appreciate the reviewers who spent a significant amount of time reviewing the manuscripts and providing guidance: Joey Goodsell (University of Southern Mississippi), Trevor Hearing (University of Bournemouth), Tom Kingdon (Emerson College), Alan Lifton (University of Sunderland), Dustin Morrow (Temple University), and Larry Scher (Rio Hondo College).

Contributors of photographs, illustrations, and advice: 20th Century Fox , Will Adams, Alan Gordon Enterprises, Alfacam, Apple, Asbury College, Audio-Technica, Avanti Group, Avid, BandPro, Greg Bandy, Dennis Baxter, BBC, Bexel, Tristan Bresnen, Austin Brooks, K Brown, Kathy Bruner, Whit Bussey, Jen Canal, Canon, Carr-Hughes Productions, CBC, Charter, Chyron, David Clement, Core Sound, Dominic Cicchetti, Kistof Creative, Paul Clatworthy, Compix, Countryman Associates, Bernard Custadio, Jon Cypher, Guillaume Dargaud, Dartfish, Datavideo, Jeff Day, DDD, Demon Fisheye Lens, Discovery Channel, Doremi, Paul Dupree, Brian Douglas, ESPN, David Eubank, Kevin Ferrara, Fifteenhundred, Fischer Connectors, Firestore, Focus Enhancements, FX Group/fxgroup.tv, Sean Franklin, Jeff Giblin, Matt Giblin, Mike Gilger, Douglas Glover, Jessica Goodall, Grass Valley, Jon Greenhoe, David Grosz, *Highdef* magazine, Matt Hogancamp, Holophone, Hoodman, Jeff Hutchens, Imagine Products, Indie-Dolly Systems, International Sports Broadcasting, Russ Jennisch, JVC, KOMU-TV, Hank Levine, Litepanels, Lowell, LPG, Manfrotto, Jim Mickle, Gary Milkis, Ben Miller, Don Mink, Shannon Mizell, MobiTV, Mole Richardson, Thom Moynahan, Brady and Andrea Nasfell, NBC, NHK, North Shore Studios, Olympic Broadcast Services, Lynn Owens, Sarah Owens, Panasonic, Andy Peters, Lee Peters, P+S Technik, Red Digital Cinema Camera Company, Ben Rogers, Scott Rohrer, Rosco, Kristin Ross, Mike Rowe, George Ruhe, Devon Salyer, Megan Scott, Sarah Seaton, Sennheiser, Josh Sheppard, Shure, Sodium Entertainment, Sony, Doug Smart, Steadicam, Mark Stokl, Strand, *Studio* magazine, Ben Taber, Josh Taber, Jennie Taylor, Tektronix, Thomson, Cherie A. Thurlby, Tiffen, *TV Technology* magazine, Uniset, U.S. Department of Defense, U.S. Navy, VFGadgets, Videosmith, Taylor Vinson, Vinten, Vortex Media, Nathan Waggoner, Doug Walker, Wescott, Adam Wilt, Adam Wilson, WLEX-TV, Luke Wertz, WOOD TV8, WOTV4 and WXSP, YouTube, Tyler Young, and Zeiss.

StoryBoard Quick was used for some illustrations: © PowerProduction Software.

"Storytelling is the most powerful way to put ideas into the world today."
Robert McAfee Brown

Changing Television

Although television technology is rapidly changing, you have to keep in mind that storytelling is still the key to a good television program: whether it is narrative, news, sports, or comedy, it always comes down to the story. Technology is very important, but it really is there only to help tell and support the storyline.

The change in the paradigms of television production has occurred quickly over the past few years and continues at warp speed. Originally, most productions took place in a studio with few shots created outside of those confines. Production was highly expensive and only a few select people got to work on those shows. Today, the majority of productions are taking place outside of the traditional studio and the transmission methods have expanded far beyond the standard television box to the Internet, iPods, cell phones, and large screens. The low cost of equipment and transmission has brought incredible technology into the hands of almost everyone, allowing a student to use his or her camera and editing software to create a production that can be watched by millions on the Internet.

What we are finding is that the various media are not really competing with each other. Instead, when done well, these media can support one another. When traveling, you look at your phone; when at the office, you check out television programming on the Web; when you want the highest-quality viewing, you watch a large-screen television in the comfort of your home.

What Is This Book About?

Many saw the future of television as HDTV on large screens in homes. Few predicted that while many countries were in the process of transitioning to the high quality of HDTV, there would also be an incredible demand for highly compressed (and thus lower-quality) video images that could be seen on cell phones, iPods, and the Internet. Although all of the related technologies are very important, we will be focusing on how to create quality video productions. We will spend very little time working through how to compress video or the specifics of various types of cameras and editing software. We will be dealing with the overall areas. For the specifics, you will have to read the instruction manuals that come with the equipment or software.

Though our goal is to focus on the creation of programs, we are in the awkward position of bridging the transition between old and new techniques and technologies. The chapters in this book have been laid out in a logical manner, starting with the foundations of television. These foundations include an overview of the industry, a discussion about the role of the various crewmembers, a look at production equipment and facilities, and a review of how television works. Once we understand what the crew does and how the equipment works together, Part 2 covers the production process and scripting. Parts 3–5 cover the various components of the production such as the camera, graphics, lighting, backgrounds, makeup, audio, recording, and editing. Part 6 covers many of the specific production techniques that are used today in the creation of programs, and Part 7 deals with engineering.

In an effort to make the various production aspects more understandable, we have added hundreds of full-color illustrations, updated the equipment and techniques areas, added new distribution methods, and made teaching resources available for faculty. Qualified instructors may access the teaching resources at http://textbooks.elsevier.com.

We have created this book in the hopes of helping you get prepared to create quality programming, whether you're using high-end professional equipment or your parent's camcorder. We want to equip you to work in a variety of situations (news, documentary, sports, narrative, comedy, and so on), as well as to use different distribution methods (Internet, broadcast, PDA, I-mag, or others). We want you to get the best out of your equipment, creating projects that have a significant impact on your audience.

Ultimately, production is not a matter of knowing "which buttons to press," but how to use your tools creatively. We hope you will discover how the techniques you use can influence and persuade your audience, hold their attention, develop their interest, and influence and kindle their emotions. For example, when your subject moves, should you move the camera to follow along, widen the lens's coverage, or cut to another camera angle? It matters which methods you choose, because each one will have a different impact on your audience.

Who Is This Book For?

This book was created for anyone who wants to create quality video productions. It is for students and beginning professionals alike. We do not assume that you have previous production experience, yet the content is deep enough that beginning professionals can profit from it. Many times, we have used photographs and illustrations from the highest levels of production. The goal is to give you examples that you can adapt to any level at which you are working.

Terminology

The majority of the terms that we use are the most common in the United States. However, as our industry becomes more global, we decided that it was important to also place the European terms in parentheses next to some of the the U.S. terms.

Summary

The story is the key to quality programs, but it is essential that you understand what is required to produce the story. You may not be required to know the features of every piece of equipment, but you do need to understand enough about the equipment that you know how to use it to creatively tell your story. The bottom line is that it all comes down to you, not the equipment.

Jim Owens, April 2009

PART 1

The Foundations of Television Production

CHAPTER 1

An Overview of Television Production

"I believe that good television can make our world a better place."

Christiane Amanpour, CNN Reporter

Terms

DVE: Digital video effect equipment, working with the switcher, is used to create special effects between video images. A DVE could also refer to the actual effect.

Linear editing: The copying, or dubbing, of segments from the master tape to another tape in sequential order.

Nonlinear editing: The process in which the recorded video is digitized (copied) onto a computer. Then the footage can be arranged and rearranged, special effects and graphics can be added, and the audio can be adjusted using editing software.

Prosumer equipment: Prosumer equipment, sometimes known as *industrial equipment*, is a little heavier-duty and sometimes employs a few professional features (such as interchangeable lenses on a camera), but may still have many of the automatic features that are included on the consumer equipment.

Switcher (vision mixer): Used to switch between video inputs (cameras, graphics, video players, etc.)

Teleprompter: A device that projects computer-generated text onto a piece of reflective glass over the lens of the camera. It is designed to allow talent to read a script while looking directly at the camera.

3

"The definition of television is changing. Let's take an iPod, which was an MP3 device a short time ago. When you put video on that device, it becomes a television. So I make the case that television is actually growing to other devices. It's because of the programming, it's the quality, it's the story line. It's all those things we associate with television programming. 'Television' was never the box—it was the programming that was on the box."

Chris Pizzuro, Vice President of Digital News Media, Turner Entertainment

TELEVISION PRODUCTION

Although the television medium has experienced transforming technical changes in the past few years, it is important to keep in mind that the key to great television is still storytelling. As equipment has evolved and become increasingly adaptable, production techniques have also evolved in order to take advantage of new opportunities.

Equipment Has Become Simpler to Use

You've probably already discovered how even inexpensive consumer high-definition (HD) camcorders can produce extremely detailed images under a wide range of conditions (Figure 1.1). Camera circuitry automatically adjusts and compensates to give you the best picture. A photographer needs to do little more than point the camera, follow the subject, and zoom in and out. To pick up audio, we can simply clip a small lavaliere microphone onto a person's jacket, give them a handheld microphone, or just use the microphone attached to the camera. As for lighting, today's cameras are so sensitive that they work in daylight or whatever artificial light happens to be around. So where's the mystery? Why do we need to study television/video techniques? Today, anyone can get results.

The Illusion of Reality

"You must use the camera and microphone to produce what the brain perceives, not merely what the eye sees. Only then can you create the illusion of reality."
Roone Arledge, Former Producer, ABC Television

4

FIGURE 1.1
Consumer HD camcorders provide an incredible amount of quality, which is now available to the amateur. (Photo courtesy of JVC)

One of the basic truths about photography, television, and film is that the camera always lies. On the face of it, it's reasonable to assume that if you simply point your camera and microphone at the scene, you will convey an accurate record of the action to your audience. But as we shall see, in practice the camera and microphone inherently transform "reality."

There can be considerable differences between what is actually happening, what your viewers are seeing, and what they think they are seeing. How the audience interprets space, dimension, atmosphere, time, and so on will depend on a number of factors, such as the camera's position, the lens angle, lighting, editing, the accompanying sound, and, of course, their own personal experience.

We can use this gap between the actual and the apparent to our advantage. It allows us to deliberately select and arrange each shot to affect an audience in a specific way. It gives us the opportunity to devise different types of persuasive and economical production techniques.

If a scene looks "real," the audience will invariably accept it as such. When watching a film, the audience will still respond by sitting on the edge of their seats to dramatic situations. Even though they know that the character hanging from the cliff is really safe and is accompanied by a nearby production crew, it does not override their suspended disbelief.

Even if you put together a disjointed series of totally unrelated shots, your audience will still attempt to rationalize and interpret what they are seeing. (Some pop videos and experimental films rely heavily on this fact to sustain interest.) If you use a camera casually, the images will still unpredictably influence your audience. Generally speaking, careless or inappropriate production techniques will usually be confusing, puzzling, and a bore to watch. The show will lack a logical and consistent form. Systematic techniques are a must if you want to catch and hold audience attention and interest.

Television versus New Media

"I would like to try to clarify the question of terminology, particularly the term 'new media.' How can we distinguish 'television' from 'new media'? The distinction is linear service or nonlinear service.

"Traditionally, television has been a linear service, that is, the broadcasting of a program service where the supplier decides on the moment those programs will be offered to the public no matter the distribution platform used.

"On the other hand, the nonlinear services equal the new media, which means making video available for on-demand delivery using any distribution platform.

"It is the demand that makes the difference."
Jean Réveillon, General Secretary of the European Broadcasting Union

It's Not Just Academic

At first thought, learning about television production would seem to be just a matter of mastering the basic equipment mechanics. But let's think for a moment. How often have you heard two people play the same piece of music yet achieve entirely different results? The first instrumentalist may hit all the right notes but the performance may sound dull and uninteresting. The second musician's more sensitive approach stirs our emotions with memorable sound.

Of course, we could simply assume that the second musician had greater talent. But this "talent" generally comes from painstaking study and effective techniques. Experience alone is not enough—especially if it perpetuates incorrect methods. Even quite subtle differences can influence the quality and impact of a performance. You'll find parallel situations in television production practices.

Techniques Will Tell

It's common for three directors to shoot the same action, and yet produce quite diverse results:

- In a "shooting by numbers" approach the first director may show us everything that's going on, but follow a dull routine: the same old wide shot to begin with, followed by close-up shots of whoever is speaking, with intercut "reaction" shots of the listener.
- The second director is busy getting "unusual" shots that actually distract us from the subject itself.
- The third director's smooth sequence of shots somehow manages to create an interesting, attention-grabbing program. The audience feels involved in what is going on.

Clearly, it's not simply a matter of pointing the camera and staying in focus.

Similarly, two different people can light the same setting. The first person illuminates the scene clearly enough, but the second somehow manages to build a persuasive atmospheric effect that enhances the show's appeal. These are the kinds of subtleties you will learn about as we explore techniques.

Having the Edge

Working conditions have changed considerably over the years. Earlier equipment often required the user to have technical understanding to operate it effectively and keep it working. Some of the jobs on the production crew camera, audio, lighting, videotape operation, and editing were all handled by engineers who specialized in that specific area.

In today's highly competitive industry, in which equipment is increasingly reliable and operation is simplified, there is a growing use of multitasking. Individuals need to acquire a variety of skills, rather than specialize in one specific skill or craft. Also, instead of permanent

FIGURE 1.2

Laptop computers allow an editor to create programming anywhere.

in-house production crews, the trend is to use freelance operators on short-term contracts for maximum economy and flexibility. Now it's even possible for a single person to go out on location with a lightweight camera, record the images and sound, use a laptop computer system to edit the results, and return with a complete program ready to put on the air (Figure 1.2).

The person with greater know-how and adaptability has an edge. Job opportunities vary considerably. The person who specializes in a single craft can develop specific aptitudes in that field. However, the person who can operate a camera today, light a set tomorrow, and subsequently handle the sound has more opportunities in today's market.

Although a single person can accomplish many roles, television still relies on teamwork. Results depend not only on each person knowing their own job, but also on their understanding of what others are aiming to do. In many shows for which the action is live or cannot be repeated, there is only one opportunity, and if that is lost—if, for instance, a camera operator misses the shot—not only will that one shot be substandard, but the whole show can be affected.

Studying this book will give you a number of major advantages:

- By taking the trouble to understand the fundamentals of the equipment that you are using, you'll be able to rapidly assimilate and adapt when new gear comes along. After that, it's just a matter of discovering any operational differences, or different features, and so on.
- It will help you to anticipate problems and avoid problems before they happen.
- When unexpected difficulties arise, as they inevitably will at some point, you will recognize them and quickly compensate. For example, when the talent has a weak voice, you may be able to tighten the shot a little to allow the sound boom to come a little closer without getting into the shot.

OVERVIEW

Before we begin our journey, let's take an overview of the terrain we will be covering. This will help to familiarize you with the areas that you are going to have to deal with and give a general idea of how they interrelate.

Organization

Although organizational basics follow a recognizable pattern for all types of television production, the actual format the director uses will always be influenced by such factors as the following:

- Whether the production is taking place in a studio or on location.
- Whether it is to be transmitted live or recorded for transmission later.
- Whether the action can be repeated (to correct errors, adjust shots) or is a one-time opportunity that has to be captured the first time around.
- Any restrictions due to shortage of time, equipment limitations, space problems, and so on.
- How the director decides to shoot the action (camera viewpoints, shot changes, and so on).
- Whether there is an audience.

In some situations, a multicamera setup is the best solution for shooting the action effectively. (This is when the cameras are controlled by a production team in a separate control room.) At other times, the director may choose to stand beside a single camera, guiding each shot from a nearby video monitor (Figure 1.3).

PLANNING AND PERFORMANCE

In order to create a smooth-flowing live television production, the director needs to understand the event; for example, what is going to happen next, where people are going to stand, what they are going to do, their moves, what they are going to say, and so on. Although there will be situations in which the director has no option but to extemporize and select shots spontaneously, quality results are more likely when action and camera treatment are planned in advance.

FIGURE 1.3
Directors using a single camera often guide the shot by viewing the camera image on a monitor.

In more complex productions, it is usually necessary for performers and crews to work following a production schedule, which is based on the script. This serves as a regulatory framework throughout the show. Action and dialogue are rehearsed to allow the production team to check their camera shots, lighting, set sound levels, rehearse cues, and so on. These rehearsals give the crew a chance to see what the director is going to do. They also allow the director to see what does or does not work. In a drama production, actors have usually memorized all their dialogue (learned their lines), and every word and move is rehearsed before the actual shoot begins.

However, in many productions, the talent does not have the time or opportunity to remember a detailed prepared script. Instead, they read their lines from a teleprompter, which displays the script in front of the camera lens (Figure 1.4). In addition, talent may also be guided by instructions or advice picked up on an inconspicuous earpiece; this is typically done in newscasts, magazine programs, and similar productions.

SHOOTING THE ACTION

You can shoot action in several ways:
- As a continuous process (live-to-tape), recording everything that happens.
- Dividing the total action into a series of separately recorded sequences (scenes or acts).
- Analyzing each action sequence, putting them into a series of separately recorded shots with variations in viewpoints and/or subject sizes. Action may be repeated to facilitate later editing.

Later, in Chapters 9 and 10, we will look at the advantages and limitations of these various methods.

FIGURE 1.4
Teleprompters put the script in front of the camera's lens.

CAMERAS

Today's cameras range from large network cameras with huge lenses to lightweight designs that are adaptable to field and studio use. Some of the new digital still cameras even have the capability of shooting HD video footage (Figures 1.5, 1.6, and 1.7). For documentaries and newsgathering, even smaller handheld units play a valuable role.

FIGURE 1.5
Cameras with large lenses are used as "fixed" or immobile cameras. (Photo courtesy of Thomson/Grass Valley)

FIGURE 1.6
HDV lightweight cameras are perfect for shooting documentaries and low-budget independent film projects.

FIGURE 1.7
Some of the newest still cameras, called DSLRs (digital single-lens reflex), shoot still photos and high-quality video, all on the same camera. (Photo courtesy of Canon)

FIGURE 1.8
Hard drives are increasingly used to record video images. (Photo courtesy of Doremi Labs)

VIDEO RECORDING

For convenience and greater flexibility, most television programs are recorded. The picture and sound are usually recorded on magnetic tape, hard drive, disc, or flash memory (Figure 1.8). In some situations, sound may be recorded on a separate audio recorder, too. The video recorder may be:

- Integrated into the actual camera unit.
- In a separate nearby portable unit, which is connected to the camera by cable or radio.
- Housed in a central video recording area in a remote van or nearby building.

In a multicamera production, the separate outputs of the cameras are to be switched or blended together. This task is usually carried out with a production switcher (Figure 1.9). The program is generally recorded on a central video recorder.

Alternatively, each camera's output may be recorded separately on individual video recording decks (called an isolated camera or ISO camera) and their shots are edited together during an editing session.

ADDITIONAL IMAGE SOURCES

Additional image sources such as graphics, animations, still shots, digital video effects (DVEs), and other picture sources may be inserted into the program during production or added to the final project recording during the postproduction editing session.

PROGRAM SOUND

Typically, a microphone is clipped to the speaker's clothing, handheld, or attached to a sound boom or other fitting. Music, sound effects, commentary, and the like can either be played into the program's soundtrack during the main taping session or added later during postproduction (Figure 1.10).

LIGHTING

Lighting can significantly contribute to the success of a presentation, whether it is augmenting the natural light or providing totally artificial illumination. Lighting techniques involve carefully blending the intensities and texture (hardness or diffusion) of the light, with selectively arranged light direction and coverage, to bring out specific features of the subject and/or scene (see Figure 1.10).

FIGURE 1.9
Production switchers are used to switch between two or more live cameras during a project.

SETS AND SCENIC DESIGN

Scenic design, or providing appropriate surroundings for the action, creates a specific ambience for the program. The setting may include an existing location, sets that are built for the program, or virtual sets that can be used to simulate an environment (Figure 1.11).

MAKEUP AND COSTUME (WARDROBE)

In larger productions, these areas are overseen by specialists. But in smaller productions, the responsibility for these areas may be given to someone else, such as a production assistant (Figure 1.12).

EDITING

There are two forms of editing:

1. *Live editing* occurs during the actual performance. A technical director, or vision mixer, cuts or dissolves between video sources (multiple cameras, graphics, etc.) using a production switcher (vision mixer) directly to air or to a record medium.
2. *Postproduction editing* occurs after all of the program materials (video, audio, and graphics) have been compiled. The chosen shots or segments are then placed together in the appropriate order to create the final program.

FIGURE 1.10
A wireless microphone is placed on the talent and lights are used to boost the natural light.

Two basic systems are used in postproduction editing:

- In *linear tape editing,* specific segments from the original footage tape are selected and then copied from one tape deck to another tape deck to form a master tape. The content is placed on the master tape in a linear order. Significant changes to the edited master are difficult, as the program was assembled in a linear fashion on a tape. Linear systems usually require separate graphics and audio equipment (Figure 1.13).

"If you don't take advantage of [interactivity], you're not maximizing the opportunity. We're asking advertisers to create something more interesting than the 30-second spot."
Rick Mandler, Disney/ABC

9

FIGURE 1.11
Set building requires skilled craftspeople.

FIGURE 1.12
The wardrobe department at a major studio.

FIGURE 1.13
Digital laptop linear editing system. (Photo by Austin Brooks)

FIGURE 1.14
Nonlinear editor. (Photo by Austin Brooks)

- In *nonlinear editing*, portions of the original footage are usually digitized or copied onto the editing computer's hard drive in order to provide a digital duplicate. Nonlinear editing systems allow random access to the individual video and audio clips and allow an unlimited number of changes to the program, as the clips can be easily reconfigured and manipulated on the hard drive. The final master is then output to a recording medium. Nonlinear systems usually include graphics and audio processing software (Figure 1.14).

POSTPRODUCTION AUDIO (PROGRAM SOUND)

In addition to the natural sound from the action, productions may include music, sound effects, and narration received from a variety of sources.

As with picture editing, the audio may be selected and mixed live during the actual production. Alternatively, the final soundtrack may be built during the postproduction session.

AUDIENCE IMPACT

It's pretty obvious that to achieve quality and professional results, we need to be able to competently use the equipment. However, it's all too easy to develop the mechanical know-how and to create cool digital effects while overlooking the most important issue: how best to communicate to your audience.

Ideally, the techniques you choose should arise from the nature and purpose of the production. The camera techniques, lighting, audio, and setting design should all be selected to communicate your story to a specific audience. For example, many an otherwise excellent documentary program has been ruined by an obtrusive, repetitive, and irrelevant musical background.

We shall be exploring various ways in which techniques can influence your audience's response to what they are seeing. There is nothing mysterious about this idea: program making is a persuasive craft, the same as marketing, advertising, and all other presentational fields. Learning how to control and adjust production techniques to achieve the kind of impact you need is one of the director's skills.

Audiences don't usually give much thought to whether the program they are watching is actually film, television/video, digitally created, or a mixture of all these media. In fact, in today's multimedia world, it is becoming increasingly difficult to discern where one medium ends and another begins. The viewer is concerned only with the effectiveness of the material: whether it holds their attention; whether it is interesting, amusing, stimulating, gripping, intriguing, entertaining; and so on.

The convergence of media has blurred the demarcations between the various communication media. The same programming can be found on a television station, in a theater, online ready for download, available on DVD at the rental store, or accessible through a mobile phone.

TELEVISION, VIDEO, OR FILM?

Whether you are involved with television, video, or film production, you will find that the program-making principles and the equipment used can be virtually identical. The terms have begun to blur over recent years:

- *Television* usually refers to a broadcast medium in which programs are distributed via land transmitters, cables, or satellites to a general audience, and seen "off-air" as part of a regular public service.
- *Video* program making usually refers to nonbroadcast television production. Traditionally, this term has included the home video market and corporate media. Most of these programs are distributed in stores, online, or internally at corporations. But even these broad distinctions do not always work in our converging media environment.
- Traditionally, *film* meant that the project was being shot on celluloid. With so many independent films being shot on video due to the financial savings, the term *film* seems to convey that it will be shown on a big screen (unless it goes directly to DVD). *Film*, using video, is generally the term employed when referring to a narrative or documentary. Videotape can be edited and then transferred to film for theater projection. Some theaters are beginning to use video projectors. It is little wonder that people talk about "filming" or "photographing" with the video camera (Figure 1.15).

FIGURE 1.15
A low-budget film is shot using the HDV video format.

Television Organizations

Traditionally, the only organizations that could transmit television programming were networks or stations. Stations were generally limited to their city or region and networks were usually limited to a region of the country, but might cover the entire country. Cable and

FIGURE 1.16
A television network production facility.

satellite transmission began to change the coverage limits by expanding the coverage outside of their usual coverage, even to other countries.

Networks and stations are generally well-equipped high-technology hubs with many staff members (Figure 1.16). Most permanent television studios are equipped with anywhere from two to six video cameras and a selection of sound and lighting equipment. Network studio operations will normally be supported by various in-house facilities (specialists, engineers and supply services, and so on). Regular production teams or crews may be allocated on a scheduled basis to cover a variety of programs ranging from newscasts to talk shows, magazine programs, comedy, and soap operas. In larger organizations, a production crew may tend to work on a specific style of show, such as comedy or drama, for—as you will see—each type of production tends to require noticeably different skills and aptitudes.

In some television studios or networks, crews may work both in the studio and away from their base on remotes/outside broadcasts. Generally, units specialize in studio production or on-location assignments such as sports or newsgathering.

Although some television stations or networks create most of the programs that they transmit, others primarily purchase programming that is created by outside production companies. Audience ratings strongly influence both subject choice and production formats. There may be less opportunity for experiment and a greater tendency to follow proven, formulaic approaches.

Today, the Internet has again blurred the lines of transmission, in that an individual can create niche programming and reach millions of viewers around the world by using some of the online video sites. These sites create niche networks of which the programs are available for viewers to view live or download to their computer, mobile phone, PDA, or iPod-type device. The power to reach individuals internationally is available to almost anyone. However, the basics of television are still the same. Individuals still must understand how to communicate their message through visual storytelling.

The Equipment Is Always Changing

If you are uncomfortable with change, you may not want to work in television on the technical side. It seems that the technology just keeps changing at an incredible speed. However, the good news is that the equipment also keeps increasing in quality and affordability. The bad news is that the viewers' expectations rise with the improvements in equipment. Mastering the equipment will leave you free to concentrate on the creative aspects of the job.

However, a word of warning. It is easy to want to try out the various "bells and whistles" available in new technology just because they are there. Directors may get tempted to introduce variety: adding a wipe here or some other exciting new effect there. Camera operators may be

"Every time a new medium comes along in the television marketplace, the feeling is that it is going to knock out the old and that we should be threatened by this new technology. Instead, as content providers, we see great opportunity from this for ourselves and also for the advertisers that use our medium to communicate to their consumers."

David Poltrack, President of CBS Vision

tempted to use their equipment with a certain "panache": an impressively rapid dolly move here, a fast zoom there. There's the temptation to dramatize the lighting treatment or add a little extra to the sound. However, keep in mind that *appropriateness* is the watchword.

Today's Equipment

Broadly speaking, the equipment used for television/video program making today tends to fall into the following three categories.

CONSUMER EQUIPMENT

Consumer equipment is intended for hobbyists and/or family use. This equipment tends to make almost everything automatic (auto focus, exposure, etc.); it usually has a lot of extra special effects (fades, masks); and it is usually very easy to use. The equipment is designed for occasional or light use. Of course, this equipment is the least expensive (Figure 1.17).

FIGURE 1.17
Consumer HD camera.
(Photo courtesy of Canon)

PROSUMER EQUIPMENT

Prosumer equipment, sometimes known as industrial equipment, is a little heavier-duty, and sometimes employs a few professional features (such as an interchangeable lens on a camera), but it may still have many of the automatic features that are included on the consumer equipment. Because of its combination of portability and quality, this type of lower-cost equipment is often used by professionals. Prosumer equipment is generally medium-priced (see Figure 1.18).

FIGURE 1.18
Prosumer HD camera.
(Photo courtesy of Panasonic)

13

PROFESSIONAL EQUIPMENT

Professional equipment is usually designed for heavy-duty everyday use, usually has many more adjustable features than the consumer/prosumer equipment, and includes the highest-quality components, such as high-quality lenses, on a camera (Figure 1.19). Professional equipment must:

- Function at the highest standards, providing high definition and color fidelity under a variety of conditions, low picture noise, and no visible defects or distortions (artifacts).
- Be extremely stable and reliable.
- Be adjusted and maintained to stringent standards, and provide consistent results. (For instance, an image recorded on one machine must reproduce identically on another machine using the same standards.)
- Withstand quite rough handling (such as vibration, bumps and jolts, dust, heat, and rain) when used under very demanding conditions.

FIGURE 1.19
Professional HD camera.
(Photo courtesy of Panasonic)

THE PRODUCTION TEAM

In a well-coordinated production group, members continually interrelate. A good director will allow for the practical problems that a set designer has to face. The designer arranges a setting to help the lighting director achieve the most effective results. Similarly, the lighting director needs to rationalize treatment with the makeup artist. Of course, there are always individuals who concentrate on their own contribution to the exclusion of others. But when you work in a cooperative team in which each member appreciates the other person's aims and problems, difficulties are somehow minimized.

The Hidden Factors of Production

As you will discover, there are many hidden factors that directly affect how a television director works on a television production, such as:

- The program's budget.
- The amount of time allocated for rehearsal and recording.
- The available studio space.
- The type of equipment obtainable, and its flexibility.
- The size and the experience of the production team.
- Support/backup facilities.

All aspects of the production must be arranged and adjusted to suit these parameters.

THE DAILY ROUTINE

In a surprisingly short time, many of the procedures and operations that mystified you not so long ago will quickly become second nature. Therein lies a trap for the unwary. It's all too easy to learn techniques by rote, and go on to apply them as a comfortable routine. In a busy schedule, it is a temptation, of course, to apply regular solutions that have been successful before, rather than to work out innovative and creative approaches. However, if your goal is programming that will interest and engage your audience, you cannot settle for the routine.

THE PRESSURES OF PRODUCTION

Program making is an absorbing, extremely satisfying process, but one is always aware of underlying practical pressures. Aspirations are one thing, but the achievable can be quite another. In the real world, one has to rationalize and cope with the various pressures that influence the form and development of program making: How much will it cost? Is there time? What happens if it overruns the scheduled time? Is there enough skilled labor available? Do we have the equipment/materials? Are there any regulations/restrictions preventing it?

Very few productions evolve without a hitch of some kind. There will always be the planned action that does not work, the last-minute hang-up, the prop that breaks, the missed cue, and so on. Particularly when things go wrong, it's very easy to become more preoccupied with the mechanics of the situation; for example, how much recording time remains, camera moves, or microphone shadows, rather than aesthetic issues or potential audience responses. These can get pushed into the background.

It is not surprising that, especially during live airing of a show, program makers can lose sight of the value and purpose of the end product their audience will see. The more fully you understand production principles and problems, the freer you are to think about the significance of what you are doing.

KEEP THE AUDIENCE IN MIND

One of the greatest difficulties that everyone working on any production will have is how to assess how the audience will respond. The viewer is seeing it for the first time, and usually the only time. The production team has become overly familiar with all its aspects. Every person in the team is concentrating on their own specific contribution. While the director is worried about the talent's performance:

The set designer has noticed where some scenic flats do not fit properly.
The lighting director is fretting about a boom shadow.
The audio person finds the air conditioning noise to be obtrusive behind quiet speech.
The makeup artist is disturbed by a perspiring forehead.
The costume designer has noticed creases in a collar.
The video operator is preoccupied with picture matching in color correction.
The producer is concerned with the costs of overrunning the scheduled time.

It is not easy to assess from the audience's viewpoint. And when you have put all that effort into a project, it's hard to accept that your audience may be watching the show with less than 100 percent attention, unaware of any of these problems.

REVIEW QUESTIONS

1. How do you define television?
2. Why do we need to study television production?
3. What are the advantages and disadvantages to being able to multitask in television production?
4. Compare the two different types of editing (live and postproduction).
5. What are the primary differences among video, television, and film?
6. What are the differences between linear and nonlinear editing?
7. What are the differences among consumer, prosumer, and professional video production equipment?

CHAPTER 2

The People Who Make It Happen

"The producer has the final word on all matters—but don't tell that to the talent; most think they do."

Joseph Maar, Director

Terms

A-1: The senior audio person on a production.

A-2: The audio assistant, who reports to the A-1. See "Audio Assistant" within this chapter.

Director: Responsible for telling the story.

EIC (engineer in charge): Responsible for maintaining and troubleshooting all equipment on a truck or in a specific studio. See "Studio Engineer" in this chapter.

Field mixer: A portable audio mixer used by audio personnel to record a quality audio signal. This term could also refer to the person operating the field mixer.

Freelance: Independent contractors who provide services to multiple organizations, hiring out their skills on an as-needed basis.

TD (technical director): Responsible for operating the television production switcher.

Visual storytelling: The use of images to convey a compelling story.

One of the reasons that this chapter is near the beginning of the book is to underscore the importance of people in production. A good crew is far more important than the latest equipment. The crew will make or break the production. It really does not matter what equipment you have if you don't have knowledgeable people running it. A great crew can make a boring event exciting. A mediocre crew can make an exciting event boring.

As you would expect, organizations differ greatly in how they describe each job. We will try to highlight the most popular descriptions of each job in this chapter. You will note that there are also overlaps between some of these positions. Each company decides how best to deal with those overlaps.

THE PRODUCTION CREW

Television production crews greatly differ in size. There is not a "perfect" size for all crews. The right size for a project depends on the type of project that you are working on and the preferences of the director.

FIGURE 2.1
Small crews have become more prevalent with the introduction of more portable high-quality cameras. (Photo courtesy of Sony)

At one end of the scale, there are directors who initiate the program idea, write the script, and even predesign the settings. They cast and rehearse the performers, guide the production team, and, having recorded the show, control the postproduction. Smaller crews have become more prevalent with the introduction of more portable and affordable equipment. This type of production crew is very popular with documentaries and low-budget productions (Figure 2.1).

At the other end of the scale, there are big-budget productions with large crews, in which the director relies heavily on the production team to provide him or her with quality sets, lighting, sound, and camera work. The director can then concentrate on directing talent and shot selection. Dramatic productions have traditionally used a larger crew (Figure 2.2).

Another type of crew includes the director in a presentational role. On projects run by these crews, a number of separate stories or segments are independently prepared by members of the production staff. The director is then responsible for visualizing the production treatment that will coordinate these various contributions. This type of situation occurs in many magazine programs, newscasts, and current affairs programs. Obviously, in this type of production, members of the crew other than the director have significant impact on the various components of the program.

There is a place for all levels of expertise in the wide spectrum of television production. Like other craftspeople, crew members become skilled in their specific field. Someone whose talent lies in drama production would probably lack the edge-of-seat intuition of a good sports director: an almost clairvoyant ability to anticipate action and to take spontaneous shot opportunities. On the other hand, someone specializing in sports might be lost in the world of drama, in which the director, with painstaking shot-by-shot planning, guides performance and develops dramatic impact. And when presenting a symphony orchestra, one needs skills that are far removed from those involved in shooting a documentary on location (Figure 2.3).

For smaller productions, the director may combine the functions of both director and producer. Having been allocated a working budget, the person in this dual role is responsible for the entire business and artistic arrangements—origination, interpretation, casting, staging, and treatment—

FIGURE 2.2
Large productions may require an army of people.

FIGURE 2.3
A dramatic director gives guidance to an actor.

subsequently directing the studio operations and postproduction editing. More often, the producer serves as the business head of a production and is thus responsible for organization, finance, and policy, serving as the artistic and business coordinator for several directors. As productions have become increasingly costly and more complicated, the workload needs to be spread out. The director is then free to concentrate on the program's interpretation, as well as the staging and direction of the subject being presented.

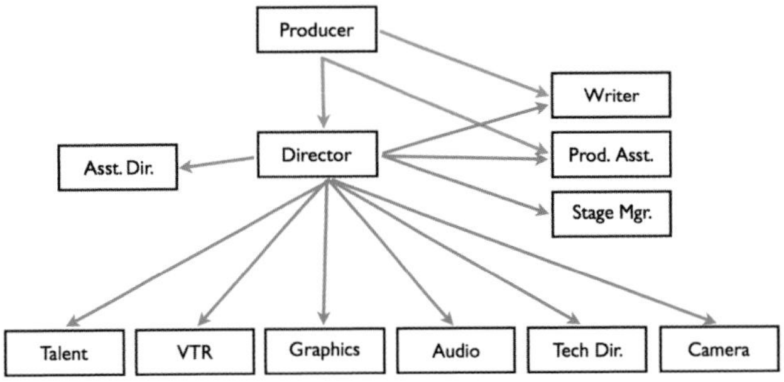

The common thread between all of these different production types is that the director is responsible for telling the story, whether it is a dramatic show or a sports production. A knowledge of visual storytelling is essential (Figure 2.4).

FIGURE 2.4
A common diagram of how a television production crew works.

Members of the Production Crew

Although (as mentioned before) crew members' job descriptions may vary from company to company, this sections provides some of the most common descriptions. Please note that some responsibilities differ between various types of programming, different companies, and different countries. For example, the producer's role in a dramatic production is different from the producer's role in sports.

EXECUTIVE PRODUCER

The executive producer is responsible for the overall organization and administration of the production group (e.g., a series of programs devoted to a specific field). He or she controls and coordinates the business management, including negotiating rights, program budget, and who gets hired, and sometimes may be involved in major creative decisions and/or concerned with wider issues such as funding, backing, and coproduction arrangements.

PRODUCER

The producer is generally responsible for the management of a specific production. Usually, the producer is concerned with the choice of supervisory staff and crew, interdepartmental coordination, script acceptance, and production scheduling. The producer may select or initiate the program concepts and work with writers. He or she may assign the production's director, and is responsible for meeting deadlines, production planning, location projects, rehearsals, production treatment, and so on. Producers may also become involved in such specifics as craft or union problems, assessing postproduction treatment, and the final program format. The producer reports to the executive producer (Figure 2.5).

Generally, the director is responsible for the visualization of the script or event and the producer stays out of the actual hands-on production. However, in sports and news, the producer generally gets more involved with working with the talent, determining replays, inserting preproduced packages, the timing of the show, and guiding the general direction of the program during a live production.

FIGURE 2.5
Phil Rosenthal (center), producer of *Everybody Loves Raymond*, reviews the script with actor Ray Romano (right) and a writer. (Photo courtesy of CBS/Ron Tom/Landov)

ASSISTANT PRODUCER/ASSOCIATE PRODUCER

The assistant producer or associate producer (AP) is responsible for assisting the producer. His or her responsibilities, as assigned by the producer, may include coordinating appointments and production schedules, making sure that contracts are completed, booking guests, creating packages, and supervising postproduction. This person may be assigned some of the same responsibilities of an associate director. The AP reports to the producer.

FIGURE 2.6

Some directors prefer to work as a director and technical director.

DIRECTOR

Ultimately, the director is the individual responsible for creatively visualizing the script or event. Directors must be able to effectively communicate their vision to the crew. They also have to be able to be team builders, moving the crew toward that vision. This role involves advising, guiding, and coordinating the various members on the production team (scenic, lighting. sound, cameras, costume, and so on) and approving their anticipated treatment. The director may choose and hire performers/talent/actors (casting), envision and plan the camera treatment (shots and camera movements) and editing, and direct/rehearse the performers during prerehearsals (Figure 2.6).

During studio rehearsals, the director guides and cues performance through the floor manager, and instructs the camera, sound crews, and technical director (vision mixer). He or she also evaluates the crew's contributions (sets, camera work, lighting, sound, makeup, costume, graphics, and the like).

In some situations, the director may choose to operate the production switcher (e.g., a local news show) and guide and coordinate postproduction editing and audio sweetening.

As mentioned before, the director's job can range in practice from being the sole individual creating and coordinating the production to a person directing a camera and sound crew with material organized by others. The director reports to the producer.

ASSISTANT DIRECTOR/ASSOCIATE DIRECTOR

The assistant director or associate director (AD) is responsible for assisting the director. Functions may include supervising prerehearsals, location organization, and similar events on the director's behalf. During rehearsal and the actual production, the AD is generally in the production control room and may be responsible for lining up shots, graphics, and tapes, so that they are ready for the director's cue. He or she may also be responsible for checking on special shots (such as chroma-key), giving routine cues (tape inserts), and so on, while the director guides the actual performance and cameras. The AD also advises the director of upcoming cues and may assist in off-line editing (timings and edit points). The AD may also check program timing and help the director with postproduction. This person may be assigned some of the same responsibilities of an associate producer. The AD reports to the director, or sometimes to the producer.

PRODUCTION ASSISTANT

The production assistant (PA) helps the director and/or producer with production needs. These may include supervising the production office (making copies, making coffee, and running errands), prerehearsals, and location organization. Their responsibilities may also include logging tapes, taking notes during production meetings, and similar tasks. During rehearsals and recording, this person may assist the producer/director with graphics or serve as a floor manager.

PRODUCER'S ASSISTANT

The producer's assistant usually works with the director. This role may be very close to a PA's responsibilities. He or she may also check performance against the script and continuity. The producer's assistant may be assigned to line up shots, prepare inserts, and so on, while the director guides the performance and camera crew. He or she may also ready the director, crew, and recorder/player regarding upcoming cues. The director may assign the producer's assistant to note the durations/time code of each take and keep the director's notes regarding changes to be made and retakes.

FLOOR MANAGER/STAGE MANAGER

The floor manager (FM)/stage manager (SM) is the director's primary representative and contact on the studio floor, in the broadcast booth (see Figure 2.6), or on the field of play. The FM may be used to cue performers and direct the floor crew. In the studio, the FM is responsible for general studio organization, safety, discipline (e.g., noise control), and security. An assistant floor manager may be used to ensure that the talent is present. The FM reports to the producer or director (Figures 2.7 and 2.8).

FIGURE 2.7
The floor manager (shown here facing away from us) is working with the talent in the broadcast booth at a sports event.

PRODUCTION MANAGER/LINE PRODUCER

The production manager is responsible to the producer and director for maintaining the production within the allocated budget. He or she also may serve in administrative functions relative to the production.

TECHNICAL DIRECTOR/VISION MIXER

The technical director (TD) generally sits next to the director in the control room and is responsible for operating the television production switcher (and perhaps for electronic effects). The TD may also serve as the crew chief. He or she reports to the director (Figure 2.9).

MAKEUP ARTIST/MAKEUP SUPERVISOR

The makeup artist designs, prepares, and applies makeup to the talent, aided by makeup assistants and hair stylists. The supervisor is generally responsible for multiple makeup artists, to ensure consistency (Figure 2.10).

COSTUME DESIGNER

The costume designer designs and selects performers' costumes (wardrobe). He or she may be assisted by dressers and wardrobe handlers (Figure 2.11).

21

GRAPHICS DESIGNER/GRAPHICS ARTIST

The graphics designer is responsible for the design and preparation of graphics for a series of shows or just one individual show (Figure 2.12).

GRAPHICS OPERATOR

The graphics operator is the person who actually implements the graphics during the production. He or she is responsible for organizing and typing on-screen text and titles for a production, either doing so during the production or storing them for later use. Operators may also serve as designers/artists (Figure 2.13).

FIGURE 2.8
The floor manager is relaying instructions to a cameraman from the director on the set of a situation comedy (sitcom).

FIGURE 2.9
Technical directors edit a live program by utilizing a production switcher.

FIGURE 2.10
A makeup artist prepares talent for a production. (Photo by Sarah Seaton)

FIGURE 2.11
A costume designer designs costumes for a production.

FIGURE 2.12
Graphics staff review production graphics.

FIGURE 2.13
Graphics operators insert data into predesigned graphics at a sports event.

FIGURE 2.14
Lighting director.

FIGURE 2.15
Video operators are responsible for matching the cameras and other input devices.

FIGURE 2.16
Camera operators are responsible for setting up the cameras, as well as operating them. (Photos by Josh Taber)

LIGHTING DIRECTOR

The lighting director is responsible for designing, arranging, and controlling all lighting treatment, both technically and artistically. This responsibility may include indoor and/or outdoor lighting situations (Figure 2.14).

VIDEO OPERATOR/SHADER/VISION CONTROL/
VIDEO TECHNICIAN/VIDEO ENGINEER

The video operator is responsible for controlling the picture quality by utilizing test equipment to adjust the video equipment. There are a variety of adjustments that can be made, including exposure, black level, and color balance. Operations are closely coordinated with the lighting director (Figure 2.15).

CAMERA OPERATOR/CAMERAMAN/CAMERAPERSON/
PHOTOGRAPHER/VIDEOGRAPHER

The camera operators are responsible for setting up the cameras (unless they are already set up in a studio situation) and then operating the cameras to capture the video images as requested by the director (Figure 2.16).

CAMERA ASSISTANT

The camera assistant is responsible for assisting the camera operator in setting up the camera. He or she is also responsible for making sure that the camera operator is safe (keeping him or her from tripping over something or falling), keeping people from walking in front of the camera when it is on, keeping the camera cable from getting tangled, and guiding the camera

FIGURE 2.17
Camera assistants may be required to push the camera dolly.

FIGURE 2.18
Camera assistants are responsible for keeping the camera operator safe and the cable untangled.

FIGURE 2.19
The person on the left is the focus puller. Having a focus puller allows the camera operator to concentrate on composition.

operator during moving shots. A camera assistant may also push a camera dolly if needed (Figures 2.17 and 2.18).

FOCUS PULLER

The focus puller is responsible for adjusting the focus so that the camera operator can concentrate on composition. The focus puller uses a marked lens to establish focus. This position is rarely used except in dramatic shooting (Figure 2.19).

AUDIO MIXER/AUDIO ENGINEER/SOUND SUPERVISOR/SENIOR AUDIO TECHNICIAN

The audio mixer (A-1) is responsible for the technical and artistic quality of the program sound. This job includes determining the number and placement of the microphones required for the production. He or she also makes sure that the audio cables are properly plu gged into the audio mixer and is responsible for the final mix (audio levels, balance, and tonal quality) of the final production. Audio personnel are also generally responsible for the intercom system used by the crew (Figures 2.20 and 2.21).

AUDIO ASSISTANT

Supervised by the A-1, the audio assistant (A-2) is responsible for positioning microphones, running audio cables, operating sound booms, troubleshooting audio problems, and operating field audio equipment (Figure 2.22).

SET DESIGNER/SCENIC DESIGNER

The set designer is responsible for conceiving, designing, and organizing the entire scenic treatment. His or her responsibilities may even include designing the graphics. The set designer is generally responsible for supervising the set crew during setting, dressing, and striking the sets (Figure 2.23).

SET CREW/STAGE CREW/GRIPS/FLOOR CREW

The set crew are responsible for the sets or scenery such as erecting, setting, or resetting scenery, props, and action cues (such as rocking a vehicle). In some organizations, they may initially set up and dress settings.

23

FIGURE 2.20
This audio mixer is using a field mixer to adjust the levels on the talent's mic.

FIGURE 2.21
This A-1 is mixing surround sound. (Photo by Dennis Baxter)

FIGURE 2.22
Audio assistants are sometimes assigned to hand-hold microphones around the field of play.

24

FIGURE 2.23
This set designer is working on a project in his shop.

ELECTRICIANS

Electricians are responsible for rigging and setting lamps and electrical apparatuses, including electrical props.

SPECIAL EFFECTS DESIGNER

The special effects designer is responsible for designing and operating mechanical illusions such as fire, snow, and explosions.

TECHNICAL MANAGER/STUDIO SUPERVISOR/ REMOTE SUPERVISOR/TECHNICAL COORDINATOR

The technical manager coordinates and is responsible for all technical operations of the production. He or she may book the facilities, check technical feasibility, make sure that everything is working correctly, and ensure safety.

STUDIO ENGINEER/MAINTENANCE ENGINEER/ENGINEER-IN-CHARGE

Engineers are responsible for maintaining and troubleshooting all camera and sound equipment in a production. Maintenance engineers usually are assigned to do regular maintenance on the equipment, the studio engineer is responsible for the studio, and an engineer-in-charge (EIC) is responsible for a production truck.

UTILITY

Utilities staff members assist the engineering staff by helping carry gear and cable, setting up equipment, and laying cables (Figure 2.24).

VTR OPERATOR/TAPE OPERATOR

The VTR (videotape recorder) operator is responsible for recording the program and playing preproduced packages or replays that will be inserted into the program. Although still referred to as the VTR or tape operator, the operator may actually be recording and playing back programming from a memory card, hard disc, or hard drive (Figure 2.25).

FIGURE 2.24
Utilities crew assist the engineers by carrying and then laying cables for cameras. (Photo by Scott Rohrer)

FIGURE 2.25
A VTR operator is using a hard drive recorder to record and play back video.

FIGURE 2.26
The editor is responsible for assembling the shot footage into a useful finished production.

WRITER

The writer is responsible for writing the script. Occasionally the producer or director will write material. At times, writers are assisted by a researcher, who obtains data, information, and references for the production writer.

EDITOR

The editor selects, compiles, and cuts video and audio to produce programs. He or she may assemble clips into segments and those segments into programs, or may just correct mistakes that occurred during the production process (Figure 2.26).

TALENT

Talent is generally defined as people who are heard or appear on television. There are a number of different types of talent. The following is a list of some of the people who are included in talent.

ACTORS

Actors generally work from an established script. By playing a role, they create a character for the audience. Actors usually rehearse before the camera rehearsal (Figure 2.27).

PERFORMERS

Performer is usually a term used to describe people who are appearing in front of the camera as themselves. This group could include interviewers, announcers, newscasters, anchor persons, hosts, and so on. Performers often address the audience directly through the camera using scripted, semiscripted, or unscripted material. Sometimes the word "performer" refers to a person providing a specific act (such as a juggler). (Figure 2.28.)

FIGURE 2.27
Actors work from an established script in CBS's *NUMB3RS*. (Photo courtesy of CBS/ Randy Tepper/Landov)

ANCHOR

The anchor generally sits at a desk or table of some type and provides the consistent talent that pulls the show together. Anchors generally open the show, introduce on-air talent such as reporters or other in-studio talent, and then end the show (Figure 2.29).

FIGURE 2.29
Anchors usually provide a level of consistency on a show by being the person who opens the show, introduces others, and ends the show. (Photo by Jon Greenhoe)

GUESTS

Guests are invited "personalities," specialists, or members of the public—usually people without experience in front of the camera. Guests could include interviewees, contestants, audience contributors, and so on.

26

FIGURE 2.28
Anchors and commentators are called *talent* or *performers* in television.

There are other people who may be involved in a production as well, depending on the size of the staff. These people may include security, prop manager, stunt personnel, catering, and others.

THE FREELANCE CREW

Today, many companies have started using a freelance crew. Freelancers are independent contractors who work for multiple organizations, hiring out their production skills on an as-needed basis. There are freelancers available who can fill every one of the previously mentioned positions.

Freelancers are generally hired when a company does not have enough work to keep a full crew busy. Many times a network or station will need a crew at a remote site. It is usually less expensive to hire a local crew than to transport and house the in-house crew.

REVIEW QUESTIONS

1. What are the main differences between shooting a scripted drama and a sports event?
2. Why do some productions require large crews, while other productions can be shot with just a couple of people?
3. What is the difference between a director and a technical director?
4. What is the difference between an actor and a performer?
5. In television productions, what is the difference between a writer and an editor?

CHAPTER 3

The Television Production Facility

"For live multicamera production, the control room is where it all comes together. The director has to be ready for anything."

Don Mink, Director

Terms

Boom pole: A pole that is used to hold a microphone close to a subject.

Camera control unit (CCU): Equipment that controls the camera from a remote position. The CCU includes adjusting the camera, luminance, color correction, aperture, and so on.

Chroma-key: Utilizing a production switcher, the director can replace a specific color (usually green or blue) with another image source (still image, live video, prerecorded material, and so on).

Control room: The television studio control room, sometimes known as a *gallery*, is where the director controls the production. Although the control room equipment may vary, they all include video and audio monitors, intercoms, and a switcher.

DVE: Digital video effect equipment, in combination with the switcher, is used to create special effect transitions between video images. A DVE could also refer to the actual effect instead of the equipment.

Flats: Free-standing background set panels.

Intercom: A wired or wireless communication link between members of the production crew.

Preview monitor: A video monitor, located in the control room's monitor wall, that is used by the director to preview video before it goes on the air.

Program monitor: Also known as the "on-air" monitor, the program monitor shows the actual program that is being broadcast or recorded.

Remote truck (also known as an outside broadcasting or OB van): A mobile television control room that is used away from the studio.

Sitcom: A situation comedy television program.

Studio: An area designed to handle a variety of productions; a wide open space equipped with lights, sound control, and protection from the impact of weather.

Switcher (vision mixer): A device used to switch between video inputs (cameras, graphics, video players, and so on).

Today, someone with a handheld camcorder and a very modest computer can produce results that not so long ago would have required the combined services of a large production team and a great deal of equipment.

Nowadays, the television camera is free to shoot virtually everywhere. The audience has come to accept and expect the camera's flexibility. Whether the pictures that they are watching are from a camera in the studio or from outer space, intense close-up shots from a microscope or from a "critter camera" attached to a swimming seal, or thrilling shots from a skydiver's helmet camera, these diverse channels are all grist for the endless mill of television programming, and they are accepted as "normal."

PRODUCTION METHODS

The way to develop a production depends on a number of factors:

- Whether the show is live (being seen by the viewers as it is happening), or whether you are recording the action for subsequent editing and postproduction treatment.
- Whether you have chosen to record continuously or selectively: respectively, in the order in which the action will be seen, or in an order arranged to suit the production mechanics.
- Whether you are able to control and direct the action you are shooting, or whether you are obliged to grab shots wherever you are able.

As new facilities have been developed, established methods of creating programs have grown. Wherever possible, productions are recorded, and have come to rely more and more on post-production editing techniques—using all kinds of digital effects to enhance audience appeal.

As you will see, although many situations involve little more than uncomplicated switching between shots, in others the editing process—which determines how shots are selected and arranged—becomes a subtle art.

All television productions have a number of common features—the specific skills required of the director and crew can vary considerably with the type of show that is being produced. The program material itself can determine how you present it. Some types of productions follow a prepared plan, and others have to rely heavily on spontaneous decisions. Let's look at some examples:

Interviews and talks shows. Approaches here are inevitably somewhat standardized, with shots concentrating on what people have to say and how they react. (See Figures 3.1 and 3.8.)

Newscasts. Most news programs follow a similar format. "Live-on-air" in the studio, newscasters present the news seated behind a central desk, reading from teleprompters and introducing stories from various contributory sources—preproduced packages, live on-site reporters, library photographs, graphics, and so on. There also may be brief interviews, either in the studio or via a display screen. As newscasts are continuously reviewed and revised, there is a behind-the-scenes urgency, particularly for late-breaking news stories. The closely coordinated team is continually assessing and editing incoming material, preparing commentary, and assembling illustrations and graphics. (See Figure 3.2.)

Sports programs. Each type of sport or game poses its own specific problems for the director. Shooting conditions vary considerably. On one hand is the relatively localized action of the boxing ring. On the other is the fast ebb-and-flow action of the football field. When presenting the wide-ranging action of a golf tournament, marathon runners, a horse race, or a bicycle race, will the cameras follow along with the action or shoot from selected vantage points? Sometimes, several different events are taking place simultaneously. Can they all be covered effectively on-air or will selective segments be shown on a delayed basis? In each case, the director's aim is to always be "in the right place at the right time." While conveying a sense of continuity, the camera must not only capture the highlights, but be ready to record the unexpected. Slow-motion replays help the commentators and audience analyze the action. (See Figure 3.3.)

Comedy. Most comedy shows follow the familiar "realistic" sitcom format. The studio production is staged to enable the studio audience (seen or only heard) to see and react to the action. They can watch any recording or preproduced inserts on hanging video monitors. Additional "appropriate" laughter/applause or even "reaction shots" may be added during postproduction editing. (See Figure 3.4.) Some sitcoms have been moved out of the studio and are being shot in the field.

Music and dance. Productions can range from straightforward performance to elaborate visual presentations in which images (and sound) involve considerable postproduction (e.g., creating montages, slow-motion sequences, color changes, or animation effects). Particularly where the sound arrangements are complex, the on-camera performance may be lip-synced to a previously recorded soundtrack. (See Figure 3.5.)

Drama. Drama productions usually follow a very carefully planned process in which the dialogue, action, camera work, and sound and lighting treatments are fully scripted. The show may be recorded continuously or in segments. Most drama today relies heavily on postproduction (e.g., adding sound effects, music, postsyncing). (See Figure 3.6.)

FIGURE 3.1
On-location interviews can be difficult, due to the lack of control of the surroundings. (Photo courtesy of Sodium)

FIGURE 3.2
The newscast studio. (Photo by Jon Greenhoe)

FIGURE 3.3
Television sports programs require the ability to predict accurately where the action is going.

FIGURE 3.4
Sitcoms are generally shot in a studio.

FIGURE 3.5
A jib is used to capture a concert. (Photo by Dave Grosz)

FIGURE 3.6
The director and producer review the storyboard for a dramatic production. (Photo by Taylor Vinson)

29

THE VENUE

Today, television productions are shot under a variety of conditions:

FIGURE 3.7

The outside of a Hollywood television studio, or soundstage.

- In a regular fully fitted television/video studio.
- In an extemporized studio, set up for the occasion.
- On location, in an existing interior (such as a public building).
- On location, in the open air.

Each locale has its specific advantages and limitations. Although a studio has all the facilities that we may need, for example, we have to face the fact that there is nothing to shoot there (except the walls) until we create a set of some sort, which then needs to be decorated and lit appropriately. The running costs of providing these conditions can be considerable.

On location, you may have a ready-made environment in which to shoot, and perhaps daylight to provide the illumination. But there are various new problems, from variable weather conditions and background noises to traffic and bystanders. You are normally away from your base, with its backup services (e.g., spare equipment, maintenance, and so on).

The Television Studio

Studios are designed to handle a variety of productions with their wide open spaces and are equipped to hang and supply power to lights. Studios are ideal, because they protect productions from the impact of weather such as snow and rain, they are independent from the time of day (productions can be lit as though it is daylight), and they allow for sound control. They are used for many dramatic productions, news shows, and talk shows. (See Figures 3.7 and 3.8.) Although in practice television studios vary from the modest to purpose-built giants, all seem somehow to share a certain indefinable atmosphere.

At first glance, a studio may have the feel of a deserted warehouse. It generally is well soundproofed in order to block unwanted sounds from being recorded on the program microphones. The acoustically padded walls are also designed to reduce echo. If you look up, you'll see that the studio has been designed with a framework of bars or battens suspended from the ceiling. These battens are designed to hold all of the required lights as well as to support scenery. (See Figure 3.9.) Once the scenery is brought in and the lights are hung, adjusted, and turned on, the atmosphere will become completely transformed.

FIGURE 3.8

Talk shows are generally shot in a studio so that the director can control the surroundings. (Photo courtesy of Fischer Connectors)

The set may be permanent in studios, or a temporary structure may be built for a specific show. Furnishings and props are added to the set by the set designer/decorator. Once the basic set is in place, a lighting crew begins to position and adjust each lamp to a meticulously prepared lighting plot designed by the lighting director. The camera and sound crews move their equipment from storage into the opening positions, preparing for the upcoming rehearsals. Everywhere is urgent action: completing tasks, tidying away, making last-minute changes.

To the first-time viewer, with the army of production personnel moving around the studio doing their own jobs, it can look like chaos. However, there really is a system in place that works. The various pieces of the production jigsaw combine to provide the show that has been planned and prepared. The cameras set up their shots and are seen on the monitor wall screens in the control room.

Within hours, the production will have completed rehearsals, the crew will have learned and practiced the director's treatment, performances hopefully will have reached their peak, and the program will have been recorded or transmitted. And then, if it is a temporary set, the whole set will be "struck" and tucked away in storage or discarded; equipment will be stored and floors cleaned. And then it changes back to the original "warehouse."

These are the conditions in which our theories and hopes become reality. And it is only when we relate our aspirations to the relentless pressure of practical conditions that we see television production in its true perspective.

THE TELEVISION STUDIO IN ACTION

During the rehearsal, the show is being monitored only internally. However, if it is a live transmission, at the scheduled time the studio video (pictures) and audio (sound) signals will be fed via the coordinating television control room to the recorders or immediately to the transmitters.

FIGURE 3.9
Sets can be stabilized by tying them to the bars in the ceiling.

Although sets can be electronically inserted, most are free-standing panels referred to as *flats*. Many studios have "permanently" built-in or arranged scenery ready for their regular newscasts, cooking programs, interviews, and the like. Sets may include three-walled rooms, a section of a street scene, or even a summer garden. Each set is lit with lights that may be suspended from the ceiling, clamped to sets, or even attached to floor stands. It is hard to appreciate how much care has gone into the fact that each light has been placed and angled with precision, for a specific purpose (see Figure 3.8).

Despite the number of people working around a set during the production, it is surprising how quiet the place usually is. Only the dialogue between the actors should be audible. Camera dollies should quietly move over the specially leveled floor, as the slightest bumps can shake the image. People and equipment move around silently, choreographed, systematically, and smoothly, to an unspoken plan.

However, if you were to put on an intercom headset, you would enter into a different world! You would hear the continuous instructions from the unseen director in the production control room: guiding, assessing, querying, explaining, cuing, warning, correcting—coordinating the studio crew through their headsets. The director uses the intercom to guide the production crew. In the studio, the crews operating the cameras, microphones, lighting, set, and so on hear the intercom through their headsets—information that is unheard by the performers/talent or the studio microphones. The floor manager, the director's link with the studio floor, is responsible for diplomatically relaying the director's instructions and observations to the performers with hand signals. (See Figure 3.10.)

Although the garden scene in the studio does not really look real in person and up close, on camera the effect can be idyllic. A quiet birdsong can be used from a sound effects CD to complete the illusion.

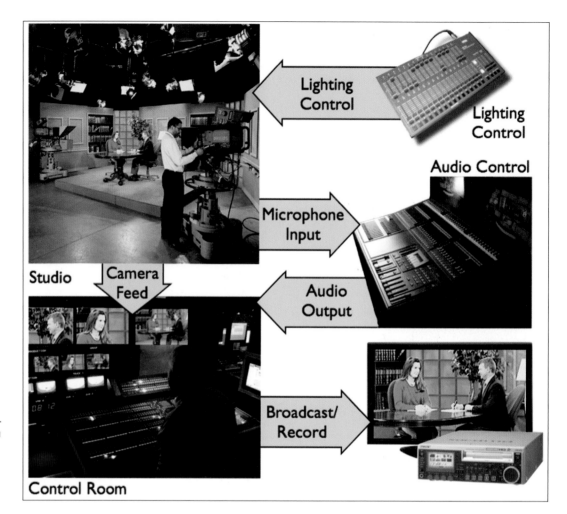

FIGURE 3.10
The studio production center. Lighting, audio, and camera signals are sent to the control room. The mixed signal is then recorded or transmitted live. (Photos courtesy of Fischer, Sony, and Panasonic)

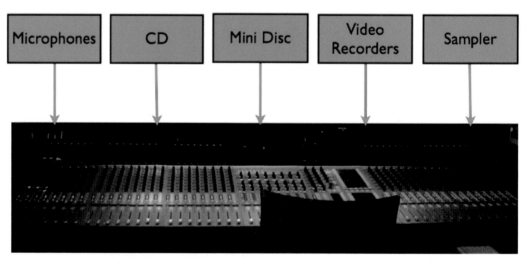

FIGURE 3.11
Audio mixers receive a wide variety of sources.

Microphones, such as an attached mic or a boom mic, are used to capture the audio. In a nearby room, an audio mixer is responsible for mixing and blending the various audio levels, from the actor's performance to the bird's song (Figure 3.11).

When shows are broadcast live, they must be shot continuously. However, during a rehearsal or a show that is going to be recorded (it can be completed in postproduction), the director has the ability to stop and start. If the director sees a bad shot, has a technical problem

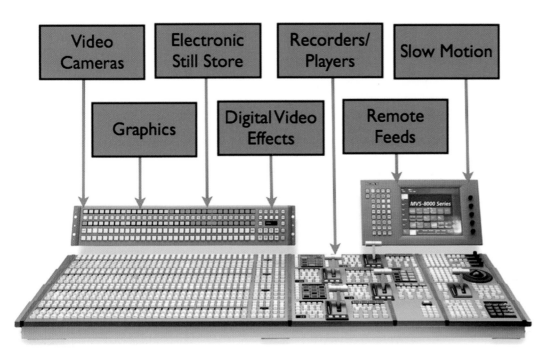

FIGURE 3.12
Video switchers can have many sources sending signals to them. Keep in mind that each area listed in blue may represent one source or many sources, such as cameras. (Photo courtesy of Sony)

in the control room, notices a problem with the talent, or doesn't like something about the shot, he or she can tell the floor manager to stop the action while the problem is sorted out. Once the situation is remedied, the show can go on.

THE TELEVISION STUDIO CONTROL ROOM

The television studio control room, sometimes known as a *gallery* in Europe, is the nerve center where the director, accompanied by a support group, controls the production. Most control rooms are segmented into separate rooms or areas. However, there are smaller control rooms, or even one-piece switchers, that merge many of these operations into one area. A large control room has more room and flexibility, but requires more people. A one-piece system can be operated by one person but is limited in the number of cameras it can include. (See Figures 3.12 through 3.15.)

The director can have many people trying to get his or her attention in the control room. Of course, there is another whole group of people in the studio. However, in the control room the director needs to review graphics, listen to the assistant director, and respond to audio personnel, video shaders, playback, the technical director, and sometimes the producer. (See Figure 3.16.)

The director usually sits in the television control room—although sometimes sitcom directors prefer to be out in the studio—watching a large group of video monitors called the *monitor wall*. (See Figure 3.17.) The smaller monitors show the displays from each camera being used, plus a variety of image sources such as graphics, animations, and satellite feeds. There are usually two larger screens. One is generally the preview monitor, which is the director's "quality control" monitor, and which allows him or her to assess upcoming shots, video effects, combined sources, and the like. The second monitor, is the "on-air" or "transmission" monitor, which shows what is actually being broadcast or recorded.

The director's attention is divided between the various input monitors, the selected output on the on-air monitor, and the program audio from a nearby loudspeaker.

FIGURE 3.13
This one-piece system includes audio mixing, graphics, video switching, and the monitor wall. (Photo courtesy of Sony)

FIGURE 3.14
Control rooms take all different forms. In this situation, it is located right off the set in the studio.

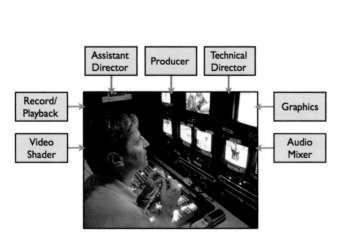

FIGURE 3.15
A small control room.

As mentioned before, the director instructs the production team and floor crew through an intercom headset (earphone and microphone). In smaller productions, the entire crew is on one intercom channel, with everyone hearing everyone else's instructions from the director. Larger productions utilize multiple channels of intercom, allowing fewer voices to be heard, which can reduce confusion.

Although some directors may prefer to switch for themselves, most directors utilize a technical director (TD). TDs are responsible for switching between the various video and graphic inputs on the switcher (see Figure 3.17). The TD enables the production director to concentrate on controlling the many other aspects of the show. The TD may oversee the engineering aspects of the production such as aligning effects, checking shots, ensuring source availability, and monitoring quality.

Depending on the size of the production, there are a variety of other personnel who may be involved in the production, such as the lighting director, producer, and so on. (See the list of personnel in Chapter 2.)

Special effects may be added live or, if the show is not live and is being recorded, it may be more convenient to leave all video effects and image manipulation until a postproduction session rather than attempt them during production.

As far as cameras are concerned, each studio camera's cable is routed via a wall outlet to its separate CCU (camera control unit), where a video operator (shader) monitors the picture quality, checking and adjusting the video equipment as necessary (see Chapter 2). The video operator is also responsible for color correcting the recorders and other image sources to

34

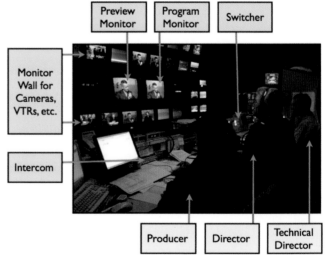

FIGURE 3.16
The director has a large group of people to deal with during a production.

FIGURE 3.17
Areas of the control room (blue) and the control room personnel (yellow). (Photo courtesy of PBS/Department of Defense.)

match (color balance, exposure, and contrast) with the cameras. Video operators generally monitor multiple sources at the same time. This video operator's position may be located in a nearby master control room or within the production control room itself. Other equipment, such as recording equipment, may be located in or outside the actual control room. These details differ from company to company.

Complex dramas and musical production require an audio mixer that not only has a good ear but also a great deal of dexterity and split-second operations. Incoming sources will include not only multiple studio microphones but discs, audio and video recordings, and remotes feeds. At the same time, the audio mixer guides the sound crew on the studio floor by using the intercom. The audio assistants may need guidance to avoid a mic appearing in a shot and to avoid boom shadows, and may need action reminders (e.g., when talent is going to move to a new position).

SERVICES AND SUPPORT AREAS

Most studios have a variety of storage and service facilities nearby that help in the smooth running of day-to-day production. Their size and scale vary, but studios typically have the following:

FIGURE 3.18
Prop rooms store a collection of props that may be needed for a production.

- Makeup rooms (for individual makeup and in-program repairs).
- A green room with rest rooms where people can wait during production breaks.
- Dressing rooms (where performers can dress, rest, and await their calls).
- Prop and set storage space (Figure 3.18).
- Technical storage: All the portable technical equipment is housed here ready for immediate use, such as camera mounts, lighting gear, audio equipment, monitors, cables, and so on. This not only helps to protect the equipment, but keeps the studio floor clear.

Various technical areas for electronic and mechanical maintenance are also usually located near the studios. The larger studios will even include a set shop, in which sets can be constructed (Figure 3.19).

Remote Production Facilities

Compared to studios, remote productions must face a myriad of difficulties, such as dealing with changes in weather, parking the remote unit, venue nonproduction personnel who may not understand the operations of a remote crew, electrical power, and unwanted audio.

FIGURE 3.19
Set shops are used by the larger studios to construct sets onsite.

However, as every event cannot happen in a television studio, mobile units have been designed to go on the road. They are really just mobile, self-contained television production control rooms. Basically, they are the same as the control rooms found within studios.

THE REMOTE PRODUCTION TRUCK

Remote trucks, sometimes called OB (outside broadcast) or production trucks, are the ultimate in mobile control rooms. These units not only contain the control room, but also storage for cameras, microphones, and other related production equipment. (See Figures 3.20 and 3.21.)

35

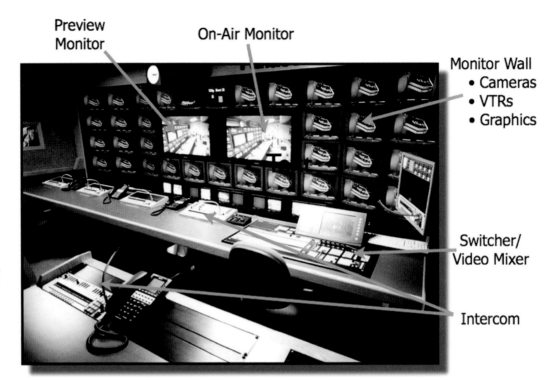

Preview Monitor

On-Air Monitor

Monitor Wall
• Cameras
• VTRs
• Graphics

Switcher/ Video Mixer

Intercom

FIGURE 3.20

The production area of a remote truck includes the same areas as the studio control room. It is the area where the director, producer, and technical director (vision mixer) are located to create the production.

Graphics

Video Record & Playback

Video Operators

Surround Audio

FIGURE 3.21

Besides the production area shown in Figure 3.20, remote trucks also have a graphics area, a video record and playback area, a video operator area, and an audio area.

Although the remote truck may include the same areas as the studio control room, they are generally much more compact. These units can take many different shapes and sizes, from 12 to 53 feet long—all depending on the need. Sports production units have a tendency to be very large, requiring large crews. (See Figure 3.22.) Remote news production units are generally small and can be run by a few people.

PORTABLE FLYPACK CONTROL ROOMS

Remote units do not always have to be contained in a truck; sometimes they come in crates. Flypacks, or portable control rooms that can be shipped or flown into a location, can take a number of different shapes. Although a small system can be a simple one-piece unit, these are generally a custom-ordered set of equipment that can allow you to do anything a remote truck can provide. However, these systems are built into portable shipping cases that can be shipped to a location, avoiding the issues of driving a truck to the location. Like building blocks, the units can be wired together with a predesigned wire harness. Because these units can be shipped by a standard shipping company, they can be a very cost-effective alternative to a full remote truck. However, they do take more time to build once they arrive onsite (Figure 3.23).

FIGURE 3.22
Remote trucks come in all different sizes and shapes.

37

FIGURE 3.23
Flypacks vary in size. (Left) An all-in-one unit that is roughly the size of a laptop computer and contains a four-camera HD switcher, four-input audio mixer, graphics, and a small LCD monitor wall. (Right) A made-to-order large flypack that could include many video and audio sources, large speakers, large monitor wall, test equipment, and so on.

FIGURE 3.24
A complex production switcher.

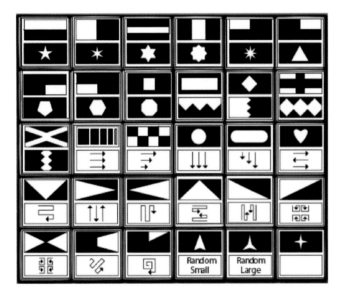

FIGURE 3.25
This illustration shows some of the wipe patterns that are available on production switchers. Video editors also have a wide variety of wipes available. (Image courtesy of Thomson/Grass Valley)

THE PRODUCTION SWITCHER

The production switcher (Figure 3.24) allows the director to edit live between the various program sources (cameras, graphics, satellite feeds, and playback units). The primary means of transition are:

Cut or take. This instant change from one image to another is the most used transition during productions. It has been said that 99% of all transitions are cuts.

Dissolve. Dissolves are a gradual change from one image to the next and are usually used to show a change of time or location.

Wipe. The wipe is a novel transition that can take many different shapes. (See Figure 3.25.) It shows a change of time, subject, or location. Although the wipe can inject interest or fun in the sequence of shots, it can be easily overused.

Fade. A fade signifies a dissolve transition to or from black. (See Chapter 17 for more information about switching.)

The Wipe

Wipes, used as a unique transition between incoming images on the switcher, can be quite flexible. Most medium- and higher-end switchers allow wipes to be customized.

Although the results are always geometrical, you can change them in several ways:

- Pattern size can be adjusted—expanded or contracted.
- Pattern shapes can be adjusted. For example, a square can be made rectangular; a circle can become an ellipse.
- The pattern can be moved around the frame: up/down, left/right, diagonally.
- You can control the speed at which the pattern changes or moves, using a fader lever or an autowipe button.
- The symmetry of the pattern can be adjusted.
- The pattern edges can be made hard (sharp) or soft (diffused). If sources are interswitched instantaneously, there will be a sharply defined division.
- A border can be placed around a pattern insert, in black, white, or color.

There are literally dozens of wipe patterns, but some typical examples are shown in Figure 3.25.

Chroma-Key

A significant option on many switchers is chroma-key. Chroma-key allows the director to insert one image onto another. (See Figure 3.26.) It has endless applications, especially when combined with other video effects. Chroma-key can simulate total reality or create magical, stylized, decorative displays. (Additional information concerning chroma-key virtual sets is provided in Chapter 13.)

FIGURE 3.26
With the subject sitting in front of a green background, a secondary image (computer-generated news set) was inserted into whatever is green in the camera shot. The combined result makes it look as though the subject is actually in front of the background scene. Subjects within the master shot must not wear or contain the keying color (blue or green) or the secondary background will insert into those areas as well. The secondary background image can be anything: colors, still images, graphics, and/or recorded or live video images.

For decades, chroma-key has been used to insert studio action "into" photographs, graphics, and video images. It has been used in all types of productions from interviews to opera, from "soap operas" to musical extravaganzas, from kids' shows to serious discussions, and from newscasts to weather forecasting. The opportunities seem boundless. Yet chroma-key has mainly been used as an incidental technique—or to provide "magical tricks." There have been a number of reasons for this:

- Some directors and actors feel uncomfortable when confronted with a studio comprising blue backdrops and floor, odd scenic pieces, and a scattering of furniture. They prefer "solid sets" that allow them to stand and see potential shots.
- Working with chroma-key and virtual sets requires imaginative anticipatory planning if it is to be wholly successful.
- Ineptly handled, chroma-key production can consume rehearsal time, as incongruous effects arise.

The opportunities for chroma-key are endless. But you need to apply chroma-key carefully, keeping in mind its problems and limitations, if you are going to achieve convincing, accurate results. Careful planning will save a great deal of time. Detailed planning and methodical setup methods pay off. Completely convincing results can be obtained and the time taken is nominal.

When preparing a chroma-key setup, begin by checking that the chroma-key area and subjects are suitable:

- Is the color of the background appropriate? Ideally, the green background (and floor, if necessary) should be of an even overall tone of chroma-key green. Another popular color used in chroma-key is blue. Some systems are more color-critical than others. Check that the painted chroma-key flats have a dull, even finish. Background or floor cloth should be stretched, without folds or wrinkles.
- The keying surfaces should be evenly lit. If they vary in brightness, it will be difficult to adjust clip levels correctly. So look out for deep shadows falling on the chroma-key green or blue surfaces (particularly from the performers or furniture).

FIGURE 3.27
This camera is synced to the chroma-keyed background imagery. Note that this syncing system uses a grid on the background to determine its positioning.

40

Synchronized Movements with the Virtual Set

In order to use a moving or zooming camera during a production that uses a virtual set, the inserted imagery must move in synchronization with the camera. (See Figure 3.27.) Otherwise, the set (background) would stay the same size, no matter which camera was used, which creates a very unrealistic-looking set situation. Some form of a servo link is required to ensure that both operate in exact synchronism. Then, as the camera moves, proportional changes will be seen in both subject and background pictures. The combined results in the composite are completely realistic. Precise information is required about the camera's floor position, height, shooting angle, and lens angle and must be fed into a computer, which correspondingly adjusts the background source. Even slight changes in the subject camera require the entire background picture to be instantly recalculated and redrawn to correspond if the composite is to be compatible. Entire scenic environments can be created artificially to enhance these shots. The background can be derived from a camera shooting, a photographic display, or a three-dimensional scale model, or computer-generated backgrounds can be used.

Practical Examples

Let's turn to a couple of examples that show the sort of thing that can be achieved with chroma-key and a little imagination. Built scenery here is minimal, and we have avoided the complications of studio settings or shooting on location:

> *What the viewer saw:* A continuous long shot shows the darkened interior of an ancient church. A cleric walks slowly across the shot from camera left. He is carrying a lighted candle and turns toward the distant altar, and moves up the aisle. He lights large candles on either side of the altar, and exits.
>
> *What was in the studio:* A green background and a green floor cloth. A photograph of a church interior provided the background scene. Corresponding with the distant altar in the photograph is a green-painted table, with a couple of regular candles on tall blue blocks.

In another totally convincing example:

> *What the viewer saw:* We are outside a small country store. A girl cycles into the shot, stops, and rests her bike against a nearby tree. She bends down to pat a sleeping dog. Reaching up to pick a blossom from the tree, she walks up steps to enter the store.
>
> *What was in the studio:* A photo slide provided the background scene, complete with store, tree, and sleeping dog beneath it. In the studio (blue cyc and floor), a blue pole on a stand corresponded to the tree in the photograph. (It had a real blossom attached to it by a thread.) The girl patted the air where the photo-dog slept. Green-painted stock treads were positioned where the store's steps were located in the photograph.

Digital Video Effects

Digital video effects (DVEs) can be designed into the switcher or may be a separate DVE piece of equipment. Like wipe patterns, some digital effects are rarely used, and others have become a regular part of production.

   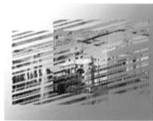

FIGURE 3.28
Here is a small sampling of the digital video effects that are available. (Images courtesy of Thomson/Grass Valley)

As you can see from Figure 3.28, an increasing range of visual effects is available. Some have a direct production value, some add an interesting new (for now) dimension to presentation, and others are for novelty.

It is not always obvious that an effect is being used. For instance, a digital effect may be used to fill the screen with a section of a still frame, or to trim the edges of its image. A perfectly normal-looking map could be a DVE composite. A "graphic" showing a series of portraits could be displaying images from a still-store, combined by digital effects.

There often are multiple names for the same movement. Technically speaking, when describing movement, the following terms generally apply:

- Horizontal movements (left/right, right/left) are along the X axis. Anything rotating around the X axis is said to tumble or flip.
- Vertical movements (up/down, down/up) are along the Y axis. Anything rotating around the Y axis is said to spin or rotate.
- Movement toward and away from the viewer is along the Z axis. (The illusion of depth actually comes from items growing larger/smaller, from expansion and compression.)

REVIEW QUESTIONS

1. Compare a studio and a remote production and explain the advantages and disadvantages of each one.
2. Explain the basic multicamera audio and video path from the camera and microphone in the studio to the final recorder.
3. What are the primary components of a control room?
4. What is the role of the director during a production?
5. List the switcher transitions and explain how each is used.
6. How can chroma-key be used effectively in television production? Give examples.

CHAPTER 4

How Television Works

"If you divide a still image into a collection of small colored dots, your amazing brain will reassemble the dots into a meaningful image . . . which makes television possible."

Marshall Brain, Professor

Terms

720p: An HDTV format that has 720 scan lines and utilizes progressive scanning. The 720p format is best for fast-moving motion scenes.

1080i: An HDTV format that has 1080 scan lines and uses an interlaced scanning system. The 1080i format has a sharper image than the 720p format.

1080p: An HDTV format that has 1080 scan lines and uses a progressive scanning system. It is often referred to as "full HD."

CCD (charge-coupled device): A type of image sensor found within video cameras.

CMOS (complementary metal-oxide semiconductor sensor): A type of image sensor found within video cameras.

Dichroic filters: Produce three color-filtered images corresponding to the red, green, and blue proportions in the scene.

Interlaced scanning: The television's electron scans the odd-numbered lines first and then goes back and "paints" in the remaining even-numbered lines.

NTSC (National Television System Committee): The television system traditionally used by the United States and Japan. It has 525 scan lines.

PAL (phase-alternating line): The television system widely used in Europe and throughout the world. It was derived from the NTSC system, but avoids the hue shift caused by phase errors in the transmission path by reversing the phase of the reference color burst on alternate lines. It has 625 lines of resolution.

Progressive scanning: This sequential scanning system uses an electron beam that scans or paints all lines at once, displaying the total picture.

RGB: The three primary colors used in video processing: red, green, and blue.

SECAM (from the French phrase for "sequential color with memory"): Television system used by France and many countries of the former USSR.

43

You don't need to study technology in depth in order to make good programs. But understanding the principles involved will certainly help you to anticipate and avoid various everyday problems. Although the actual electronics are extremely sophisticated, the basics that you need to know are really surprisingly straightforward.

THE VIDEO SIGNAL

The picture from the lens is focused onto an image sensor within the video camera. This is usually a charge-coupled device (CCD) or a complementary metal-oxide semiconductor (CMOS) sensor. The CCD is the original chip used since the move from tubes in cameras (Figure 4.1). Although the CCD is still used in the majority of the cameras made, the CMOS chip has rapidly become increasingly popular. One of the primary advantages to the CMOS chip is that it uses less power consumption, saving energy for longer shooting times.

A pattern of electrical charges forms on the light-sensitive area of the sensor, which corresponds in strength at each point to light and shade in the lens image. As special scanning circuits systematically read across this charge pattern in a series of parallel lines, a varying signal voltage or video is produced relating to the original picture tones. After amplification and electronic corrections, the video signal from the camera (with added synchronizing pulses) can be distributed.

Looking at the apparently endless range of colors and shades in the world around us, it seems incredible that they can be reproduced on a television screen simply by mixing appropriate proportions of red, green, and blue light. Yet, that is the underlying principle of color television.

FIGURE 4.1
CCD sensor.

The chips in the television camera can only respond to variations in brightness. They cannot directly detect differences in color. However, if a color filter is placed in front of the light sensor in the camera, the video signal that it produces will then correspond to the proportions of that color in the scene.

The simplest video camera systems use a multicolored striped filter fitted over a single light sensor (CCD or CMOS chip). These single-chip cameras are generally used for consumers. However, in professional cameras, which are required to provide more accurate color and detail, three separate sensor chips are used. In these, the image from the lens passes through a special prism block with dichroic filters (Figure 4.2). These filters produce three color-filtered images corresponding to the red, green, and blue proportions in the scene. The video signals from the respective sensors correspond to the three primaries needed to reproduce a picture in full color.

Light and Shade

Although the sensors and filters provide the full range of colors for the television image, what about its light and shade and its brightness variations? If the red, green, and blue are added together, they equal white. If they are all equal but very weak, they will result in a very weak white, or what we would call a dark gray. If the signals are stronger, the area on the screen will be brighter. If most parts of the screen are energized by strong video signals, we interpret this as a bright picture, and vice versa.

To summarize: The effective color (hue) results from the actual proportions of red, green, and blue, and the brightness of each part of the screen depends on the overall strength of the mixture.

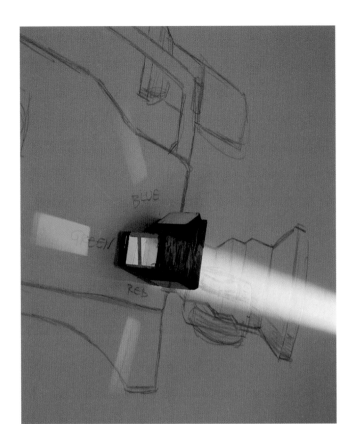

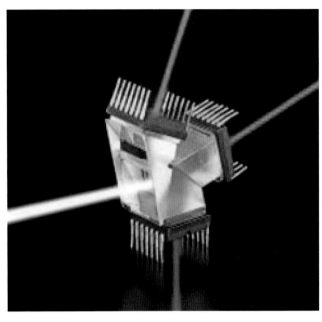

FIGURE 4.2

In a three-chip camera, light passes through the lens to a special prism block with dichroic filters. These filters produce red, green, and blue signals that go to sensors. (Images courtesy of Adam Wilt and Panasonic)

Distributing the Signal

Some cameras create a specially encoded signal that incorporates all of the color and brightness information into one signal for distribution. This encoded signal must be decoded at the receiver and then reconstituted as separate color signals for the monitor. Other camera formats send three separate RGB signals from the camera to the receiver in order to obtain a higher quality. The sound (audio) signal is usually sent separately.

Television Standard Compatibility

As standard-definition (SD) television technology has evolved over the years, different countries or areas of the world have created their own television systems. This has resulted in three different incompatible SD television systems that are now used worldwide: NTSC, PAL, and SECAM. Unfortunately, pictures transmitted or recorded on one system cannot reproduce directly onto another. Subsequently, standards converters have been developed that have enabled material originating in one system to be translated into another (e.g., from NTSC to PAL or vice versa).

These systems are primarily used in the following countries/regions:

NTSC—United States, Canada, Japan, Mexico, South Korea, and Taiwan.
PAL—Western Europe, United Kingdom, Ireland, Hong Kong and Macau, most of Eastern Europe, and China.
SECAM—Africa and parts of Asia and Europe.

Although there are a number of different HD standards, the currently most popular are 720p, 1080i, and 1080p. All of these individual formats are compatible around the world. They are not limited to specific countries as are NTSC, PAL, and SECAM.

THE TELEVISION PICTURE

There are times when television engineers may seem to be obsessed with "picture quality"—with color fidelity, definition, tonal gradation, gamma, and so on. The reason that the image quality of the pictures we produce is so important is that it—just like the accompanying sound—directly affects the viewer's enjoyment of the production. If a camera's picture is not sufficiently sharp, the viewer will not be able to see detail or texture clearly. If color varies from one camera to the next, changes will distract the viewer when cutting between the shots. If tones are not reproduced successfully, subtle variations will be lost, and surfaces will appear to be flat and unmodeled.

Clearly, picture quality matters, but how good can a television picture be? Initially, it depends on the system used. At best, it can be superb. But there are inevitably various losses between the camera lens and the home screen that degrade the picture.

Picture Detail

All video systems have a maximum limit to the amount of detail they can convey. In television, the definition (resolution) is initially influenced by the number of picture lines the system uses. But it is also affected by system design. As the image of the scene is scanned into the camera, the video should ideally be able to change in strength to correspond with tonal differences. The faster it can change, the finer the detail that it can resolve. This rate of change is measured as *frequency*.

Apart from these technical parameters, many other factors can affect picture clarity, including the lens performance. It may be dirty or badly focused. Lighting may produce lens flares. The glass of a prompter attached to the camera can degrade picture quality. Or the viewer may be watching a poor video recording. There can be many reasons for low-quality images!

Picture Tones

Although it is not immediately obvious in most pictures, the range of tones that a television system can normally reproduce is quite restricted compared with those in the original scene.

Our eyes appear to detect subtle tonal differences over a remarkably wide range—even when the lightest areas are as much as a thousand times brighter than the darkest (a 1000:1 contrast range). This impression, however, is largely due to the human brain's adaptation—that is, its ability to readjust instantaneously to the brightness of localized areas that we are looking at. Image reproduction systems have considerably less accommodation. Color negative film, for example, can handle a contrast range of only about 100:1 (10 stops) and still reproduce subtle half tones in between. If the subject contrast is greater than this range, it will result in tonal gradation and details being lost in the highlights and/or shadows.

Most electronic sensor cameras can easily handle a 40:1 range. Home television receivers are more likely to be limited to a range of around 20:1. Any picture tones that exceed this range (e.g., bright highlights, deep shadows) will appear as detail-free white or black areas on the screen. If the television receiver itself has not been adjusted for optimum contrast/brightness, or light is falling on its screen and diluting darker tones, reproduced picture quality can be considerably impaired. Many televisions display little more than a 10:1 or 15:1 range.

Whether such limitations matter in practice depends on how important tonal subtlety is in your shot. If a map that you are showing reproduces as a blank sheet because lighter tones have been blocked off, it is embarrassing! On the other hand, if dark clothing lacks subtle modeling, this may not be too important. Compensatory circuits (gamma adjustments, exposure compression) have been created that can prevent this restricted range from being too obvious. However, they do not enable you to extend the system's inherent tonal limits. Sometimes you may have to adjust the lighting contrast or the actual tones of the subjects (costumes, scenery) to keep within the limits to improve the overall image.

REVIEW QUESTIONS

1. What is the difference between a CCD chip and a CMOS chip?
2. What role do the dichroic filters play in a television camera?

PART 2

The Process, Script, and Production Plan

CHAPTER 5

The Production Process

"In TV we've used something that I love . . . it's called 'process.' I love process."

Jerry Bruckheimer, Producer

Terms

Goals: Broad concepts of what you want to accomplish in a production.

I-mag: Image magnification; refers to video on large television screens next to a stage in order to help the viewers see the stage action.

Objectives: Measurable goals.

Postproduction: Editing, additional treatment, and duplication of the project.

Storyboard: A series of rough sketches that help someone visualize and organize the desired camera treatment.

As you would expect, in the real world there are a broad spectrum of approaches to television production. One end of the spectrum is a "get me a good shot" approach, largely relying on the initiative of the camera team to find the best shots. At the other extreme are directors who know precisely what they want, and arrange the talent and cameras to get exactly that.

THE THREE STAGES OF PRODUCTION

Most television productions go through three main stages:

1. *Planning and preparation.* The preliminaries, preparation, organization, and rehearsal before the production begins. Ninety percent of the work on a production usually goes into the planning and preparation stage (Figure 5.1).
2. *Production.* Actually shooting the production.
3. *Postproduction.* Editing, additional treatment, and duplication.

The amount of work at each stage is influenced by the nature of the subject. One that involves a series of straightforward "personality" interviews is generally a lot easier to organize than one on an Arctic exploration or an historical drama. But in the end, a great deal depends on how the director decides to approach the subject.

Working at the highest quality level, directors can create incredible programming by using simple methods. Treatment does not have to be elaborate to make its point. If a woman in the desert picks up her water bottle, finds it empty, and the camera shows a patch of damp sand where it rested, the shot has told us a great deal without any need for elaboration. A single

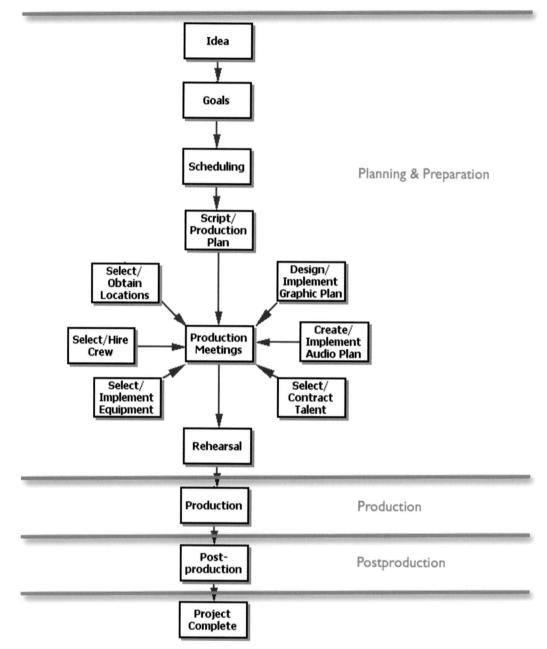

Idea

Goals

Scheduling

Planning & Preparation

Script/
Production
Plan

Select/
Obtain
Locations

Design/
Implement
Graphic Plan

Select/Hire
Crew

Production
Meetings

Create/
Implement
Audio Plan

Select/
Implement
Equipment

Select/
Contract
Talent

Rehearsal

Production

Production

Post-
production

Postproduction

Project
Complete

FIGURE 5.1
During the flow of the video production process, roughly 90 percent of the work goes into the planning and preparation stage.

look or a gesture can often have a far stronger impact than lengthy dialogue attempting to show how two people feel about each other.

It is important to understand the complexity of the production. Some ideas seem simple enough, but can be difficult or impossible to carry out. Others look very difficult or impracticable, but are easily achieved on the screen.

STAGE 1: PLANNING AND PREPARATION

"A production's quality will be in direct proportion to the quality and quantity of preproduction. Every single element in the video or audio channel of a production must be controlled, because every single element will affect the audience's reaction."

Ronald Hickman, Director

Why Plan?

Some people find the idea of planning very restrictive. They want to get on with the shooting. For them, planning somehow turns the thrill of the unexpected into an organized commitment.

But many situations must be planned and worked out in advance. Directors need to get permission to shoot on private property, to make appointments to interview people, to arrange admissions, and so on. They might occasionally have success if they arrive unannounced, but do not assume this. However, directors also need to be prepared to take advantage of unexpected opportunities. It is worth taking advantage of the unexpected, even if you decide not to use it later.

The television production process is sometimes linear and sometimes nonlinear. Sometimes the concept starts with a piece of music and sometimes a script. Other times the concept may originate with a writer, the producer, the director, or even a production assistant. So, even though the steps in the process may be in a different order at times, the most common process is described in the following sections—and it always starts with an idea.

The Idea: Starting with a Concept

Something triggers the idea. Usually, it comes from an interesting personal experience, a story you heard, something you read in a book or newspaper—some interesting incident that gave you the idea for your production. After the idea, you have to begin to formulate your goals and objectives.

Setting the Goals and Objectives

What do you really want your audience to know after they have viewed your production? It could be that you want the program to be educational, to entertain, or to inspire. The answer to this question is essential, as it guides the entire production process. The goals and objectives will determine what is used as a measuring stick throughout the rest of the production process. *Goals* are broad concepts of what you want to accomplish. Here's a sample goal: *I want to explain how to field a Formula One racing team.*

Objectives are measurable goals. That means something that can be tested to see whether the audience reacted the way you wanted them to react to the program. Take the time to think through what the audience should know after seeing your program. Following are some sample objectives.

When the viewers finish watching the program, 50 percent of them should be able to:

- Identify three types of sponsorship.
- Identify four crew positions.
- Identify two scheduling issues.

All three of these are objectives, because they are measurable. The number of objectives is determined by the goals. This means that sometimes only one objective is needed; other times, five may be required.

The Target Audience

Whether your program is a sitcom, a news program, educational television, or a sports production, it is essential to determine *whom* the program is for, and its chief *purpose*:

- Who is the viewing audience? Are they senior citizens, teens, or children?
- Is it for the general public, for specific groups, or for a local group?
- What level of content is required: basic, intermediate, or advanced? If the audience consists of children who cannot read, relevant images may be required.
- Is any specific background, qualification, language, or group experience necessary for the audience? If the audience is new to the language, carefully chosen words will need to be used.

FIGURE 5.2
The intended audience should determine how the director covers the subject. In this situation, generally a younger crowd would favor a different style of coverage than elderly people. (Photo by Paul Dupree)

- Are there specific production styles that this audience favors? Teens lean toward an MTV television style, yet older viewers may appreciate a *CBS Sunday Morning News* production style. The target audience should determine your program's coverage and style. It is self-evident that the sort of program you would make for a group of content experts would be very different than one made for young children (Figure 5.2).

The conditions under which the audience is going to watch the program are important too. Today, most video programs are not made to be broadcast. They are viewed as DVDs or streamed into homes, classrooms, corporate offices, and many other locations. So the wise director tries to anticipate these conditions because they can considerably affect the way the program is produced. How and where is your audience going to see the program (Figure 5.3)? Consider:

- Will they be watching a traditional television screen in their homes?
- Will they be a seated group of students watching a large screen in a darkened classroom?
- Will the viewer be watching a streamed video over the Internet while at the office?
- Will the program be viewed on an iPod while riding in a car (Figure 5.4)?
- Will the video be projected on large screens next to a stage in order to help the viewers see the stage action? This is known as image magnification (I-mag).

How will your audience view your production?
Historically, television productions were created for a moderately sized television set. Today, you need to know what medium your audience will be watching, as it significantly impacts how the production is made.

Cell Phone

Television

FIGURE 5.3
Different ways to watch television. Photos by Panasonic, Jon Cypher and You Tube.

Internet

Large Screen

If the program will be viewed in direct daylight, directors may want to avoid dark or low-key scenes. The images displayed on many receivers/monitors in daylight can be of poor quality: tonal gradation can be coarse, lighter tones are over-exposed, smaller lettering bleeds and actually may be indecipherable, color is often either too pale to see or over-emphasized. All this is frequently due to incorrect monitor adjustment, as viewers try to get the brightest possible picture.

Try to anticipate the problems for an audience watching a distant picture monitor. Long shots have correspondingly little impact. Closer shots are essential, as they add emotion and drama. Small lettering means nothing on a small distant screen. To improve the visibility of titles, charts, maps, and other items, keep details basic and limit the information.

If your target audience may be watching on an iPod or other very small-screen device, directors should lean toward more close-ups than usual, as the long shots may not be as discernable on the small screen (Figure 5.5).

Here are a number of reminder questions that can help you anticipate your audience's potential problems:

- Does the program rely on their previously established knowledge?
- How much do they know about the subject already?
- Will the program be watched straight through, or will it be stopped after sections for discussion?
- Will there be any accompanying supporting material (maps, graphs, or statistics) to which the audience can refer? (You cannot expect them to hold detailed data in their heads as they follow the program's story line.)
- Will there be other competing, noisy attractions as they watch, such as at an exhibition?
- Will the program soon be out of date?
- What is the time limit for the program?

The Budget

It is essential to create an accurate cost estimation of the project. Without a budget in front of the director, costs can become wildly out of control. Each expenditure needs to be tracked in order to remain within the budget. Decisions made in every aspect of the production are usually somewhat based on the budget. Figure 5.6 shows a sample television budgeting sheet.

Limitations/Restrictions

There are also a number of obvious factors that determine what you can do, and how you go about the production, such as budget restrictions; the amount of time available; money and legal issues; the time of day or season; weather; limitations or shortages of equipment or personnel; the experience and adaptability of the performers/talent/anchors/commentators/interviewers; and any local intrusions, such as location noises.

FIGURE 5.4
Small iPod-type devices with the ability to play hours of video are rapidly becoming the video player of choice for many people.

FIGURE 5.5
Close-up shots add emotion and drama to a production and add needed detail to small-screen productions such as those seen on an iPod-type device.

55

TV PRODUCTION BUDGET SUMMARY SHEET		
Name of Program:		
Number of TV Episodes & Duration:		
Previous Funding		
Development	$	$
Production	$	$
TV DEVELOPMENT/SCRIPT		
Concept & Rights:	$	
Research:	$	
Story/Script/Writer's Fees:	$	
Other (specify):	$	
Development Subtotal		$
TV PRODUCTION		
Producer Fees (total incl. EP)	$	
Director Fees (total):	$	
Presenters/Actors/Talent:	$	
Production Staff & Crew:	$	
Studio/Locations:	$	
Equipment Hire:	$	
Wardrobe/Makeup/Art Department:	$	
Travel/Accommodations/Living:	$	
Production Office/Administration:	$	
Other (specify):	$	
Production Subtotal		$
TV POSTPRODUCTION		
Music & Copyright:	$	
Library Footage & Copyright:	$	
Film/Tape Stock:	$	
Picture Postproduction:	$	
Audio Postproduction:	$	
Titles/Graphics:	$	
Postproduction Labor:	$	
Other (specify):	$	
Postproduction Subtotal		$
TV MARKETING & ADMINISTRATION		
Marketing/Delivery:	$	
Administration/Overheads:	$	
Legal:	$	
Insurance:	$	
Sundry (e.g., finance, ACC etc.)	$	
Other (specify):	$	
Marketing/Administration Subtotal		$
Total Above the Line:		$
Total Below the Line:		$
Contingency:		$
Production Company Overhead:		$
TOTAL TELEVISION PRODUCTION BUDGET		$
Total Cost per Episode		$

FIGURE 5.6

An example of a simple television budget sheet. (Courtesy of Kristof Creative, Inc./KristofCreative.com)

The Production Plan

Every program needs a production plan. As mentioned earlier, sometimes the program may be an unscripted event unfolding live, right in front of you. Although some live events cannot be scripted, a production plan is still a necessity. Going through almost the same process as creating a script, the director must know the event and create the best coverage plan. After reviewing

FIGURE 5.7
A sports event is an example of an unscripted event that still requires a production plan. (Photo by Josh Taber)

the various outcomes of the event, it is important to come up with enough contingency plans that will allow you to continue covering the event, no matter what happens (Figure 5.7).

Production Methods

Great ideas are not enough. Ideas have to be worked out in realistic, practical terms. They have to be expressed as images and sounds. In the end, the director has to decide what the camera is going to shoot, and what the audience is going to hear. Where do you start?

There are two quite different methods of approaching video production:

- The *unplanned* method, in which instinct and opportunity are the guides.
- The *planned* method, which organizes and builds a program in carefully arranged steps.

THE UNPLANNED APPROACH

Directors following the unplanned approach get an idea, then look around for subjects and situations that relate to it. After shooting possible material, they later create a program from whatever they have found. Their inspiration springs from the opportunities that have arisen.

An example would be that the director decides to make a program about "safety at sea." Using the unplanned approach, the director might go to a marina and develop a production based on the stories heard there. Or the idea could be discussed with the lifeguards, and the director might then decide to follow an entirely different plan. A commercial dock could also be visited, and the director might discover material there of an entirely different kind.

After accumulating a collection of interesting sequences (atmospheric shots, natural sound, interviews, etc.), the content is reviewed and then put into a meaningful order. A program could then be created that fits the accumulated material, probably writing a commentary as a "voiceover" to match the edited pictures.

FIGURE 5.8
Some documentaries are shot using the unplanned approach, in which instinct and opportunity are the guides. (Photo by Will Adams)

At best, this approach is fresh, uninhibited, improvises, makes use of the unexpected, avoids rigid discipline, and is very adaptable. Shots are interestingly varied. The audience is kept alert, watching and interpreting the changing scene.

At worst, the result of such shot-hunting is a haphazard disaster, with little cohesion or sense of purpose. Because the approach is unsystematic, gaps and overlaps abound. Good coherent editing may be difficult. Opportunities may have been missed. The director usually relies heavily on the voiceover to try to provide any sort of relationship and continuity between the images (Figure 5.8).

THE PLANNED APPROACH

The planned method of production approaches the problem quite differently, although the results on the screen may be similar. In this situation the director works out, in advance, the exact form he or she wants the program to take and then creates it accordingly.

Fundamentally, you can either:

- Begin with the environment or setting and decide how the cameras can be positioned to get the most effective shots. (See Figure 5.9.)
- Envision certain shots or effects that you want to see, and create a setting that will provide those results. (See Figure 5.10.)

A lot will depend on which of the following scenarios applies:

- *Interpreting an existing script* (as in drama). This will involve analyzing the script: examining the story line and the main action in each scene and visualizing individual shots.
- *Building a treatment framework.* That is, considering how you are going to present a specific program subject and working out the kinds of shots you want.

At best, the planned approach is a method in which a crew can be coordinated to give their best. There is a sense of systematic purpose throughout the project. Problems are largely ironed

FIGURE 5.9
Production and engineering staff review a venue for a television production using the planned approach. They begin with the setting and then decide where to place the cameras.

FIGURE 5.10
Narrative directors use the planned approach to production by utilizing a storyboard. However, they create the setting to fit the story. (Photo by Josh Taber)

out before they develop. Production is based on what is feasible. The program can have a smooth-flowing, carefully thought out, persuasive style.

At worst, the production becomes bogged down in organization. The program can be stodgy and routine and lack originality. Opportunities are ignored, because they were not part of the original scheme, and would modify it. The result could be a disaster.

In reality, the experienced director uses a combination of the planned and unplanned approaches, starting off with a plan and then taking advantage of any opportunities that become available.

Schedule

It is imperative to sit down and establish a schedule that includes the essential deadlines. These deadlines usually revolve around the following issues: When does the script need to be completed? When do locations need to chosen? When does the talent need to be selected and contracted? Deadlines are also selected for the crew, equipment, rehearsals, graphics, props, rehearsals, and rough production and postproduction schedule. Keep in mind that at this stage you are not actually doing any of these things; you are determining the schedule and setting the deadlines as to when they must be completed.

Any time the schedule is not met, there will be a ripple effect on the other areas of the production, because one of two things is going to happen: the production will either go over budget or some elements will need to be cut in order to make up for lost time and/or money.

Coverage

What do you want to cover in the available time? How much is *reasonable* to cover in that time? If there are too many topics, it will not be possible to do justice to any of them. If there are too few, the program might seem slow and labored. There is nothing to be gained by packing the program full of facts, for although they may sound impressive, audiences rarely remember more than a fraction of them. Unlike with the printed page, the viewer cannot check back to confirm something, unless the program is designed to be stopped and rewound or is frequently repeated.

The kind of subject that is being covered, as well as who makes up the audience and the content that needs to be featured, will influence how the camera is utilized in the program, where it concentrates, how close the shots are, and how varied they are. As a director, here are some of the areas that need to be considered in advance:

- What are the content areas that need to be covered?
- Is the subject (person, event, or object) best seen from specific angles? Does a specific angle help communicate the message more effectively? (See Figure 5.11.)
- Would the addition of graphics help the audience understand the content of the production?
- If possible, watch a preliminary unfilmed rehearsal so that the best viewpoints and shots can be determined.
- Give the talent and crew the vision and goals for the production and then help them know what they can do to assist in attaining the goals.
- If considered helpful, create a shot list for each camera operator. A shot list is a description of each shot needed from the camera operator, listed in order, so that the operator can move from shot to shot with little instruction from the director. Other camera operator supports may include team rosters to help the operator find a specific player for the director.

FIGURE 5.11
This producer is determining the best camera angles for coverage in a stadium.

Building an Outline

The program outline begins with a series of *headings* showing the main themes that need to be discussed.

Let's use the example of an instructional video about "building a wall." In this case, the topics that might be covered could include: tools needed, materials, foundation, making mortar, and methods of laying bricks and pointing. We can now determine how much program time can be devoted to each topic. Some will be brief and others relatively lengthy. Some of the topics will need to be emphasized; others will be skipped over to suit the purpose of the program.

The next stage is to take each of the topic headings and note the various aspects that need to be covered as a series of *subheadings*. Under "tools," for instance, each tool that must be demonstrated should be listed. Now there is a structure for the program and the director can begin to see the form it is likely to take.

Research

Some programs, such as dramas (especially period dramas), documentaries, news, interviews, and others need to complete research in order to create the program's content or make sure that the existing content is accurate. This research may involve going to the library, doing online research, or contacting recognized experts in the content area of the show. Travel may even be required.

Cam 1

Cam 2

Cam 3

FIGURE 5.12
In a formal interview, there are relatively few shots.

The important thing to remember here is that research is time consuming and may affect the production budget—especially if a content expert wants an appearance fee or flights and lodging are included for the crew or guest.

Regular Studio Formats

There are a number of regular formats used in studios today: interviews, panel discussions, piano and instrumental performances, singers, and newscasts. These are usually familiar to a studio production crew and meaningful shooting variations are limited. What the talent is saying (or playing) is more important than straining to achieve new and original shots. Consequently, these productions follow normal patterns so that the director often starts off with planned angles and then may introduce a specific treatment as it becomes desirable (Figures 5.12 and 5.13).

Planning for regular productions is primarily a matter of coordinating staff and facilities; ensuring that the video packages or clips are available (with known timing and cue points); graphics, titles, and similar features are prepared; and any additional material organized. The production itself may be based on a series of key shots and some spontaneous on-the-fly decisions.

Top Shot

Long Shot

Reaction Shot

Medium Long Shot

Hands

Over the Shoulder

Through the Lid

FIGURE 5.13
There is often a broad range of shot options. (Photos by Austin Brooks)

Complex Productions

Whether you are shooting in the studio or on location, time is money and it must be used efficiently. Although smaller shows may get by with a preliminary talk-over a few days before the production date, for more complex projects comprehensive planning is essential. The team must be briefed and organized, which requires discursive agreement; there are sundry factors to consider, such as time estimates, costing, manpower, safety, union agreements, and others.

Treatment Breakdown

For many shows, the action is predetermined by the program format—the talent is going to enter by walking down a staircase and sitting in a specific chair to be interviewed, then move over to a table to talk about the product on display. The shots are straightforward. The director checks over the studio plans, and with an eye to the program script, places cameras in regular positions that fit the treatment (long shots, group shots, singles, reaction shots). Any variations can be worked out during rehearsals.

However, if you are directing a more complicated production, planning will need to be more detailed. You begin by reading through the script, with the sets and layouts in the studio. As you read, you visualize each scene and consider issues such as whether talent is going to make an entrance or exit, what they are going to do, where they will be doing it, and whether they will need props such as a map. Are they going to speak to the camera? Are other people in the scene, and what are they doing? Are they going to move around (look out a window on the set)? Although these questions sound very obvious, they don't just happen. Everything has to be planned, arranged, and learned.

The next step is to systematically block out the action. For example, you might ask yourself, "Would it be better if the hostess is seen entering the room and moving over to the desk, or should we discover her already seated? Because the show is about dress design, would it be preferable if the audience saw her clothing as she enters rather than opening with a head and shoulders shot at the desk? Is the idea of a desk too formal anyway? Would an easy chair be preferable?" and so on.

After determining the action, consider what type of shots would be appropriate and where the cameras should be to get them. If one camera moves into the set to get a close shot of the item they are discussing, will the camera now be in the second camera's shot? Would it be better to record some shots of the product after the formal interview and then edit in the insert shot during postproduction? This is how a director builds a continuous succession of shots, noting them in the script margin, either as abbreviated reminders or as tiny sketches. The same situation can often be tackled in various different but equally successful ways. Let us look at an example for a dramatic production:

Returning husband enters door, wife has an unexpected guest.

This could be broken down as:

Shot 1: Husband enters door, hangs up hat . . . medium shot shows who it is and orientates the audience.
Shot 2: Wife looks up, greeting him . . . medium two-shot showing her with guest.
Shot 3: Husband turns and sees the guest . . . close-up shot of husband's reaction.
Shot 4: The guest rises, walks to greet the husband . . . from medium two-shot; pans with guest, dollying in for tight two-shot of guest and husband.

Developing the Camera Plan

Depending on the type of production, the director may need to determine the type of lenses required for a specific type of shot. In order to plan the specifics, it is very helpful to have a scale-accurate floor plan or ground plan. The other option is to visit the location and measure it. These issues arise especially often when working at remote sites. One of the ways to calculate the lenses needed is to use a lens calculator (a chart or PDA software). You can also judge the types of shot (close-up, full length, etc.) that a certain lens angle will give.

The resultant production plan (camera plan), together with margin action notes or sketches, will form the basis for all technical planning and subsequent rehearsals. Even the biggest productions can be analyzed into shots or sequences in this way.

Storyboards

Directors need to think through each scene in their minds, capturing the images and turning them into a storyboard. A storyboard is a series of rough sketches that help the director visualize and organize their camera treatment. It is a visual map of how the director hopes to arrange the shots for each scene or action sequence. Storyboards will be covered in more detail in Chapter 6. (See Figure 5.14.)

Once the script and/or production plan, and possibly even storyboards, are completed, there is a whole series of planning and preparation that needs to be completed. These tasks are not linear; that is, the production staff can be working on all of them at the same time. The producer and director often act as coaches, reviewing the work by each segment of their staff, encouraging, giving feedback, providing quality control, and challenging them to move forward at a brisk pace. The producer or the director has to juggle all of these aspects at the same time. Each of these areas will be developed in more detail in later chapters.

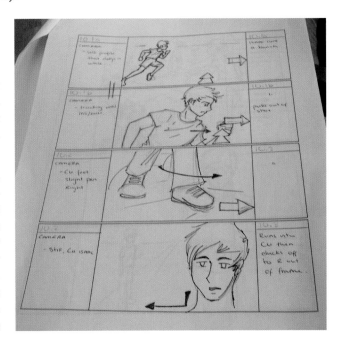

FIGURE 5.14
A storyboard on the set of a production. The storyboard roughly visualizes what the program will look like. (Photo by Taylor Vinson)

63

Production Aspects

There are many aspects that need to be considered during the planning stage. Following are a few of them.

SELECT AND OBTAIN LOCATIONS

Shoot locations must be chosen. A location may be a studio, a sports venue, a house, or some other location. Permits or contracts may need to be obtained. Later in this chapter, we will discuss the location site survey.

DETERMINE CAMERA LOCATIONS

By determining the specific camera locations, you can calculate cable lengths, contract equipment if needed, and plan other steps.

SELECT AND CONTRACT THE TALENT

Anchors, narrators, actors, or anyone else who will be appearing in front of the camera must be chosen and then contracted.

SELECT AND HIRE THE CREW

The appropriate production and engineering crew must be hired. This may or may not involve contracts. Each person needs to know their start and end dates as well as their pay, instructions, and a multitude of other details.

DECIDE ON THE TALENT

Once the talent has been chosen, then you look at contracts, costuming, makeup, and similar related details.

CREATE AND IMPLEMENT THE AUDIO PLAN

Audio specifications must be determined. For example, what needs to be heard? Once you know what must be heard, an audio plan is created. This plan would include the placement plan for each microphone, needed sound effects, and any other required audio inputs.

DESIGN AND IMPLEMENT THE GRAPHIC PLAN

Working with designers and decorators, graphics will need to be designed to create a mood or look for the production. These graphics may include text, animations, and even set graphics. It is imperative that the graphics are consistent.

EQUIPMENT MUST BE CHOSEN AND CONTRACTED

The equipment needs must be determined. This may include cameras, audio gear, lights, and so on. This equipment may already be owned or may need to be rented, which would then require contracts.

FIGURE 5.15
Production meetings allow the staff from the various areas to get together to be updated on a regular basis. These joint meetings also provide an opportunity for the staff to ask questions.

64

The Production Meeting

Production meetings are an essential part of the planning process. These meetings should include representatives from each of the production areas listed previously, as well as engineering, the production manager, and location personnel. Each person participating in the meeting will then have the opportunity to stay informed and ask questions, with all of the other area representatives present. This approach allows them to work out complicated situations that arise when changes are made. (See Figure 5.15.)

Once the meeting is complete, each individual follows up on the issues raised in the meeting. This may include documentation, budgeting, staffing, scheduling, and so on. This production planning meeting forms the basis for efficient teamwork. Problems anticipated and overcome at this stage prevent last-minute compromises. Camera cable routing, for example, is a typical potential hazard. Cables get tangled and can impede other cameras, or drag around noisily.

FIGURE 5.16
Site surveys allow you to check out the actual location to make sure that it will meet the production needs.

Location Surveys (Recce)

Fundamentally, there are two types of shooting conditions: at your *base* and *on location*. Your *base* is wherever you normally shoot. It may be a studio, theater, room, or even a stadium. The base is where you know exactly what facilities are available (equipment, supplies, and scenery), where things are, the amount of room available, and so on. If you need to supplement what is there, it usually can be easily done.

A *location* is anywhere away from your normal shooting location. It may be just outside the building or way out in the country. It could be in a vehicle, down in a mine, or in someone's home. The main thing about shooting away from your base is to find out in advance what you are going to deal with. It is important to be prepared. The preliminary visit to a location is generally called a *remote survey*, *site survey*, or *location survey* (Figure 5.16). It can become anything from a quick look around to a detailed survey of the site. What is found on the survey may influence the planned production treatment. The following checklist gives more remote survey specifics.

Checklist: The Remote Survey	
The amount of detail needed regarding a specific location varies with the type and style of the production. Information that may seem trivial at the time can prove valuable later in the production process. Location sites can be interiors, covered exteriors, or open-air sites. Each has its own problems.	
Sketches	___ Prepare rough maps of route to site that can ultimately be distributed to the crew and talent (include distance, travel time). ___ Rough layout of site (room plan, etc.). ___ Anticipated camera location(s). ___ Designate parking locations for truck (if needed) and staff vehicles.
Contact & Schedule Information	___ Get location contact information from primary and secondary location contacts, site custodian, electrician, engineer, and security. This includes office and mobile phones as well as email. ___ If access credentials are required for the site, obtain the procedure and contact information. ___ Obtain the event schedule (if one exists) and find out whether there are rehearsals that you can attend.
Camera Locations	___ Check around the location for the best camera angles. ___ What type of camera mount will be required (tripod, Steadicam, etc.)? ___ If it's a multicamera production, cable runs must be measured to ensure that there is enough camera cable available. ___ What lens will be required on the camera at each location to obtain the needed shot? ___ Any obstructions? Any obvious distractions (e.g., large signs, reflections)? ___ Any obvious problems in shooting? Anything dangerous?
Lighting	___ Will the production be shot in daylight? How will the light change throughout the day? Does the daylight need to be augmented with reflectors or lights? ___ Will the production be shot in artificial light? (Theirs, yours, or mixed?) Will they be on at the time you are shooting? ___ Estimate the number of lamps, positions, power needed, supplies, and cabling required.
Audio	___ What type of microphones will be needed? ___ Any potential problems with acoustics (such as a strong wind rumble)? ___ Any extraneous sounds (elevators, phones, heating/air conditioning, machinery, children, aircraft, birds, etc.)? ___ Required microphone cable lengths must be determined.
Safety	___ Are there any safety issues that you need to be aware of?

65

Continued

Checklist: The Remote Survey (*Continued*)	
Power	___ What level of power is available and what type of power is needed? The answer to this question will differ greatly between single camera and multicamera production.
	___ What type of power connectors are required?
Communications	___ Are walkie-talkies needed? If so, how many?
	___ How many mobile phones are needed?
	___ If a multicamera production, what type of intercom and how many headsets are required?
Logistics	___ Is there easy access to the location? At any time, or at certain times only? Are there any traffic problems?
	___ What kind of transportation is needed for talent and crew?
	___ What kind of catering is needed? How many meals? How many people?
	___ Are accommodations needed (where, when, how many)?
	___ If the weather turns bad, are there alternative positions/locations available?
	___ Have a phone number list available for police, fire, doctor, hotels, and local (delivery) restaurants.
	___ What kind of first-aid services need to be available (is a first-aid kit enough, or does an ambulance need to be onsite)?
	___ Is location access restricted? Do you need to get permission (or keys) to enter the site? From whom?
	___ What insurance is needed (against damage or injury)?
Security	___ Are local police required to handle crowds or just the public in general?
	___ What arrangements need to be made for security of personal items, equipment, props, etc.?
	___ Do streets need to be blocked?

FIGURE 5.17

The director works with the actors during a rehearsal.

Setup

All of the production equipment—which may include the cameras, mounting gear, lights, microphones, graphic generators, and related cabling—must be set up early enough to leave time for troubleshooting. This means that the setup begins hours before it is needed. If everything works, then the crew gets a break before the production begins. If there are problems, the crew may still be troubleshooting when the production begins. Once everything is operational, rehearsals may begin.

The Rehearsal

Depending on the type of production, one or many rehearsals may occur. These rehearsals give the director, crew, and talent the chance to see how everything flows, whether the equipment works the way it was planned, and whether changes need to be made. When the rehearsals are complete, it is generally time to begin the production (Figure 5.17).

STAGE 2: PRODUCTION

We have finally reached the production! Hard work in the planning and preparation stage should diminish the number of problems that occur during the production. It does not mean that you won't have problems, but it should at least reduce the number of problems.

The Director During the Production

During production is when the director finally gets to direct the crew to capture the audio and video needed to communicate the message. The director visually interprets the script or event, motivates the crew to do their best work, and guides the talent to get the best performances (Figures 5.18 and 5.19).

The Producer During the Production

The producer's responsibilities vary based on the type of production. However, he or she always keeps an eye on the budget and the production schedule and ensures that the production is meeting the originally stated goals.

Production Emphasis

You can use images and sounds to report events simply, undramatically, and unobtrusively. For some types of production, the best kind of staging and camera treatment provides a quiet, sympathetic background to the performance—such as an opera or an interview. However, there are program subjects that need as much "hype" as possible—flashing, swirling light effects, arresting color, unusual sound quality, bizarre camera angles, and unpredictable cutting—to create an exciting production.

Although some productions have a relatively loose format, others require split-second timing, with accurately cued inserts coming from live remotes. Some programs effectively use a compilation of prerecorded material woven together by commentary and music. Other types of productions concentrate on action; others on reaction. Dialogue may be all-important—or quite incidental.

Away from the studio, productions can be anything from a one-camera shoot trailing wildlife to a large-scale remote (outside broadcast) covering a vast area with many cameras. Unforeseen problems are inevitable, and the restrictions of the environment and the weather affect the director's opportunities.

Selective Tools

The camera and microphone do not behave like our eyes and ears, but substitute for them. Our eyes flick around with a knowledge of our surroundings, providing us with an impression of unrestricted stereoscopic vision; in fact, we can detect detail and color over only a tiny angle, and our peripheral vision is monochromatic and quite blurred. In daily life, we build up an impression of our environment by personally controlled sampling: concentrating on certain details while ignoring others. The camera and microphone, on the other hand, provide us with only restricted segments. And the information provided in these segments is modified in various ways, as we have seen, by the characteristics of the medium (distorting space, proportions, scale, etc.).

FIGURE 5.18
The director directing a studio show. (Photo by Jon Greenhoe)

FIGURE 5.19
The director of this sitcom is directing from the floor of the studio, reviewing the camera shots on a quad-split monitor.

67

Selective Techniques

If you simply set up your camera and microphone overlooking the action and zoom in close for detail, the viewer progressively loses the overall view and struggles to understand the big picture. If you go with a wide shot, showing more of the scene, some detail will become indiscernible. The choice of suitable viewpoint and shot size provides the concept of guided selection—the beginnings of techniques.

Good production techniques provide variety of scale and proportion; of composition pattern; of centers of attention and changing subject influence. You achieve these things by variation in shot size and camera viewpoint, by moving the subject and/or the camera, or by altering the subject that is seen.

Although you may sometimes encourage the viewer to browse around a shot, you will generally want him or her to look at a particular feature, and to follow a certain thought process.

The Screen Transforms Reality

The camera and microphone can only convey an impression of the subject and scene. Whatever the limitations or inaccuracies of these images, they are the only direct information our viewer has available to them. And, of course, interpretation must vary with one's own experience and previous knowledge. Whether you are aiming to convey an accurate account (newscast) or to conjure an illusion (drama), the screen will transform reality.

You could fill the screen with a shot of a huge aircraft, or with a diminutive model. The pictures would look very similar. Yet neither conveys the subjective essentials—that is, how you feel standing beside the giant plane or handling the tiny model. Introducing a person into the shot would establish scale, but it would still not include our characteristic responses to such a situation: the way we would be awed by the huge size, or intrigued by the minute detail.

The camera can be used to select detail from a painting or a photograph and the television screen puts a frame around it, transforming this isolated area into a new complete picture; an arrangement that did not originally exist; or an arrangement that if sustained in a close-up can easily become detached and dissociated in the audience's minds from the complete subject.

When a solid sculpture is shot in its three-dimensional form, it becomes reproduced as a flat pattern on the television screen. Planes merge and interact as they cannot do when we examine the real sculpture with our own eyes. Only on the flat screen can a billiard ball become transformed into a flat disc under diffused lighting. In practice, you can actually make use of this falsification of reality. The very principles of scenic design heavily rely on it. Keep in mind that the camera and microphone do inevitably modify the images they convey; and that these images are easily mistaken for truth by the viewer.

Interpretative Production Techniques

It is one of those production paradoxes that although your camera can show what is happening, it will often fail to convey the atmosphere or spirit of the occasion. You can often achieve more convincing representative results by deliberately using selective techniques than by directly shooting the event.

Straightforward shots of a mountain climber may not communicate the thrills and hazards of the situation. But use low camera angles to emphasize the treacherous slope—show threatening overhangs, straining fingers, slipping feet, dislodged stones, laboring breath, slow ascending music—and the illusion grows. Even climbing a gentle slope can appear hazardous if strong interpretative techniques are used.

Sometimes the audience can be so strongly moved by this subjective treatment that sympathetic bodily reactions set in when watching such scenes—even dizziness or nausea. Even situations outside the viewer's personal experience (e.g., the elation of freefall or the horror of quicksand) can be conveyed to some degree by carefully chosen images and audio.

Techniques can also be introduced obtrusively for dramatic effect, or so unobtrusively that the effect appears natural, and the viewer is quite unaware that the situation is contrived:

Obtrusive: The camera suddenly drops from an eye-level shot to a low-angle shot.
Unobtrusive: The camera shoots a seated actor at eye level. He stands, and the camera tilts up with him. We now have a low-angle shot.

When situations seem to occur accidentally or unobtrusively, they are invariably more effective. For example, as an intruder moves toward the camera, he becomes menacingly underlit by a nearby table lamp.

Many techniques have become so familiar that we now regard them as the norm—a natural way of doing things. But they are really illusions that help us convey specific concepts:

- "Chipmunk" voices (high-pitched audio) for small creatures
- Echo behind ghostly encounters
- Rim light in "totally dark" scenes
- Background music

If the program was live, the production process generally ends at the completion of the production segment of the process. However, if it was recorded for later distribution, the next stage is postproduction.

STAGE 3: POSTPRODUCTION

Everything that was shot earlier is now assembled together in a sequential fashion. Mistakes can be corrected and visual effects, sound effects, and music added. Postproduction will be covered in detail in Chapter 17.

The goal is a final show that is polished, without any noticeable production issues. If the production meets the originally stated goals, then it is a success!

REVIEW QUESTIONS

1. Explain the three stages of a television production.
2. Where do concepts come from for a production?
3. What are the advantages to setting goals and objectives?
4. What are some of the different ways that a viewer can watch television?
5. Describe the differences between the planned and unplanned approaches to production.
6. What is the value of a production meeting? Who attends this meeting?

CHAPTER 6

The Script and Production Plan

"Stories can take us places of which we can only dream. An audience will suspend their disbelief in order to be swept into a story. We have to put aside the idea that 'men can't fly' to enjoy *Superman*."

Barry Cook, Director

Terms

Breakdown sheet: An analysis of a script, listing all of the production elements listed in order of the schedule.

Camera script: A revised script for camera rehearsals, including the details of the production treatment: cameras and audio, cues, transitions, stage instructions, and set changes.

Fact sheet/rundown sheet: Summarizes information about a product or item for a demonstration program, or details of a guest for an interviewer.

Outline script: Usually includes any prepared dialogue, such as the show opening and closing.

Preliminary script/writer's script: Initial submitted full-page script (dialogue and action) before script editing.

Rehearsal script: Script prepared for television and used for prestudio rehearsal. Script details the settings, characters, action, talent directives, and dialogue.

Running order: In a live production, the program is shot in the scripted order.

Shooting order: When taping a production, the director can shoot in whatever order is most convenient for the crew, actors, and/or director.

Show format: Lists the items or program segments in a show, in the order in which they are to be shot. It may show durations, who is participating, shot numbers, and so on.

Synopsis: An outline of the characters, action, and plot. This synopsis helps everyone involved in the production understand what is going on.

Once an idea is conceived, it must be transformed into a message, a script, and/or a production plan. Generally, the script must be created before anything else is done, because it will be the source that every other area draws from.

THE SCRIPT'S PURPOSE

Planning is an essential part of a serious production and the script forms the basis for that plan. Scripts do the following:

- Help the director clarify ideas and develop a project that successfully communicates to the viewers.
- Help the director coordinate the entire production team.
- Help the director determine what resources will be needed for the television production (Figure 6.1).

Although some professional crews on location (at a news event, for instance) may appear to be shooting entirely spontaneously, they are usually working through a tried-and-true process or pattern that has been proven successful in past situations.

For certain types of production, such as narratives, the script usually begins the production process. The director then reads the draft script, which usually contains general information on characters, locations, stage directions, and dialogue. He or she then visualizes the scenes and assesses the possible treatment. The director must also anticipate the script's potential and possible difficulties. At this stage, changes may be made to improve the script or make it more workable. Next, the director goes on to prepare a camera treatment.

Another method of scripting begins with an outline. In this method, you decide on the various topics you want to cover and the amount of time that you can allot to each topic. A script is then developed based on this outline and decisions are made concerning the camera treatment for each segment.

When preparing a documentary, an extended outline becomes a shooting script, showing perhaps the types of shots that the director would like. It usually also includes rough questions for on-location interviews with participants. All other commentary is usually written later, together with effects and music, to finalize the edited production.

In order to have a concise, easy-to-read script, abbreviations are usually used. These abbreviations significantly reduce the amount of wordage on the script, which also reduces the number of required pages (Table 6.1).

FIGURE 6.1
The director uses the script to coordinate the production.

Table 6.1	Television Script Abbreviations			
Many organizations duplicate the rehearsal script on white paper. Operational information is added to the original to provide the camera script on yellow paper. Often, script revisions change color with every update.				
All camera shots are numbered in a fully scripted show. Inserts are not numbered (stills, prerecorded video, graphics, etc.), but are identified in the audio column. Where possible, cutting points are marked in the dialogue with a slash mark: _____ /				
Equipment	CAM	Camera	CG	Character generator
	MIKE, MIC	Microphone	BOOM	Mic boom
	G	Graphic	VT, VTR	Videotape
	ESS	Electronic still store	CP, CAP	Caption*
	DVE	Digital video effect	Crawl	Crawl

Continued

72

Table 6.1	Television Script Abbreviations (*Continued*)			
Position	L/H, R/H	Picture lefthand, righthand	B/G, F/G	Background, foreground
	C	Center	X	Move across
	U/S, D/S	Upstage, downstage	POV	From the point of view of person named
	O/C	On-camera		
Cueing	Q, I/C, O/C	Cue, in cue, out cue	RUN	VT
	S/B	Stand by	F/X	Cue effects
Cameras	ECU, CU, MS, LS, XLS (see Chapter 8 for more shot details)		DI	Dolly in
	2-S, 3-S	Two-shot, three-shot	P/B, D/B	Pull back, dolly back
	O/S	Over-the-shoulder shot	FG/BG	One person foreground; another background
Switching (vision mixing)	CUT	Not marked, but implied unless other transition marked	LOSE GRAPHICS	Cut out graphics
	MIX (DIS)	Mix (dissolve)	FI, FO	Fade-in, fade-out
	WIPE	Wipe	T	Take
	S/S	Split screen	KEY (INSERT)	Electronic insertion (chroma-key, CSO)
	CK	Chroma-key		
Audio	F/UP	Fade up audio	Spot FX	Sound effect made in studio
	FU	Fade audio under	STING	Cue strong musical chord emphasizing action
	P/B	Playback	OS, OOV	Over scene, out of vision (audio heard where source not shown)
	REVERB	Reverberation added	ANNCR	Announcer
	ATMOS	Atmosphere (background sounds)	SOT	Sound on tape
General	TXN	Transmission	ID	Station identification
	ADD	An addition (to a story)	MOS, VOX, POP	Man-on-street interview
	EXT	Exterior	INT	Interior
	PROP	Property	LOC	Location
	RT	Roll titles		
*U.K. term.				

THE LIVE EVENT PRODUCTION PLAN

There are some types of programs that cannot be scripted. For example, sports events cannot be controlled; you never know where they are going to go. However, the director still needs to think through a quasi script or what is often known as a *production plan*. These production plans are designed to map out the general flow of the production, with contingency plans taking into consideration that the event could take many unexpected turns along the way.

The Outline Script: Semiscripted Production

The type of script used will largely depend on the kind of program being made. There will be some production situations—particularly where talent improvises as they speak or perform—when the "script" simply lists details of the production group, facilities needed, and scheduling, and shows basic camera positions, and so on.

An *outline script* usually includes any prepared dialogue, such as the show's opening and closing. When people are going to improvise, the script may just list the order of topics to be covered. During the show, the list may be included on a card held by the talent, a cue card positioned near the camera, or a teleprompter in order to remind the host. If the show is complicated with multiple guests or events occurring, a show format is usually created (Table 6.2). This lists the program segments (scenes) and shows the following:

- The topic (such as a guitar solo).
- The amount of time allocated for this specific segment.
- The names of all talent involved (hosts and guests).
- Facilities (cameras, audio, and any other equipment and space needed).
- External content sources that will be required (such as tape, digital, satellite, and so on).

When segments (or edited packages) have been previously recorded to be inserted into the program, the script may show the opening and closing words of each and the package's duration. This step assists accurate cueing.

Fully Scripted Shows

When a program is fully scripted, it includes detailed information on all aspects of the production, as described in the following subsections.

SCENES

Most productions are divided into a series of *scenes*. Each scene covers a complete continuous action sequence and is identified with a number and location (Scene 3—Office set). A scene can involve anything from an interview to a dance routine, a song, or a demonstration sequence.

Table 6.2 Sample Show Format	
The show format lists the items or program segments in a show in the order in which they are to be shot. It may show durations, who is participating, shot numbers, and the like.	
Example:	
CARING FOR THE ELDERLY	Total duration: 15 min
1. OPENING TITLES & MUSIC	00:10
2. PROGRAM INTRO.	00:30
3. PROBLEMS OF MOBILITY	02:20
4. INJURIES	02:15
5. DIET	02:45
6. DAILY ACTIVITIES	03:40
7. EXERCISES	01:20
8. AIDS THAT CAN HELP	01:15
9. CLOSING	00:25
10. END TITLES	<u>00:10</u>
	15:00

SHOTS

When the director has decided how he or she is going to interpret the script, each scene will be subdivided into a series of *shots*; each shot shows the action from a specific viewpoint. The shots are then numbered consecutively for easy reference on the script, in the order in which they will be screened.

In a live production, the program is shot in the scripted order (*running order*). When taping a production, the director can shoot in whatever order is most convenient (*shooting order*) for the crew, actors, and/or director. The director may decide to omit shots ("drop Shot 25") or to add extra shots (Shots 24A, 24B, etc.). He or she may decide to record Shot 50 before Shot 1 and then edit them into the correct running order at a later time.

DIALOGUE

The entire prepared dialogue, spoken to the camera or between people. The talent may memorize the script or read it off teleprompters or cue cards.

EQUIPMENT

The script usually indicates which camera/microphone is being used for each shot (Cam. 2 Fishpole).

BASIC CAMERA INSTRUCTIONS

Details of each shot and camera moves (Cam. 1 CU on Joe's hand; dolly out to long shot).

SWITCHER (VISION MIXER) INSTRUCTIONS

For example: cut, fade.

CONTRIBUTORY SOURCES

Details of where videotape, graphics, remote feeds, and so on appear in the program.

When is it necessary to fully script a production?

1. When the dialogue is to follow a prescribed text that is to be learned or read from a prompter or script.
2. Where action is detailed, so that people move to certain places at particular times and do specific things there. (This can affect cameras, sound, and lighting treatment.)
3. When there are carefully timed inserts (prerecorded materials) that have to be cued accurately into the program.
4. When the duration of a section must be kept within an allotted time slot, yet cover certain agreed-upon subject points. (The speaker might otherwise dwell on one point, and miss another altogether.)
5. Where there are spot cues—such as a lightning flash and an effects disc sound of thunder—at a point in the dialogue.

The fully scripted show is developed in several stages, as described in the following subsections.

PRELIMINARY SCRIPT/DRAFT/ OUTLINE SCRIPT/WRITER'S SCRIPT

The initial submitted full-page script (dialogue and action) before script editing.

REHEARSAL SCRIPT

A script prepared for television and used for prestudio rehearsal. The script details the locales (settings), characters, action, talent directives, and dialogue (Table 6.3).

75

Table 6.3	The Rehearsal Script		
SCENE	**INT/EXT**	**LOCATION**	**TIME OF DAY**
3	INT	LOUNGE	NIGHT
		(GEORGE ENTERS, WALKS TO TABLE, SWITCHES ON LAMP.)	
GEORGE: (CALLS) The lights are okay in here. It must be your lamp.			
		(GEORGE TAKES GUN FROM DRAWER.) SLIPS IT INTO HIS POCKET: PULLING OUT TELEGRAM. HOLDS IT UP.	
"SORRY CANNOT COME WEEKEND, BRIAN SICK, WRITING . . . JUDY."			
		(HAND WADS IT UP, THROWS IT INTO FIRE.) (DOOR OPENS: EILEEN ENTERS.)	
EILEEN: Really, these people are not good. They promised to be here tonight. Look how late . . . GEORGE: It's probably the storm that has delayed them. They'll be here all right.			
		(EILEEN SITS ON COUCH: GEORGE JOINS HER.)	
EILEEN: If Judy knows you're here, it'll take wild horses to keep her away. GEORGE: How many more times do I have to tell you . . . EILEEN: Why do you keep pretending?			
		LIGHTNING FLASH	
GEORGE: I've warned you. You'll go too far.			

CAMERA SCRIPT

A revised script for camera rehearsals, augmented with details of production treatment: cameras and audio, cues, transitions, stage instructions, and set changes (Table 6.4).

FULL SCRIPT

The *full script* is not, as some people believe, an artistically inhibiting document that commits everyone concerned to a rigid plan of procedure. It can be modified as the need arises. It simply informs everyone about what is expected at each moment of the production. Rehearsal time is too precious to use up explaining what is expected of everyone as you go. It is far better to have a detailed script that shows the exact moment for the lighting change, to cue the graphics, or to introduce a special effect. The full script is a changeable plan of how the production will proceed that has details added to it as the production develops.

Fully scripted approaches can be found in newscasts, drama productions, operas, situation comedy shows, documentaries, and commercials. When dialogue and/or action are spontaneous, there can be no script—only an outline of where the show is headed (e.g., discussions). A formal talk is scripted.

The more fragmentary or disjointed the actual production process is, the more essential the script becomes. It helps everyone involved to *anticipate*. And in certain forms of production (such as chroma-key staging), anticipation is essential for tight scheduling.

In a complex production that is videotaped out of sequence, the production crew may be unable to function meaningfully without a full script, which makes it clear how shots/sequences are

| Table 6.4 | The Camera Script | | | | | | |

SHOT	CAM.	(POSITION)	SCENE	INT/ EXT	LOCATION	TIME OF DAY	F/X
			CAMS. 2A, 3A, 4B. SOUND BOOM B1				
			3	INT	LOUNGE	NIGHT	TAPE:
10.	F/U 2.	A					WIND RAIN
		LS PAN/ZOOM on GEORGE to MS	(GEORGE ENTERS, WALKS TO TABLE, SWITCHES ON LAMP.)				
11.	3.	A.	GEORGE: (CALLS) The lights are okay in here. It must be your lamp.				
12.	2.	A.	(GEORGE TAKES GUN FROM DRAWER.)				
13.	4.	MS B	SLIPS IT INTO HIS POCKET: PULLING OUT TELEGRAM, HOLDS IT UP				
		CU of telegram	"SORRY CANNOT COME WEEKEND. BRIAN SICK. WRITING . . . JUDY."				
14.	3.	PULL FOCUS on fire as he throws A	(HAND WADS IT UP, THROWS IT INTO THE FIRE.)				
		LS	(DOOR OPENS: EILEEN ENTERS.)				
			EILEEN: Really, these people are not good. They promised to be here tonight. Look how late . . .				
			GEORGE: It's probably the storm that has delayed them. They'll be here all right.				
		DOLLY IN to MS as EILEEN X's to couch.	(EILEEN SITS ON COUCH: GEORGE JOINS HER.)				
			EILEEN: If Judy knows you're here, it'll take wild horses to keep her away.				
			GEORGE: How many more times do I have to tell you . . .				
			EILEEN: Why do you keep pretending?				
			LIGHTNING FLASH				
15.	2.	A					
		CU	GEORGE: I've warned you. You'll go too far.				DISC: THUNDERCLAP

interrelated and reveals continuity. The lighting director may, for example, need to adjust the lighting balance for a scene so that it will cut smoothly with the different shots that were previously captured.

The full script can be a valuable coordinating document, enabling you to see at a glance the relationships between dialogue, action, treatment, and mechanics. During planning, of course, it helps the team estimate how much time there is for a camera move, how long there is for a costume change, whether rearranging shooting order will give the necessary time for a makeup change, the scenes during which the "rain" should be seen outside the windows of the library set (i.e., the water spray turned on and the audio effects introduced)—and the thousand and one details that interface in a smooth-running show.

The full script is used differently by various members of the production team. For the director, the script has two purposes: as a reference point when developing treatment, estimating the duration of sequences, planning camera moves, and so on, and to demonstrate to members of the team what he or she requires. The director's assistant(s) follows the script carefully during rehearsals and taping, checking dialogue accuracy, noting where retakes are needed, timing sections (their durations, where a particular event occurred), perhaps readying and cuing contributory sources, as well as "calling shots" on the intercom—for example, "Shot 24 on 2. Coming to 3." The person operating the production switcher follows the script in detail, preparing for upcoming transitions, superimpositions, effects, and so on, while checking the various monitor pictures.

Others in the team for whom a script would be too distracting (e.g., camera and boom operators) use it as a detailed reference point when necessary, but are guided by simplified outlines such as *breakdown sheets* and *camera cards* as they memorize their operations (Table 6.5).

Table 6.5	Breakdown Sheet/Show Format/Running Order

Script Breakdown Sheet

Color Code
Day Ext. - Yellow
Night Ext. - Green
Day Int. - White
Night Int. - Blue

Production Company: _____

Production Title: _____

Date: _____

Breakdown Page # _____

Page Count _____

Scene # | Scene Name | Int. or Ext.

Description | Day or Night

CAST Red	**STUNTS** Orange	**EXTRAS/ATMOSPHERE** Green
	EXTRAS/SILENT BITS Yellow	
SPECIAL EFFECTS Blue	**PROPS** Purple	**VEHICLE/ANIMALS** Pink
WARDROBE Circle	**MAKE UP/HAIR** Asterisk	**SOUND EFFECTS/MUSIC** Brown
SPECIAL EQUIPMENT Box	**PRODUCTION NOTES** Underline	

Basic Script Layout Formats

Television scripts follow several standard layouts. Other studios prefer a single-column cinematic format, with transitions in a left margin, and all video and audio information in a single main column. Other versions use two vertical columns, with picture treatment (cameras, switching) on the left, and action and dialogue on the right, together with studio instructions and lighting/effects cues. Directors often mark up their script by hand with their own instructional symbols to indicate transitions and shots.

SINGLE-COLUMN FORMAT

Although there are different variations of the single-column format, all video and audio information is usually contained in a single main column. Before each scene, an explanatory introduction describes the location and the action.

Reminder notes can be made in a wide lefthand margin, including transition symbols (for example: X=cut; FU=fade-up), cues, camera instructions, thumbnail sketches of shots or action, and so on.

This type of script is widely used for narrative film-style production and single-camera video, in which the director works alongside the camera operator. It is perhaps less useful in a multicamera setup, in which the production team is more dispersed, with everyone needing to know the director's production intentions (Table 6.6).

TWO-COLUMN FORMAT

Like the one-column format, there are many variations of the two-column format. This traditional television format is extremely flexible and informative. It gives all members of the production crew shot-by-shot details of what is going on. They can also add their own specific information (e.g., details of lighting changes) as needed. See Table 6.7.

Table 6.6 Sample Single-Column Shooting Script/Single-Camera Format
FADE-IN:

1. EXT: FRONT OF FARMHOUSE—DAY
   Front door opens. FARMER comes out, walks up to gate.
   Looks left and right along road.

2. EXT: LONG SHOT OF ROAD OUTSIDE FARM (Looking east)—DAY   POV shot of FARMER looking along road, waiting for car.

3. EXT: FARM GATE—DAY
   Medium shot of farmer leaning looking over gate, looking anxiously.
   He turns to house, calling.
       FARMER:
       I can't see him. If he doesn't come soon, I'll be late.

4. INT: FARMHOUSE KITCHEN—DAY
   Wife is collecting breakfast things. Sound of radio.
       WIFE:
       You're too impatient. There's plenty of time.

5. EXT: FARM GATE—DAY
   Medium shot of FARMER, same position. He looks in other direction.
   Sound of distant car approaching. Sudden bang, then silence.

		Table 6.7 — Sample Two-Column Shooting Script/Multi-Camera Shooting Script
SHOT	**CAM (Position)**	**SCENE/ACTION/AUDIO**
CAMS:	1B, 2D, 3A	SOUND: BOOM POLE
		Scene 4. INT. BARN—NIGHT
15.	FU 2D	(FARMER ENTERS, HANGS TAPE 7: WIND
	LS DOORWAY	LAMP ON WALL-HOOK DISC 5: RAIN
	Zoom in to MS	BESIDE DOOR)
		FARMER: It's getting late.
		How is the poor beast doing?/
16.	1B O/S SHOT	SON: I don't think she'll last the night.
		SON'S POV She has a high fever./
17.	3A LS FARMER	(FARMER WALKS FORWARD TO THE STALL)
	He comes	FARMER: I called Willie. He's on his way.
		(FARMER KNEELS BESIDE COW)/
18.	CU SON	SON: D'you think he'll be able to get here?
19.	1C CU FARMER	FARMER: If the bridge holds.
		But the river's still rising./

Abbreviations used:
CU: Close-up
MS: Medium shot
LS: Long shot
FU: Fade-up
O/S: Over the shoulder
POV: Point of view
___/:   Indicates point to "cut to next shot"

Two versions of the script are sometimes prepared. In the first (*rehearsal script*), the right column only is printed. Subsequently, after detailed planning and preproduction rehearsals, the production details are added to the left column to form the *camera script*.

Keep It Brief

The stage loves words; television and the cinema love movement. The goal is to say what you want to say in the briefest way possible. If that means taking out an entire speech, and replacing it with an arched eyebrow, do so. If you have to choose between the two, the arched eyebrow probably packs the greatest punch. A nod speaks volumes; a facial tick can bring down an empire. This approach can guide writers to write more effective dialogue in all genres. The dialogue can be qualitative, not quantitative.

Adapted from Sabastian Corbascio, Writer and Director

THE DRAMA SCRIPT

The dramatic full script may be prepared in two stages: the *rehearsal script* and the *camera script*.

The *rehearsal script* usually begins with general information sheets, including a cast/character list, production team details, rehearsal arrangements, and similar details. There may be a synopsis of the plot or story line, particularly when scenes are to be shot/recorded out of order. The rehearsal script generally includes the following types of details:

- Location: The setting where the scene will be shot.
- Time of day and weather conditions.

- Stage or location instructions: (The room is candlelit and a log fire burns brightly.)
- Action: Basic information on what is going to happen in the scene, such as actors' moves (Joe gets in the car).
- Dialogue: Speaker's name (character) followed by their dialogue. All delivered speech, voiceover, voice inserts (for example, phone conversation), commentary, announcements, and so on. (Perhaps with directional comments such as "sadly" or "sarcastically.") (See Figure 6.2.)
- Effects cues: Indicating the moment for a change to take place (lightning flash, explosion, Joe switches light out).
- Audio instructions: music and sound effects.

The *camera script* adds full details of the production treatment to the left side of the rehearsal script, and usually includes:

- The shot number.
- The camera used for the shot and possibly the position of the camera.
- Basic shot details and camera moves (CU on Joe. Dolly back to LS as he rises.)
- Switcher instructions (cut, dissolve, etc.).

FIGURE 6.2
Talent discuss and rehearse the script for the opening of a sports event for ESPN. The director usually listens to the rehearsal to give feedback. (Photo by Josh Taber)

SUGGESTIONS ON SCRIPTWRITING

There are no shortcuts to good scriptwriting, any more than there are to writing short stories, composing music, or painting a picture. Scriptwriting techniques are learned through observation, experience, and reading. But there are some general guidelines that are worth keeping in mind as you prepare your script, as explained in the following sections.

Be Visual

Although audio and video images are both very important in a television production, viewers perceive television as primarily a visual medium. Material should be presented in visual terms as much as possible. If planned and shot well, the images can powerfully move the audience—sometimes with very few words. Other times programs rely almost entirely on the audio, using the video images to strengthen, support, and emphasize what is heard. Visual storytelling is difficult but powerful when done well.

When directors want their audience to concentrate on what they are hearing, they try to make the picture less demanding. If, for instance, the audience is listening to a detailed argument and trying to read a screen full of statistics at the same time, they will probably not do either successfully.

Pacing the Program

Keep in mind that writing for print is totally different than writing for television. In print, the reader can read at their own pace, stop, and reread whenever they want to. In a television program, the viewing audience generally has to watch the program at the director's chosen pace. An essential point to remember when scripting television is that the difference between the rates at which the viewer can take in information. A lot depends, of course, on how familiar the

"Being a good television screenwriter requires an understanding of the way film accelerates the communication of words."

Steven Bochco, Producer

audience already is with the subject and the terms used. Where details are new to the audience, and the information is complicated, more time will be required to communicate the information in a meaningful way. Ironically, something that can seem difficult and involved at the first viewing may appear slow and obvious a few viewings later. That is why it is so hard for directors to estimate the effect of material on those who are going to be seeing it for the first time. Directors become so familiar with it that they know it by heart and lose their objectivity.

The key to communicating complex subjects is to simplify. If the density of information or the rate at which it is delivered is too high, it will confuse, bewilder, or just encourage the audience to switch it off—mentally, if not physically.

As sequences are edited together, editors find that video images and the soundtrack sometimes have their own natural pace. That pace may be slow and leisurely, medium, fast, or brief. If editors are fortunate, the pace of the picture and the sound will be roughly the same. However, there will be occasions when they find that they do not have enough images to fit the sound sequence, or they do not have enough soundtrack to put behind the amount of action in the picture.

Often when the talent has explained a point (perhaps taking 5 seconds), the picture is still showing the action (perhaps 20 seconds). The picture, or action, needs to be allowed to finish before taking the commentary on to the next point. In the script, a little dialogue may go a long way, as a series of short pieces cut into the program, rather than a continual flow of verbiage.

The reverse can happen, too, when the action in the picture is brief. For example, a locomotive passes through the shot quickly in a few seconds, taking less time than it takes the talent to talk about it. So, more pictures of the subject are needed, perhaps from another viewpoint, to support the dialogue.

Even when picture and sound are more or less keeping the same pace, do not habitually cut to a new shot as soon as the action in the picture is finished. Sometimes it is better to continue the picture briefly, in order to allow time for the audience to process the information that they have just seen and heard, rather than move on with fast cutting and a rapid commentary.

It is all too easy to overload the soundtrack. Without pauses in a commentary, it can become an endless barrage of information. Moreover, if the editor has a detailed script that fits in with every moment of the image, and the talent happens to slow down at all, the words can get out of step with the key shots they are related to. Then the editor has the choice of cutting parts of the commentary, or building out the picture (with appropriate shots) to enable picture and sound to be brought back into sync.

Style

The worst type of script for television is the type that has been written in a formal literary style, as if for a newspaper article or an essay, where the words, phrases, and sentence construction are those of the printed page. When this type of script is read aloud, it tends to sound like an official statement or a pronouncement, rather than the fluent everyday speech that usually communicates best with a television audience—not that we want a script that is so colloquial that it includes all the hesitations and slangy half-thoughts one tends to use, but certainly one that avoids complex sentence construction.

It takes some experience to be able to read any script fluently, with the required natural expression that brings it alive. But if the script itself is written in a stilted style, it is unlikely to improve with hearing. The material should be presented as if the talent were talking to an individual in the audience, rather than proclaiming on a stage, or addressing a public meeting.

"The biggest misconception about writing for television is that it's just like *The Dick Van Dyke Show*. Writers are almost never home by 5:30. Only the actors have those hours."
Carmen Finestra, Co-creator and Executive Producer, *Home Improvement*

The way the information is delivered can influence how interesting the subject seems to be. The mind boggles at: "The retainer lever actuates the integrated contour follower." But we immediately understand if it is written this way: "Here you can see, as we pull this lever, the lock opens."

If the audience has to pause to figure out what is meant, they will not be listening closely to what is being said immediately afterwards. Directors can often assist the audience by anticipating the problems with a passing explanation, or a subtitle (especially useful for names), or a simple diagram.

Hints on Developing the Script

How scripts are developed will vary with the type of program and the way individual directors work. The techniques and processes of good script writing are a study in themselves, but we can take a look at some of the guiding principles and typical points that need to be considered.

WRITER'S BLOCK

There will be times when you "hit a wall" when writing. When you have been working for awhile and realize that you are not getting any traction on the script, take a break and do something else for a while to help clear your mind. Then go back with a fresh perspective (Figure 6.3).

THE NATURE OF THE SCRIPT

The Script May Form the Basis of the Entire Production Treatment

Here the production is staged, performed, and shot as indicated in the script. As far as possible, dialogue and action follow the scripted version.

The Scriptwriter May Prepare a Draft Script (i.e., a Suggested Treatment)

This is studied and developed by the director to form a shooting script.

FIGURE 6.3
Two writers from the television series *Monk* take a break during a scriptwriting session to play air-hockey. On the wall behind them are notecards filled with ideas for the show. (Photo courtesy of NNS/Landov)

The Script May Be Written after Material Has Been Shot

Certain programs, such as documentaries, may be shot to a preconceived outline plan, but the final material will largely depend on the opportunities of the moment. The script is written to blend this material together in a coherent story line, adding explanatory commentary/dialogue. Subsequent editing and postproduction work is based on this scripted version.

The Script May Be Written after Material Has Been Edited

Here the videotape editor assembles the shot material, creating continuity and a basis for a story line. The script is then developed to suit the edited program. Occasionally, a new script replaces the program's original script with new or different text. For example, when the original program was created in a different language from that of the intended audience, it may be marketed as an *M&E version*, in which the soundtrack includes only "music and effects." All dialogue or voiceover commentary is added (dubbed in) later by the recipient in another language.

SCRIPTWRITING BASICS

A successful script satisfies two important requirements:

- *The program's main purpose:* to amuse, inform, intrigue, persuade, and so on.
- *It must be practical.* The script must be a workable vehicle for the production crew.

Fundamentally, we need to ensure that:

- The script meets its deadline. When is the script required? Is it for a specific occasion?
- The treatment is feasible for the budget, facilities, and time available. An over-ambitious script will necessarily have to be rearranged, edited, and have its scenes rewritten to provide a workable basis for the production.
- The treatment usually must fit the anticipated program length. Otherwise, it will become necessary to cut sequences or pad the production with added scenes afterwards to fit the show to the allotted time slot.
- The style and the form of presentation are appropriate for the subject. An unsuitable style, such as a lighthearted approach to a very serious subject, may trivialize the subject.
- The subject treatment is suitable for the intended audience. The style, complexity, concentration of information, and other details are relative to their probable interest and attention span.

ASK YOURSELF

Who Is the Program For? What Does Your Audience Already Know?

Analyzing your audience is covered in Chapter 5.

What Is the Purpose of This Program?

Examples: entertainment, information, instruction, or persuasion (as in advertising, program trailers, propaganda). Is there a follow-up to the program (such as publicity offers or tests)?

Is the Program One of a Series?

Does it relate to or follow other programs? Do viewers need to be reminded of past information? Does the script style need to be similar to previous programs? Were there any omissions, weaknesses, or errors in previous programs that can be corrected in this program?

What Is the Length of the Program?

Is it brief? (Must it make an immediate impact?) Is it long enough to develop arguments or explanations for a range of topics?

How Much Detail Is Required in the Script?

Is the script intended to be complete with dialogue and action? (Actual visual treatment depends on the director.) Is the script a basis for improvisation (e.g., by a guide or lecturer)? Is it an ideas sheet, giving an outline for treatment?

Are You Writing Dialogue?

Is it for actors to read, or inexperienced performers? (For the latter, keep it brief, in short "bites" to be read from a prompter or spoken in their own words.) Is the dialogue to be naturalistic or "character dialogue"?

Is the Subject a Visual One?

If the subjects are abstract, or no longer exist, how will you illustrate them?

Have You Considered the Script's Requirements?

It takes only a few words on the page to suggest a situation, but to reproduce it in pictures and sound may require considerable time, expense, and effort (e.g., a battle scene). You may have to rely on available stock library video. Does the script pose obvious problems for the director? For example, a script involving special effects, stunts, and the like?

Does the Script Involve Costly Concepts That Can Be Simplified?

An intercontinental conversation could be covered by an expensive two-way video satellite transmission, or can it be accomplished by utilizing a telephone call accompanied by previously acquired footage or still images?

Does the Subject Involve Research?

The script may depend on what researchers discover while investigating the subject. Do you already have information that can aid the director (have contacts, know of suitable locations, availability of insert material, etc.)?

Where Will the Images Come From?

Will the subjects be brought to the studio? (This allows maximum control over the program treatment and presentation.) Or will cameras be going on location to the subjects? (This may include situations like shooting in museums.) Script opportunities may depend on what is available when the production is being shot.

REMEMBER

Start Scripting with a Simple Outline

Before embarking on the main script treatment, it can be particularly helpful to rough out a skeleton version, which usually includes a general outline treatment, covering the various points that need to be included, in the order in which the director proposes dealing with them.

Be Visual

- Sometimes pictures alone can convey the information more powerfully than the spoken word.
- The way a commentary is written (and spoken) can influence how the audience interprets a picture (and vice versa).

- Pictures can distract. People may concentrate on looking instead of listening!
- Avoid "talking heads" wherever possible. Show the subject being talked about, rather than the person who is speaking.
- The script can only *indicate* visual treatment. It will seldom be specific about shot details, unless that is essential to the plot or situation. Directors have their own ideas!

Avoid Overloading

- Keep it simple. Don't be long-winded or use complicated sentences. Keep to the point. When a subject is difficult, an accompanying diagram, chart, or graph may help make the information easier to understand.
- Do not give too much information at a time. Do not attempt to pack too much information into the program. It is better to do justice to a few topics than to cover many inadequately.

Develop a Flow of Ideas

- Deal with one subject at a time. Generally, avoid cutting between different topics.
- Do not have different information on the screen than in the commentary. This can be very distracting and confusing to the viewer.
- Aim to have one subject or sequence lead naturally into the next.
- When there are a number of separate different topics, think through how they are related and the transitions necessary to keep the audience's interest.

Consider Pace

- Vary the pace of the program. Avoid a fast pace when imparting facts. It conveys an overall impression, but facts do not sink in. A slow pace can be boring or restful, depending on the content.
- Remember that the audience cannot refer to the program later (unless it is interactive or they have a video recorder). If they miss a point, they may fail to understand the next—and will probably lose interest.

Watch Your Style

- Use an appropriate writing style for the intended viewer. Generally, aim for an informal, relaxed style.
- There is a world of difference between the style of the printed page and the way people normally speak. Reading from a prompter produces an unnatural, stilted effect.
- Be very careful about introducing humor in the script!

Storyboards

Many directors need to think through each production scene in their minds, capturing the images and turning them into a storyboard. The storyboard is primarily used for dramatic productions, but is used for other events as well. An example would be the opening ceremonies at the Olympics (Figure 6.4).

The storyboard is a series of rough sketches that help the director visualize and organize his or her camera treatment. It is a visual map of how the director hopes to arrange the key shots for each scene or action sequence (Figures 6.4–6.7).

Directors find that the storyboard can be a valuable aid, whether they are going to shoot action:

- Continuously, from start to finish.
- In sections or scenes (one complete action sequence at a time).
- As a series of separate shots or "action segments," each showing a part of the sequence (Figure 6.8).

"Olympic Flag / Olympic Hymn"

Opening Ceremony * XIX Olympic Games * Salt Lake 2002   Page 1

Time	Length	Camera	Audio	Comm. Cue	Image
8:50:46	0:00:10	6		WIDE SHOT of flag carriers as they approach the flag pole.	**1** ANNOUNCE OLYMPIC FLAG
		2		People carry the flag.	**2** ENTRANCE OF OLYMPIC FLAG
8:53:46	0:03:00	mini come n go		Flag goes over camera.	**3** ENTRANCE OF OLYMPIC FLAG
8:55:46	0:02:00	24		Flag arrives. Music segues. Olymp Flag raised.	**4** OLYMPIC HYMN

FIGURE 6.4
This storyboard was a page from the opening ceremony at the Olympics. Hand-drawn, it served as a guide to the staff involved in the broadcast of the production. (Image courtesy of International Sports Broadcasting)

Shot 18:

-The group gathers around the phone and waits while it rings.

Shot 19:

-John answers the phone outside on his cordless phone.

-His grandkids play in the BG.

Shot 20:

-GO TO *SPLIT SCREEN*.

-Conversation begins with office.

-He tells them about the *MetLife LifeLong Income* plan.

FIGURE 6.5
This storyboard was created for a television commercial. (Image courtesy of Jim Mickle)

87

Storyboards can be designed a number of different ways. There are software programs that assist the director in visualizing ideas; someone can roughly sketch them out; or a storyboard artist can create detailed drawings that can even be animated to be shown during the fundraising period (Figure 6.9).

Hand-drawn storyboards usually begin with a grid of frames. Start to imagine your way through the first scene, roughly sketching the composition for each shot. You don't have to be able to draw well to produce a successful storyboard. Even the crudest scribbles can help you organize your thoughts and show other people what you are trying to do. If the action is complicated, you might need a couple of frames to show how a shot develops. In our example, the whole scene is summarized in just five frames.

Let's look at a very simple story line, to see how the storyboard provides you with imaginative opportunities.

The young person has been sent to buy her first postage stamp.

There are dozens of ways to shoot this brief sequence. You could simply follow her all the way from her home, watching as she crosses the road, enters the post office, goes up to the counter . . . the result would be totally boring.

88

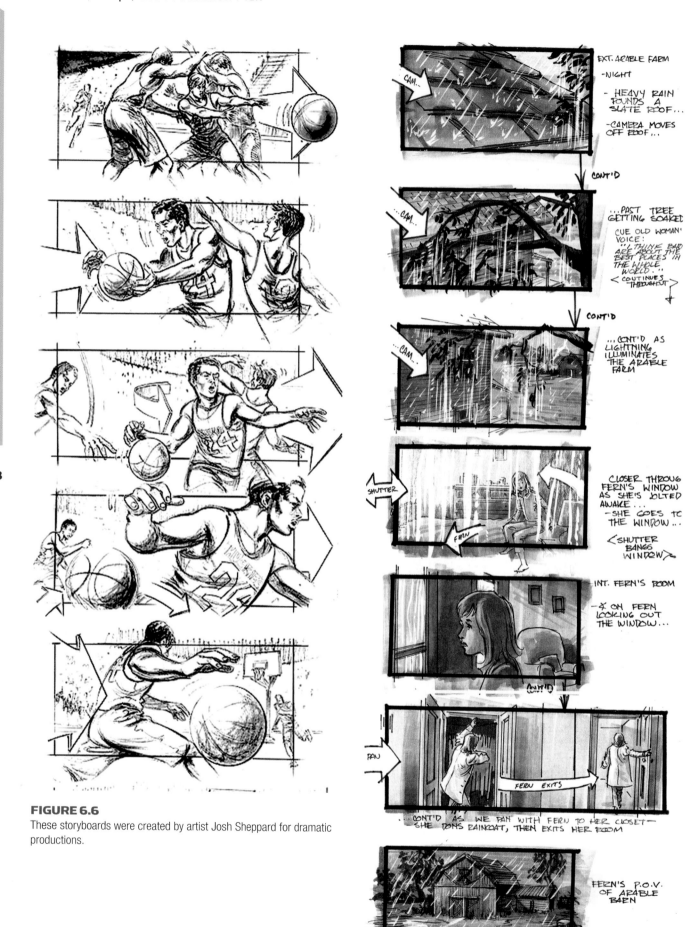

FIGURE 6.6
These storyboards were created by artist Josh Sheppard for dramatic productions.

FIGURE 6.7
(Left) A frame from a storyboard. (Right) How the camera shot that specific scene. (Photo by Taylor Vincent)

FIGURE 6.8
A storyboard is consulted during a production. The storyboard helps keep the crew focused on the project.

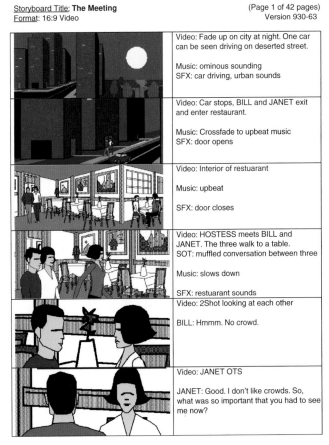

FIGURE 6.9
A storyboard used for a dramatic production that was created by computer software designed for nonartists. (Image created using StoryBoard Quick/Power Productions)

1

ANALYZING ACTION

Let's think again. We know from the previous scene where she is going and why. All we really want to register are her reactions as she buys the stamp. So let's cut out all the superfluous footage, and concentrate on that moment. (See Figure 6.10.)

1. The child arrives at the counter, and looks up at the clerk.
2. Hesitatingly, she asks for the stamp.
3. She opens her fingers, to hand the money to the clerk.
4. The clerk smiles and takes the money and pulls out the stamp book.
5. A close shot of the clerk tearing the stamp from a sheet.

2

You now have a sequence of shots, far more interesting than a continuous "follow-shot." It stimulates the imagination. It guides the audience's thought processes. It has a greater overall impact. However, if this type of treatment is carried out poorly, the effect can look very disjointed, contrived, and posed. It is essential that the treatment matches the style and theme of the subject.

3

The whole sequence could have been built with dramatic camera angles, strong music, and effects. But would it have been appropriate? If the audience knows that a bomb is ticking away in a parcel beneath the counter, it might have been. It is all too easy to over-dramatize or "pretty-up" a situation (such as star filters producing multiray patterns around highlights, and diffusion filters for misty effects). So much is now done in postproduction, but resist the temptation.

4

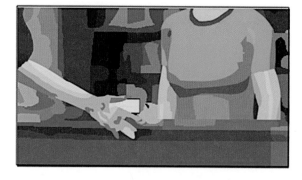

This breakdown has not only helped you to visualize the picture treatment, but allowed you to begin to think about how one shot is going to lead into the next. You can start to deal with practicalities. You see, for example, that shots 1 and 3 are taken from the front of the counter, and shots 2, 4, and 5 need to be taken from behind it. Obviously, the most logical approach is to shoot the sequence out of order. The storyboard becomes a shooting plan.

To practice storyboarding, review a motion picture carefully, making a sketch of each key shot. This way, you will soon get into the habit of thinking in picture sequences, rather than in isolated shots.

5

FIGURE 6.10
When edited together correctly, a sequence looks natural. But even a simple scene showing a person buying a stamp needs to be thought through. Note how shots 1 and 3 are taken on one side of the counter, and shots 2, 4, and 5 on the other. (Illustration created by StoryBoard Quick software)

Additional Production Plan Information

In addition to the script and possibly a storyboard, there are a number of other production/scripting tools that may be helpful.

Synopsis: An outline of characters, action, and plot. Appended to a dramatic script, particularly when shot out of sequence, or to coordinate a series. This synopsis is helpful to assist everyone involved in the production to understand what is going on.

Fact sheet/rundown sheet: Summarizes information about a product or item for a demonstration program, or details of a guest for an interviewer. Provided by a researcher, editor, or agency for guidance.

Breakdown sheet/show format/running order: Lists the events or program segments in order, allowed durations, participants' names, cameras, and audio pickup allocated, setting used, video and audio inserts, and so on. (This is sometimes also called a rundown sheet, but is not to be confused with the fact sheet.) Invaluable for unscripted, semiscripted, and scripted shows that contain a series of self-contained segments (sequences, scenes). Also as a summary of a complex dramatic script to show at a glance: shot numbers for each scene, operational details, inserts, break for major resetting (clearing props, redressing set, moving scenery), costume, makeup changes, and so on. (See Table 6.5.)

Individual camera information:

Shot sheet: The shot sheet is a list of all of the individual camera's required shots. Shot sheets reduce the amount of communication between the director and the camera operators during the actual production, as the shots are already on the sheet.

Team roster: In sports production, it is often helpful for camera operators to have a list of team members with their jersey numbers. That way, if the director tells them to shoot a specific person (by name), they can see what their number is (Figure 6.11).

FIGURE 6.11
Camera operators often use information, such as a shot sheet or a team roster, that assists them in doing their job.

91

REVIEW QUESTIONS

1. What is the script's role in a production?
2. What are the different types of scripts and how are they used in a production?
3. Why is a show format used during a production?
4. When is it necessary to fully script a production?
5. How is a storyboard used in a production?

PART 3

Visualizing the Story

CHAPTER 7

What the Camera Can Do

"While cameras with lots of features are nice, it is not the camera that creates incredible images—it is what you do with the camera that is important."

Jeff Hutchens, Photographer

Terms

Convertible camera: Can be used in a variety of configurations. This type of camera generally starts out as a camera "head." A variety of attachments can then be added onto the camera head, including different kinds of lenses, viewfinders, recorders, and so on, to suit a specific production requirement.

EFP (electronic field production) camcorders: Used for non-news productions such as program inserts, documentaries, magazine features, and commercials. Can also be used for a multicamera production.

ENG (electronic news gathering) camcorders: Generally used for news gathering. Often these cameras are equipped with a microphone and camera light and are used to shoot interviews and breaking news.

Focal length: An optical measurement—the distance between the optical center of the lens and the image sensor, when you are focused at a great distance such as infinity. Measured in millimeters (mm) or inches.

Focus puller: The person responsible for keeping the camera in focus using a follow-focus device.

Follow-focus device: A device that is attached to a film-style camera's lens, allowing a focus puller to adjust the focus on the camera.

POV (point-of-view) camera: These small, sometimes robotic cameras can be placed in positions that give the audience a unique viewpoint.

Telephoto lens: A narrow-angle lens that is used to give a magnified view of the scene, making it appear closer. The lens magnifies the scene.

Wide-angle lens: A lens that shows us a greater area of the scene than normally seen. The subject looks unusually distant.

Video/television cameras have become increasingly user-friendly over the years. Various controls that previously needed watchful readjustments can now be left to clever automatic circuitry that tweaks them automatically. On the face of it, there may thus seem to be little point in getting involved with the technicalities of its controls. It looks as if you only need to point

95

the camera and zoom in and out to adjust the size of the shot—leaving circuitry to take care of all other issues such as exposure, light quality, and so on. Why do we need to learn about lens apertures, depth of field, lens angles, and other details?

Frankly, it really depends on how critical you are of the results. When you want successive pictures to match in brightness, contrast, and color quality, with consistent perspective and controlled focusing, you need to understand the effects of the various camera controls. Although automatic compensatory circuits (autocircuits) can certainly ease pressures when working under difficult conditions and are valuable fall-back devices that can be helpful, they do have their limitations. Good camera work involves making subtle artistic judgments, and autocircuits simply can't do that for you.

Knowing about the various camera adjustments and the effects that they can have on your images will not only enable you to make the best judgments, but will also prepare you for problems that arise under everyday conditions.

TELEVISION CAMERAS

A wide range of television/video cameras are available today, from modestly priced designs for consumers to very sophisticated state-of-the-art cameras. The market spread of models suits a variety of applications; as you would expect, both design and performance vary with cost. Although cameras at the lower end of the range can provide very satisfactory image quality under optimum conditions, the more advanced equipment designs produce consistently excellent pictures for long periods, even in difficult circumstances (Figure 7.1).

96

FIGURE 7.1
Cameras have been designed for a wide variety of users and situations. (Photos courtesy of Sony, Panasonic, and Thomson)

A number of factors can influence one's choice of camera:

- Cost: initial and running costs.
- Physical aspects: weight, portability, method of mounting, and reliability.
- Operational features: available options, controls, handling, and flexibility (e.g., zoom range).
- Image performance: resolution, color quality, any picture impairment (artifacts), performance stability, and sensitivity.

Determining the features that are most important to you depends on how you are going to use the camera. Are you shooting live or recording? Are you working with a single-camera setup or as part of a multicamera production? Are you editing what you shoot as you go or will the material be edited later? Some camera systems are more appropriate than others for specific situations.

One factor can strongly outweigh others. If, for instance, a news unit is working under hazardous conditions where the likelihood of equipment loss or damage is high, it may be wiser to use a small, low-cost consumer/small-format camcorder rather than a larger, expensive camera!

TYPES OF CAMERAS

Historically, there have been many different types of cameras, generally sorted into one of three categories: consumer, prosumer/industrial, and professional. Generally, the categories were assigned according to the level of quality and the features each camera provided. Of course, there are still some high-end professional cameras and some low-resolution/low-feature consumer cameras that are aimed at specific markets. However, the quality of today's cameras have blurred the lines between these three categories, sometimes allowing lower-end/lower-cost cameras to be used in high-end professional productions. Some of the different styles of cameras are discussed in the following sections.

Camcorders

Camcorders are the main type of camera used today in television productions. As high-quality camcorders have became available at lower prices, these have been adopted by many organizations throughout the world, for both studio and location production (Figures 7.2 and 7.3). Although camcorders can record their own signal, they can also be used in multicamera productions. These cameras have proven to be not only convenient, but adaptable, with lower operating costs than many other cameras.

FIGURE 7.2
Small handheld portable cameras are used in situations where larger cameras cannot be used. (Photo courtesy of JVC)

FIGURE 7.3
High-end professional cameras are used in situations where absolute control is needed over every aspect of the image. (Photo courtesy of Panasonic)

FIGURE 7.4
The camera used to shoot *Guiding Light*. (Photo courtesy of Canon)

Case Study: *Guiding Light*

Guiding Light, the longest-running scripted television series in broadcast history, strategically enhanced its look in 2008 by becoming the first series of its kind to be filmed exclusively with small, handheld, highly portable digital camcorders, which enable the show to be shot inside actual homes and offices, or on location practically anywhere. The camcorder chosen for this new production model was a Canon prosumer camera.

The key to *Guiding Light*'s new production model of exclusively using compact, handheld Canon camcorders is what Janet Morrison, the producer of the show's digital department, described as "Four walls and a ceiling. Its purpose is to make the show more intimate for the viewer and to really bring them into Springfield, so they can be a part of these characters' lives in a way they haven't been before." Springfield, *Guiding Light*'s fictional locale, is portrayed by a suburban New Jersey town several miles west of the series' Manhattan studios. "In our old production model [using pedestal-style cameras to shoot actors performing in traditional three-sided sets,] our two studios in Manhattan had room for seven sets at a time," Morrison added. Now, however, using these compact camcorders, producers of *Guiding Light* can shoot in as many locations as they wish. "This has opened up our 'canvas' in ways we weren't able to imagine before. Our writers have so many more places where scenes can happen. They can write people in the park, or at the municipal building, or using cars that actually drive, as opposed to cars that just sit on a studio floor. This new production model has completely changed the way the show looks and the way stories can be told."

Jennie Taylor, *Highdef* magazine

FIGURE 7.5
ENG cameras.

Camcorder Styles

Camcorders are often known as ENG (electronic news gathering) or EFP (electronic field production) cameras.

ENG camcorders are generally used for news gathering. These are often the cameras that are equipped with a microphone and camera light and are used to shoot interviews and breaking news (Figure 7.5).

EFP cameras are used for non-news productions such as program inserts, documentaries, magazine features, commercials, etc. (Figure 7.6). EFP cameras can also be used for a multicamera production.

FIGURE 7.6
EFP cameras.

The Convertible Camera

Convertible cameras can be used in a variety of configurations. This type of camera generally starts out as a camera "head." The camera head is the part of the camera that creates the image—primarily the chips. Figure 7.7A shows a camera head with a studio back attached, which allows it to be used in a multicamera situation. A variety of attachments can then be added onto the camera head, including different kinds of lenses, viewfinders, and recorders, to suit a specific production requirement. Here are a few examples:

Studio, stationary, or hard camera: This configuration utilizes a long lens, a studio back, a large studio/EFP viewfinder, and remote controls for the zoom and focus. Due to the weight of the large lens, this camera is fairly stationary unless also attached to a dolly (Figure 7.7B).

Handheld camera: When maximum mobility is required, a shoulder-supported handheld camera can be used. This camera utilizes a small eyepiece viewfinder, the EFP/ENG lens, and no remote controls for the zoom and focus (Figure 7.7C). A convertible handheld camcorder can also be created by replacing the studio back with a recorder (Figure 7.7D).

EFP camera: The electronic field production camera can be set up in a number of different ways. In Figure 7.7E, the camera is configured as part of a multicamera production with an EFP lens, zoom controls, and the large viewfinder. This type of camera is lighter to transport than the studio/stationary camera. However, the EFP's lens is not as long.

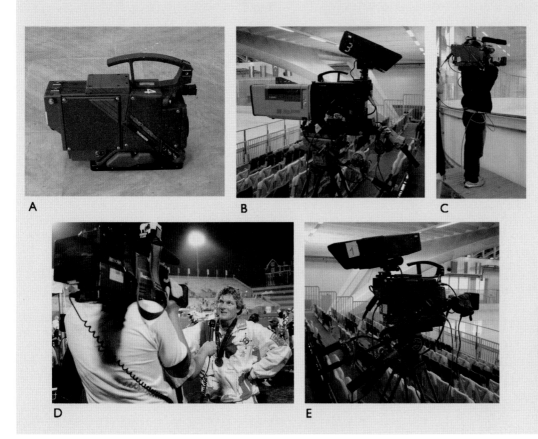

A   B   C   D   E

FIGURE 7.7
Convertible cameras provide maximum flexibility for the camera crew, allowing them to configure the camera for the specific needs of the production.

99

Studio Cameras

Studio productions make use of a wide range of camera designs, from handheld cameras in a studio configuration to the large traditional studio cameras (Figures 7.8 and 7.9). However, this type of camera is not limited to the studio; you will also see it at sports events and other multicamera productions. The large "studio" viewfinder is usually intended to make it easier for the camera operator to accurately focus and compose the images.

Studio cameras are usually mounted on heavy-duty wheeled dollies—pedestals or rolling tripods—on a pan and tilt head, which enables it to turn (pan) and tilt (Figure 7.10). Its focus and zoom controls are usually fixed to the panning handles (pan handles), which position the head.

FIGURE 7.8
This studio configuration utilizes a small camcorder with studio back, large studio monitor, remote controls, and an ENG lens. (Photo courtesy of JVC)

FIGURE 7.9
The traditional studio camera does not have a built-in recorder and is heavy and large. (Photo courtesy of Sony)

FIGURE 7.10
Wheeled dollies are often used with studio cameras. (Photo by Jon Greenhoe)

Case Study: National Geographic Films

Among the highest echelon of international wildlife cinematographers, Dereck Joubert and producer wife Beverly Joubert, both Explorers-in-Residence at the National Geographic Society, have a lot of experience shooting film of lions in the wilds of Botswana.

Joubert shoots with a run-and-gun style with two Panasonic P2 HD camcorders when shooting the lions on location in Botswana's Duba Plains. "We have worked in terrible conditions with the cameras," Joubert said. On one project, "it rained solidly for two months while we were following lions, getting bogged in, getting drenched, and generally fighting the elements. This is an electronic camera, and yet I have felt more confident with it, not less, because of its tapeless mechanics. The fewer moving parts to take on moisture, the better. When it isn't raining, it is 120 degrees in the shade."

FIGURE 7.11
Tapeless cameras are increasingly being used on some of the National Geographic film projects. (Photo courtesy of Panasonic)

Joubert explained, "As a veteran film cameraman, with every HD camera I use I try to set it up as much like a film camera as possible. In my mind, this is an electronic film camera: I expose for the highlights and mostly let the dark areas take care of themselves, because in film terms the camera's latitude can handle it. I expose the same way as with film, I use short depths of field because I think we see in shorter depths of field, and movie audiences expect that." (See Figure 7.11.)

Specialty Cameras

There are all kinds of specialty cameras available. Figures 7.12 and 7.13 show some of the types.

FIGURE 7.12
Two different types of 3D cameras are shown. (Left) This type uses small miniature cameras on a bracket, which send the images to software that merges the images. (Right) This camera uses two much larger cameras and a two-way mirror to merge the images.

FIGURE 7.13
Both of these video camera packages provide a 360-degree view of a scene. (Left) This set uses seven cameras to provide a left/right view of the scene. (Right) This set uses ten cameras, combined in one ball, to provide a 360-degree left/right view, as well as an up/down view of the scene.

FIGURE 7.14
This POV camera was mounted onto a referee's helmet in order to give viewers a chance to see what the referee was seeing.

Miniature or Point-of-View Cameras

Miniature or POV (point-of-view) cameras are being utilized on a regular basis by directors who need to get a camera into a location that would be extremely difficult for a normal camera. These difficulties may be size (the camera may not fit into a tight location), safety (it may not be safe to have a camera and operator in a dangerous location), or visibility (the director may not want the camera to be seen). Generally, these cameras are remotely controlled by a camera operator (Figures 7.14, 7.15, and 7.16).

CAMERA BASICS

Let's now take a closer look at the various features found on cameras (Figures 7.17, 7.18, and 7.19) and how they can affect the way you use them:

- The camera's viewfinder.
- The camera's main controls.
- The camera lens and how it behaves.
- The techniques of adjusting exposure for the best picture quality.
- Methods of supporting the camera.

FIGURE 7.15
Camera operators can use a POV camera to get into small areas. This operator used a POV camera attached to a pole to get a shot in a bull's pen at a rodeo. Note that a lavalier mic has been taped to the camera to capture the audio. (Photo by Ben Miller)

FIGURE 7.16
The Discovery Channel's Mike Rowe uses a small HD POV camera taped to a light to capture tight areas in a cave. In this situation, Mike is both the host and one of the camera operators for the show *Dirty Jobs*. (Photo by Douglas Glover)

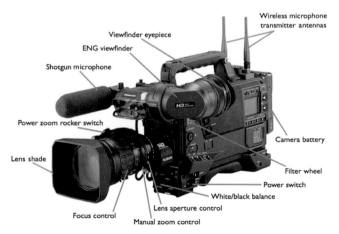

FIGURE 7.17
Parts of an ENG/EFP camera. (Photo courtesy of Panasonic)

The Viewfinder

An effective viewfinder is essential for successful camera work. It enables you to select, frame, and adjust the shot; to compose the picture; and to assess focus adjustment. When you are working alone, with a portable camera, the viewfinder will usually be your principal guide to picture quality and exposure, as well as providing continual reminders about videotaping, the battery's condition, and other relevant factors.

Traditionally, most viewfinders are fitted with a black-and-white monitor, displaying a high-grade black-and-white image. Although LCD screens do have the advantage that you can see the shot in color (although it's not necessarily identical to that on the picture monitor), one cannot see fine detail as easily on the LCD, and manual focusing may be more difficult. However, color screens have gotten much higher quality and have gained in popularity.

Some camera systems show just a little more than the actual shot being transmitted so that the camera operation can see whether there is anything just outside the frame that might inadvertently come into the picture. Although the viewfinder shows exactly the same shot area as the transmitted picture, the camera operator has no warning if an unwanted subject (a microphone, a bystander) is about to intrude into the shot.

Because the viewfinder is a monitoring device, any adjustments made to its brightness, contrast, sharpness, or switching will not affect the camera's video output. Normally, a viewfinder is fed with the camera's own video, but when necessary, it may be able to be switched to display another camera's picture as well. This feature lets you compare two or more cameras' shots, or to show them combined in a composite effect. You can also use the viewfinder to display test patterns (e.g., color bars), which allow you to check the camera's performance.

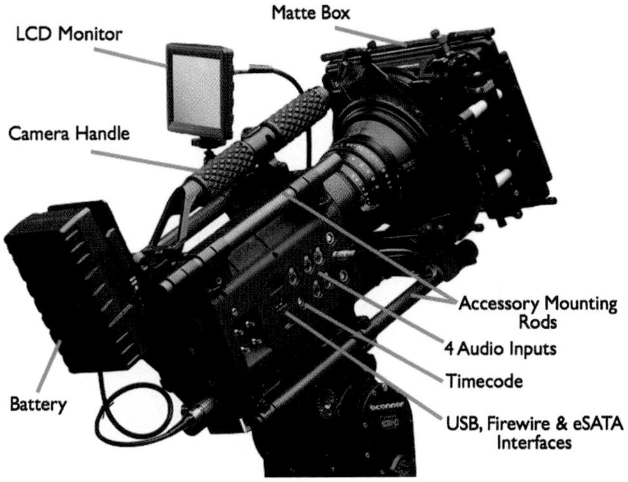

Viewfinders often have a number of indicators that aid in framing the image, such as a safe area line around the viewfinder's edges to remind the camera operator how important information and titles near picture edges can be lost inadvertently through edge cutoff on overscanned TV receiver screens. Other viewfinders may keep the camera operator informed about the camera or recorder's settings and status. These may include light or audio meters, shutter speeds, a tally light showing when the camera is recording or "on-air," zoom lens settings, "zebra" (refers to a camera feature that displays all over-exposed areas of the image with diagonal stripes warning the operator to reduce the exposure), battery status, and other displays. Various indicators keep you informed about the camera and recorder's settings and status. Some monitors even place a red line around all sharply focused subjects (Figure 7.20).

FIGURE 7.18
Parts of a studio-configured camera. (Photo courtesy of JVC)

FIGURE 7.19
Parts of a high-quality (4K) HD camera. (Photo courtesy of Red)

103

The Camera's Controls

Television cameras have three different categories of controls:

- Those that need to be continually readjusted while shooting, such as focus.
- Occasional adjustments such as compensating for changing light.
- Those involved in aligning the camera's electronics in order to obtain optimum consistent performance.

Production
monitor/
viewfinder

Film-style
viewfinder

Focus
puller

Matte
box

FIGURE 7.20
A film-style video camera configuration may include two
viewfinders. The film-style viewfinder is used by the camera
operator. The production monitor or viewfinder can be used by the
operator or by the focus puller. The focus puller is a person who
uses a follow-focus device to keep the image sharply focused.
These camera configurations generally also include a matte box
used to hold filters and shield the lens from light glares. (Photo
courtesy of Panasonic)

FIGURE 7.21
A video operator adjusts a camera that is part of a multicamera
production utilizing a CCU.

Once these are set up, they should not be casually tweaked! There are really two quite distinct
aspects to picture making: camera work and image quality control. These can be controlled
manually, semi-automatically, or even completely automatically. Let's look at some practical
cases.

MULTICAMERAS

Camera operators who are part of a multicamera production concentrate on the subtleties of camera work. They spend their time selecting and composing the shots, selectively
focusing, zooming, and controlling dolly movements. The quality of the video image is
remotely controlled by a video operator utilizing a camera control unit (CCU) or remote
control unit (RCU), as shown in Figure 7.21. There are basically two types of camera adjustments made by the video operator:

Preset adjustments: During the setup period, camera circuitry is adjusted to ensure
optimum image quality. This may include color and tonal fidelity, definition, and
shading (adjusting the aperture). These adjustments can be done manually using test
signals displayed on test equipment, or, in digital systems, the process can be semi-
automated by inserting programmable memory cards.

Dynamic adjustments: During the actual television production, the video operators,
sometimes known as "shaders," continually adjust the camera's images (in terms
of exposure, black level, gamma, color balance) to optimize the subjective quality
of shots and match the various camera's images. This approach not only leaves the
camera operator free to concentrate on effective camera work, but results in the highest and most consistent image quality.

SINGLE CAMERAS

Single-camera operators are not only required to ensure that they obtain well-composed images, but must also adjust the camera to obtain the highest-quality image possible. There are a number of options for adjusting the camera:

- The camera's built-in automatic circuitry can be used to readjust the camera's performance as conditions change. Although this is a good option when in a hurry to capture the images, it gives the least amount of quality control to the camera operator—and may not provide the optimum quality in every situation.
- Preview the scene before shooting and adjust the controls until pictures appear optimum in the viewfinder or a nearby monitor.
- Readjust the camera controls while shooting.

THE CAMERA LENS

"Never make the mistake of thinking that a lens is a mere accessory to the camera—especially in HD imaging. The HD lens has the primary role in shaping the image and giving it critical performance attributes that, in turn, will determine the ultimate digital performance of your camera."

Larry Thorpe, Canon U.S.A.

Lens Systems

PRIME LENS

Occasionally, for special purposes, a *prime* or *primary lens* may be required. Prime lenses have fixed optics; that is, their focal length or scene coverage cannot be varied. The prime lens is particularly useful when:

- The highest optical quality is necessary.
- Creating a special optical effect such as an extremely wide-angle fish-eye lens.
- Shooting in low-light situations. Primes have lower light losses, and thus are able to obtain a quality image in low light.

Because its focal length is fixed, the prime lens will cover only a specific angle of view, according to whether it is designed as a narrow-angle (or telephoto or long) lens, a wide-angle (or short) lens, or as a normal lens system. You can change a prime lens coverage only by adding a supplementary lens. Prime lenses are available with fixed focal lengths ranging from just a few millimeters (for wide-angle work) to telephoto lenses with focal lengths of more than 1000 mm (Figure 7.22).

ZOOM LENS

Most television/video cameras come with the familiar zoom lens system, which is a remarkably flexible production tool. A zoom lens system has the great advantage that its focal length is adjustable. You can alter its coverage of the scene simply by turning a lever. This change gives the subjective impression that the camera is nearer or farther from the subject, at the same time modifying the apparent perspective. At any given setting within its range the zoom lens behaves like a prime lens of that focal length (Figure 7.23).

105

FIGURE 7.22
Prime lenses are used when the highest optical quality is required. (Photo courtesy of Ziess/BandPro)

FIGURE 7.23
The zoom lens is a variable–focal length lens. (Photo courtesy of Canon)

Lens Controls

Most lens systems have three separate adjustments that can be made manually or semi-automatically:

- Focus—adjusting the distance at which the image is sharpest.
- *f*-stop—adjusting a variable iris diaphragm inside the lens system.
- Zoom (if utilizing a zoom lens)—altering the lens focal length to adjust how much of the scene the shot covers.

Generally, how the lens controls are adjusted will affect the following:

- How sharp the detail in the image is (focusing).
- Exactly how much of the image appears sharply defined in the shot (depth of field).
- How much of the scene appears in the shot (focal length/angle of view).
- The impression of distance, space, and size that the picture conveys.
- The overall brightness of the picture, and the clarity of lighter tones and shadows (exposure).

Focal Length

The distance between the optical center of the lens and the image sensor (CCD or CMOS) in the camera, when focused at a great distance such as infinity, is the *focal length* of the lens. Focal length is simply an optical measurement and is generally measured in millimeters (mm). In a prime lens, the focal length is fixed. In a zoom lens, the focal length can be adjusted within limits.

How much of the scene and subject the lens shows will depend on several areas:

- The size of the subject itself.
- How far the camera/lens is from the subject.
- The focal length of the lens being used.
- The size of the camera's image sensor (such as $^2/_3$, $^1/_2$, or $^1/_3$ inch).

The coverage of a prime lens is fixed according to its specific focal length. So, in order to alter the shot, the camera needs to be moved and a supplementary lens attached or the lens changed.

Because the angle of view (field of view) of a zoom lens varies as its focal length is altered, camera operators have the choice of moving the camera either nearer or farther away from the subject, or controlling the lens focal length to alter the shot size.

Why bother? Does it really matter what focal length setting is used on a zoom lens? Apparently all one has to do is to stand wherever it happens to be convenient, zoom in and out on the subject until you get the size of shot you want—and there we are!

But if you really care about the quality of the image, the focal length of your lens is not a mere technicality. As you will see, the focal length you choose will simultaneously affect:

- How much of the scene your shot shows.
- The apparent proportions, sizes, and distances of everything in the shot (perspective).
- How much of the scene is in focus and how hard it is to focus accurately.
- Camera handling, such as how difficult it is to hold the shot steady.

FOCAL LENGTH AND IMAGE SIZE

Let's suppose that you set your lens focal length to 20 mm (0.8 in.) and then change the focal length to 40 mm. As the focal length is altered, the subject appears to get closer (zoom in). Its image will now be twice as large on the screen. But now the shot shows less of the scene—only half the previous overall height and width is shown in the viewfinder.

What if instead you had changed from the 20 mm focal length to a 10 mm setting? Then the subject would appear further away—only half as big—but the shot would now cover twice the previous height and width.

A long focal length lens setting (telephoto lens) covers only a narrow segment of the scene—however, it shows a correspondingly larger image of the subject.

A short focal length lens (wide-angle lens) gives you a wide view, but subjects usually appear quite small and far away.

WORKING PRACTICES

There are several ways of working out the sort of shot you will get at various distances:

Trial and error: A "try it and see" approach, in which the camera is moved around to potential positions, changing the lens focal length setting until you get the result you want. This is a very laborious process.

Director's viewfinder: In this approach, the director stands in the planned camera position and checks out the scene through a handheld portable viewfinder. After its zoom lens has been adjusted to provide the required shot size, the corresponding focal length is then read off the viewfinder's scale and the camera's lens is set to this figure (Figure 7.24).

Computer calculators: There are a number of tools available that will calculate lens angles, depth of field, and other measurements. Some, such as the one shown in Figure 7.25, work on a PDA device, making it very easy to take into the field. These computer-based calculators are especially good for preplanning a shoot.

Experience: When working regularly in certain surroundings, such as a news studio, you soon come to associate various shot sizes with specific camera positions and focal length settings. However, these proportions will be altered if you happen to change to a camera with a different CCD/CMOS chip size.

LENS ANGLE

Lens angles have a distinct impact on the final image. There are three basic types of angles: normal, telephoto, and wide angle.

Normal Lens

A *normal lens* gives a viewpoint that is very close to what is seen by the human eye. It has very little distortion.

Telephoto Lens

A *telephoto lens*, or *narrow-angle lens*, is designed to have a long focal length. The subject appears much closer than normal, but you can see only a smaller part of the scene. Depth and distance can look unnaturally compressed in the shot (Figures 7.26 and 7.27).

Using a telephoto lens angle has some major advantages:

- When you cannot get the camera near the subject because of obstructions.
- When the subject is out of reach.
- When there is insufficient time to move the camera closer to the subject.
- When the camera is fixed in position.
- When the camera operator is unable to move smoothly and unobtrusively.

FIGURE 7.24

A director's viewfinder can be used to determine the camera position and the appropriate lens. (Photo courtesy of Alan Gordon Enterprises)

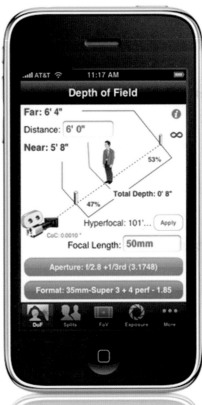

107

FIGURE 7.25

This screenshot is from the software program pCAM, which runs on a PDA. The software helps the director or cameraperson (video, film, and photography) calculate the correct lens, depth of field, and settings. (Photo by David Eubank)

Wide-angle lens view   Telephoto lens view

FIGURE 7.26
The angle of the lens determines what is captured in the camera.

FIGURE 7.27
The red lines show a wide-angle lens while the blue lines show a narrow-angle/telephoto lens. (Camera photo courtesy of JVC)

There are often occasions, both in the studio and in the field, when the only way that you can hope to get an effective shot of the subject is by using a telephoto lens.

However, the telephoto lens also has some drawbacks (Figure 7.28):

- Depth can appear unnaturally compressed—foreground-to-background distance seems much shorter than it really is. Solid objects look shallower and "depth-squashed."
- Distant subjects look much closer and larger than normal. Things do not seem to diminish with distance as we would expect.
- Anyone moving toward or away from us seems to take an interminable time to cover the ground, even when running fast. At the racetrack, horses gallop toward us, but appear to cover little ground despite their efforts.
- When the camera uses a telephoto lens to shoot a subject head-on lengthwise, the subject will look much shorter than it really is. For example, a large oil tanker may look a few yards long.

If a long telephoto lens is utilized to capture close-up shots of people who are a good distance away, you will notice that their features are unpleasantly flattened and facial modeling is generally reduced. Shot from the front (full face) or when slightly angled (three-quarters face), this effect can be very obvious.

Camera handling becomes increasingly more difficult as the telephoto lens focal length is increased. Even slight camera movement, caused by a shaky handheld or dollying over an uneven floor, causes image jerkiness. It is no easy feat to follow a fast-moving subject, such as a flying bird, in a close shot with a telephoto lens and keep it accurately framed throughout its maneuvers! Apart from handling difficulties, there is the additional focusing hazard of working with a shallow depth of field!

When using a telephoto lens, it is difficult to hold the camera still for any length of time without shake from one's breathing, heartbeat, or tiring muscles. A gust of wind can be a disaster! But it is virtually impossible to hand-hold a camera with a long telephoto lens. Telephoto lenses usually require the camera operator to use a tripod or other camera support, and lock the pan and tilt head to keep the image steady.

In hot weather, close shots of distant subjects taken with a telephoto lens can be marred by heat haze rising from the ground. Light diffraction produces an overall shimmering that distorts the picture and destroys the detail. The only remedy in this situation is to move the camera closer to the subject and use a wider lens angle.

Wide-Angle Lens

A *wide-angle lens* has a short focal length that takes in correspondingly more of the scene. However, subjects will look much further away and the depth and distance appear exaggerated. The exact coverage of any lens will depend on its focal length relative to the size of a camera CCD/CMOS chip image size. As you might expect, wide-angle (short-focus) lenses have the opposite characteristics of telephoto lenses.

WIDE-ANGLE LENS DISTORTION

The wide-angle lens exaggerates perspective. Depth and space are over-emphasized. Subjects in the image seem further away than they really are (Figures 7.28 and 7.29). Anyone approaching or walking away from a camera with a wide-angle lens seems to be moving much more quickly than normal.

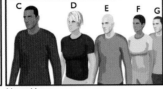

Total Scene

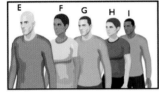

Wide-Angle Lens

Normal Lens

Telephoto Lens

FIGURE 7.28
Lens angles distort the perspective of the scene. Wide-angle lenses expand the subjects and telephoto lenses compress the subjects.

FIGURE 7.29
This image was shot with a fish-eye wide-angle lens. The camera operator was standing very close to the building, but the lens was still able to capture this shot. However, note the distortion that takes place in this situation. (Photo courtesy of Demon Fisheye Lens)

109

This distortion can be used to your advantage. A wide-angle lens can give a wide overall view of the scene, even when it is relatively close. This can be a great help when shooting in restricted spaces. Occasionally, when setting up a shot, you may find that something nearby is visible as a blur in the foreground of the shot. If the camera is moved closer until the obstruction is out of the shot, the subject may appear too large or too close. Moving closer with a wider lens angle can be the answer.

Even a small room can look quite spacious when shot on a wide-angle lens—a very useful deception when you want to emphasize space, or make small settings in the studio appear more impressive.

There are times when the wide-angle lens distortion can be an embarrassment. If, for instance, you are shooting within a very confined area such as a cell, only a wide-angle lens will give you a general view of the location. (Any other lens angle would provide only close shots.) But at the same time, the wide-angle lens exaggerates perspective and makes the surroundings seem very spacious. In these circumstances, the only alternative is to use a normal lens angle, and move outside the room, shooting in through a window or door.

FIGURE 7.30
Although super-wide-angle shots can give a good view of a very confined area, faces can become incredibly distorted. (Photo by Guillaume Dargaud)

If you take close shots of people through wide-angle lenses, you will get extremely unreal, bizarre distortions: odd-shaped heads, large protruding noses, stumpy legs, and enlarged chests (Figure 7.30)—fine for grotesques, but totally unacceptable for flattering portraiture!

Never use wide-angle lenses for close shots of geometrical subjects such as pages of print, graph paper, or sheet music. The geometrical distortion can become very noticeable. When panning a shot containing straight vertical or horizontal lines, wide-angle lenses bend the lines near the picture edges. The wider the lens, the more obvious these effects become. The fish-eye lens, which has a coverage from 140 degrees to 360 degrees, can be used only for those odd situations where the gross distortion can be accepted or artistic.

Table 7.1	Lens Characteristics	
	Advantages	**Disadvantages**
Normal lens	■ Perspective appears natural. Space/distance appears consistent with what the eye sees. ■ Camera handling feels natural and is relatively stable. ■ Focused depth is generally satisfactory, even though it can be fairly shallow for close-up shots.	■ May not provide the image needed when shooting in confined spaces. ■ Camera must move closer to the subject in order to capture detail; may be seen by other cameras taking longer shots of the same subject.
Telephoto lens	■ The field of view is restricted. ■ Brings distant subjects closer. ■ Permits "closer" shots of inaccessible subjects. ■ Compresses objects into a more cohesive group, such as a line of cars. ■ Defocuses distracting background. ■ Camera handling and focusing become more difficult.	■ The compressed image may be distracting. ■ Can flatten the subject's modeling, which can appear unnatural. ■ Camera handling is much more difficult (pan, tilt, smooth dollying) due to image magnification. ■ The restricted depth of field makes focusing highly critical.
Wide-angle lens	■ Can obtain wide views at closer distances, especially in confined space. ■ Lens reduces the "jerkiness" of a handheld shot. ■ Provides considerable depth of field. ■ The extended depth of field makes focusing less critical. ■ Space, distance, and depth of field are exaggerated.	■ Depth appears exaggerated. ■ Produces geometric distortion (such as buildings) at the widest lens angles. ■ Susceptible to lens flares.

FIGURE 7.31
This supplementary wide-angle lens is screwed onto the front of the camera lens. (Photo courtesy of VF Gadgets)

WIDE-ANGLE CAMERA HANDLING

On the plus side, camera work is much easier when using a wide-angle lens. Camera movements appear smoother, and any slight bumps as the camera moves are less likely to cause jerky shots. As an extra bonus, focusing is less critical, as the available depth of field is much greater.

The advantages and disadvantages of the three types of lenses are outlined in Table 7.1.

Supplementary Lenses

By adding an extra, "supplementary" lens onto the front of a camera lens, you can alter its focal length. These supplementary lenses can be used with both a prime lens and a zoom lens, and can change the lens so that it becomes more of a telephoto, wide-angle, or close-up lens (Figure 7.31).

Lens Care
Camera lenses are very sensitive tools. Although we may begin by handling new camera equipment with tender-loving care, familiarity can result in casual habits. Experienced camera operators develop a respect for their lens systems. They appreciate that a moment's distraction can cause a great deal of expensive damage to these precision optical devices, especially when working under adverse conditions. Liquid, dust, or grit can in a moment wreck the lens or degrade its performance.

Zoom Lens

Let's take a closer look at the operating features of the zoom lens. Its main advantage is that you can select or change between any focal lengths within its range without interrupting the shot. You can zoom out to get an overall view of the action and zoom in to examine details (Figures 7.32 and 7.33). The fact that in the process you are playing around with the spatial impressions your picture conveys is usually incidental to the convenience of getting shot variations from a camera viewpoint.

In order to alter the focal length of a zoom lens, it is necessary to move specific lens elements to adjust the overall magnification while still maintaining sharp focus. This involves very precise mechanical readjustments. If the focal length of the lens when zoomed completely in (telephoto) is, for example, 14 times that when fully zoomed out (wide angle), it has a zoom ratio of "fourteen to one." This can be written in a number of different ways such as 14× or 14:1. With this lens, you can change the size of a subject's image size in a picture by a magnification factor of 14. You might, for instance, zoom from a full-length of a person to a close shot of the face. A really high ratio—such as 44:1—could fill the screen with a person's eye, then zoom back until they became a speck in the landscape. Zoom lenses with the lower ratios (10:1 and 18:1) are usually on handheld cameras. The longest ratios (44:1 and 100:1) are usually on sports or remote production cameras.

ZOOM LENS CONTROLS

There are basically two methods of adjusting the focal length of a zoom lens:

Direct control: By turning a ring or a lever on the lens barrel. Although subtle zooming action is not easy with this type of direct control, it is simple and allows rapid zoom changes. The major advantage of this form of control is that it does not make any noise, unlike motorized systems. On most ENG/EFP cameras, you can override the motorized lens servo-switch control and operate the zoom action manually.

Servo control: The lens zoom action is controlled by a small forward/reverse variable-speed electric motor.

On ENG/EFP cameras, a rocker switch forms part of the lens housing. When the camera is handheld or shoulder-mounted, fingers on the right hand can easily operate the two-way rocker switch to adjust the zoom. Pressing W (wide-angle) causes the lens to zoom out toward its widest angle; when the T (telephoto) is pressed, the lens zooms in to the longest focal length. By releasing the rocker switch, the zoom can be stopped at any point within the zoom range. Most zoom lenses also have an adjustable zoom speed (Figure 7.34).

On large cameras, such as the larger studio and field cameras, a servo remote control is usually located on one of the tripod pan handles. These controllers provide a smooth, even change, particularly during a very slow "creep-in." The spring-loaded thumb-lever control is turned

FIGURE 7.32
Zooming in progressively fills the screen with a smaller segment of the scene.

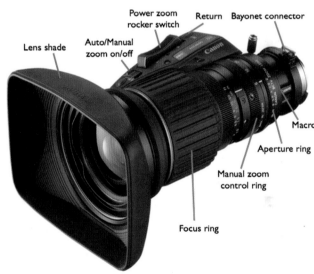

FIGURE 7.33
Parts of a zoom lens.
(Photo courtesy of Canon)

FIGURE 7.34
The fingers on the left are positioned on a rocker switch, allowing the camera operator to zoom in or out.
(Photo by Josh Taber)

111

to the left to zoom out, and to the right to zoom in. Light thumb pressure results in slow zooming, and heavier pressure gives a fast zoom. You soon learn to adjust thumb pressure to control the zoom rate (Figure 7.35).

Remote Focus Control   Remote Zoom Control

FIGURE 7.35

Larger cameras incorporate zoom and focus controls that are located on the tripod's pan handles.

112

ZOOM LENS ADVANTAGES

Zoom lenses have unquestionably added an important dimension to camera work:

- Zooms provide a wide selection of lens' focal length.
- Camera operators can rapidly select any focal length within the lens' range.
- Zooming can be controlled manually or by a motor driven at various preset speeds.
- They allow the camera operator to slightly adjust the size of the shot to improve composition/framing without having to move the camera nearer or farther away from the subject.
- Zooming is much easier and more precise than dollying (although the final effect may not be as good as a dolly shot).

ZOOM LENS DISADVANTAGES

Although a zoom has many advantages, it also has some disadvantages:

- Depth of field, perspective, and camera handling vary as the lens is zoomed in and out.
- If you are continually varying the zoom settings during a rehearsal, it is important to repeat the same angles and camera positions when recording. Suppose, for instance, that you are now further away than previously and you zoom in to compensate. This "corrected" shot will not have the same relative subject proportions. You might now be in the way of another camera or a boom mic in the studio. To avoid this type of discrepancy, note the details of the lens angle on a card, shot sheet, or script, and mark or tape the camera's floor positions during rehearsal.
- Zooming can easily be misused as a lazy substitute for more effective camera movement. Sometimes a dolly shot would be much more effective than a zoom, but the zoom is easier.

ZOOM LENS HANDLING

Focusing and camera handling are very easy when you have the lens set to a wide angle. But things become increasingly difficult as the lens is zoomed in to longer telephoto shots. Fast-moving subjects are harder to follow and frame accurately. When they're shooting on a wide-angle setting and the subject moves away, camera operators will find it necessary to both move and zoom in at the same time to capture the subject effectively. However, one of the problems in the telephoto setting is that it is difficult to keep the shot steady.

ZOOMING THE LENS VERSUS THE DOLLY SHOT

Why bother to move the camera when it can simply be zoomed in and out to get the shot? The reason is that there is a significant difference between a zoom shot and a dolly shot (unless you are shooting a flat surface). When shooting a flat surface, such as a painting, the effect of zooming is identical with that of dollying—an overall magnification or reduction of the image.

There are important differences when shooting three-dimensional situations. Although the zoom shot shows the magnification or reduction of the image, a dolly shot shows a different

Zoom Lens Shot

Dolly Shot

1a

2a

1b

2b

1c

2c

1d

2d

FIGURE 7.36

Zooming simply magnifies and reduces the picture. It does not produce the changes in the scene that arise as the dolly is moved through a scene. Increasing the focal length narrows the lens angle, filling the screen with a smaller and smaller section of the shot. The photographs illustrate the difference between the zoom and dolly. Notice that there is not much of a difference between images 1b and 2b. However, as the dolly continues in 2c, it begins to show a different perspective, showing that there is a table between the two chairs on the left. Photo 1d zooms past the table, while the dolly perspective in 2d takes the viewer up to the table and allows them to see the top of it.

perspective. In Figure 7.36, you can actually see that the camera moved down the aisle, showing more information to the viewer than is possible with a zoom shot. Zooming is seldom a completely convincing substitute for moving the camera.

EXTENDER LENS

Some zoom lens systems include a built-in supplementary lens that is called a *2x extender*. The extender can be flipped in or out of use and is available in sizes other than 2x, but that is the most common configuration. The 2x extender doubles the focal length of the lens, allowing the camera operator to zoom in much closer to the subject (Figure 7.37).

There are a few drawbacks to using an extender lens:

- The extender lens cannot be switched in or out when shooting because it disrupts the visual image. It must be changed between shots.
- There can be a substantial loss of light when utilizing an extender, which causes camera operators to adjust their aperture.
- The minimum focusing distance on the zoom lens can substantially change when switching in the extender. A zoom lens generally focuses on closer subjects when not using the extender.

FIGURE 7.37
A 2x extender doubles the focal length of the zoom. (Photo courtesy of Canon)

Focusing

When you focus the camera, you are adjusting the lens to produce the sharpest possible image of the subject. With a prime lens, this involves altering the distance between the lens and the camera's sensor chip. With the zoom lens, focus adjustment is done by readjusting the positions of internal lens elements.

WHY FOCUS?

Simple photographic cameras do not have a focus control, yet everything in the shot looks reasonably sharp. Why do television cameras need to be continually focused? There are several reasons why fixed-focus systems do not work with television cameras:

- They do not provide maximum sharpness of the subject.
- Because the lens aperture is reduced (small stop) in order to provide a large depth of field, high light levels are needed for good images.
- Everything in the shot is equally sharp. That means there is no differential focusing in which subjects can be made to stand out against a defocused background (Figure 7.38).
- The camera cannot focus on close subjects (although a supplementary lens may help).

If needed, a camera can be put into fixed focus by using a lens with as wide an angle as possible and using the smallest possible aperture. This combination will give you the best images your camera can provide in that situation.

FIGURE 7.38
Focusing with a shallow depth of field will allow you to make your subject stand out against a defocused background.

FOCUSING METHODS

Two different methods are generally used to focus the camera's lens system:

Focus ring: Lens systems on handheld and lightweight cameras can be focused by turning a ring on the lens barrel, until subject details are as sharp as possible (Figure 7.39).

Remote focus control: When a camera is attached to a tripod (or other mount), pan handles are usually attached to its pan and tilt head to allow the operator to pan and tilt the camera. Some type of rotating control is usually clamped onto one of the pan handles to adjust the lens focus by remote control. Designs vary. Some allow you to readjust the focused distance rapidly. A single turn of the grip moves the focus from the closest to the furthest point, allowing the camera operator to change the focus instantly between a subject in the foreground and another in the distance. Other focus controls require two or three complete turns to cover the full focus range. The remote focus control is linked to the lens focusing mechanism through a flexible cable (Figures 7.40 and 7.41).

FIGURE 7.39
This cameraman is focusing an ENG/EFP camera by adjusting the lens' focus ring with his left hand.

Some types of cameras have a servo-motor focusing system that adjusts the lens focus mechanism utilizing a remote control. This system has some considerable advantages: it can be located on the side of the camera, attached to a pan handle, or even from a long distance away from the camera.

Dramatic projects often shoot with a focus puller (Figure 7.42). The focus puller is in charge of the sharpness of the image, letting the camera operator concentrate on framing the subject.

Consumer and prosumer cameras usually have automatic focusing features. Ideally, you just point the camera, and it focuses on the subject. Autofocus is particularly useful when moving around with a handheld camera, as it maintains focus wherever you move, allowing

115

FIGURE 7.40
This camera operator is focusing a stationary or fixed camera with a couple of fingers on his left hand while using his other fingers on the left pan handle to tilt or pan the camera. (Photo by Shannon Mizell)

FIGURE 7.41
There are a variety of remote focus controls that attach to the pan handle. The type in this photo, different from the twist handle in Figure 7.35, requires that the operator turn the spoked wheel, often called a *capstan control*, in order to focus the lens.

FIGURE 7.42
In situations where the camera operator needs to concentrate on framing, a focus puller (in the yellow shirt) may be used. This person attaches a follow-focus mechanism to the lens in order to adjust the focus from the side of the camera.

you to concentrate on framing the shot and checking out your route. However, it is best to think of the autofocus feature as an aid instead of thinking that it relieves you of all focusing worries.

FIGURE 7.43
Autofocus struggles to focus if shooting through other objects such as this cage or branches, railing, and in similar situations.

Autofocus Problems

There are a number of inherent problems that happen with autofocus. Here are some of the most common issues:

- If the subject is not central, autofocus may adjust on whatever happens to be there, leaving your subject defocused.
- Although you may want two subjects at different distances from the camera to appear equally sharp, the autofocus may indiscriminately sharpen on one or neither.
- If you are shooting through a foreground framework of, for example, branches, a grille, netting, or railings, the system will focus on this, rather than on your subject beyond (Figure 7.43). If the subject is behind glass or beneath the surface of a pool, the autofocus system can also be fooled by this.
- If someone or something moves in front of the camera, the system may automatically refocus on it, defocusing your subject. If, for instance, you pan over a landscape, and a foreground bush comes into the shot, the lens may defocus the distant scene and show a well-focused bush. Similarly, when following a moving subject, such as someone in a crowd, the system may continually readjust itself, focusing randomly on passing subjects. Of course, this effect is incredibly distracting.
- When shooting in rain, snow, mist, or fog, autofocusing may not be accurate.
- Subjects that are angled away from the camera may produce false results.

Although these problems may not occur, it is good to be aware of their possibility. When in doubt, switch to manual focusing.

DEPTH OF FIELD

The distance between the nearest and farthest areas of focus is called the *depth of field*. In the right situation (such as lots of bright light or a wide-angle lens), the depth can be huge (Figures 7.44 and 7.45). In other situations, the depth can be incredibly shallow (low light or shooting, a close-up shot, or a telephoto lens), requiring the camera operator to readjust the focus every time the subject moves forward or backward (Figure 7.46).

FOCUSING THE ZOOM LENS

If a shot is correctly focused, zooming in or out should have no effect. It is important to zoom in on the subject as close as you can, focus, and then zoom back out. The image should stay in focus now for zooms in and out of that subject. Focusing during a wide-angle shot is easy, as there is plenty of depth. However, when you zoom in, the focused depth becomes progressively shallower as the lens angle narrows; then, the focus becomes much more critical.

ADJUSTING THE ZOOM'S BACK FOCUS

If the image does not stay focused during the zoom, once the lens has been focused during the close-up as mentioned earlier, it usually means that the lens needs the back focus adjusted. To ensure that the zoom lens maintains focus as it is zoomed (referred to as "correct focus tracking"), the lens system has to be carefully adjusted:

- With the lens set at the maximum aperture, zoom in close and adjust the lens for maximum sharpness using the focus ring on the lens.
- Zoom out to the widest angle, and adjust the internal back focus (flange) control for the sharpest image (Figure 7.47).

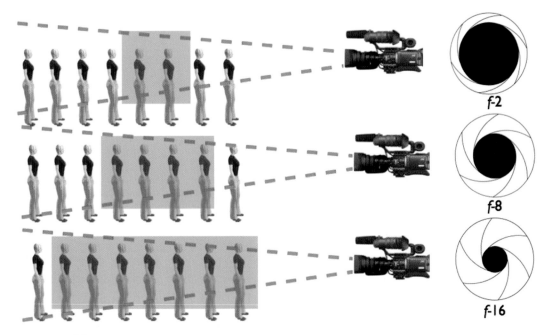

FIGURE 7.44
By adjusting the aperture (*f*-stops), the depth of field can be increased or decreased. The larger the *f*-stop number, the larger the depth of field.

Back Focus Flange

FIGURE 7.45
The shallow depth of field was achieved by using a telephoto (narrow-angle) lens, along with a fairly small-numbered *f*-stop such as *f*/4. (Photo by Josh Taber)

FIGURE 7.46
A large depth of field is achieved by using a wide-angle lens and a large-numbered *f*-stop, such as *f*/22. The bright sunlight in this photo allowed the large-numbered aperture.

FIGURE 7.47
The back focus flange needs to be adjusted whenever the zoom does not stay in focus when zooming in or out on the same subject. We are assuming that the lens was focused on the close-up of the subject. (Photo courtesy of Panasonic)

Now the zoom lens should be working effectively. If not, repeat the adjustment for optimum results.

LENS APERTURE (*f*-STOP)

If you look directly into a lens, you will see an adjustable circular diaphragm or iris made up of a number of thin overlapping metal blades. The size of the hole formed by these plates is carefully calibrated in graduated stops (Figure 7.48). These *f*-stops are usually marked

FIGURE 7.48
The aperture is the opening in the lens that allows light to fall on the sensors. Each opening is carefully calibrated into a series of *f*-stops. These *f*-stops significantly affect the scene being shot by varying the amount of light and the depth of field. The larger the number (smaller the opening in the lens), the larger the depth of field.

around a ring on the lens barrel. Turning the ring alters the effective diameter of the lens opening over a wide range (Figure 7.49).

When the lens aperture is adjusted, two quite separate things happen simultaneously:

- It changes the brightness of the lens image falling on the image sensor (exposure of the image).
- It alters the depth of field in the shot—which is also affected by the lens focal length.

f-STOPS (*f*-NUMBERS)

The larger the opening in the lens, the more light the lens will let through to the sensor. As the lens aperture is reduced (referred to as stopping down) the corresponding *f*-stop number increases. The lens smallest aperture may be around *f*/22, and the largest aperture opening may be around *f*/1.4. For each complete stop that you open the lens, its image brightness light will double (halved when stopping down). The standard series of lens markings is:

f/1.4 2 2.8 4 5.6 8 11 16 22 32

In reality, many intermediate points such as *f*/3.5, *f*/4.5, and *f*/6.3 are also used.

Focus ring   Aperture ring

FIGURE 7.49
The aperture ring is used to adjust the *f*-stops. (Photo courtesy of Zeiss/BandPro)

Exposure

There is a lot of misunderstanding about "correct exposure." A picture is considered to be correctly exposed when the subject tones you are interested in are reproduced the way you want them. Obviously, this may vary in different situations and is ultimately up to the director.

Because the camera's image sensor can respond accurately over only a relatively restricted range of tones, brighter areas will *crush out* (become white) above its upper limits; darker tones are *lost* (turn black) below the sensor's lower limits. The goal is to adjust the lens aperture to fit the director's vision (Figure 7.50).

If more details are needed in the shadows, the lens aperture will need to be open in order to increase the exposure. But, of course, this will cause all the other tones in the picture to appear brighter, and the lightest may even crush out to a blank white. Occasionally, the director may choose to deliberately over-expose a shot to create a special high-key effect with bleached-out lighter tones.

Conversely, if you want to see better tonal gradation in the subject's white dress, you may need to reduce the exposure by closing down to a slightly smaller *f*-stop. This will, however, cause all the other tones in the image to appear darker, and the darkest might now merge or even be lost as black.

Under-exposed

Correctly Exposed

Over-exposed

FIGURE 7.50
Exposing the image appropriately is incredibly important.

118

As you can see, exposure is an artistic compromise. But it is also a way in which the image can be manipulated. The director may choose to deliberately over- or under-expose the image to achieve a certain effect such as stormy skies, mystery, or night effects. It is quite possible to set the exposure to suit the prevailing light levels, and shoot everything in the scene with that stop. But for more sensitive adjustment of picture tones, one really must be alert and continually readjust the exposure for the best results.

AUTOMATIC IRIS

Consumer and prosumer cameras are usually fitted with an auto-iris. When turned on, it automatically adjusts the lens aperture to suit the factory-set average light levels. The auto-iris can actually be quite helpful at times. The auto-iris can be used as a "light meter" to get the most accurate reading, as long as you know about some lighting situations that can fool it (explained next). Without it, you would have to continually check tonal gradation in the viewfinder picture and open the iris until the scene was correctly exposed. The auto-iris can also be especially helpful if the camera operator is very mobile, moving around quickly and concentrating on framing the shot.

Unfortunately, like any automatic function, the auto-iris cannot make artistic judgments, and can be easily fooled. Ideally, you want the exposure of your main subject to remain constant. But an auto-iris is activated by all other tones in the picture. Here are some examples of problem issues that will require the camera operator to manually adjust the aperture:

- Move in front of a light background, bring a newspaper into shot, or take off a jacket to reveal a white shirt, and the iris will close and reduce the exposure even though it is not important that there is detail in those white areas. The problem is that all of the other picture tones will now appear darker (Figure 7.51).
- If a large dark area comes into shot, the iris may open up "to compensate," and all picture tones appear lighter.
- Walk through trees, where areas of sky and foliage come and go, and exposure can open and close, becoming very distracting to the audience.
- If shooting a concert where the lead singer is in a very bright spotlight, the auto-iris will usually adjust the camera so that the stage is black and the lead singer is pure white, with no detail.

In some camera designs, the auto-iris adjusts both the lens aperture and the shutter speed to "correctly" expose the picture. However, this adjustment can cause problems, such as when the subject approaches the camera and moves into shade. The auto-iris will open up, reducing the depth of field and leaving the subject defocused!

FIGURE 7.51
The auto-iris was used for both of these images. (Left) The bright white sky threw off the iris, making the subjects too dark. (Right) However, by adjusting the shooting angle and getting rid of the bright sky, the auto-iris was able to capture a well-exposed image.

Auto-iris systems work by measuring the brightness of the lens image falling on the sensor chip. Most auto-iris systems concentrate on the center area of the frame. Some are designed to avoid being over-influenced by the top of the frame, where bright skies, for example, could falsely reduce the exposure. The best systems judge exposure by sampling all parts of the image.

MANUAL IRIS ADJUSTMENT

Turning the iris/diaphragm ring on the lens barrel (see Figure 7.41) allows the camera operator to decide exactly how the image should be exposed. The overall picture brightness can be adjusted and compensation can be made for features in the scene that would fool the auto-iris system.

REMOTE IRIS CONTROL

When a camera is connected to a CCU (see Figure 7.21), usually in a multicamera situation, its lens aperture is usually set to suit prevailing light conditions by the video operator, who is also known as a shader. During a production, the lens aperture of each camera can be remotely controlled, either with coarse adjustment (several stops) or more usually with a fine control (e.g., ± half a stop) to vary exposure subtly for the best image quality.

FIGURE 7.52

Filters come in a variety of shapes, sizes, colors, and effects. (Photo courtesy of Tiffen)

Camera Lens Filters

Filters of various kinds can be attached to the front of the lens, located in the camera's internal filter wheel or inserted into a matte box on the front of the camera (Figure 7.52). Another option for filters is applying them to recorded video during the editing process. The following subsections describe some of the most common lens filters.

NEUTRAL-DENSITY FILTERS

When the scene is too bright for the aperture you want to work at, a neutral-density (ND) filter is used to cut down the overall intensity. These transparent gray-tinted (neutral) filters do not affect the colors—just the overall brightness. Most cameras come with one or more of these filters built into the camera. If the camera does not have them, they must be attached to the front of the lens.

ND filters may be used when shooting in very strong sunlight to prevent over-exposure. Should you want to open up the aperture of the lens to restrict the focused depth for artistic reasons, an ND filter can be used to bring down the light level, allowing you to open up the aperture, which will give a smaller depth of field.

FIGURE 7.53

The blue color-correction filter shown can be used to get rid of the warm tungsten light in the scene. (Photos courtesy of Tiffen)

CORRECTIVE FILTERS

When there are changes in the color temperature of light sources, corrective filters can be used to compensate. For example, when moving from a daylight scene to a tungsten-lit area, a correction filter should be used (Figure 7.53).

STAR FILTERS

Star filters are clear disks with closely scribed grid patterns. These diffraction-effects filters can produce four- to six-point stars from bright points of light, including flames, reflections, and lamps. The star's directions change as the filter is turned (Figure 7.54).

DIFFUSION DISKS

Available in various densities, these filters provide general image softening through fine surface scratches or dimpling on a clear disk. Sharp detail is reduced and highlights develop glowing halos (Figure 7.55).

FIGURE 7.54
The scribed grid pattern on the filter creates a star pattern at each point of bright light. (Photos courtesy of Tiffen)

FIGURE 7.55
A diffusion filter softens the image. (Photos courtesy of Tiffen)

UV (HAZE) FILTERS

The UV filter reduces haze blur (due to ultraviolet light) when shooting daylight exteriors, and protects the lens surface.

POLARIZING FILTERS

Polarizing filters are occasionally used to reduce strong reflections or flares from smooth or shiny surfaces such as glass or water. (They have very little effect on rough materials.) Polarizing filters can be used to darken an overly bright sky without affecting overall color quality, although there will be some light loss. By rotating the filter, you can selectively reduce or suppress specific reflections (Figure 7.56).

FIGURE 7.56
Polarizing filters are used to reduce or remove distracting reflections, such as this window. (Photos courtesy of Tiffen)

GRADUATED FILTERS

When shooting in the field, there are times when the main subject is properly exposed, but distant skies are far too bright and distracting. This can be a particular problem when the foreground subjects are dark-toned. A graduated filter can often overcome this dilemma. Its upper section has a neutral gray tint that reduces the brightness of the image in that part of the picture. So it will "hold back" the overly bright skies while leaving anything in the clear lower section unaffected.

Graduated filters have a gradual tonal transition, giving a soft blend between the treated and untreated areas. There are also graduated filters than can be used to create a deliberate effect. One half of the filter may be orange and the other half clear or blue-tinted. Some color filters have a central horizontal orange or yellow band, which, with care, can simulate the effect of a sunset (Figure 7.57).

Camera Filter Wheel

Professional cameras generally include an internal filter wheel. The filter wheel can be rotated, placing the desired filter in front of the sensor chips. The filters in the wheel usually include a 5600-degree daylight color-correction filter (used when shooting outdoors), a 3200-degree tungsten color-correction filter (for shooting indoors under tungsten light), and a couple of different ND filters. There are also usually blanks in the wheel so that additional filters can be added.

Video Gain Adjustment

Video gain is the amplification of the video signal in order to shoot in extremely low light. Although there are times when this may be necessary in order to capture an image, it can substantially deteriorate the image. Some cameras allow the camera operator to set different levels of gain, such as +3, +9, and +18. However, it is important to know that the higher the gain level, the poorer the quality of the final video image. In summary, the gain

FIGURE 7.57
(Left) This is a graduated filter. (Center) This image is a scene without a filter. (Right) In this shot, the camera operator used a graduated filter to enhance the sky and mountains. (Photos courtesy of Tiffen)

should be adjusted only in situations where you *must* capture an image—even if you have to compromise some of the quality.

Shutter Speeds

Selecting the correct shutter speed is very important in capturing the best video image. In some instances, a fast shutter speed should be used in order to get the clearest images of a speeding car. However, a slower shutter speed may be very appropriate for the same situation—although the final project will have some blurriness to it. In other situations, a specific shutter speed is needed in order to increase or reduce the depth of field in an image. Adjustment of shutter speeds is one of the creative tools available for the camera operator.

Supporting the Camera

When shooting while moving over uneven ground, climbing stairs, or in the middle of a crowd, the audience expects pictures to bounce around a bit. At times this "point-of-view" style of shooting can even add to the mood of the program. However, images that weave around, bounce up and down, or lean to one side soon become tiring for the audience to watch. Smooth subtle movement and rock-steady shots are usually essential for effective camera work, and there are various forms of support to help achieve this.

WHAT TYPE OF SUPPORT?

Before beginning any project, consider whether you have an appropriate camera mount (or a suitable substitute). Otherwise, you may not be able to get the kind of shot that the director would like. The kind of camera support you need will depend on a number of very practical factors:

- The size and weight of your camera. Do you intend to hand-hold or shoulder-mount the camera? Will the shots be brief, or are you shooting sustained action?
- Are you shooting from a fixed position, moving only while "off-shot," or moving while shooting (on-shot)? Will there be any quick moves to other camera positions?

FIGURE 7.58
The shoulder-mounted handheld camera is steadied by the right hand, positioned through the strap on the zoom lens. That same right hand also operates the record button and the zoom rocker (servo zoom) switch. (Photos courtesy of Josh Taber and Sony)

- Will you want high/very high or low/very low shots? Will you be raising/lowering the camera to these positions or even swooping or gliding within the action?
- Your surroundings can influence the type of mounting you use—the floor surface, operational space, height. Does the mounting have room to move around within the scene, around furniture, through doorways, and between trees?
- Is the camera likely to be unsteady? Are you shooting while walking/running or from a moving vehicle?
- In some situations, the solution is a remotely controlled camera mounted on a rail system, a robotic pedestal, or even a self-propelled camera car.

THE HANDHELD CAMERA

If you are hand-holding an ENG/EFP camera, the goal is to support it firmly, but not so tightly that your slightest movements are transmitted to the shot. Your right hand is usually inserted through an adjustable support strap near the zoom control. Your left hand usually holds the lens barrel. Holding the eyepiece viewfinder against an eye can even help to steady the camera (Figure 7.58). Whether you make hand adjustments or rely on auto-controls (auto-focus and auto-iris) will largely depend on the camera design and shooting conditions.

There are a number of devices designed to help you hand-hold a camera more steadily. One of those devices is a wrist support system, designed to keep the wrist stiff when holding the camera (Figure 7.59).

The lighter the camera, the more difficult it is to hold it steady. Make use of a nearby stable structure such as a wall, if you can. (You'll see various regular ways of steadying a handheld camera in Figure 7.60.) When you need to rest your camera on a rough or uneven surface, a

123

FIGURE 7.59
A wrist support system designed to help support a small video camera. (Photo courtesy of Hoodman Corporation)

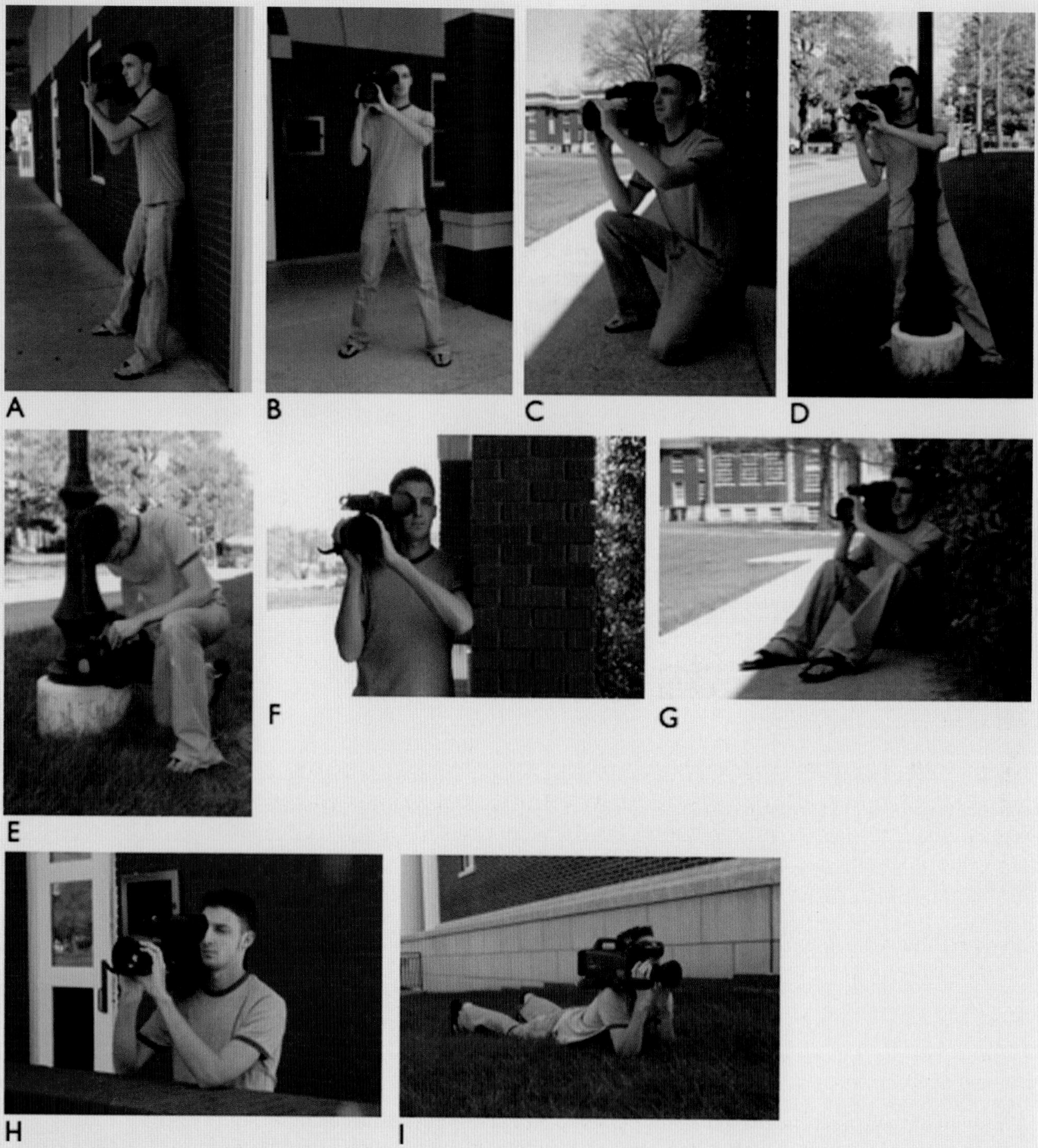

FIGURE 7.60
Keeping the handheld camera steady takes practice. Here are some techniques to hand-hold a camera:
A. Rest your back against a wall.
B. Bracing the legs apart provides a better foundation for the camera.
C. Kneel, with an elbow resting on one leg.
D. Rest your body against a post.
E. Lean the camera against something solid.
F. Lean your side against a wall.
G. Sit down, with elbows on knees.
H. Rest your elbows on a low wall, fence, railings, car, etc.
I. Elbows resting on the ground. (Photos by Josh Taber)

small bag containing sand (sandbag) or filled with foam balls (a type of bean bag) will help to support it firmly.

Some camera lens systems include an image stabilizer that is built in or attached to the lens system to steady slight picture movements.

Camera Stabilizers

The widespread technique of supporting the camera on one shoulder has its limitations. Its success largely depends on the camera operator's stamina! Some people can continue shooting over long periods, without their pictures leaning over to one side, wavering, or drooping. But arms tire and back muscles ache after a while, and it is not easy to sustain high-grade camera work, particularly when shooting with a telephoto lens.

BODY BRACE OR SHOULDER MOUNT

A body brace or shoulder mount can be attached under the camera to make it more comfortable to support and keep the camera steady (Figure 7.61).

MONOPOD

The monopod can be easily carried and is a very lightweight mounting. It consists of a collapsible metal tube of adjustable length that screws to the camera base. This extendable tube can be set to any convenient length. Braced against a knee, foot, or leg, the monopod can provide a firm support for the camera, yet allow it to be moved around rapidly for a new viewpoint. Its main disadvantage is that it is easy to accidentally lean the camera sideways and get sloping horizons. And of course, the monopod is not self-supporting (Figure 7.62).

STEADICAM/GLIDECAM SUPPORT

The most advanced form of camera stabilizer, such as the Steadicam or Glidecam system, uses a body harness with ingenious counterbalance springs. Stabilizers of this kind will not only absorb any camera shake but actually allow you to run, climb stairs, jump, shoot from moving vehicles—while still providing smooth, controlled shots! The operator uses a small electronic viewfinder attached to the stabilizer. Near-magical results are possible that are unattainable with other camera mountings. But underneath it all, there is still a vulnerable human operator, and extended work under these conditions can be very tiring (Figures 7.63 and 7.64).

THE PAN AND TILT HEAD

As you might expect, there are several types of camera head designed to suit different types and weights of camera.

If you simply bolted the camera onto a mounting, it could be held firmly, but would be unable to move around to smoothly follow the action. Instead, a pan and tilt head/camera head is needed, which goes between the camera and the top of the camera mount. It firmly anchors the camera, yet allows it to be turned (panned) and tilted, or fixed at any required angle (Figure 7.65).

Panning handles are attached to either side of the pan and tilt head for the camera operator to support and guide the camera. Zoom and focus controls are clipped to the panning handles (Figure 7.66).

If the camera head moves around too easily, it can be difficult to make smooth pans and tilts. So drag controls allow the camera operator to introduce a controlled amount of friction to steady movements. They should never be over-tightened to "lock-off" the camera. The separate head locks should be used to prevent panning or tilting (such as when leaving the camera).

FIGURE 7.61
A body brace helps to firmly support the camera. (Photo courtesy of Videosmith)

125

FIGURE 7.62
The monopod shown has additional support with the base. (Photo courtesy of Manfroto)

Balance adjustments ensure that the camera remains level. Careful balancing is absolutely essential when you have large zoom lenses, prompting devices, and camera lights attached to the camera; otherwise, the camera will be front-heavy and very difficult to operate. In some situations, it might even over-balance the mount, causing the camera to fall.

Choosing the Right Camera Mount

CAMERA TRIPODS

Although the tripod can't always be repositioned quickly, it does have advantages. It is simple, robust, and can be folded up and easily transported. It can be used in a wide variety of situations: on rough, uneven, or overgrown surfaces; on stairs; and so on.

Basically, a tripod has three legs that each have independently adjustable length. The legs are spread apart to form a stable base for the camera. When moving to a new location, the tripod legs can simply fold together. The camera can be screwed directly to the tripod pan and tilt head or a quick-release mounting plate can be used, which allows the camera to be detached in a moment (Figure 7.66).

Tripods are a great help when used properly, but they are not foolproof. Here are some useful warnings:

- Don't be tempted to use the tripod legs partly open, as it can easily fall over. Instead, always adjust the camera height by altering the leg length, not by changing the spread.
- Fully extended tripods can be a bit unstable at times, especially in windy conditions. It may be necessary to use a sandbag to provide stability or fasten the tripod to the ground or a platform.
- Don't leave the camera standing unattended on a high tripod. People (or animals) may knock it over or a pulled cable may over-balance it. It is much safer to drop the tripod to its lowest level (Figure 7.67).

Tripods usually have two types of feet: retractable spikes for use on rough surfaces and rubber pads for floors. Spikes can easily damage carpets and wooden floors.

FIGURE 7.63
Small cameras can be supported by a handheld steady device like this Steadicam. (Photo courtesy of Steadicam/Tiffen)

126

FIGURE 7.64
Larger cameras need to be attached to a brace on the body in order to spread the weight over the body and not just the camera operator's arms.

FIGURE 7.65
Parts of a pan and tilt head. (Illustration courtesy of Vinten)
1. Wedge adapter operating lever
2. Sliding plate adjustment handle
3. Carrying handle
4. Center lock plunger
5. Balance knob
6. Tilt brake lever
7. Pan brake lever
8. Center lock release lever
9. Illuminated level bubble
10. Timer button
11. Digital display
12. Illumination button
13. Graduated sliding plate
14. Wedge adapter
15. Wedge adapter mounting screw

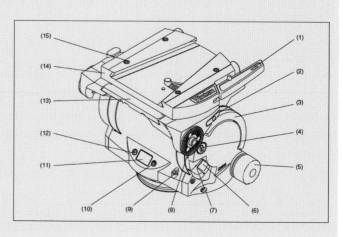

The feet of a tripod can be fitted onto a "spreader" or "spider" in order to prevent its feet from slipping. (See the spreader in Figure 7.67.)

If you have a wide pan shot, stand with your body at the midpoint of the pan, ready to twist from side to side.

TRIPOD DOLLY

A tripod dolly, which can be folded for transportation, is added to the bottom of a tripod in order to allow it to roll across a floor (Figure 7.68).

Although the dolly moves around quite easily on a flat, level floor, uneven surfaces will cause a jerky image, especially when a telephoto lens is used.

CAMERA PEDESTALS

A pedestal (ped) is the most widely used studio camera mount. Fundamentally, it consists of a central column of adjustable height, fixed to a three-wheeled base that is guided by a steering wheel.

The rubber-tired wheels can be switched into either:

- A "crab" mode, in which all three wheels are interlinked to move together.
- A "steer" or "dolly" mode, in which a single wheel steers while the other two remain passive.

Pedestal designs range from lightweight hydraulic columns on casters to heavyweight designs for large cameras. The ideal pedestal is stable, easy to move, and quickly controlled by one person (see Figure 7.10).

CAMERA JIBS AND CRANES

Jib Arms

As filmmakers have demonstrated so successfully over the years, a large camera crane offers the director an impressive range of shot opportunities. It can hover, then swoop in to join the action. Or it can draw back, rising dramatically, to reveal the broader scene. It allows

FIGURE 7.66
The collapsible tripod, a three-legged stand with independently extendable legs. (Photo by Paul Dupree)

FIGURE 7.67
When not in use, the camera operator dropped the tripod to its lowest position in order to provide maximum stability for the camera.

FIGURE 7.68
A tripod dolly is attached to the legs of the tripod to enable it to roll over smooth surfaces.

the camera to travel rapidly above the heads of a crowd, or to sweep around near floor level as it follows dancers' movements. But such visual magic is achieved at a price! Larger camera cranes are cumbersome, need a lot of room to maneuver, and require skilled and closely coordinated crews. Today, relatively few TV studios make use of such camera cranes. Instead, the modern jib arm can satisfy most directors' aims (Figures 7.69, 7.70, and 7.71).

Smaller lightweight jibs are easily disassembled and transported, and have proved to be extremely adaptable both in the studio and in the field. All the camera controls, including focus, iris, zoom, tilt, and pan, are adjusted by hand or by a remote control.

A jib is more compact than the traditional camera crane, much more portable, and a lot less costly to buy or hire. The camera on a jib arm may be handled by a single operator. It can stretch out over the action (like a crane), reaching over any foreground objects. It can support the camera at any height within its range, moving smoothly and rapidly from just above floor level up to its maximum, and swing around over a 360-degree arc.

FIGURE 7.69
Camera jibs provide directors with an impressive range of shot opportunities. This large jib requires a specially trained operator.

FIGURE 7.70
The smaller jib shown in the foreground of this photo is much easier to use than the large jib shown in Figure 7.69.

FIGURE 7.71
Cranes, different from the jib, usually provide a seat for the camera operator.

Camera Dollies

Camera mountings that have been widely used in filmmaking have been equally successful in television production. Camera dollies work incredibly well at capturing "dolly in," "dolly out," and "tracking" shots. Dollies can use wheels that work on a smooth floor or can be designed to run on a track.

There are a variety of dollies available, from very small dollies to larger systems designed to be ridden on (Figures 7.72–7.75).

Sky Cam/Cable Camera

There are a number of different names for this type of camera: cable cam, sky cam, and flying camera. This specialty camera has been used successfully over sports fields to provide a "flying camera." The remotely controlled camera (which is gyro-balanced) is suspended on

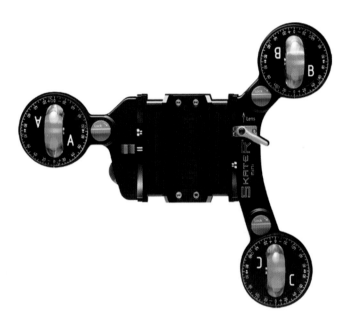

FIGURE 7.72
This "skater" dolly provides an extremely low-angle dolly shot. (Left) The top of the skater shows that it uses three skateboard-type wheels in order to glide silently and smoothly over the floor. (Photos courtesy of P+S Technik)

FIGURE 7.73
The camera operator is standing on this dolly, which is rolling on a dolly track.

FIGURE 7.74
This dolly utilizes a pivoting seat and camera support (or *turret*), allowing the camera operator to control camera pans by moving his or her feet. (Photo by Will Adams)

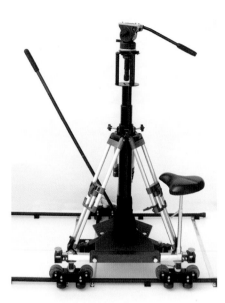

FIGURE 7.75
Dollies come in all shapes and sizes, based on the camera weight and movement requirements. (Photo courtesy of Indie-Dolly Systems)

FIGURE 7.76
The cable camera provides high-angle shots that allow the audience to view a sport from unique angles.

overhead cables. The camera can utilize a motor on the camera mount to move along cables or use independent computer-controlled winches that simultaneously adjust cable lengths, to rapidly reposition the camera at rates up to 27 mph anywhere over the action area. The camera's wide-ranging aerial views can go from zoomed-out vista shots to zoomed-in detail (Figure 7.76).

REVIEW QUESTIONS

1. What is the difference between an EFP camera and an ENG camera?
2. Why use a POV camera?
3. How does a wide-angle lens optically adjust the scene?
4. What are some of the challenges experienced when using a telephoto lens?
5. What are some of the advantages of using a zoom lens?
6. What are the advantages and disadvantages of automatic focus?
7. What are some of the types of camera supports, and what are their advantages?

CHAPTER 8

Using the Camera

"In the hands of even a moderately skilled photographer who knows the capabilities of the camera, even a cell phone can produce reasonable pictures. Unfortunately, owning a camera and knowing which button to push doesn't make you a photographer, any more than owning an automobile makes you a Formula One racecar driver."

Andy Ciddor, TV Technology

Terms

CU: Close-up shot.

ECU/XCU: Extreme close-up shot.

ELS/XLS: Extreme long shot.

f-**stop:** Regulates how much light is allowed to pass through the camera lens by varying the size of the hole the light comes through.

I-mag (image magnification): I-mag is when you are shooting for large video screens positioned near a stage to allow the viewers to get a better view of the action on the stage.

LS: Long shot.

MS: Medium shot.

Tally light: Cameras, or their viewfinders, usually have a tally light on the front. The front light is to let the talent know that the camera is recording. There is also a tally on the back that lets the camera operator know when his or her camera has been chosen to be recorded by the director.

Now that we have examined the camera's features, let's take a look at the techniques that are the foundation of good camera work.

STANDARD SHOTS

As filmmaking developed, a fairly universal system for classifying shots evolved. This system provides convenient quick reference points for all members of the production team, especially the director and the camera operator.

This series of shot terms are defined relative to the size of the subject. However, the overall concept works for any subject. Figure 8.1 demonstrates the various terms with each shot. Terminology does vary from place to place, but the most widely recognized ones are included here. When framing, it is important to avoid shots that cut through the body at natural joints.

131

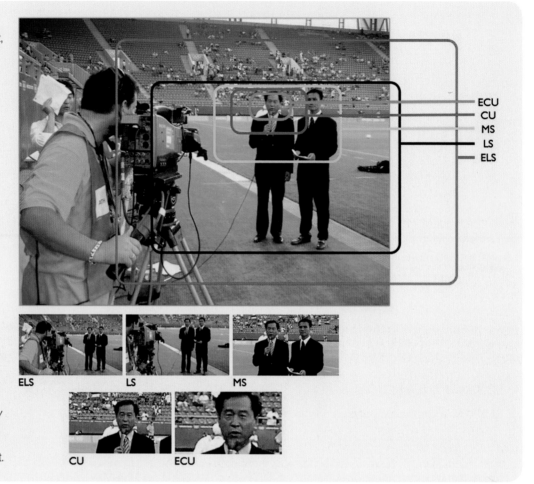

FIGURE 8.1
When shooting any subject, shots are classified by the amount of the subject taken in. Following are the shots of a person:

- *Extreme close-up* (ECU or *XCU*) or *big close-up* (BCU) is a detail shot.
- *Close-up* (CU) is generally framed just above the head to the upper chest.
- *Medium shot* or *mid-shot* (MS) cuts the body just below or above the waist.
- *Long shot* (LS) or *wide shot* (WS) generally features the entire person in the frame, just above and below the body. The European term for a long shot of a person is a *full shot* (FS).
- *Extreme* (or extra) *long shot* (ELS or XLS) or *very long shot* (VLS) shows significant space above and/or below the subject.

Exactly how you get a specific shot does not affect the term used. For instance, you can take a close-up shot with a camera that is close to the subject with a wide-angle lens or it can be shot with a camera that is quite a long distance from the subject using a telephoto lens. Of course, there will be differences in perspective distortion and camera handling depending on which method you use.

Selecting the Shot

Part of the issue when selecting a shot is knowing where that shot is going to end up. For example, if your final project will primarily be seen on a home television, a variety of shots from extreme long shots to extreme close-ups are appropriate. If you are shooting for large video screens positioned near a stage to allow the viewers to get a better view of the stage action (also known as image magnification or I-mag), medium shots and close-ups are used, as the viewer can already look at the stage and get their long shot (Figure 8.2). If the main use is for something like a video iPod or a small video area for the Internet, the small viewing screen requires more close-ups, so the viewer can really understand the nuances of what is going on.

FIGURE 8.2
Image magnification (I-mag) requires a different type of shot sequence than a standard television. Note the screen on the right side of the stage that is used to help the audience get a better view of the stage action.

Checking the Shot

Once a shot has been established, a review of the overall scene can be very helpful.

FIGURE 8.3
Note the tree growing out of this person's head. Background objects like the tree can be distracting.

FIGURE 8.4
Camera operators need to be careful not to include a boom mic into the frame. Boom operators have to be careful not to allow the mic to drift downward into the frame.

133

- Check for potential problems such as a light that will come into the shot if you pan right. It will let you know if someone is going to move into the shot and that you may need to recompose the picture to include that person.
- Check your viewfinder image to see if something is about to move out of shot, or is going to be partly cut off at the edge of the shot.
- Check the composition of the shot (framing, headroom, etc.), subtly correcting for changes that develop such as people moving to different positions in the shot. Composition will be discussed in Chapter 10.
- Watch for the unexpected, such as objects "growing out" of subjects (Figure 8.3). Are microphones, cameras, lamps, or their shadows appearing in the shot? You can often reframe the shot slightly to avoid them (Figure 8.4).

FIGURE 8.5
When accurately focused (A), the most important part of the subject should be the sharpest. The specific focus point (as represented by the darker blue line in the illustrations) should have a large enough depth of field (represented by the light blue field) to keep the subject in focus as she moves a little forward or backward. Note that the incorrect focus points, as demonstrated in B and C, would make it easier for the subject to move out of focus. (Camera photo courtesy of JVC)

CAMERA OPERATION

Focusing

Focusing is not always as straightforward as it looks. When the subject has well-defined patterns, it is fairly easy to detect maximum sharpness. However, with less well-defined subjects, you can rock the focus to either side of optimum, and somehow, they may still look soft-focused.

The exact point at which you focus can matter. There is usually more focused depth beyond the actual focused plane than there is in front of it. So in closer shots there can be advantages in focusing a little forward of the true focusing point (nearer the camera) to allow for subject movement (Figure 8.5). If you are focused too far back (away from the camera), the problem worsens. When shooting people, the eyes are a favorite focusing point.

Dealing with a Limited Depth of Field

FIGURE 8.6
When a limited depth of field creates problems (A), here are a few solutions:

- If the aperture is stopped down (a higher *f*-stop number), the depth of field will increase (B).
- If there is not enough depth to cover two people (C), it is possible to split focus (D). However, both subjects may be slightly soft-focused.
- Wide-angle lenses have a much wider depth of field than a telephoto lens (E).
- The closer the camera is to the subject, the shallower the depth of field. By moving the camera farther back, a wider depth of field will be created. However, the subject will be smaller. (Camera photo courtesy of Panasonic)

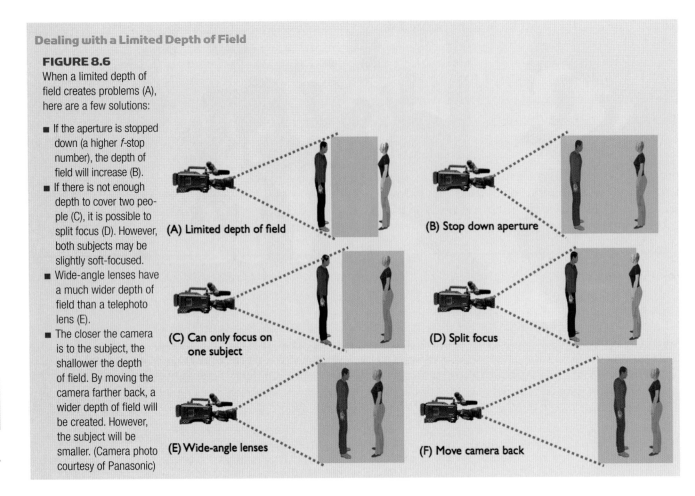

(A) Limited depth of field

(B) Stop down aperture

(C) Can only focus on one subject

(D) Split focus

(E) Wide-angle lenses

(F) Move camera back

Depth of field continually changes as you focus at different distances, select different lenses, or zoom in or out. This is something you quickly become accustomed to, but it can't be ignored. Focusing is much easier in longer shots and more complicated with close-up shots. You shoot two people speaking, yet can get a sharp image of only one of them at a time. In very large close-ups, focusing can be so critical that only part of a subject is sharp, while the rest is completely defocused. Figure 8.5 illustrates some of the solutions to this dilemma.

Camera Moves

There are a couple of things that you'll need to think about as a camera operator when moving the camera:

- Always check around you to make sure that you don't run over cables, bump into the set or props, move in front of other cameras, or run into people.
- When part of a multicamera production, make sure that you have enough cable by ensuring that you have sufficient slack before the move begins. Never pull a cable that has a tight loop in it. Cables can be easily damaged.

PRODUCTION FORMAT STYLES

Camera operators working on a single-camera production have many different responsibilities than those working on a multicamera shoot. Multicamera camera operators usually have someone in the control room adjusting their camera's aperture (so that the image quality is the same as the other cameras involved in the production) and a director telling them exactly what he or she wants, in real time. Single-camera production camera operators have to adjust their own cameras in many different ways, as they are usually not being monitored from a control room or production truck. The single-camera operator has more individual control over the image, making shot decisions on a continual basis.

The Single-Camera Shoot

If you are on a shoot for a documentary or a news story, there will always be quite a bit of improvisation (Figure 8.7). You need to make the most of any opportunity that presents itself. Clearly, a lot depends on whether you are working indoors or in the open, and whether you are on your own or backed by a team. The weather, audio, and light conditions will affect the shoot. It is very important to ensure that your camera is fault-free in any situation. Single-camera productions usually use ENG or EFP equipment. See Table 8.1 for suggestions of things to look at when checking out ENG/EFP equipment.

FIGURE 8.7
ENG/EFP productions require the camera operator improvise in many situations. (Photo courtesy of Sony)

Table 8.1 Checklist for Taking Out the Camera	
Although the exact procedures will depend on the design of your specific camera, here is the most common areas to review before taking a camera into the field.	
Camera support	If using a quick-release plate, make sure that it is present. Otherwise, make sure that all other supports are operational.
Lens	Examine the lens surface for dust, dirt, and fingerprints. Clean dust off surfaces with a lens brush or an air can. Then breathe gently on surfaces and clean them with clean lens tissue. If the lens is regularly removed from the camera, the rear element of the lens will need to be inspected as well.
Power	Batteries and AC power adapters are the most common power supplies. Check to ensure that they are fully charged and operational.
Viewfinder	Most viewfinders that come with an ENG/EFP camera are called ENG viewfinders, although studio viewfinders are also occasionally used. Adjust the viewfinder position to your comfort level. The eyepiece on the ENG viewfinder may need to be adjusted to suite your eyesight. Check the viewfinder's performance to make sure that the image is good (sharp detail, brightness, and contrast). (See Figure 8.8.)
Preset Controls	■ Check the macro position to make sure it is operational. ■ If the lens is equipped with a 2x extender, make sure that it is working properly. ■ Check aperture settings in manual and automatic settings. Manually underexpose the picture, and check if auto-iris mode compensates. ■ Watch the exposure indicator (zebra) for over-exposure or under-exposure. ■ Check the gain (leave at 0 or OFF). When shooting in low-light areas, increase the gain, and check changes in iris settings. ■ Check shutter speeds to make sure they are operational. Generally the shutter is set at 1/60. ■ Test the white balance setting to make sure it responds to the lighting situation. A white card or surface is used for this test. ■ Do a test video recording, making sure that an image and audio are recorded.

FIGURE 8.8
The ENG viewfinder is specifically designed for handheld cameras. (Photo courtesy of Panasonic)

Some people on a single-camera shoot prefer to travel light, setting off with just a camcorder, a spare battery, and recording media. However, for peace of mind, there's a lot to be said for using a systematic checklist routine. This list can be as brief or comprehensive as you like, including whatever gear you personally find invaluable on that kind of project. (The item that you'll need in an emergency is sure to be the one you've left behind!) Lists also help to avoid losses when hurriedly repacking equipment after a shoot (Table 8.2).

The Multicamera Shoot

Whether you are working out on a remote location or in a television studio, you will find that all multicamera setups have a common theme. Unlike a single-camera unit,

Table 8.2 Have You Forgotten Anything?
Camcorder
Standard zoom lens
Supplementary lens
Filters (UV, sky, ND, fluorescent, and any others)
Matte/filter box
Lens cleaning kit
Viewfinder (ENG or studio)
White card (used for white balance)
Camera protection
Carrying case
Weather and/or water protection (from rain, sand, dust, etc.)
Underwater camera housing
Batteries (fully charged)
Camera battery (on-board)
Battery charger
AC power (mains) adapter
Recording media (ready to use)
Camera mount equipment
Tripod
Pan and tilt head, and quick release
Panning handle(s)
Remote zoom/focus controls
Shoulder support
Body brace

Table 8.2	Have You Forgotten Anything? (*Continued*)
Monopod
Audio equipment
Camera microphone
Handheld (interview) mic
Shotgun mic
Wireless microphone and receiver
Headphone
Portable audio mixer
Audio cables
Lighting equipment
Camera light
Lamp power supply (batteries or AC power supply)
Portable light kit
Additional lights
Reflectors (white, silver, gold)
Sandbags
Lighting cables with extensions
Spare lamps
Diffusers (spun glass, scrim)
Color filters (daylight, tungsten)
ND filters
Supplementary
Portable video monitor with light hood
Teleprompter
Gaffer tape
Small tool kit

which often relies on a spontaneous and improvised approach, a multicamera team is essentially a closely coordinated group, working to a planned pattern. We will look at the ways in which these teams are organized and managed (Figure 8.9).

THE CAMERA OPERATOR IN A MULTICAMERA PRODUCTION

Productions vary considerably in their complexity. Some follow a familiar routine, with cameras taking standard shots from limited angles. In other shows, cameras are mobile and follow very complicated action, such as sports productions (Figure 8.10). These action productions can require the skilled, highly controlled camera work that comes only with experience.

FIGURE 8.9
Multicamera productions may utilize a camera operator for each camera or, as shown in this image, they may be robotically controlled by one remote operator. (Photo by Jon Greenhoe)

FIGURE 8.10
Remote multicamera productions include their own set of problems once they move out of the controlled studio.

138

FIGURE 8.11
Shot sheets help the camera operators know how the director needs them to compose specific shots. Some sheets, like the photo sheet shown here, help the camera operator identify specific people.

Each camera operator is on his or her own, required to get the best shots possible, despite having to find ways around specific problems. At the same time, the operator is part of a crew, working together to achieve a coordinated, excellent program for the viewing audience. In some productions, the camera operator can help the director by offering potential shots; in others, this would be a distraction from a planned treatment, as you don't really know what shots other cameras have.

If the production has been planned in meticulous detail, the camera operator's role may be to reproduce exactly what the director drew in storyboard sketches weeks before. On the other hand, the entire show may be "off-the-cuff," with the director relying on the camera crew to find the best shots of the action.

Usually directors will have a camera meeting before the production to explain the types of shows that they want from each camera person. During the breaks, the director may discuss specific shot problems or new shots. Many times directors will use a shot sheet that lists the shots that will be needed throughout the production (Figure 8.11). From then on, the camera crew relies on intercom instructions to guide their camera work.

PREPARING FOR REHEARSALS

It is possible to simply move your camera into the opening position, focus, and wait for the director's instructions. However, if you did that, you would probably get burned. The camera must be checked before the production, or even the rehearsal, begins. Table 8.3 lists the majority of the issues that need to be considered in advance and tested. Once this checkout becomes routine, it can be quickly accomplished.

Table 8.3	Multicamera Prerehearsal Checklist
Camera	___ Is the camera switched on? ___ Are the cables tightly attached on both ends? ___ Is there sufficient cable for the camera moves? ___ Is the lens clean?
Viewfinder	___ Are the viewfinder's focus, brightness, contrast, and picture shape (aspect ratio) correct? ___ Are the tally lights working?
Lens	___ Check the smoothness of focusing action from close-up to infinity. ___ Check focus when fully zoomed in, and when zoomed out. ___ Prefocus on a distant subject and then slowly zoom out, checking that focus does not wander.
Zoom	___ Is the zoom action smooth throughout the range? ___ Is the 2x extender working (if your lens has one)?
Filters	___ Is the correct filter being used in the filter wheel?
Camera Mount	___ Is the camera head firmly attached to the pan and tilt head? ___ Are the pan and tilt head handles firmly attached and at a comfortable angle? ___ Is the pan and tilt head accurately balanced? ___ Is the drag/tilt friction working and adjusted? ___ Are the tripod's legs firmly in place (if you're using one)? ___ If using a pedestal, is it smooth and easy to move when you raise/lower it slowly? Check to make sure that it does not drift up or down. ___ Are the camera support's wheels easily steerable (if there are wheels)?
Intercom	___ Can you hear the director and others over the intercom?
Teleprompter	___ Is the teleprompter (if there is one) secure and working?
Shot Sheets	___ Have you read through the shot sheet and do you understand what the director wants?

THE CAMERA OPERATOR DURING THE PRODUCTION

Although there are no specific rules for being an effective camera operator, there are some basic guidelines that can make life a lot easier, and produce more consistent results.

You can tell an inexperienced camera person at a glance—standing poised, rigid, and tense, eyes glued to the viewfinder, gripping controls tightly. Relax! The best posture is an alert, watchful readiness; you should be very aware of what is going on around you—not so relaxed as to be casual, but continually waiting to react.

In a multicamera show, you need to keep a watchful eye on the tally light on the camera. It shows that your camera has been selected on the production switcher, which means that your camera is on-air. When the light is out, you can move to new positions, adjust zooming or focus, check composition, and so on (Figure 8.13). It is important not to move the camera until the tally light goes off. It is also useful to check other cameras' lights when moving around, to ensure that you are not going to get into their shots.

Make sure that the viewfinder is at a comfortable angle and easy to see. The viewfinder must be adjusted to give optimum detail in both the shadows and the lightest tones.

Always prefocus the lens whenever you move to a new position. Zoom in, focus sharply, and then zoom out to the shot that was requested by the director. You will then be ready to zoom in from a wide shot to closer detail if needed.

For most shots utilizing talent, the lens should be around the talent's eye level—unless the director wants higher or lower angles for some reason (Figure 8.14). If the camera is slightly lower, at chest height, this tends to give the talent a more authoritative look. A higher camera can make the talent look a bit inferior.

If you have received a shot sheet, be ready to move to the next position once each shot is completed.

Listen to all intercom instructions, including those for other cameras.

FIGURE 8.12
It is important that camera operators check out their cameras before the production begins.

Problems generally occur during rehearsals that only the director can solve by making changes or reorganizing the camera shots. These problems may include situations in which one camera blocks another's shot, there is insufficient time for camera moves, compositional problems arise, focusing difficulties crop up, and so on. Let the director know the issues—it may even mean stopping rehearsal to work things out. Don't assume that it will be all right the next time. It may be worse.

Occasionally, an experienced camera operator can help the director by suggesting slight changes in the camera angle that would improve a sequence or simplify a complicated situation. What is obvious on the floor may not be evident on monitors in the control room. However, you must avoid appearing to "subdirect" the show.

Things go wrong during a busy production. When that happens, you have to quickly determine whether someone will handle it quickly or whether you need to inform others (such as about a lamp knocked out of position by moving scenery). In most cases, the floor manager is your on-the-spot contact. Teamwork is the essence of good production.

"Studio" viewfinder tally light

FIGURE 8.13
Viewfinders usually have a tally light on the front and the back. The front one is to let talent know that the camera is on-air. The back tally lets the camera operator know when his or her camera is on-air.

PRODUCTION TECHNIQUES THAT AFFECT THE CAMERA OPERATOR

Directors can tackle productions in a variety of ways. The techniques vary with the personality and experience of the director and with the content and the intended audience. These techniques may include the following:

- An improvised spontaneous approach.
- An outlined shooting plan that cannot be rehearsed before taping or transmission, such as a dance group who are arriving during air-time.
- A rehearsal with stand-ins in place of the actual performers. This allows you to check the shots in advance.

- A closely planned show in which the director explains the action/shots to camera and sound crew before beginning rehearsals.
- A "stop and start" approach in which the action is rehearsed on camera while the director guides shots, stopping and correcting errors/problems as they arise. After a complete run-through rehearsal, the show is usually recorded or transmitted from beginning to end.
- A "rehearse and record" approach, in which each shot, segment, or scene is rehearsed and recorded before going on to the next. Shots will not necessarily be in the final program order, because they will be edited together later.

As you will see, the problems and opportunities for the production crew can be very different with each method, ranging from a "one-chance-only" situation to the "retake-until-we-get-it-right" approach.

FIGURE 8.14
The camera operator shooting this NBC cooking segment has his camera at the talent's eye level.

AFTER THE SHOW

At the end of a production, when any retakes have been completed and checks made, the director and the technical director will announce on intercom that the crew is cleared. The floor manager will repeat this for everyone, including performers.

At the end of a studio production, as the camera operator, you should lock off the camera's pan and tilt head. Make sure that the cable has been arranged in a neat pattern so that it will not tangle the next time and place the lens cap on the camera. Some multicamera-production camera operators, especially on remote productions, may need to tear down and put away their camera. Their job also may include rolling up long cables and then loading all of the gear into a truck. Once you have been released, you are done.

141

REVIEW QUESTIONS

1. How do you select the right shots?
2. Why does the medium (such as an iPod versus an I-mag screen) make a difference in the shots that are used?
3. What significance does the tally light have?
4. Why is it important to look around the scene (away from the viewfinder) before recording?
5. What are some ways of dealing with a limited depth of field?
6. How does a shot sheet help the camera operator?

CHAPTER 9

The Persuasive Camera

"A film is never really good unless the camera is an eye in the head of a poet."

Orson Welles

Terms

Deep focus: A very wide depth of field.

Dutch: Tilting the camera is called a "dutch" or a "canted" shot. This movement increases the dynamics of the shot.

Eye-level shot: Provide an image that is roughly at the eye level of the talent (in a studio show) or the average viewing audience.

High-angle shots: Provide a view from above the subject.

Low-angle shots: Provide a view from below the subject.

Pan shot: The pivoting of a camera to the left or right.

Tilt: Moving the camera up or down.

Presenting a subject effectively can sometimes be a challenge. This chapter will cover some of the most common techniques.

SHOOTING STYLE

The simplest way to shoot a subject is to aim it at your subject and then zoom between long shots showing the general action and close-up shots showing detail. However, this mechanical, less-than-stimulating routine soon becomes very boring to watch. Creative techniques add to the subject's appeal and hold the viewer's interest.

When pointing a camera at a scene, you are doing much more than simply showing your audience what is going on there. You are selecting specific areas of the scene (Figure 9.1). You are drawing their attention to certain aspects of the action. The way you use your camera will influence the impact of the subject on the audience.

In an interview, for example, the guests can be shot from a low angle, which will give them a look of importance or self-confidence. From a high angle, they might look diminished, unimportant. Concentrating on detailed shots of their nervous finger movements helps build a sense of insecurity.

The camera interprets the scene for the audience. How the camera is used affects the audience's responses. If the scene is just shot with no understanding of the impact of techniques, the result will be a haphazard production.

143

FIGURE 9.1
The camera isolates. The camera shows only what is going on in its frame of the scene. The audience does not really know what is outside the field of view. (Photo by Josh Taber)

144

FIGURE 9.2
"Pulling focus" can be used to guide the viewer through a scene. Notice the change of focus in the two photos. The audience can also be directed where to look, because the eye is drawn to what is in focus. (Photos by Josh Taber)

Whenever a camera is pointed at action, you have to make a series of fundamental decisions, such as:

- Which is the best angle? Can the action be seen clearly from there?
- Which features of the scene need to be emphasized at this moment? (See Figure 9.2.)
- Do you want the audience to concentrate on a specific aspect of the action?
- Do you want to convey a certain impression?

SCREEN SIZE

As discussed in previous chapters, the size of the screen on which the audience watches the production can influence how they respond to what they see there. It is more difficult to distinguish detail on a small screen (or a larger screen at a distance). The picture is confined and restricted, and we tend to feel detached as we closely inspect the overall effect. On the other hand, when watching on a large screen, we become more aware of detail. Our eyes have greater freedom to roam around the shot. We feel more closely involved with the action. We are onlookers at the scene.

At typical viewing distances, most television receivers allow us to effectively present a wide range of shot sizes, from vistas to microscopic close-ups. Although wide shots of large-scale events, panoramic views, or spectacular situations are not particularly impressive on television, this limitation is not too restrictive in practice.

SHOOTING FOR THE INTERNET

Compressing video to be used on the Internet deteriorates the overall quality of the video. Anytime footage is compressed, a bit of the quality has to be sacrificed. Here are a few things to keep in mind when shooting something that will be streamed on the Internet:

- Do not use more camera motion than needed. Whenever there is camera motion, the result is more compression.
- Use a tripod to give the most stable shot possible (this usually should be done anyway). Camera pans and tilts should be limited and, when used, slow and smooth.
- Light the subject well.
- Keep the background simple. The more detailed it is, the more compression that needs to happen.

SELECTING THE SHOT

Each type of shot has its specific advantages and disadvantages. Some are best for setting the scene; others allow the audience to see intense details and emotions. For example, long shots can be used to:

- Show where all of the action is taking place
- Allow the audience to follow broad movements
- Show the relative positions of subjects
- Establish mood

However, long shots do not allow your audience to see details, and you can leave them aware of what they are missing. For example, in a wide shot of an art gallery, audience members may feel that they are being prevented from seeing individual paintings clearly (Figure 9.3).

Closer shots are usually used to:

- Show detail
- Emphasize certain areas
- Reveal people's reactions/emotions
- Dramatize the event

If too many close shots are used, the effect can be very restrictive. The audience can be left feeling that they were prevented from looking around the scene, from seeing the responses of other performers, from looking at other aspects of the subject, and from following the general action.

Occasionally, it is important to shoot both a wide-angle shot as well as the close-up. This technique enables the director to show both shots at the same time. The benefit to the viewer is that they can see the whole situation as well as the close-up detail. This method is sometimes called a *combination shot* (Figure 9.4).

FIGURE 9.3
Although long shots are beautiful, viewers want to see the close-up details.

145

FIGURE 9.4
Combined shots can show detail and the bigger picture simultaneously. This can be achieved by inserting a detail, or clarifying, shot. (Photos courtesy of Panasonic and Canon)

FIGURE 9.5
Although the extreme long shot (ELS) does not provide detail, it definitely establishes the scene for the viewer. Most of the time, the ELS shows the viewer the entire field of play, plus the audience.

If the action in the scene is incidental to the purpose of a sequence, such as someone speaking about their forthcoming vacation while they happen to be making an omelette, then shots should concentrate on the people involved, watching their interactions. However, if the purpose of the sequence is to show us how to cook, then we need detail shots of the action, with little or no interruption from reaction shots. Although this seems obvious, directors do make the wrong choice at times and may confuse or annoy the audience.

A shot that is appropriate at one moment could be very unsuitable the next. In fact, there are times when an inappropriate or a badly timed shot can totally destroy an entire sequence.

The Extreme Long Shot

The extreme long shot (ELS or XLS) enables you to establish the location and to create an overall atmospheric impression. It can be used to cover very widespread action, or to show various activities going on at the same time. It is usually a high shot from a hilltop or an aerial view, such as from a blimp at a sports venue (Figure 9.5). With extreme long shots, the audience takes a rather detached, impersonal attitude, surveying the scene without any sense of involvement. The extreme long shot is generally wider than the long shot. It usually shows much more than just the "field of play."

The Long Shot

Often used at the start of a production, the long shot (LS) immediately shows where the action is happening. This establishing shot sets the location and broad atmospheric effect. It allows the audience to follow the purpose or pattern of action (Figure 9.6).

As the shot is tightened, and shows less of the scene, the audience is influenced less by the setting and the lighting. The people within the scene have a greater audience impact; their gestures and facial expressions become stronger and more important.

Medium Shots

Medium shots (MSs) are generally mid-shots, although they may be framed a little larger or smaller. Their value lies in the idea that you are close enough to see expressions and emotions but far enough away to understand the context that the subject is in. Gestures can usually be captured in this type of shot. The medium shot is thought to be the one shot that "tells the story" (Figure 9.7).

FIGURE 9.6
Both of these shots are long shots. They set the scene. (Left) A long shot of the venue and (right) a long shot of a person. In contrast, an extreme long shot of the first photo would have probably included the entire venue. (Derby photo by Josh Taber)

147

FIGURE 9.7
These medium shots, one from a sitcom and the other from a concert, demonstrate that the shot roughly cuts the subject in half. Generally, it is framed above or below the waistline of a person. (Concert photo by Paul Dupree)

The Close-Up

An extremely powerful shot, the close-up (CU) concentrates interest. With people, it draws attention to their reactions, responses, and emotions. Close-ups can reveal or point out information that might otherwise be overlooked, or only discerned with difficulty. They focus attention or provide emphasis (Figures 9.8 and 9.9).

The Extreme Close-Up

The extreme close-up (XCU or ECU) adds drama to the situation or clarifies a situation. By filling the screen with the face, it easily communicates the emotion of the situation. A close-up of an object allows the viewer to understand the detail a bit more (Figure 9.10).

When using a close-up, you have to ensure that the audience wants to look that close, and do not feel that:

- They have been cheated of the wider view, where something more interesting may be happening.

148

FIGURE 9.8

Close-ups of people are generally framed from mid-chest up. Note that you can see the framing of the interview on the stage's I-mag screen to the far right. It is a close-up.

FIGURE 9.9

Close-up shots of a scene allow the viewer to see more detail as compared to the long shot of this same scene in Figure 9.5. (Photo by Josh Taber)

FIGURE 9.10

The extreme close-up generally cuts into the face and is a great tool for adding drama by communicating the emotion of the moment. (Photo by Paul Dupree)

- They have been thrust disconcertingly close to the subject—the audience may become overly aware of facial blemishes in enlarged faces.
- Detail that is already familiar is being over-emphasized.
- Through continually watching close-up fragments, they have forgotten how these relate to the main subject, or have become disorientated.

Where shots do not contain enough detail to maintain the audience's continued interest, do not hold them long enough that their attention begins to wander.

Instead of beginning a sequence with a long establishing shot, anticipation can be built gradually, shot by shot, satisfying curiosity a little at a time. This encourages a sense of expectation and speculation.

However, you have to be cautious that piecemeal introductions do not confuse the audience, especially when they are unfamiliar with the subject. There must be sufficient material for the audience to be able to interpret the time, place, and action correctly. When action has been seen from close-up viewpoints for a period of time, longer shots may be required to re-establish the scene in the viewer's mind.

Deep-Focus Techniques

As you saw earlier, the depth of field in a scene varies with the lens *f*-stop, type of lens (wide-angle/telephoto), and focused distance. You can change it by altering any of these parameters.

Stopping down the lens (such as *f*/11 or *f*/16), everything from foreground to far distance appears sharply focused. The camera has no problems in following focus and there is little danger of subjects becoming soft-focused. There is an illusion of spaciousness and depth, enabling shots to be composed with subjects at various distances from the camera. However, higher light levels are necessary (Figure 9.11).

One weakness of this technique is that when there is little camera movement or few progressively distant planes in the picture, it can appear unattractively flat. Surfaces or subjects at very different distances can merge or become confusing to the audience.

Shallow-Focus Techniques

Using a wider lens aperture (e.g., *f*/2) restricts focused depth. It enables you to isolate a subject spatially, keeping it sharp within blurred surroundings, and avoids the distraction of irrelevant subjects. You can display a single sharply focused flower against a detail-free background, concentrating attention on the bloom and suppressing the confusion of foliage. Sharply defined detail attracts the eye more readily than defocused areas.

By deliberately restricting depth of field, you can soften obtrusive backgrounds, even if these are strongly patterned, so that people or other subjects stand out from their surroundings. On the other hand, restricted depth can prove embarrassing when essential details of a close object are out of focus. The camera must continually refocus in order to keep a close-up of a moving subject sharp. For instance, close-up shots along a piano keyboard can demand considerable dexterity when trying to follow and focus on quickly moving fingers.

Occasionally, by changing focus between subjects at different distances (pulling focus, throwing focus) you can move the viewer's attention from one to another; however, this trick easily becomes disturbing unless coordinated with action. Blurred color pictures can be frustrating. Whereas in monochrome, defocused planes merge; in color, the viewer may be unable to decipher unsharp detail and the effect can be less acceptable. (See Figure 9.12.)

MOVING THE CAMERA HEAD

In everyday life, we respond to situations by making specific gestures or movements. These reactions and actions often become very closely associated. We look around with curiosity; move in to inspect an object; withdraw or avert our eyes from a situation that we find embarrassing, distasteful, or boring.

149

FIGURE 9.11
A deep depth of field is possible by using an aperture of *f*/11 or greater.

FIGURE 9.12
When a wider lens aperture is used, such as *f*/2, a very shallow depth of field occurs.

Table 9.1	Why Change Between Telephoto and Wide-Angle Lenses?
Why use lenses other than a normal lens?	■ When you want to exclude (or include) certain foreground objects, and repositioning the camera or subject would spoil the proportions. ■ Where a normal lens would not provide the required size or framing without repositioning the camera or subject.
A telephoto lens can be used	■ When shooting subjects that are a long distance away. ■ When the camera is isolated—on a camera platform (tower) or shooting through some foreground subject. ■ When the camera cannot be moved—stationary camera—or the camera cannot be moved closer.
A wide-angle lens can be used	■ When the normal lens does not provide a wide enough shot of a scene. ■ To maintain a reasonably close camera position (so talent can read the prompter) yet still provide wider shots.
The perspective of an image can be adjusted as follows:	■ By changing the lens from telephoto to wide angle, and changing the camera distance to maintain the same subject size, which alters relative subject/background proportions and effective distances (Figure 9.14). ■ Wide-angle lenses increase the depth of field and enhance the spatial impression. ■ The telephoto lens reduces the spatial impression, compressing the depth in the image. ■ To increase production flexibility. ■ When dollying the camera would distract the talent or obscure the action from the audience. ■ When using only one camera.

150

FIGURE 9.13
Different lens angles create a variety of views of the same subject. (Photo courtesy of Canon)

It is not surprising to find that certain camera movements can evoke associated responses in the audience, causing them to have specific feelings toward what they see on the screen. These effects underlie the impact of persuasive camera techniques.

Panning the Camera

The pan shot is the smooth pivoting of the camera from left to right on the camera support, which might be a tripod or even a person (Figures 9.15 and 9.16). Panning shows the audience the spatial relationship between two subjects or areas. Cutting between two shots does not provide the same sense of continuity. When panning over a wide area, the intermediate parts of the scene help us to orient ourselves. We develop an impression of space. However, it is important to avoid panning across irrelevant areas, such as the "dead" space between two widely separated people.

Unless you are creating a special effect, panning should be smooth—neither jerking into action nor abruptly halting. Erratic or hesitant panning irritates the audience. If the pan and tilt head is correctly adjusted, problematic pan shots usually only occur when using long telephoto lenses or when the subject makes an unpredicted move.

FIGURE 9.14
The background changes in size are due to the lens used. Note that the first photo was shot with a telephoto lens and the final shot was taken with a wide-angle lens. The camera had to be moved closer to the subject for each shot, as a wider lens was attached so that the subject would stay the same approximate size. (Photos by K. Brown)

FIGURE 9.15
The pan shot is the pivoting of a camera to the left or right. (Photo courtesy of Vortex)

FIGURE 9.16
The pan shot, as shown, smoothly moves from the red frame to the black frame, providing one continual shot when the action moves beyond the original red frame. (Photo courtesy of Dartfish)

FOLLOW PAN

The *follow pan* is the most common type of camera move. The camera pans as it follows a moving subject. In longer shots, the viewer becomes aware of the interrelationship between the subject and its surroundings. Visual interaction can develop between the subject and its apparently moving background pattern, creating a dynamic composition. In closer shots, the background becomes incidental, or even often indecipherably blurred (Figure 9.17).

SURVEY PAN

In the *survey pan*, the camera slowly searches the scene (a crowd, a landscape), allowing the audience to look around at choice. It can be a restful anticipatory action—providing that there is something worth seeing. It is not enough to pan hopefully.

The move can also be dramatic, building anticipation: The shipwrecked survivor scans the horizon, sees a ship . . . but will it notice him? But the surveying pan can build to an anticlimax, too; the fugitive searches to see whether she is being followed.

FIGURE 9.17
When following the subject in a wide arc with a handheld camera, the feet should face the mid-point of the arc. This will allow the camera operator to smoothly pan with the action.

152

INTERRUPTED PAN

The *interrupted pan* is a long, smooth movement that is suddenly stopped (sometimes reversed) to provide visual contrast. It is normally used to link a series of isolated subjects. In a dance performance, the camera might follow a solo dancer from one group to the next, pausing for a short while as each becomes the new center of interest.

In a dramatic application, you might see escaping prisoners slowly trek through treacherous marshland. One man falls exhausted, but the camera stays with the rest. A moment later it stops and pans back to see what occurred to the person.

WHIP PAN

The *whip pan* (also known as the *swish*, *zip*, or *blur pan*) moves so rapidly from one subject to the next that the intermediate scene becomes a brief, streaking blur. Whether the effect generates excitement or annoyance is largely determined by how the preceding and following shots are developed. As our attention is dragged rapidly to the next shot, this pan gives each subject transitory importance. The whip pan usually produces a dynamic change that continues the pace between two rapidly moving scenes. A whip pan has to be accurate as well as appropriate to be successful: no fumbling, reframing, or refocusing at the end of the pan.

Tilting the Camera Head

Tilting refers to moving the camera up or down (Figure 9.18). Tilting, like panning, allows you to visually connect subjects or areas that are spaced apart. Otherwise, you would need to intercut different shots, or use a longer shot to include both subjects.

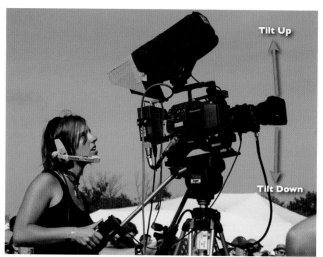

FIGURE 9.18
A camera tilt is when the camera is pointed up or down.

Tilting can be used:

- To emphasize height or depth—tilting up from a climber to show the steep cliff face to be climbed.
- To show relationships—as the camera tilts from the rooftop spy down to the person in the street below; or from the person in the street up to the rooftop, revealing that he is not alone.

Camera Height

Camera height can have a significant influence on how the audience perceives your subject. How you get the angle is immaterial. You can use a jib, suspend a camera on wires, or use any other mechanism. The key is whether the image does what you want it to do. There are three general categories that deal with camera height:

Eye-level shots provide an image that is roughly at the eye level of the talent (in a studio show) or of the average viewing audience. This is the most common shot used in television and provides a sense of normalcy (Figure 9.19).

High-angle shots provide a view from above the subject. This high vantage point can provide the viewer with additional information, such as showing the actions and

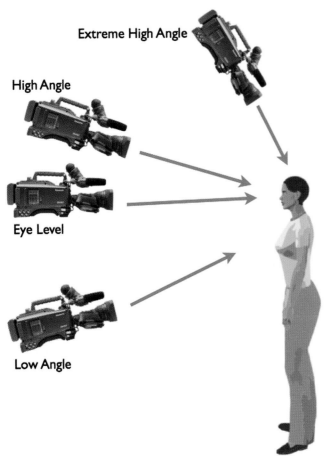

FIGURE 9.19
The eye-level angle is used more than any other angle. The other angles are used when appropriate.

FIGURE 9.20
Although high-angle shots can help the audience see what is on the desk in this shot from NBC's *The Office*, they can also make the subject look inferior or unimportant. (Photo courtesy of Kobal)

context of the subject. However, these shots can also give the viewer an impression that the subject is not important or even inferior (Figures 9.20, 9.21, and 9.23).
Low-angle shots make the subject appear more important and very strong. These shots make the viewer feel inferior (Figures 9.22 and 9.24).

Extreme Camera Angles

Extreme angles can be creative and attention-grabbing. If appropriate, they can add a lot to the production. However, they sometimes draw attention to the abnormality or ingenuity of the camera's position. If the audience is wondering how we got that shot, techniques have obscured artistic purpose (Figure 9.25).

Where extreme angles appear naturally, viewers accept them readily: looking down from an upper-story window; looking up from a seated position; even an eavesdropper peering through plank flooring to the room below. But an unexplained extreme shot usually becomes a visual stunt.

MOVING THE CAMERA

How freely the camera can be moved around is determined by the type of camera mount used. Although a jib offers incredible flexibility, it may not be able to relocate as rapidly as a handheld camera. Well-chosen camera moves add visual interest, plus influence certain

FIGURE 9.21
All high-angle shots do not make the subject look inferior. This shot allows the audience to see the drummer's movements. (Photo courtesy of Sennheiser)

FIGURE 9.22
Low-angle shots generally make the subject look important, strong, or powerful. (Photo by Josh Taber)

FIGURE 9.23
High-angle shots can be obtained in a number of ways, such as holding the camera high, using a jib, climbing onto a higher area, or shooting from a helicopter. (Photos courtesy of Sony and Jeff Hutchens)

FIGURE 9.24
Low-angle shots are obtained by placing the camera lower than the subject. Even jibs, primarily used for high-angle shots, can be used to obtain low-angle shots. (Photo by Paul Dupree)

FIGURE 9.25
Extreme angles, like this photo of a cameraman, sometimes draw attention to the novelty of the shot, distracting the audience from the main subject. (Photo by Bill Miller)

audience reactions. However, camera movement needs to be motivated, appropriate, smoothly controlled, and done at a suitable speed, or it can become distracting and/or disturbing (Figures 9.26 and 9.27).

155

The Moving Close-Up

Close-ups of people allow the subject to dominate the image; its strength is determined by the position of the camera. Although the influence of the environment can be limited with the close-up, the pace varies with dynamic composition. When the subject is slightly off-center in the direction of movement, a sense of anticipation and expectancy is created. The following are some thoughts about close-ups of people:

a. Profiles of people are weak against a plain background. However, there is an impression of speed and urgency if shot against a detailed background.
b. A three-quarter frontal shot can be dramatically strong. By preventing the viewer from seeing the subject's route or destination, a sense of anticipation can be built.
c. A high-angle elevated frontal shot weakens the subject but still allows him or her to dominate the environment.
d. A low-angle shot makes the subject look powerful and dominating.
e. A three-quarter shot from behind the subject can be subjective, because the viewer moves with the subject, expectancy developing during the movement.
f. A high-angle shot from behind is not only highly subjective but also produces an increased anticipation—almost a searching impression.
g. and h. In level and low shots, there is a striking sense of depth. The subject is strongly linked to the setting and other people, yet remains separate from them.

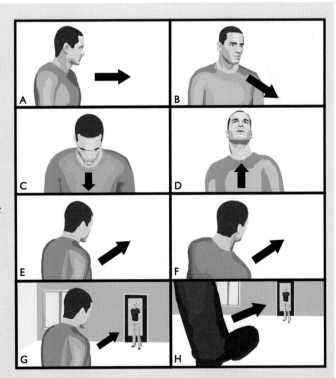

FIGURE 9.26
The moving close-up shot.

Subjective Camera Treatment

When you use the camera subjectively, you are portraying an individual's perception of the event. The subjective camera makes it look as if the viewer is actually walking around the scene, following the action. The camera can walk through a crowd, move up to inspect something, and then glance up at nearby details. We encounter this approach regularly when shoulder-mounted or Steadicam-type cameras are used instead of shooting from a stationary position on a tripod.

Subjective camera movement creates a participatory effect for the audience. But if the director moves the camera when the audience is not ready, or fails to show them something they wish to see, the audience will probably feel resentful. The skilled director persuades the audience to want a change of view or a move. The unskilled director thrusts it upon the audience.

Imitative Camera Movement

Cameras can be moved to suggest jogging or the rolling movement of a ship. The camera can significantly affect the dynamics of the subject. If used effectively, camera movements can even provide subjective influence on the action itself (Figure 9.28).

Using the Zoom Lens

As discussed earlier, the zoom lens brings both advantages and pitfalls for the unwary. It is too easy to change the lens angle just to change subject image size. There is always the temptation to stand and zoom, rather than move around with a normal lens. Zooming demands little of the camera operator or director. There is just the need for a prezoom focus check before zooming in for the shot.

Zooming is extremely convenient. However, the zoom only simulates camera movement. The zoom optically isolates a section of the scene. There are no natural parallactic changes as you zoom in; scale, distance, and shape become distorted through zooming. A slow zoom

FIGURE 9.27
Dollying in causes increased interest and a buildup of tension. However, the close-up may result in diminished interest. Dollying back usually results in lowered interest or relaxed tension—unless unseen subjects are revealed, or when curiosity, expectation, or hope have been aroused. Attention tends to be directed toward the edges of the picture. Dollying appears faster than it really is on a wide-angle lens, and slower on a narrower lens angle.

FIGURE 9.28
In order to increase the dynamics of this shot, the camera was tilted, which is usually called a "dutch" or "canted" shot, for ABC's broadcast of *Alias*. (Photo courtesy of Touchstone TV/The Kobal Collection)

FIGURE 9.29
Zooming can provide a bridge between close-ups and long shots. In these shots, zooming out from the CU to an LS provides the context for the subjects.

made during panning, tilting, or subject movement may disguise these discrepancies. A rapid zoom during an exciting fast-moving ball game can make the image more dynamic. Much depends on the occasion.

Zooming can provide a visual bridge from the wide view to the close-up, without the time and effort involved in dollying or the interruption (and possible disorientation) of cutting (Figure 9.29). A rapid zoom-in produces a highly dramatic swoop onto the subject. An instant (snap) zoom-in flings subject detail at the audience (Figure 9.30). Such effects can be incredibly dynamic, or just plain annoying—it has to be done right.

Zoom should be smooth and decisive. Use zoom shots to direct attention, to increase tension, to give powerful emphasis, or to restrict the coverage. But the zooming action itself should be used discriminately for specific occasions.

Directors use different terms when calling for a zoom in or out. Some of the most commons terms for zooming out are "zoom-out," "pull-out," or "widen." When needing a zoom-in, the director may ask for a "zoom-in," "push-in," or "tighten."

FIGURE 9.30
A snap zoom quickly moves the audience from an CU to an LS or vice versa. (Photo by Will Adams)

157

REVIEW QUESTIONS

1. Each type of shot (CU, MS, and LS) conveys different information. Explain those differences.
2. How does the camera interpret the scene for the audience?
3. What are some of the challenges of shooting for the Internet?
4. How is deep focus obtained in an image?
5. How do you change the perspective of an image without moving the camera?
6. What are some of the issues to consider when taking close-up shots of people?
7. What are two of the types of pan shots and how can they be used?

CHAPTER 10

Creating an Effective Image

"There are three main responsibilities for the camera operator: First is the ability to work well with others. Secondly, you must know your equipment well. Thirdly, the application of the operator's own talents, physical ability, intuition and patience."

Martin Goldstein, Camera Operator

Terms

Animation (image composition): The video images should give the audience the same emotional response that you had while shooting.

Axis of action line: Often called the "action line" or "eye line," this is an imaginary line along the direction of the action in the scene. Cameras should shoot from only one side of this line.

Composition: Creating an image that is attractive or that captures and keeps the audience's attention and effectively communicates the production's message.

Context: Making sure that the content of the image allows the viewer to understand the subject better; composing the shot in such a way that it includes a background or foreground that adds additional information or context to the image.

Continuity: Making sure that the shots will edit together in the final production to avoid ending up with a series of shots that do not fit together smoothly. This happens especially often when repositioning the camera to shoot a repeated scene from a different location.

Cutaway shot: Used to cover edits when any video sequence is shortened or lengthened. Generally it is a shot of something outside of the current frame.

Headroom: The amount of space above the head. This changes proportionally with the length of the shot, lessening as the shot tightens.

Symbolism (image): Creating an image that is meaningful to the viewer.

159

At the end of the day, it's how you see the world—the camera, no matter how simple or complex, is just the means to record your vision, not the producer of it.

Why do some pictures look very attractive, while the eye passes over others disinterestedly? Why do some draw the eye to a specific subject, while in others we look around? Effective images are much more than just a pretty picture: They are images that effectively communicate the mood, emotion, meaning, symbolism, and/or context needed to communicate the intended message. This chapter will explore what makes an effective image.

BEHIND THE PICTURE

Most people think that the process of creating an image is the responsibility of the camera operator. For the single camera operator, that is largely true. But in the studio, where the entire environment is contrived, the final image is usually the outcome of a combination of different people's talents. The design of the setting, the way it has been lit, and the angle selected by the director can all be controlled to provide the appropriate conditions for maximum impact on the audience.

The camera operator's opportunities to create a meaningful composition depends directly on the way the scene has been developed and how action has been arranged. Stand someone in front of a flatly lit plain background, and the prospects for interesting shots are very limited. However, sit the same person in a well-designed, attractively lit setting, and the camera can explore the situation, producing effective shots.

Persuasive images are the result of successful planning. If the lighting is inappropriate, or the director selects an ineffective camera position, the result will be inferior images—and lost opportunities.

COMPOSING THE PICTURE

The goal of composition is to create an image that is attractive or that captures and keeps the audience's attention and effectively communicates the production's message. It is a way of arranging pictures so that the viewer is directly attracted to certain features (Figure 10.1). You can influence how viewers respond to what they are seeing. The image can be composed to create anticipation, unease, apprehension, excitement, restful calm. The mood can be anywhere from depressing to exciting—and anywhere in between.

It is always tempting to devise shots that are *different*—shots that make the eye stop and wonder. Wildly distorted perspectives from a close wide-angle lens, very-low-angle shots, or

160

FIGURE 10.1
Why be concerned with composing the image? The unguided eye will wander around the scene, finding its own areas of interest.

pictures using weird reflections are fine when you need them for a dramatic or comic effect. But extremely unusual viewpoints don't just make a picture look different; they also draw attention to themselves. They may distract the audience from the real subject.

Composition principles or "rules" are really guides. Composition is up to the person creating the image. It is his or her responsibility to create an image that meets the needs of the intended audience. That means that effective composition can be translated different ways based on the interests, styles, and age of the viewers.

Practical Composition

Camera operators or directors can adjust an image's composition in a number of ways:

Adjust framing: Positioning the shot to deliberately include/exclude parts of the scene, or to alter the subjects' position in the frame.

Increase or decrease the lens angle of view: The lens angle of view (wide angle or telephoto) will determine how much of the scene appears in the picture from that viewpoint.

Adjust the camera position: As the camera moves up/down or sideways, foreground objects change position in the frame more noticeably than distant ones. So even slight readjustments can considerably alter the compositional relationships.

Change the shot proportions: By altering the lens angle, and changing the camera distance to compensate, you can keep the same size shot but adjusting proportions within it. (See Figure 9.14.)

COMPOSING THE SHOT

Good composition does not have to be difficult. However, it does take careful planning to get the best image. Here are some key factors used to shoot images that effectively communicate the message of the production:

Symbolism: Does the image have meaning to the viewer? When the viewer sees the image, what does he or she immediately think of? Is that what you are trying to communicate?

Context: The content of the image should allow the viewer to understand the subject better. Compose the shot in such a way that it includes a background or foreground that adds additional information or context to the image (Figure 10.2).

Animation: The video images should give the audience the same emotional response that you had while shooting. Does the image portray emotion or motion in some way?

FIGURE 10.2
Since this image was shot within a meaningful context, the viewer knows that it was shot in Italy. (Photo by Sarah Owens)

The Director and Composition

Directors vary on how they deal with composition. For many productions, the director is so preoccupied with what is being said and with performance, continuity, and techniques, that he or she does not arrange the specific composition of shots. Instead, the director indicates the shot size required (CU, two-shot, group shot) and leaves the details of lens, exact framing, and so on to the camera operator.

In other types of production, the director deliberately groups actors to provide specific compositional arrangements for the camera—for dramatic effect, or to direct the audience's attention. In some cases, the director may have prepared a storyboard sketch (see Chapter 6) showing the detailed composition of certain key shots.

Composition Principles

Composition principles are not laws. They are indications of how people respond to a specific design of the image. These are important, in that if you do not organize images appropriately, your audience may react by looking at the wrong things, interpreting the picture inappropriately, or becoming bored by unattractive shots. Composing shots is not just a matter of stunning images but a method of controlling the continuity of thought.

THE EFFECT OF THE PICTURE FRAME

The camera does much more than just "put a frame" around a segment of the scene. It inherently modifies whatever it shows. Because the screen totally isolates its subjects so that the viewer cannot see whatever else is happening (Figure 10.3), and because the resulting image is flat, unique relationships develop within it that are not present in the actual scene.

Few shots directly portray reality. Former U.S. President Richard Nixon once said that "while a picture does not lie, it does not necessarily tell the truth." In many cases, our own experience enables us to rationalize and interpret, so that we make a pretty accurate assessment of what we are seeing.

Unfortunately, there is no formula for the perfect image. However, there are some basic composition guidelines, described in the following sections.

Framing

You choose exactly what the viewer is going to see: what is to be included within the picture, and what is to be excluded from it. You may be selecting to concentrate attention, to avoid distractions, or to show more subject detail. You might even omit information deliberately—and then reveal it in a later shot.

As all parts of the frame do not have equal pictorial value, the effect of the image changes depending on where you place the main subject. How the shot is framed will not only alter compositional

FIGURE 10.3
Because you can isolate the viewer from the rest of the scene, the first photo looks like a normal house. However, the audience has no idea that the scene is actually part of a back lot of a film studio and is part of a soundstage, as shown in the second photo.

FIGURE 10.4

The first image has too little headroom, the second image has too much headroom, and the third one is correct. (Photo by Josh Taber)

balance but can also influence the audience's interpretation of events. Framed in a certain way, a two-shot might lead the viewer to expect that someone is about to enter the room, or that an eavesdropper is right outside the door.

Headroom (the amount of space above the head) changes proportionally with the length of the shot, lessening as the shot tightens. In a multicamera production, the headroom can vary considerably between different cameras. So it is important for the director to check that comparable shots match (Figure 10.4).

One of the problems with monitors across the world is that they are not all the same size. Different manufacturer's technologies differ and the images on the monitors sometimes drift with age. With that in mind, it is important that the audience does not miss any important details, such as titles. Always compose the shot so that everything essential fits into the "safe area" shown in Figure 10.5. The safe area should include all graphics and video images that are essential for the viewers.

Framing the image within the video screen is a framing guideline. Framing occurs when the camera operator selects something that will appear in the foreground, creating a frame made of a fence, a building, a window or doorway, a tree, and so on. The frame object must not distract the viewing audience from the primary subject on the screen (Figures 10.6 and 10.7).

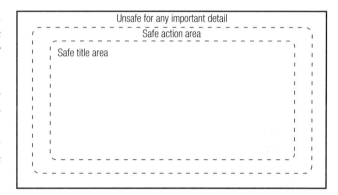

Unsafe for any important detail
Safe action area
Safe title area

FIGURE 10.5

The picture edges are sometimes lost on the screen due to different sizes of monitors and the aging of monitors. To ensure that no important action, or titling is lost, keep it within the borders shown.

163

FIGURE 10.6

Framing the image can take place many different ways: windows, trees, foreground objects, and so on. (Lamb photo by Sarah Owens)

FRAMING PEOPLE

Don't let the frame cut people at natural joints; intermediate points are much more attractive (Figure 10.7).

- Avoid having people seem to lean or sit on the edge of the picture.
- If the shot is framed too close to contain the subject's motion, the subject will keep moving in and out of the picture. The result is very disconcerting and distracting (Figure 10.8).

FIGURE 10.7
Avoid framing people at natural joints. It looks more natural to go above or below bends of the body.

FIGURE 10.8
If shooting too close, the camera operator may not be able to keep up with the movement of the subject. (Photo by Josh Taber)

Pictorial Balance

Good camera operators and directors strive for balanced composition: not the equal balance of formal symmetry, as that can be boring, but an image with equilibrium.

Balance in an image is affected by:

- The size of a subject within the frame
- Its tone
- Its position within the frame
- The relationships of the subjects in the shot

A balanced picture unifies the subjects within a shot. Although images can be deliberately arranged so that they are unbalanced to create a dynamic tension, make sure this is done sparingly. Balanced arrangements do not have to be static. Shots can be continually readjusted to balance the image by moving a person, altering the framing, and so on. This readjustment allows you to redirect attention to a different subject, or to alter the picture's impact. Balance is a very subjective effect. You cannot measure it. But there are a number of useful guiding principles:

- While centering the object in the center of the frame is okay and safe, it can be very dull to watch (Figure 10.9).
- A subject or object on one side of the frame usually requires some type of counter-balancing in the remainder of the shot. This can be an equal opposite mass, giving symmetrical balance, or a series of smaller areas that together counterbalance the area (Figure 10.10).
- Tone significantly influences visual weight.
  - ❏ The darker-toned subjects look heavier and smaller than light-toned subjects.
  - ❏ A small darker area, slightly offset, can balance a larger light-toned one further from the picture's center.

FIGURE 10.9
(Left) The subject is centered, causing the subject to be unbalanced and thus a bit boring for the viewer. (Right) By moving the subject slightly to the left, or panning the camera to the right, the subject has more room to talk and the image has more scene depth and image balance.

A

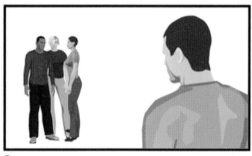

B

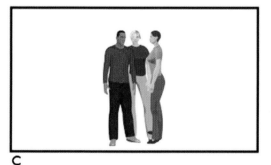

C

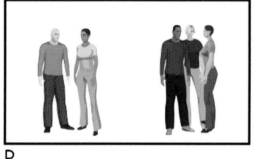

D

FIGURE 10.10
A group that would look lop-sided and unbalance the picture (A) can be counterbalanced by another mass in another part of the screen (B). If centered (C), the picture is balanced, even without other subjects, but continual centering gets monotonous. Different-sized masses can balance each other, but take care not to split the audience's attention (D).

FIGURE 10.11
Darker areas at the bottom of a picture project stability and solidity.

- ❑ Darker tones toward the top of the frame produce a strong downward thrust—top-heaviness, or a depressed closed-in effect. At the bottom of the frame, they introduce stability and solidity (Figure 10.11).
- ❑ People's eyes are always drawn to the brightest area of the image. That means that the audience can be told where to look by making that area a little brighter (Figure 10.12).
- ■ Regularly shaped subjects have greater visual weight than irregular ones.
- ■ Warmer colors (red, orange) appear heavier than cooler ones (blue, green); bright (saturated) hues look heavier than desaturated or darker ones.

There are many ways to change the balance and emphasis in an image:

- ■ Change the lens (zoom in or out).
- ■ Adjust the aperture to adjust the focus (depth of field).
- ■ Alter the camera position, which also may require changing the lens (zoom).
- ■ Move or adjust the subjects.
- ■ Change the camera height.
- ■ Adjust the lighting so that it is correct.

Unity (Order)

When the composition of a shot is unified, all its components appear to fit together and form part of a complete pattern (Figure 10.13). Without unity, one has the impression of randomness, of items being scattered around the frame.

Visual Patterns

The eye is attracted to a variety of patterns. A solemn, quiet mood is suited by slow, smooth-flowing lines; a rapid, spiky staccato would match an exciting, dramatic situation (Figures 10.14, 10.15, and 10.16).

Lines can create specific feelings:

- ■ Horizontal lines can portray calm and tranquility.
- ■ Vertical lines show strength and dignity.
- ■ Diagonal lines can show movement and speed.
- ■ Curved lines can portray serenity.
- ■ Converging lines show depth.

FIGURE 10.12
Note that your eye is always drawn to the brightest spot in the photo.

FIGURE 10.13
By slightly moving the talent and/or changing the camera's position, the separated people in the image on the left became more of a unified subject, as shown on the right

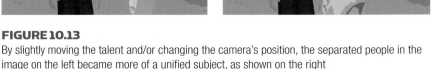

FIGURE 10.14
Horizontal and curved lines provide a feeling of rest, leisure, beauty, and/or quiet.

FIGURE 10.15
Vertical lines give a feeling of strength and dignity.

167

FIGURE 10.16
Dynamic (diagonal) lines provide a feeling of speed, vitality, excitement, or drama.

Leading Lines

Leading lines occur when the lines within the image lead the viewer's eyes to whatever the director wants them to look at. The eyes naturally follow the lines to the subject at the convergence point (Figure 10.17).

Rule of Thirds

If the screen is divided into even proportions (halves, quarters), either vertically or horizontally, the result is generally pretty boring. For example, a horizon located exactly halfway up the frame should be avoided.

The *rule of thirds* is a useful aid to composing the picture. Divide the screen into thirds both horizontally or vertically (Figure 10.18). The main subject should be on one of those lines, or ideally, on the intersection of two of the lines. The rule of thirds suggests that the

FIGURE 10.17
Converging leading lines portray depth in this image.

main subject should not be in the middle of the image (Figures 10.19, 10.20, and 10.21). Instead, it should be placed before or after the center of the image, depending on the effect the director would like. Keep in mind that the rule is merely a guideline—sometimes it may be closer to a fifth or somewhere in between. Good camera operators instinctively compose shots with these features at the back of their mind.

Scale

We judge how large or small a thing is by comparing its size and proportions with familiar items that we recognize in the picture. Without a comparative scale, we can only guess. A finger moves into shot, and we realize that a chair we are looking at is a skillfully made miniature. The eye is easily fooled, as you can see in Figure 10.22.

Perspective lines can influence our impression of scale and relative size. Again, although there is no relationship between shot size and the size of the subject, we often assume when an unfamiliar subject fills most of the frame that it is larger than it really is.

Subject Prominence

A subject's surroundings have a considerable influence on our attitude toward it. Consider the difference between a coin imposingly displayed on a velvet cushion and one heaped with others in a rusty junk box. Depending on how you present a subject, it can appear important or trivial. It can look powerful or weak; interesting or incidental. It can even be overlooked altogether!

168

FIGURE 10.18
The rule of thirds suggests that the main subject should not be in the exact center of the image. (Photo by Sarah Owens)

FIGURE 10.19
Although placing the main subject in the exact center of the image allows formal balance, it can be very boring. By placing the subject slightly to the left or right of the frame's centerline, the image becomes more dynamic. Notice that the structure is also "framed" by the lantern in the foreground.

FIGURE 10.20

When shooting a moving subject, it is important to put space before or after it, providing subtle meaning and balance. Image A shows the subject in the center, which lacks meaning. By moving, putting space in front of the subject (B), it looks as though the subject is going somewhere. Placing space behind the subject (C) makes the audience believe he or she is coming from somewhere, or being followed.

FIGURE 10.21

When a subject moves, it should be kept slightly behind the center of the frame (the red line). The amount of offset should increase as the speed increases.

FIGURE 10.22

If shooting something unusually small or large, show it next to something that the audience is familiar with so that the audience can understand that size.

FIGURE 10.23
(Left) By isolating the pin, all attention is drawn to it. (Right) Even though the pin is still prominent, the coins are distracting to the audience.

FIGURE 10.24
The low-angle shot of this horse makes it look incredibly strong and powerful. (Photo by Sarah Owens)

Isolation gives a subject emphasis. You can create this emphasis in many ways:

- By contrasting tones.
- By the camera height.
- By the composition of the picture.
- By the subject's position and size relative to its surroundings.
- By using background pattern or form to make the subject look more prominent (Figure 10.23).

Impressions of the Subject

How talent is shown by the camera can modify his or her on-screen strength as understood by the viewer—whether they look forceful, scared, or submissive. The subject's general posture is significant, too. Weak attitudes include side or rear views, lying down, looking down, bowed, stooping, clasped hands, and slow movements. Strong attitudes include frontal view, up-tilted head, hands clenched, stamping feet, and fast movement.

Camera treatment can have a considerable influence on our reactions to a subject. Shooting a ranting dictator in a high-angle long shot would make his or her gestures appear futile, weak, and ineffective. However, a low-angle mid-shot would give him or her a powerfully dramatic force (Figure 10.24). When you use a strong camera treatment on a weak character, you actually strengthen him or her. For example, an elderly woman making weak submissive gestures could seem to have a dignity and an inner strength against adversity when shot from a low viewpoint.

Composition and Color

The shades of color in an image can significantly impact the viewer: color and emotion are inextricably interlinked. It is important to think about color as images are composed, graphics created, and sets designed. Here are a few examples (Figure 10.25):

Red—warmth, anger, excitement, power, strength
Green—spring, macabre, freshness

Yellow—sunlight, treachery, brilliance
White—snow, delicacy, purity, cold

Composition and Motion

Composition that appears so forceful in a "frozen moment" still photograph often goes unnoticed during motion. For example, a photograph of a horse leaping a fence can look dynamic, strong, and graceful. However, a moving image of the same action may seem quite commonplace and unexciting.

A still photograph seldom holds the attention for long; the moving picture offers continued interest. Movement attracts. Through change, the director can introduce variety into the image, holding the audience's attention on the chosen subject. Changes enable a director to:

- Alter a subject's prominence.
- Redirect the viewer's attention.
- Add or remove information as the audience watches.
- Transform the mood of the scene.
- Show movement, growth, and development.

This brief list reminds us of the potential persuasive power of the moving image.

FIGURE 10.25
White and blue are generally associated with coldness. Viewers take that stereotype with them when viewing other images that are white and blue, allowing the director to manipulate a shot so that the audience reacts the way he or she wants them to react.

The still photograph allows viewers freedom to scrutinize and assess; the moving image often gives them time to grasp only the essentials, before it is replaced by the next—particularly if action is fast or brief.

If the information in a succession of images is obvious, simple, or familiar to the audience, changes can be rapid. (An informed audience may actually find the fast pace exciting as they rapidly assess each new shot.) However, if the pace is too fast for the audience, they are likely to get frustrated as each shot disappears before they have finished looking at it. In the long run, their attention and interest will deteriorate.

Movement can be dynamic and stimulating—or confusing and tiring. It depends on the subject, and on your audience.

A Theory of Dynamic Composition

In daily life, we continually make very subjective judgments as we assess the movements and speed of things around us. As we drive through flat, featureless country, we feel that the car is traveling at a much slower speed than the speedometer shows. Driving along a tree-lined road, the reverse happens, and we tend to overestimate speed. (See Figure 10.26.)

Watching moving pictures, we carry over these arbitrary interpretations. We cannot see speed and movement in the picture; we can only make interpretations from the clues that are present in the scene. Against a plain white sky, a fast-moving aircraft appears stationary. When we see the landscape beneath streaking past, we have an impression of speed (Figure 10.27).

Here are a few typical ways in which we react to movement in an image:

Effort: Slower speeds can suggest effort, or that motion is difficult, especially if it is accompanied by sounds that are similarly associated (low-pitched, forceful, percussive). By replaying a normal action in slow motion, the impression of effort involved can be increased. We also interpret the amount of effort, from signs of strain, tension, slipping, and so on, even when these have been faked.

Relative speeds: We assess the speed at which someone is running toward us by the rate at which his or her image size grows. (Shot with a long telephoto lens, this increase is slow, so we lose our sense of speed.)

Gravity: Although gravity is irrelevant, we subconsciously associate movement and position within the frame with gravitational forces. Something moving from top to

171

DIRECTION AND SPEED

FIGURE 10.26
Direction and effective speed:

A. Talent moving across the screen quickly passes out of the shot.

B. Diagonal moves are more interesting (and take longer).

C. Moves toward (or away from) the camera are sustained the longest. However, they may take too long.

172

FIGURE 10.27
Seeing that the background is blurring by, the viewer understands that the carnival rider is going fast.

bottom appears to be moving downwards, sinking, falling, or collapsing. Moving from bottom to top of the shot, it is rising against gravity, floating, or climbing.

Fixation point: The visual impact of movement can depend on where we happen to fix our attention. Looking skyward, we see moving clouds and static buildings—or static clouds and toppling buildings.

Strength: Something that is large in the frame and is moving toward the camera appears to grow stronger and more threatening. Seen from a side viewpoint, the same action (e.g., a truck backing up) can seem quite incidental.

Using Dynamic Composition

Dynamic composition is used by the media daily. Some widely accepted working principles have emerged:

Direction of movement: Like vertical lines, vertical movement is stronger than horizontal.

- ❑ A left-to-right move is stronger than a right-to-left action (Figure 10.28).
- ❑ A rising action is stronger than a downward one. For example, a rise from a seated position has greater attraction than a downward sitting movement.
- ❑ An upward move generally looks faster than a horizontal one.

Diagonal movement: Like diagonal lines, this is the most dynamic movement direction (Figure 10.29).

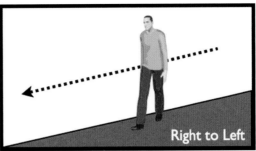

FIGURE 10.28
The direction of the slope can alter an image's attractiveness to the viewer. The left-to-right version has a tendency to be more interesting than a right-to-left version.

FIGURE 10.29
Diagonal movement is the most dynamic movement direction.

FIGURE 10.30
Movements toward the camera are more powerful than movements away from the camera.

173

Movement toward the camera: All forward gestures or movements are more powerful than recessive action away from the camera: a glance, a turned head, a pointing hand. Similarly, a shot moving toward a subject (dolly/zoom-in) arouses greater interest than one withdrawing from it (dolly back/zoom-out). (See Figure 10.30.)

Continuity of movement: A moving subject attracts attention more readily than a static one, but continuous movement at constant speed does not maintain maximum interest. When action is momentarily interrupted or changes direction, the impact is greater than one carried straight through. Converging movements are usually more forceful than expanding ones.

Crossing the Line

Camera angles can easily confuse the audience's sense of direction and their impression of spatial relationships if care is not taken when selecting camera positions. For example, during a basketball game, if cameras are placed on both sides of the court, it is confusing to see a player running toward the left side of the screen and then, when the director cuts to the camera on the other side of the court, to see the player running toward the right side of the screen.

To avoid this happening, draw an imaginary line along the direction of the action (called the *action line*, *axis of action*, or *eye line*), as shown in Figure 10.31. Then be careful that the cameras shoot from only one side of this line—generally it is not crossed. It is possible to

FIGURE 10.31
Crossing the line: By moving the camera across the line of action the direction of the walk appears to change, confusing the audience. (Photos by Josh Taber)

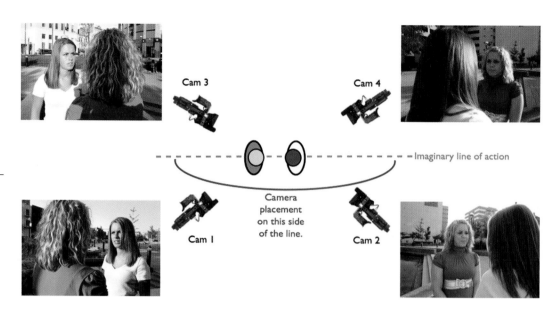

FIGURE 10.32
The line of action: Shots can be cut between cameras located on the same side of the imaginary line of action—between 1 and 2, or 3 and 4. Cutting between cameras on opposite sides of this line could cause a jump cut (1 and 3, 1 and 4, 2 and 3, 2 and 4). (Photos by Josh Taber)

dolly across the line, shoot along it, or change its direction by regrouping people, but cutting between cameras on both sides of this imaginary line produces a *reverse cut* or *jump cut* (Figure 10.32).

ANTICIPATING EDITING

It is very important to think about the editing process when shooting. If proper preproduction planning has taken place, the director and camera operator should have a good idea of how the shots should be created.

Continuity

Every time the camera is set up to take the next action shot, think about future editing. Otherwise, it is possible to end up with a series of shots that do not fit together smoothly. This happens often when repositioning the camera to shoot a repeated scene from a different location.

The most frequent problems are:

- Part of the action is missing.
- The action shot from another angle does not match that from a previous shot of the subject.
- The direction of the action has changed between successive shots.
- The shot sizes are too similar or too extreme.
- Action leaves the frame, and re-enters it on the same side.
- Successive shots show continuity differences, such as with and without eyeglasses, different attitudes/expressions, or different clothing.

Improving Editing Flexibility

When shooting, editing flexibility can help in various ways.

AVOID BRIEF SHOTS

- Always record the beginning and end of the action, to allow editing flexibility. Do not wait to record until the instant the action starts. Extra footage on each side of the action, also known as *heads* or *tails*, will give the editor the opportunity to utilize dissolves, fades, and allow him or her to trim the footage in an optimal way.

- Where possible, start and finish a long panning shot with a still shot.

EXTRA EDITING MATERIAL (USUALLY CALLED "B" ROLL)

- Always shoot some *cutaways* showing the surroundings, general scene, bystanders' reactions, and so on.
- Determine whether specific reaction shots would be appropriate.
- It is sometimes helpful to shoot the same scene at a leisurely pace and at a faster pace (slow pan and faster pan) to allow editing flexibility.

FAULTY TAKES

- Do not record over an unsuccessful shot. Parts of it may be usable during the editing process.
- If an action sequence goes wrong, it is sometimes better to retake it entirely. At other times, just change the camera angle (or shot size), and retake the action from just before the error was made (called a *pickup shot*).

ESTABLISHING SHOTS

- Always begin shooting with a wide shot of the scene (called an *establishing shot*), even if it is not used eventually. This shot allows the editor to understand the placement of the other shots.
- Consider taking a long shot (*cover shot* or *master shot*) of all of the action in a scene, then repeat the action while taking closer shots.

Table 10.1	Common Faults While Shooting
Wrong color temperature (the image is bluish or yellowish)	Make sure that the camera was white-balanced proper ly and that the appropriate color-correction filter was used.
Soft focus	The camera operator must take the time to make sure that the lens is properly focused.
Camera shake, unsteady camera	The camera may need to be secured with some type of a camera mount. It is a good habit to use a tripod, or some other mount, as much as possible. Most people cannot hand-hold a camera very steadily, especially for an extended period of time.
Sloping horizons	Leveling the camera may be time consuming but is essential.
Headroom wrong (too little or excessive)	Each time the camera is repositioned, the headroom must be reviewed.
Cut off top of head or feet	Make sure that the subject is properly framed. Do not cut on the natural bend of a body.

Continued

Table 10.1	Common Faults While Shooting (*Continued*)
Subject size (too distant or close to see properly)	The size of the subject may be problematic when successive shots are too similar, inappropriate camera height for the situation occurs, disproportionate number of long shots or close shots, or focus is on the wrong subject. Advanced planning, including storyboarding, is essential.
All subjects composed center-frame	Keep the rule of thirds in mind when shooting.
Shots do not interrelate (too many isolated subjects)	Think "transitions" as you shoot the project.
Subject obscured (foreground intrusion), background objects sprouting from heads, background distractions (posters, traffic)	Carefully review the foregrounds and backgrounds of a scene for distraction objects.
Shots too brief (or too lengthy) or start of action missed	It is better to have a clip that is too long than too short. Make sure that you begin shooting before the action begins and continue shooting briefly after the action is complete.
Zooming excessive or distracting	Zoom shots must be motivated; that is, they need to be there for a reason.
Panning not smooth, too fast, or over-shoots	The tripod may require some fine adjustment.
Person handling objects badly (obscuring, moving around)	Practicing with the talent is important so that they understand what you are trying to do.
Poor lighting (such as black eyes, half-lit face)	Lighting may need to be adjusted for maximum impact.

REVIEW QUESTIONS

1. When dealing with composition, what are the three key factors, and how do they impact the final image?
2. Why is composition important?
3. What are some of the common faults while shooting?
4. How can shooting improve the editing process?
5. What are some of the practical ways to adjust composition?
6. How is balance in an image affected by the subject?
7. Visual patterns can significantly affect the image. Give three examples and explain their impact.

CHAPTER 11

Television Graphics

"Trendy title styles are often hot today but stone cold tomorrow."

Morgan Paar, Producer

Terms

CG (character generator): A generic name for any type of television graphic creation equipment. CGs can change fonts, shape, size, color, and design of the lettering.

Credits: Recognize those appearing in and contributing to the program.

End titles: Draw the program to its conclusion.

Opening titles: Introduce the show to the audience.

Subtitles: Identify people and places.

First impressions are important. And the first impressions the audience gets from your production may come from the opening graphics. They help set the style and ambiance of the program; they inform; they guide. Well-designed graphics make a direct contribution to the success of any production. Poorly designed graphics immediately discredit the entire production. Graphics don't have to be elaborate—they just need to clearly communicate, and help grab the audience's attention. However, they do need to be brief, clear, and appropriate in style.

Effective television graphics require the graphic operator or designer to think through a number of stages in the production process:

- How does this graphic help the audience understand the subject or story better?
- What is the purpose or goal of the graphic?
- Would words, illustrations, photographs, or video imagery work best to communicate to this audience?

TELEVISION GRAPHIC GOALS

Television graphics should:

Convey information clearly and directly. They should be prepared for maximum communication impact. This means that television graphics should be simply created, not elaborate. Because television graphics move quickly and cannot be studied for a long period of time, the font should be bold and straightforward.

Establish the show's overall mood and tone through the graphic style. The font and presentation style can do much to advance the "story" being told. These can set the scene for the rest of the program (Figures 11.1 and 11.2).

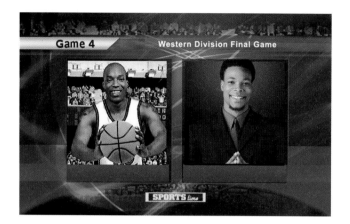

FIGURE 11.1
Television graphics can help establish the mood and tone for the whole program. (Photo courtesy of Compix)

FIGURE 11.2
Graphics for television often create the look and style of the program. Note that the logo in this photo was used as a set graphic; it is showing up (probably animated) on the set's video screen in the back and a graphic generator is being used so that it appears as part of the credit design. (Photo courtesy of KOMU-TV)

FIGURE 11.3
Graphics need to be organized in a way that can be easily understood by the viewer. (Photo courtesy of KOMU-TV)

Present fact, concepts, or processes visually so that the viewer will understand the program content. Keep the graphics organized and presented in a way that holds the audience's attention and makes it simple for them to follow the process or understand the concept being presented (Figure 11.3).

Aim to keep graphic information to a minimum, particularly if it is combined with a detailed background. A screen full of written information can be daunting to most viewers and tiring to read. People are easily discouraged from reading rapid graphics. Leave information on the screen long enough to allow it to be read aloud twice, so that even the slowest reader can assimilate it.

Tips on Making Great TV Graphics
(Adapted from Al Tompkins, Poynter Institute)

1. What is the context of this graphic? How does the information compare with previous studies or surrounding areas? Is the information really important for the viewer to know?
2. Think shapes, not just numbers. It is sometimes difficult to read with the relative nature of numbers when they are presented quickly on the TV screen. But it is easy to understand the growth of a budget when a bag of money is shown growing on the screen. Imagine that you have no words—that the graphic is all the viewer can see. How clearly would they understand what you are trying to show?
3. Think clearly about the purpose of the graphic. Ask yourself: What exactly do I want the viewer to learn from this graphic?
4. Write after you make the graphic, not the other way around. This will ensure that the copy and graphic match exactly.
5. Get other people to look at it. Let them tell you what the graphic conveys to them. It is no different than copy editing.

Types of Graphics

Graphics add clarity to a show's presentation. They are used to announce the place or time, to identify a plant, to display data, to clarify how food should be cooked, and so on. There are a number of different types of graphics:

178

- *Opening titles* announce the show.
- *Subtitles* identify people and places.
- *Credits* recognize those appearing in and contributing to the program.
- *End titles* draw the program to its conclusion.

FORMS OF GRAPHICS

Graphics can make a valuable contribution to all types of television program:

- Statistical graphics in the form of bar graphs and charts can show, in a moment, information that would be hidden in columns of figures. They enable you to simplify complex data, to compare, to show developments, to demonstrate relationships, and so on.
- Pictorial graphics can be used to illustrate a children's story, to set the scene in a drama, to explain scientific principles, to provide an atmospheric background to titling, and so on (Figure 11.4).

Animated Graphics

Animation can bring a graphic to life. Even the simplest movement, such as panning over it from one detail to another, zooming in/out on details, or cutting between sections of it, can sustain interest in what would otherwise be a static display (Figure 11.5). Such techniques are an effective way of illustrating a documentary, or any program that relies heavily on graphics or photographs (or maps or paintings in historical sequences).

Animation can take place in a number of different ways. For instance, you can build a graphic on the air by progressively adding details or sections. Character generators can usually save the animation, which can be replayed at a later time.

Interactive 3D Graphics

There are a number of interactive three-dimensional (3D) graphics that are used to help the audience understand situations and also hold their attention. One example is sports production. Some of the networks are creating 3D characters, which represent actual players, to illustrate the various plays in sports. The goal of these graphics is to illustrate the nuances and variations in a play that could have occurred or has occurred (Figure 11.6).

DESIGNING GRAPHICS

Video and television productions today may use either of two screen formats. Standard-definition television (SDTV) has an aspect ratio of 4:3 (4 units across and 3 units high). High-definition television (HDTV) has an aspect ratio of 16:9 (16 units across and 9 units high). If viewers have both types of formats, all graphics need to be designed so that they fall into the 4:3 area. Otherwise, 16:9 viewers may not be able to see important graphics (Figures 11.4, 11.7, and 11.8).

Some things to consider when designing graphics are as follows:

- Keep titling well away from the edge of the frame to avoid edge cutoff. Graphics should be designed so that they fall within the middle 80 percent of the television's scanning area. This center area of the screen is referred to as the *safe title area* (Figure 11.8).

FIGURE 11.4
Backgrounds can provide a context for the titles. (Photo by Tristan Bresnen)

FIGURE 11.5
Animated graphics hold the viewer's attention better than static graphics. (Photo courtesy of WLEX-TV)

FIGURE 11.6
ESPN analyst Merril Hoge breaks down real-life NFL matchups and plays using virtual interactive technology. The monitor on the right shows what viewers will see at home—Hoge in the middle of computer-generated football players. (Photo courtesy of George Ruhe/*The New York Times*/Redux)

- Simple, bold typefaces are best. Avoid thin-lined, elaborate lettering. Although HDTV's resolution can handle the thin lines, the majority of the world is still in SDTV, which struggles with thin lines.
- Limit the number of different fonts within a program.
- Lettering smaller than about $1/10$ screen height is difficult to read. It is important for directors to determine what media the audience will use to see the final production, or at least what the dominant media will be.
- Outlining and drop shadows often makes lettering easier to read by preventing bleeding and providing contrast (Figure 11.9).
- However, avoid placing a black-edged outline around smaller letters, because it becomes hard to read. The holes in the letters B, O, A, and R tend to fill in.
- Punctuation is not normally used, except in the following instances: quotations, hyphens, apostrophes, possessives, and names.
- Abbreviations are never punctuated on television graphics. However, if abbreviations make the title ambiguous, use three lines if necessary and spell out the words.
- Leave a space between title lines of around $1/2$ to $2/3$ the height of capital letters.
- Lettering should generally contrast strongly with its background. The lettering is usually much lighter than the background (Figure 11.10).
- Don't fill the screen with too much information at a time. It is often better to use a series of brief frames, or to use a *crawl* (continuous information moving vertically into the frame and passing out at the top).
- Warm bright colors will attract the most attention.

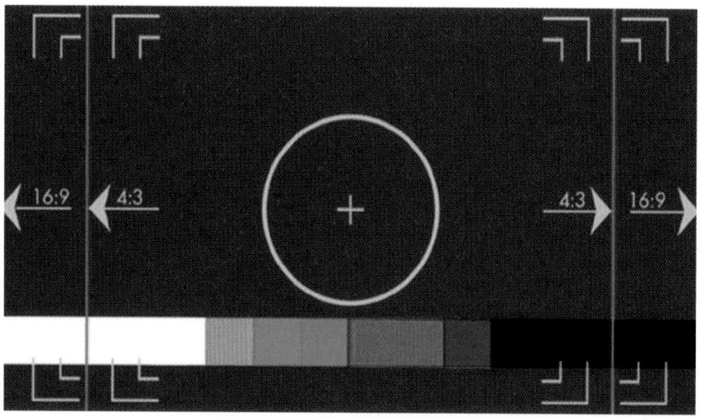

FIGURE 11.7
Today the viewing audience may be viewing on 4:3 (SDTV) or 16:9 (HDTV) televisions. Graphics need to be created so that they work on both formats.

FIGURE 11.8
Essential graphics should stay within the middle of the television's scanning area. Note that this graphic can be used on 4:3 or 16.9 televisions. (Photo courtesy of KOMU-TV)

FIGURE 11.9
Outlining the letters often makes them easier to read. (Photo courtesy of Compix)

Backgrounds for Graphics

Choosing a suitable background for a graphic can be as important as the foreground graphic. When creating full-screen graphics, graphic operators need to be careful when choosing graphic backgrounds. If the wrong background is used, it may compete for attention with the graphic. For example, don't use a sharply focused shot of a group of people in the background. Viewers will look through the words and look at the people (Figure 11.11). There are a number of different strategies that can be successfully used for backgrounds:

- Create a simple color background.
- Freeze the video background in order to not have a moving background.
- Unfocus the video image so that it is blurry.
- Select a single-color background (grass, water, sky, etc.).

FIGURE 11.10
Lettering will be more readable if it contrasts with the background. (Photo courtesy of Compix)

FIGURE 11.11
The backgrounds behind the graphics should not compete with the graphics. Note how the graphics operator here blurred and darkened the area behind the text in order to keep the attention on the graphics. (Photo courtesy of Compix)

When using a scenic background, such as the closing shots of a drama, the background content or meaning may actually help determine the style and weight of the lettering that can be used.

Plain backgrounds can prove very effective, as they are unobtrusive and emphasize the lettering. However they can also be dull and uninteresting. Ornamental backgrounds, which include patterning, texture, and abstract designs, may increase the graphic's visual appeal. However, they can look confusing. Clearly, background selection requires careful choice.

Lettering against a multihued or multitoned background is invariably harder to read. If graphics are inserted over location shots, such a street scene, the eye may have some difficulty in discerning information, and may also be tempted to wander around the background instead.

In most cases, by using larger type in light tones (white or yellow) with strong borders or shadows, legibility is considerably improved. As a general rule, avoid introducing lettering over backgrounds of similar tones or hues, or over printed matter (e.g., titles over a newspaper page). Light lettering is usually more easily read than dark, and pastel or neutral backgrounds are preferable to saturated hues.

GRAPHIC EQUIPMENT

Character generator (CG) is a generic name for any type of television graphic creation equipment. CGs can change the fonts, shape, size, color, and design of lettering. They can make it flash, flip, crawl (move sideways across the screen), roll (move vertically across the screen), and animate. Lettering can be presented as outlines or as solid characters, given a black border (black edge), or a surrounding drop shadow. Once the graphic is created, it

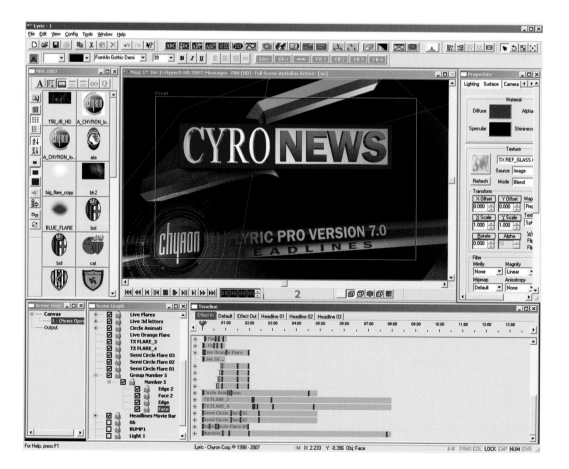

FIGURE 11.12
This is the composition screen of a high-end graphics system. The system allows almost unlimited manipulation of the graphics. (Photo courtesy of Chyron)

FIGURE 11.13
A standalone CG in use at a television station. (Photo by Jon Greenhoe)

FIGURE 11.14
Laptop CGs have become popular for graphic operators who are on the road a lot. (Photo courtesy of Compix)

can be rearranged, stored, and kept ready to appear on the screen at the press of a button (Figure 11.12).

Standalone graphic generator systems used to hold 99 percent of the market in professional television. They are still widely popular in larger markets and sports production. However, computers with graphic generation software have cornered a significant portion of the market. Today, computers are used in all markets and provide sophisticated on-screen graphics. Some mobile production crews have moved to laptop systems (Figures 11.13 and 11.14).

REVIEW QUESTIONS

1. What do graphics do for a production (in terms of its goals)?
2. What are some of the issues that need to be considered when designing a graphic for television?
3. How do screen ratios affect television graphics?
4. What can be done to letters to make them "pop" on the screen?
5. What can be done to backgrounds to make the letters more visible?

PART 4

Lighting, Backgrounds, and Sets

CHAPTER 12

Lighting for Television

"Pore over artwork and other films. Study the lighting and consider how it serves the story being presented."

Thomas McKenney, Director of Photography

Terms

Barn doors: Metal flaps attached to the front of a lighting instrument; used to control where the light falls on a scene.

Diffuser: Some type of a translucent material (wire mesh, frosted plastic, or spun-glass sheet) that diffuses and reduces the light's intensity.

Flood light: Also known as *soft light*; the scattered, diffused, shadowless illumination that in nature comes from a cloudy overcast sky, and is reflected from rough surfaces of all kinds.

Gels: Color gels (filters) can be placed over lights to enhance the color of the light.

Incident light: Also known as *direct lighting*; what's measured with a handheld light meter—that is, the amount of light falling on a subject. When measuring incident lighting, the light meter must be positioned next to the subject, pointed at the light sources.

Lighting plot: A plan that shows where each light will be placed on the set.

Reflected light: Measured with a handheld light meter or a camera's built-in meter; the light bouncing off of a subject. In this situation, the meter is aimed directly at a subject.

Spotlights: Spotlights are a directional or hard illumination that produces sharp shadows.

Three-point lighting: Also known as *photographic lighting* and *triangle lighting*; use of two spotlights (keylight and back light) and a flood light (fill) to illuminate the subject.

Zebra: Some video cameras include a zebra indicator in the viewfinder. The zebra allows camera operators to evaluate the exposure of the image in the viewfinder by showing all over-exposed segments of a scene with stripes.

Effective lighting makes a vital contribution to a television production. We quickly recognize bad lighting when we see it, but good lighting is so unobtrusive and "natural" that we usually take it for granted. In this chapter, you will learn some successful lighting techniques.

THE GOALS OF LIGHTING

Lighting in television and film is about much more than just making things visible. It has to also satisfy a number of often-conflicting objectives:

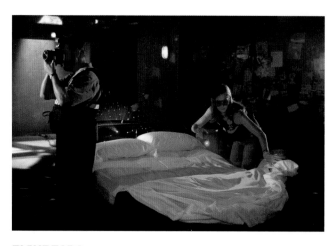

FIGURE 12.1
In this scene from CBS's *CSI*, the lighting creates a specific mood for the show. (Photo courtesy of The Kobal Collection/ CBS-TV/Ron Jaffe)

- The lighting must be bright enough to enable all the television cameras to produce pictures of the highest quality. This is usually referred to as *base lighting*.
- Lighting should convey to the viewer the time, mood, and atmosphere of the story (Figure 12.1).
- The lighting must provide a consistent look, as chosen by the director. That means it must look consistent from each camera angle.
- The lighting must fit in with the other components of the studio or location: scenery, camera placement, mic placement, and so on. Badly positioned lights can prevent the talent from reading the teleprompter, cause flares in a camera lens, result in shadows, spoil a skillfully designed setting, and degrade makeup.
- Good lighting creates a three-dimensional illusion in a flat image. It provides an impression of solidity and depth in subjects and surroundings.
- Lighting should lower the contrast ratio between the light and dark areas. By adding more light to the dark areas or dimming the extremely light areas, it is possible to get more detail in both areas.
- Successful lighting guides the audience's interest. It directs their attention toward important features, because the viewer's eyes are generally attracted to the brightest area of the screen. Lighting can create compositional opportunities for the camera.
- Lighting is used to increase or reduce the picture's depth of field.

WHY IS LIGHTING NECESSARY?

Technical Reasons

As you know, the camera needs a certain amount of light reflected from the scene to be able to produce a good tonal range in the image. If there is too little light, the lens aperture has to be opened up to compensate, and the available depth of field is considerably reduced. When there is too much light, the images become over-exposed, unless the lens is stopped down (the depth may now be too great) or a neutral-density filter is used to reduce the light. In the studio, excess light wastes power, causes ventilation problems, and is unpleasant to work in. Light levels need to be related, wherever possible, to the preferred working *f*-stop.

Unlike film, the television camera can handle and reproduce only relatively limited tonal contrasts. If the lighting is contrasty, details in the lightest and darkest tones will be lost.

On location, the existing lighting may not be suitable. From the camera position, it may prove to be:

- Too bright: strong sunlight causing performers to squint their eyes.
- Too dim: insufficient for well-exposed shots.
- Too flat: diffused light in which subjects lack form or definition.
- Too contrasty: lighter tones burned out (pure white) and shadows too black.

Under these conditions, we need to augment or replace the natural lighting—or tolerate the results. Sometimes the only solution is to alter the camera position (Figure 12.2).

Artistic Reasons

Lighting plays a major part in how we interpret what we see. Even when structure and outline give us leading clues, the play of light and shade strongly influences our judgments of size, shape, distance, surface texture, and contours.

Lighting is strongly associated with mood. Through carefully chosen light direction and contrast, you can change a scene's entire atmosphere. It can portray fun, fantasy, mystery, or dramatic tension. Lighting can enhance a setting and create pictorial beauty, or it can deliberately create a harsh, unattractive setting.

You can use light selectively to emphasize certain aspects of the scene while subduing others, or avoiding or reducing distracting features. You can exaggerate form, and draw attention to texture or suppress it. Through shadow formations, lighting can suggest structures that do not exist, or hide what is there.

FIGURE 12.2
Shooting outdoors often requires the use of lights to lighten the shadows or to illuminate the talent against a bright background. (Photo by Josh Taber)

THE NATURE OF LIGHT

Light can be applied with large "brush strokes," or with fine delicate attention to detail. It can be washed across the scene, or used to pick out and emphasize certain features. But to exercise this control, you must be able to appreciate the subtleties of light itself. Let's take a look at the practical basics of illumination:

Light intensity: The strength of light that we require on the subject and the surroundings will determine how powerful the lamps need to be, relative to the area they have to cover.
Color temperature: The color quality of the light. Light and camera performance should be matched to avoid poor color quality.
Light dispersion: Some light sources produce hard light, which casts strong shadows; others create soft light, which is diffused and has few shadows. This range of tools offers us the choice of bold brush strokes or subtly graded halftones.
Light direction: The direction of the light affects the way light and shade fall on a subject. It determines which features are highlighted, and which fall into shadow.

Light Intensity

The amount of light needed to illuminate a set or location and the action within it is partly a technical decision and partly an artistic one. You might, for example, use one strong keylight to cover both the action and the background, or a series of restricted lamps, each lighting a carefully chosen area.

Camera systems are usually quoted as having a specific sensitivity, requiring a certain light level (intensity) for a given *f*-stop. But this is only a general guide. A lot depends on the nature of the surroundings and the mood the director wants to create. To reveal detail in the walls of a dark-paneled room will require much more light than would be needed with light-toned walls.

Lighting intensities can be influenced by the surface finish: whether walls are smooth or rough textured, and whether they are plain or strongly contoured. The contrast range of the set dressings used can also affect the amount of light needed to illuminate a situation effectively.

Interestingly, a spacious light-toned setting may require less-intense lighting than much smaller dark-toned surroundings. Lighting quality cannot be judged by the watts of the lights.

189

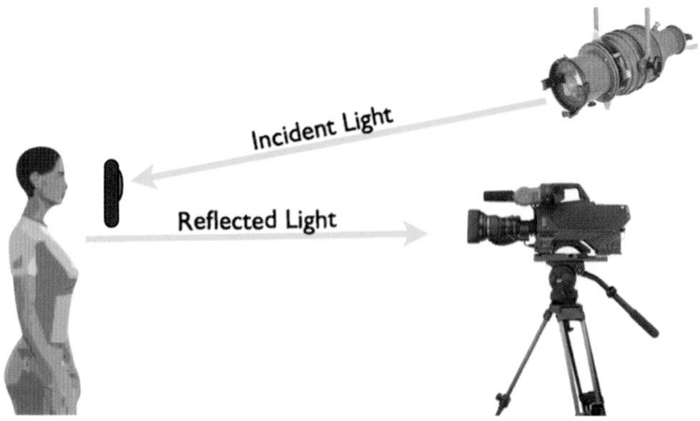

FIGURE 12.3

Standalone light meters are used to measure incident or direct lighting. Cameras have built-in reflected light meters. (Photos courtesy of Sony and Mole-Richardson)

The most helpful way to review the lighting is on an actual monitor, on which we can assess its artistic effect and judge its technical qualities.

When first lighting, or when lighting under unfamiliar conditions, it is advisable to make careful measurements of light levels. With experience, one becomes accustomed to lamp performance at various distances. Minor adjustments can be easily made with a dimmer or the lens aperture.

There are two primary ways of measuring the lighting in a scene (Figure 12.3):

- *Incident* light measurement helps to assess the relative intensities of lighting from various directions. When measuring incident lighting, the light meter must be positioned next to the subject, pointed at the light sources. It is measuring the amount of light that is falling on the subject, from the subject's perspective.

- *Reflected* light measurement provides a general indication of the amount of reflected light reaching the camera. Reflected light measurements average the amount of light reflected from the scene, arriving at the camera's lens. In this situation, the meter is aimed directly at the subject. Television cameras use reflected light metering. Today's more advanced cameras can adjust the meters to average the light, center-weight the sensor (use the center of the image to meter the lighting), in addition to other options.

Zebra Exposure Indicator

Higher-level video cameras generally include a zebra indicator in the viewfinder (Figure 12.4). The zebra allows camera operators to evaluate the exposure of the camera in the viewfinder by showing all over-exposed segments of the scene. It offers a very simple way to ensure that the lens' iris is set correctly. Although most zebras are set at between 102 and 105 IRE (a unit used in the measurement of video signals) in order to show which areas are over-exposed, some people like to set their zebras lower, for example, at 80 or 90 IRE.

FIGURE 12.4

When looking through the camera viewfinder, some cameras have zebra stripes that show the over-exposed areas of the image. (Photo by Austin Brooks)

The Color Quality of Light

The eye and brain are astonishingly adaptable. We appear to see effects that are not really there (as in optical illusions), and we overlook effects that can be clearly measured by an instrument. An everyday example of the latter is the way we accept a very wide range of quite different light qualities as representing "white" light. If we analyze "white" light, we find that it is really a mixture of a range of colors. The spectrum is red, orange, yellow, green, blue, indigo, and violet light in similar proportions. In many forms of illumination, some parts of the spectrum are much more prominent than others, and the result is far from true white. For example, light from candles or dimmed tungsten lamps actually has a warm yellowish-red color quality; or, as we say, a low color temperature. Daylight can vary considerably, from cold, bluish north-sky light to the warm quality of light around sunset. Yet our brains compensate, and accept all these sources of illumination as white light. Television cameras are not fooled in this way. They do not self-compensate. If the lighting has bluish or yellowish characteristics, the images will show this as a pronounced color cast. There are basically two ways to correct the color when shooting:

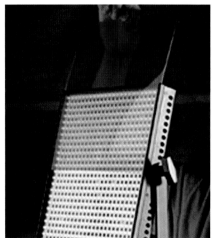

FIGURE 12.5
Gels (filters) can be placed over lights in order to color-correct a scene. (Photo courtesy of Litepanels)

- Adjust the camera to compensate for the color variations of the prevailing light, by using a suitable color-correction filter (in the filter wheel) and/or by adjusting the white balance. The white balance is usually adjusted by aiming the camera at a white surface while pressing the white balance button.
- Adjust the color temperature of the light to suit the camera's color balance. If you are using tungsten lights when shooting in daylight to illuminate shadows, blue filter material can be used to raise their color temperature from 3200 degrees K (tungsten) to around 5600 degrees K (daylight). Conversely, if daylight is illuminating a room in which you are using quartz or tungsten lamps, a large sheet of amber-orange filter can be stretched over the window to reduce the effective color temperature of the daylight to match the interior lighting (Figure 12.5).

Cameras are usually balanced for the dominant light source in the scene. However, different light sources have different qualities. Tungsten-halogen lamps (quartz lights) usually are at 3200 degrees K, and tungsten lamps can have a noticeably lower color temperature of around 3000 degrees K. High-powered HMI (hydrargyrum medium-arc iodide) lamps produce light of 5600 degrees K, which blends well with daylight but does not mix with that of tungsten sources.

Another issue is that as tungsten and quartz lamps are dimmed, their color temperature falls—the light lacks blue, and develops a "warmer" yellowish-red quality.

Light Dispersion

FLOOD LIGHT

Flood light, also known as *soft light*, is the scattered, diffused, shadowless illumination that in nature comes from a cloudy overcast sky, and is reflected from rough surfaces of all kinds (walls, sand, snow). You can create soft light artificially by using the following:

- Large-area light fittings (e.g., multilamp banks; Figure 12.6).
- Diffusion material in front of light sources (Figure 12.7).
- Internal reflection light (Figures 12.8 and 12.9).
- Light bounced from large white surfaces (e.g., matte reflector boards, or a white ceiling).

FIGURE 12.6
Multilamp bank. (Photo courtesy of Mole-Richardson)

Flood lights include scoops, broads, flood light, banks, internally reflected units, strip lights, and cyclorama lights. They are used mainly for fill light and for broad lighting of backgrounds. They can be hung, supported on light stands, or rested on the ground.

FIGURE 12.7
Diffusion material can be placed in front of a light in order to create a softer light. Lights can also be aimed at a white ceiling in order to bounce light onto a scene.

FIGURE 12.8
Weighing three pounds, the LED (light-emitting diode) light panel projects a bright soft light. It is extremely lightweight, offers low power consumption, provides accurate color reproduction, is heat-free, and can be dimmed. (Photo courtesy of Litepanels)

FIGURE 12.9
The LitePad is nicknamed the "Everywhere Light." At ⅓-inch (2.5-cm) thick, it can be placed anywhere to add a little soft light. (Photos courtesy of Rosco)

Adjustment of soft light sources is limited. Egg-crate shields and barn doors are usually used to restrict the coverage to some extent. Otherwise, diffusers or dimmers are used to control their light intensity (Figure 12.10).

Soft lights are usually used to:

- Illuminate shadows without creating additional shadows.
- Avoid emphasizing modeling and texture.

However, soft light does have practical disadvantages:

- Really diffused light can be difficult to control, because it spreads around and is not easy to restrict.
- Badly used soft light can produce flat unmodeled illumination. Texture and form can be difficult to see in the picture. If used as an overall baselight, it can reduce the impression of depth, over-light the walls of settings, destroy atmosphere, and produce flat, uninteresting pictures.

Spotlights

A spotlight is a directional or hard illumination that produces sharp shadows. This type of light comes from any concentrated light source, such as the sun or a spotlight (Figure 12.11). Spotlights produce well-defined shadows and are used to:

- Create well-defined modeling.
- Cast pronounced shadows (e.g., tree-branch shadows).
- Localize light to specific areas.
- Produce coarse shading or an abrupt brightness fall-off.
- Project light over some distance at a reasonably constant intensity. The light from focused spotlights does not "fall off " quickly with distance.

Spotlights are generally used as keylights, as back lights, as background/set lighting, and for effects (sunlight, broad decorative patterns, dapples). The light spread of the spotlight's beam is adjustable and can be focused. Ideally, the beam intensity should remain even overall as the beam width is altered However, many designs do develop hot spots or "dark centers." A couple of types of spotlights include:

Effects/pattern projectors: These spotlights, which include the ellipsoidal spotlight, can project patterns on the set or scene to simulate windows, branches, and so on.

Follow spots: Used for isolating static subjects or following moving performers (singers, skaters, dancers) in a confined pool of light. These large spotlights are carefully balanced for continuous accurate handling and are usually mounted on a stand.

However, spotlights do have practical disadvantages:

- The shadows from a spotlight may prove to be unattractive, inappropriate, or distracting.
- Spotlights can over-emphasize texture and surface modeling.
- High contrast can produce harsh, unsubtle tones.
- Multiple shadows arise when the subject is lit by more than one hard light source.

Clearly, for effective lighting treatment, you need a suitable blend of spotlights and soft diffused light. Usually the spotlight reveals the subject's contours and textures, and the soft light reduces undue contrast or harshness and makes shadow detail visible. You may deliberately emphasize contour and texture, or minimize them, depending on the blend and direction of the illumination.

The Direction of the Light

The effects of lighting will vary as you alter the angle at which it strikes the subject. Raising or lowering a lamp, or moving it round the subject, will change which parts are lit and which are thrown into shadow. It will affect how contours and texture are reproduced. Surface markings and decoration become more or less obvious. If you reposition the light, or alter the camera's viewpoint, the appearance of various features of the subject can change.

Three-Point Lighting

Three-point lighting, also known as *triangle* or *photographic lighting*, utilizes both directional and diffused lighting to obtain the best results (Figure 12.12).

FIGURE 12.10
Egg-crate shields can be used to restrict the light coverage—to a certain extent. (Photo courtesy of Westcott)

193

FIGURE 12.11
Spotlights provide distinct shadows. (Photo courtesy of Mole-Richardson)

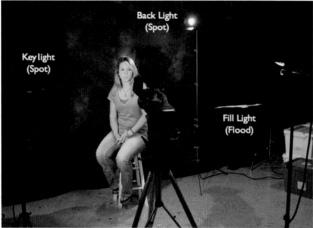

FIGURE 12.12
Three-point lighting is also known as triangle lighting or photographic lighting. Three lights are used to create the lighting treatment: the key, fill, and back lights. (Photo by Josh Taber)

The main light, or *keylight*, is positioned slightly above and to one side of the camera. This is normally a spotlight and it reveals the shape and surface features of the subject. The keylight produces distinct, harsh shadows.

The *fill light* is a flood light that is placed on the opposite side of the camera from the keylight. It reduces the shadows (made by the keylight) but should not eliminate them. The fill light also reduces the lighting contrast. The more the keylight is offset, the more important this soft *fill light* (also known as *filler* or *fill-in*) becomes. If the key is nearly frontal, you may not need fill light at all. Note that in the subject's image in Figure 12.12, the shadows on her face have not been eliminated. This helps give the face texture and shape.

Finally, a *back light* is angled down onto the subject from behind to give some separation between the subject and the background. The back light emphases the shape of the subject.

The keylight and back light are generally the same intensity. However, the back light may need to be reduced due to light hair color. The fill light is usually one-half or three-quarters the intensity of the keylight and back light.

Wherever possible, additional lights can be used to illuminate the background behind the subject. But where space or facilities are limited, spill illumination from the keylights and fill lights may be used to cover the background areas.

Lighting Terms

Base light or foundation light: Diffused light uniformly flooding the entire setting. Used to prevent under-exposure of shadows or excessive contrast.

Rim light: Illumination of the subject's edges by back light.

Modeling light or accent light: A loose term for any hard light revealing texture and form.

Kicker, cross-back, or ¾ back light: A back light that is roughly 30 degrees off the lens axis.

Bounce light: Diffused illumination obtained by reflection from a strongly lit surface such as a ceiling or a reflector.

Set light or background light: Light illuminating the background alone.

Eye light or catch light: Eye reflection (preferably one only) of a light source, giving lively expression. Sometimes from a camera light.

Camera light: Small light source mounted on a camera to reduce contrast for close-up shots.

Hair light: Lamp localized to reveal hair detail.

Top light: Vertical overhead lighting (edge lighting from above). Undesirable for portraiture.

Side light: Light located at right angles to the lens axis. Reveals subject's contours.

Contrast control light: Soft fill light from camera position illuminating shadows and reducing lighting contrast.

Edge light: Light skimming along a surface, revealing its texture and contours.

General Maxims for Lighting People

There are a number of generally accepted principles when lighting people:

- Place the keylight within about 10–30 degrees of a person's nose direction.
- Avoid steep lighting (above 40–45 degrees).

- Avoid a very wide horizontal or vertical angle between the fill light and the keylight.
- Do not have more than one keylight for each viewpoint.
- Use properly placed soft light to fill shadows.

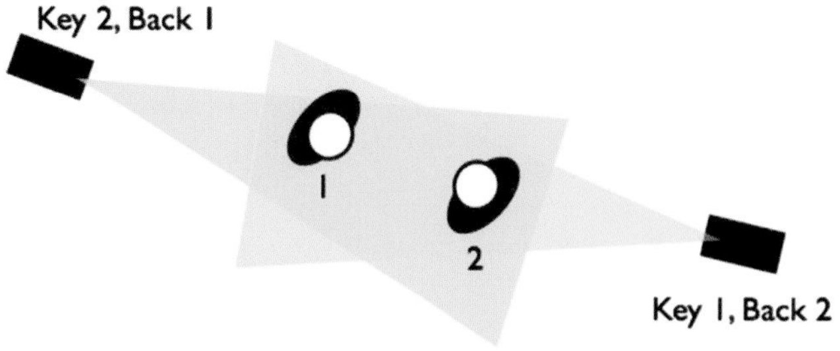

Lighting Groups of People

Check the direction in which each person is looking, and arrange their key/back/fill lights to fit. One appropriate lamp may suit a whole group, but problems can arise if there are big differences in the relative tones of their clothing, skin, and hair. Light intensity may be too strong for one, yet too weak for another. In such situations, localize the light reductions with diffusers or shading light off with a barn door or flag.

Where subjects are close, or you have few lamps, one light may have to serve two different purposes, such as a keylight for one and a back light for someone else (Figure 12.13).

Where there are groups of people (audience, orchestra), you can either light them as a whole or in subdivided sections, still using three-point lighting principles and keeping overlaps to a minimum.

Lighting Areas of the Scene

It is best to avoid flooding areas with light. The most attractive picture quality usually comes from analyzing the performance area into a series of locating points (by the table, at the door, looking out the window) and tailoring the three-point lighting at each to suit the action. One lighting arrangement will often suit other shots or action in that area (perhaps with slight light adjustments). Given sufficient lighting facilities (enough lights, dimmers, etc.) and adequate time to readjust lights, you could light to suit each individual shot. But such elaboration is not normally feasible. Where action is more general or widespread, you must cover the area in a systematic pattern of lamps (Figure 12.14).

LIGHT SOURCES

There are many different types of light sources. Each one can be used in different situations. Here are some of the most common:

Tungsten (or incandescent): The regular tungsten filament lamp is relatively cheap, has a reasonably long life, exists in a wide range of intensities (power ratings), is generally reliable, and can be mounted in many types of fittings. However, tungsten lamps waste much electrical energy as heat. Their typical color temperature is around 3000–3200 degrees K.

Quartz (tungsten–halogen): In these lamps, the tungsten filament is enclosed within a quartz or silica envelope filled with a halogen gas. This restricts the normal filament evaporation, providing a longer lamp life and/or a higher, more constant light output, of increased color temperature—around 3200 degrees K. The bulb must not be handled, as body acid attacks the surface, and the lamp becomes brittle and extremely hot in use (Figure 12.15).

HMI: The HMI is also known as a type of gas discharge lamp. These lamps are extremely efficient light sources, using a mercury arc ignited within argon gas. The HMI lights'

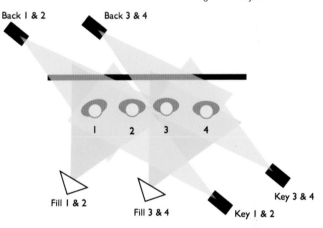

FIGURE 12.13
Lights can be shared when practical. In the illustration, one spotlight is used as a keylight for subject 1 and a back light for subject 2. The second spotlight is used as the keylight for subject 2 and the back light for subject 1.

FIGURE 12.14
Sets can be lit with a series of three-point lighting setups.

195

FIGURE 12.15
Quartz light.

abilities result in near-daylight illumination (5600–6000 degrees K). The highly efficient HMI lamp is particularly convenient for use on location to fill shadows in exteriors and to light within large daylit interiors, because its color temperature blends well with daylight. It provides about three to five times as much light as a quartz light of equivalent power, while producing less heat. A single 2.5-kilowatt (kW) HMI lamp can give as much light as two color-corrected 10-kW tungsten lamps. The lights require auxiliary circuitry (ignitors and ballast units), and there is usually a 1.5- to 3-minute buildup time from switch-on (striking) to full light. Dimming methods are restricted and a lamp cannot usually be struck again quickly after switch-off, which is a disadvantage for "shoot-and-run" productions (documentaries, ENG). (See Figure 12.16.)

Fluorescent tubes: The traditional tubular fluorescent lamp consists of a sealed gas-filled glass tube with a phosphor-coated inner surface. When switched on, the mercury vapor within the tube ionizes, causing the phosphor coating to glow brightly (fluoresce); the color depends on the specific materials used. The fluorescent lamp is three to four times more efficient than a tungsten source (more light per watt), so power consumption is correspondingly lower for the same light intensity. There is little radiant heat in the light beam. (Half of the power used by tungsten light sources may be wasted as heat!) Because fluorescent lights provide a broad light source, the illumination is relatively soft and easier on the eyes than intense spotlights. Fluorescent tubes have a relatively long life.

However, the lights can be somewhat bulky and rather fragile. The main shortcoming of this type of source lies in the light spread, for even with shutters and grilles (egg-crates, louvers), it is not easy to direct or confine light and avoid spill or over-lit backgrounds (Figure 12.17).

LED: LED lighting instruments are the newest addition to television lighting. They are made up of a series of LED lights, available as a flood or spot light. Although they

FIGURE 12.16

HMI lights have an extremely high light output. This HMI is being used to simulate daylight coming through a window. Note that it must be attached to a ballast unit (on right), which makes it quite bulky.

FIGURE 12.17

Fluorescent lights provide a broad light source. (Photo courtesy of Mole-Richardson)

are not the brightest lights, they are extremely energy efficient (cool to the touch), lightweight, and durable. They can also be easily powered by a camera battery when needed. These lights generally have a knob that allows the light intensity to be easily adjusted (see Figures 12.5 and 12.8).

LIGHTING INSTRUMENTS

Camera Light

A small portable light can be attached to the top of a video camera. These camera lights are generally powered by an AC adapter, an exterior battery pack, or the camera's battery.

Its main advantage is that it always illuminates whatever the camera is shooting, and does not require another pair of hands. Portable lighting of this sort can provide a very convenient key-light when shooting under difficult conditions, especially when following someone around. The light can also provide modeling light for close exterior shots on a dull day, or fill light for hard shadows when shooting someone in sunlight.

The disadvantages of these lights is that they add to the camera's overall weight, and their light is extremely frontal and thus tends to flatten out the subject. This light will reflect in glasses and shiny surfaces near the subject as an intense white blob. People facing the camera may also find the light dazzling.

Some camera lights have fixed coverage; others are adjustable. The illumination is invariably localized, and when using a wide-angle camera lens, subjects may move out of its light beam. Another problem is that the illumination may not really be appropriate for the scene. Though anything near the camera is easily over-lit, anything farther away remains virtually unlit, which can be very obvious in long shots. Some camera light systems even have an autosensor intensity control, which nominally adjusts their intensity to match exposure to the prevailing lighting conditions. Like all automatic systems, its performance is variable (Figures 12.18 and 12.19).

197

FIGURE 12.18
On-camera lights can draw their power from an external battery pack, the camera's battery, or an AC power supply. (Photo courtesy of Grass Valley/Thomson)

FIGURE 12.19
This LED 6000 K energy-efficient on-camera ring light is designed to provide an overall shadow-less shot or can utilize individual sections of the ring. (Photo courtesy of VF Gadgets)

Scoop

The *scoop* is an inexpensive and simple light instrument, requiring little maintenance and working well when a flood light (fill) is required. However, it can be inefficient and bulky. Unfortunately, the light from the scoop spreads uncontrollably, spilling around over nearby scenery (Figure 12.20).

Broad Light

The lightweight *broad light* (also known as a *V-light* or *broadside*) has a short trough containing a reflector and a tubular quartz light of usually 500–1000 W. The bulb may have a frontal shield to internally reflect the light. Although the broad is widely referred to as a soft light source, due to its small area, it produces quite discernible shadows. Nevertheless, it is an extremely useful wide-angle broad light source that can be hung conveniently in various ways, supported on stands, or laid on the floor.

Two-leaf or four-leaf barn door shutters that can be closed to reduce the spread of the light are often fitted to broads (Figure 12.21).

Soft Light

Soft lights are available in two primary types: the studio soft light and the portable soft light. Soft lights generally utilize a central lamp that is reflected off of the back of the lighting instrument. Although this device spreads its illumination uncontrollably, it is a very handy lighting tool (Figure 12.22).

The *portable soft light* is designed to be carried easily into the field. It provides a large amount of soft light. The portable soft light is available in different models. Some of these diffusion attachments fit on standard lights; others can be purchased with special lighting instruments (Figure 12.23).

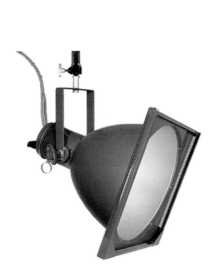

FIGURE 12.20
The scoop is a simple flood light. It is inexpensive, usually not adjustable, lightweight, and does not have a sharp outline. The scoop works well as a fill light and is great for lighting large areas on a set. (Photo courtesy of Mole-Richardson)

FIGURE 12.21
The V-light, or broad light, is a very compact light source. This powerful light source can be used as a key or fill and folds small enough to fit into a camera case. (Photo courtesy of Lowell)

FIGURE 12.22
Studio soft light. (Photo courtesy of Mole-Richardson)

FIGURE 12.23

The portable soft light is lightweight, may work with existing lighting instruments, and provides a large level of soft light. (Photos by Mole-Richardson and Taylor Vincent)

Multilamp Sources

Several soft light sources use groups of lamps, which combine so that the shadows cast by each are "lit out" by its neighbor light.

A *strip light* or *cyc light* consists of a row of light units joined in a long trough. Each unit has a bulb with a curved metal reflector. The strip light can be used to illuminate backgrounds or translucent screens from the floor. In a studio, strip or eye lights are often suspended to light backgrounds from above (Figure 12.24).

FIGURE 12.24
Strip lights or cyc lights are used primarily to light sets from the floor up. (Photo courtesy of Mole-Richardson)

Multilamp *banks* are excellent soft light sources. A typical design has multiple panels of grouped internal reflector lamps. Each panel can usually be independently switched and turned to adjust the brightness and spread of the unit. The *flood light bank* is mainly used as a booster light for exteriors and for large-area illumination. Large side-flaps may be fitted to restrict the light spread (Figures 12.6 and 12.25).

Soft light sources that rely on internal reflection to produce light scatter produce quite diffused light, but are relatively inefficient.

Large units fitted with a bank of fluorescent tubes are favored by some people as an inexpensive soft light source. Although these lights can be a bit fragile in use, one of their main advantages is that they produce little to no heat, use much less energy than a normal television light, and put out a large amount of light (Figures 12.17 and 12.26).

FIGURE 12.25
A bank of lamps provides a highly diffused light source and can easily work as a daylight booster. This lighting instrument acts like a series of scoops and houses a series of switchable PAR lamps. There is very little control over the beam coverage. These banks are available in many different light configurations. (Photo courtesy of Mole-Richardson)

FIGURE 12.26
Fluorescent tube soft lights are often used as a soft light source. (Photo courtesy of Mole-Richardson)

FIGURE 12.27
This open-face adjustable light unit can be used as a spot or flood light. (Photo courtesy of Mole-Richardson)

Open-Face Adjustable Light

The *open-face adjustable light* is widely used in the field. It has a variety of names, including *lensless spotlight*, *open-bulb spot*, *external reflector spot*, and *reflector spotlight*. This light has many advantages. It is extremely portable, compact, and efficient. Diffuser and/or corrective color gels are easily clipped to its barn doors (Figure 12.27).

Fresnel Spotlights

In television studios, where the lights have to be positioned a fair distance from the subjects, the large heavy-duty *fresnel* spotlight is universal, suspended from ceiling bars or battens. It is lighter than the other studio spotlight (the *ellipsoidal*), sometimes has an adjustable beam, and provides an unfocused spotlight beam. The fresnel is probably used more in studios than any other light (Figure 12.28).

Reflectors

The easiest and least-expensive way to improve a subject's lighting when shooting in sunlight is to use a *reflector*. This is simply a surface such as a board, screen, cloth, or even a wall that reflects existing light onto the subject from another angle. The quality of the reflected light depends on the surface you use.

There are many commercial reflectors available, such as the one shown in Figures 12.29 and 12.30. These lightweight cloth reflectors, sewn onto a spring-metal frame, can be easily folded and transported. Available surfaces include silver, gold, white, and combination reflectors. A mirrored surface, such as metal foil, will reflect a distinct beam of light from a

FIGURE 12.28
The fresnel light is a nondefined spotlight. It is lightweight, less expensive than an ellipsoidal, and has an adjustable beam. (Photo courtesy of Mole-Richardson)

FIGURE 12.29
Commercially produced cloth reflectors can be purchased that have a variety of colors. This specific reflector is designed with six different colors, for six different lighting effects. (Photo courtesy of Wescott)

FIGURE 12.30
An umbrella reflector can be attached to a light source in order to create a soft lighting instrument. (Photo by Josh Taber)

hard light source, creating sharp, well-defined shadows. This light travels well, even when the subject is some distance away. (A mirrored surface will even reflect soft light to some extent, if placed fairly near the subject.) The angle of a mirror-finish reflector can be critical. When the light shines directly at its surface, the maximum effect is obtained. However, as the surface is angled toward the light, the reflected beam, which covers only a restricted angle anyway, narrows and becomes less effective. In a long shot, its limited coverage is seen as a localized patch of light.

If the reflector has a matte-white surface, it will produce a soft diffused light, which spreads over a wide angle. But this soft reflected light is much weaker, and will travel only a relatively short distance, which depends on the intensity and distance of the original light source.

Reflectors can be easily made from a board covered with aluminum foil (smooth or crumpled and flattened) or matte-white painted, according to the type of light reflection required. (A board with a different surface on each side can be very useful.) These "boards" can be made of wood, foam core (which is extremely lightweight), or cardboard. The bigger the reflector, the more light that will be reflected over a broad area. Even a large cloth can be used. However, cloth reflectors of this size can be cumbersome to hang and are likely to blow in the wind if outdoors. However, since the only alternative is to use powerful lamps, or lights close in to the subject, it is certainly worth trying reflectors, when the sun's direction is appropriate.

Indoors, reflectors can be used to redirect light from windows or spotlights into shadowy corners. When using backlight, a low reflector can be used near the camera to reduce the shadows under people's chins and eyebrows. (See Figure 12.31.)

REFLECTORS IN USE

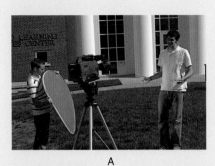

A   B   C

FIGURE 12.31

Reflectors can be used in many situations, using different techniques:
A: The sun provides the keylight and the reflector is the fill light.
B: A reflector is being used to reflect additional light into a building through its window.
C: Two reflectors are being used to increase the illumination. One of the reflectors is silver (the keylight) and the other is white (the fill light).
How effective a reflector is depends on its surface and on its angle to the sun or other light sources. If a reflector is used beside the camera, and reflects a source directly ahead of the camera, the intensity and coverage of the reflected light is at a maximum. As the reflector is angled to the source, its output and its coverage fall. (Photos by Josh Taber (A) and Nathan Waggoner (B))

FIGURE 12.32

"Furniture clamps" and "gator" clamps are used to attach a light to anything around the shooting location. (Photos courtesy of Mole-Richardson)

LIGHT SUPPORTS

Grip Clamps

There are a number of different clamps or grips available on the market in order to hold lights on location or in the studio. All of them include "mounting spuds" where lights can be attached. These clamps clip a light to any firmly based object, such as a door, table, chair, rail, post, window, or ladder. In the studio, they can also be clamped to a light stand and set flat. These clamps can be a very useful compact device to secure lamps in out-of-the-way places, especially when space is restricted (Figure 12.32).

Light Stands

Light stands come in all different sizes and shapes and are generally telescopic three-legged stands. They can be collapsed, folded, and/or dismantled into sections for transport. The size of the light will determine how sturdy the light stand needs to be. If the stand is too flimsy, it will be top-heavy and easily upset, even by the weight of the light's cable. With more robust types of stands, two or more lights can be attached to a stand when necessary.

Light stands have the disadvantages of occupying valuable floor space (perhaps impeding camera or sound-boom movement), casting shadows onto backgrounds, having trailing cables, and being vulnerable. But they do permit easily adjusted precision lighting (Figure 12.33).

In fact, most television lighting is suspended, in order to leave floor space uncluttered by lamps or cables.

Studio Ceiling Supports

Smaller studios and temporary sets in larger studios frequently use pipes to hang the lights on in the studio. These pipes enable lamps to be clamped or suspended as required (Figure 12.34).

Large studios frequently use "battens," "bars," or "barrels" arranged in a parallel pattern over the studio area, and individual battens may be counterbalanced by wall weights or motor

FIGURE 12.33
Light stands can be collapsed and folded into a compact size for storage and transport. (Photo by Josh Taber)

FIGURE 12.34
Pipes are often used on temporary sets to hang lights from. This set was used for CBS's *Without a Trace.*

FIGURE 12.35
Battens in studios allow the lights to be hung on them and generally provide electrical power receptacles. (Photo by Jon Greenhoe)

winches to allow lamps to be rigged. Battens are usually a type of hanging bar that allows the lights to be hung and then plugged directly into the batten (Figure 12.35).

Portable Light Kits

Portable light kits are available for the remote production crew. These kits usually come in two- to four-light packages, which include lighting instruments, light stands, power cables, barn doors, and so on. There is a wide variety of kits available from different vendors (Figure 12.36).

CONTROLLING THE LIGHTS

Lights can be controlled in a number of ways, including dimmer boards, cookies, filters, diffusers, barn doors, and flags. Each of these types of controllers can be used for different purposes, based on where the shoot is taking place, the equipment available, and the skills of the person doing the lighting.

Dimmer board: There are many different styles of dimmer boards, from fairly inexpensive simple manual fader boards to highly technical computer-driven boards (Figure 12.37). These systems are extremely adaptable and can be suitable for portability. Faders (control levers) and channel switchers are grouped on a lighting board (console), remotely controlling the lights. Intensity adjustments are smooth and proportional over their range, even for varying electrical loads. Generally, the lights are attached to dimmer units, which are controlled by the dimmer board.

Barn doors: Barn doors have independently adjustable flaps (two or four) on a rotatable frame; these selectively cut off light beams. They are used to restrict light, shade walls, and prevent back light from shining into the camera lens (causing lens flares). Barn doors are attached to the front of the lighting instrument and are most commonly used to control where the light falls on the scene (Figure 12.38).

203

FIGURE 12.36
Many different types of portable light kits are available. (Photo courtesy of Mole-Richardson)

FIGURE 12.37
Dimmer boards are available in a variety of styles, from simple manual fader boards to highly sophisticated computer-driven units. (Photos courtesy of Strand)

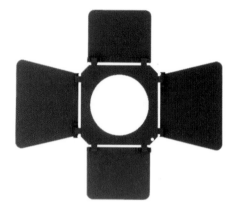

FIGURE 12.38
Barn doors.

204

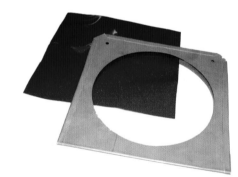

FIGURE 12.39
Flags are available individually or in kits such as the one shown here. Generally, flags are mounted on light stands. (Photos courtesy of Wescott)

FIGURE 12.40
Color filters, also called *gels*, are used to create effects or balance the color of the light falling on the scene. The gel is placed in the metal frame and slid into a holder in the light.

Flags: Flags are often used to control spill light from light sources. Flags are generally made of cloth that is stretched over a metal frame. The flags are usually mounted on a light stand placed in front of the light source (Figure 12.39). Flags can also be constructed by using any material that can block the light.

Light filters/gels: Color gels (filters) can be placed over lights to enhance the color of the light. They are added to create special effects or control the type of light falling on the subject. Note the filter being used in Figure 12.5. Gels are usually placed into gel holders and then placed onto the light (Figure 12.40).

Diffuser: Diffusers consists of some type of a translucent material (wire mesh, frosted plastic, or spun-glass sheet). They diffuse light (overall or locally) and reduce the intensity. (See Figure 12.7 and the wire-mesh diffusers on the bottom of Figure 12.36.)

Cookies/gobos: Cookies (or gobos) are perforated opaque or translucent sheets that create dappling, shadows, light break-up, or patterns that can be projected onto a set by a spotlight. Cookies can be inserted onto the front of some spotlights (Figure 12.41).

BASIC LIGHTING PLAN

Before lighting any production, a number of preliminary questions should be answered. Whether you get these answers at a preproduction meeting with the director, set designer, or audio engineer, or from a chat in the studio while looking around the set will depend on the size and type of the production.

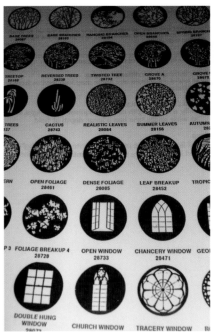

FIGURE 12.41
A sheet from a catalog of cookies.

What Is Going to Happen?

The subject: The main subjects in most programs are people. Even for a single person speaking to the camera, or a seated interview, you must know where people are going to be positioned and the directions they will be facing. You will need details of the action. The answers will decide where you place keylights. If keys are badly angled, it can considerably affect portraiture. All subjects tend to have optimum directions for the main light direction.

The cameras: Where are the cameras going to be located? Lighting must suit the camera's position. If the subject is to be shot from several positions, the lighting has to take this into account. However, that does not mean flooding light onto the set from all directions.

The surroundings: You will need to know about the general tones of the surroundings. Are they light-toned (then they could easily become overly bright) or dark-toned (in which case more light may be needed to prevent lower tones from becoming detail-free shadows)? Will the subjects stand out from their background or tend to merge with it?

Atmosphere: Are you aiming at a specific atmospheric effect (upbeat, cozy evening interior, intriguing mystery, etc.)? The answer to this question will influence how the light and shade are distributed in the scene.

Production mechanics: These include such things as:

❏ **Sound-boom positions** to avoid casting shadows that will be seen in the shot.

❏ **Lighting cues** such as someone apparently switching room lights on.

❏ **Lighting effects,** which include effects such as a fire flicker, lightning, moonlight, and so on.

There will be times when you will have to light a setting without knowing any of these details. In those circumstances, you can provide only a general pattern of lighting and check the images during the rehearsal to see where changes will be needed to improve the situation. Results under these conditions can be unpredictable.

The Lighting Plot

Most people find the basics of lighting easy enough to understand, but are very apprehensive when it comes to the actual lighting process. How do you begin? Creating a *lighting plot* will help you think through your lighting plan. An accurate lighting plot will enable you to immediately identify every lamp during rehearsal. Without a plot, you will be left wondering which lamp is causing the boom shadow, or why there is a hot spot on the set. Work systematically through the project step by step. Break the set into different areas, analyzing where the action is going to take place, and place the lights as needed (usually a type of triangle lighting).

Lamp Care and Safety

- Avoid moving lights when they are lit. Filaments are very fragile when hot.
- Use gloves when handling hot lamps. Never touch quartz lamps or HMI bulbs with a bare hand (body acids destroy the envelope).
- Allow plenty of ventilation around lamps to avoid over-heating. (Drapes, cloths, and other scenery can burn if they are too close to lamps.) If you place diffuser material or color medium too close to a fresnel lens you may crack the lens, so always use proper holders.
- Beware of over-balancing floor stands! Weigh the bottoms (weights, sandbags). Secure cables to prevent accidents.
- Always utilize safety chains or wires to secure all hanging lamps and accessories in case they fall.
- Switch off lamps whenever possible to reduce heat, lengthen lamp life, and minimize power costs.

Table 12.1 The Techniques of Setting Lamps	
The subject	■ Scrutinize the subject and consider the specific features that you want to emphasize or suppress. ■ Will there be any obvious problems with that subject (such as a person with deep-set eyes or a peaked cap, who needs a lower keylight)? ■ Anticipate troublesome light reflections (for example, on an oil painting). Will a carefully positioned key avoid bad light flare or is dulling spray needed? ■ How critical will the shots be? If revealingly close, will there be sufficient depth of field? Will there be possible camera shadow problems? ■ Is the subject stationary, or is it moving around? ■ Is it being shot from several angles? If so, from which directions? ■ Are shadows likely to fall on the subject from people nearby, or parts of the scenery (hanging chandeliers, arches, tree branches)? Lighting angles may need to be adjusted to suit the situation.
The keylight	■ Arrange a keylight, suitable for the camera's position(s), subject direction(s), and action. ■ Does the keylight cover the subject? If the subject moves, will it still be suitable? ■ Does the key need to cover more than one subject—an area, perhaps? ■ Does the light coverage need restricting? Is there any unwanted spill light onto nearby areas (people, settings)? Use barn doors or flags. ■ Does the keylight suit the various camera angles? ■ Is the keylight likely to cause boom shadows?

Table 12.1	The Techniques of Setting Lamps (Continued)
The keylight (continued)	■ Is the keylight position too steep (i.e., too high)? Look for dark eye sockets and long nose and neck shadows. ■ Is the keylight's position too shallow (i.e., too low)? It can blind talent, reflect in glasses, cause background hot spots, throw subject shadows onto the background, or cast camera shadows onto people.
The fill light	■ Generally avoid high-intensity overall fill light (base light). It flattens modeling, reduces contrast unduly, and over-lights backgrounds. ■ Position the fill to illuminate the shadows, not to add illumination to the keylight level. ■ Fill light must be diffused. If necessary, place diffuser over light sources. ■ Typical fill light intensity is around half of the keylight level.
The back light	■ Avoid a steep back light. It becomes an ugly "top light"—flattening the head and hitting the nose tip. If someone is close to a background and cannot be backlit properly, omit it. Do not use top light or side light instead. ■ Avoid very shallow back light. Lamps come into the shot. Lens flares may develop. ■ Avoid excess back light. Intensity is roughly the same as the keylight level. Excess light creates unnatural hot borders to subjects and over-lights hair.
Background lighting	■ Is the background associated with a specific style, atmosphere, or mood that needs to be carried through in the lighting treatment? ■ Is there any danger that the subject might blend into the background tones? ■ Plan to light the subject before lighting the background. Any subject lighting falling on the background may make extra background lighting there unnecessary. However, keep the subject and background lighting separate, as they usually require quite different treatment. ■ Whenever possible, relate the light direction to the environment, such as visible windows and light fixtures.

Lighting and Camera Rehearsal

The camera rehearsal is the moment of truth. Now you can see the results of your labors. Keep an eye on all preview monitors and look out for lighting defects, such as distracting shadows, hot spots, unsatisfactory contrast, wrong light direction, unattractive portraiture, boom shadows, and the like. If possible, readjust dimmers to improve the lighting balance directly as you see inaccuracies; rebalancing could affect all subsequent shots.

The director will also be arranging and readjusting shots. Many shots will be as expected; some may be quite different and could require total relighting. Whether you correct lighting problems as they arise (and miss continuing rehearsal pictures while doing so) or list them to be corrected during a break depends on the circumstances. It is reasonable to quietly adjust a barn door with a lighting pole during rehearsal, but diffusers and gels or hanging lamps cannot be changed unobtrusively.

Mic boom
shadow

FIGURE 12.42
Sound boom shadows can
be a challenge on a set.

Sound Boom Shadows

Shot anticipation and coordination are necessary to prevent boom shadows from falling across people and backgrounds. The normal trick is to throw the inevitable shadow out of the shot by careful keylight positioning. Obviously, difficulties arise when this lamp position is artistically incompatible (Figure 12.42).

Lighting on Location

When you are shooting away from the studio, you will encounter a wide range of lighting conditions:

Day exteriors. These vary from overcast skies to strong blinding sunlight with deep shadows.

Night exteriors. Anything from pitch-black night to strong moonlight; from the odd street lamp to "bright-as-day" surroundings.

Day interiors. These can range from locations where sunlight through windows embarrassingly overwhelms any interior lighting to those where you need to provide a high-power lamp to simulate sunlight on a dull day!

Night interiors. Conditions here can vary considerably, from total darkness to an extensively lit environment. Sometimes the interior lighting is quite unsuitable for the camera and must be switched off.

In Table 12.2, you will find a useful summary of typical equipment and techniques that you can use when lighting on location.

Table 12.2	Lighting Treatment on Location
Exterior shots: Day	
Sunlight	■ Avoid shooting into the sun or having the talent look into the sun. ■ Reflect sunlight with a hard reflector (metallic-faced) as keylight, or soft reflector (white-coated) for fill light. ■ In closer shots, color-corrected lamps can fill shadows. ■ Bright backgrounds are best avoided, especially when using auto-iris.
Dull day, failing light	■ Color-corrected light can provide keylight or fill shadows.
Exterior shots: Night	■ Quartz lighting can provide key, fill, and back lighting for most situations. For larger areas, higher-powered sources are necessary, such as HMI lights. ■ Large lens apertures are often unavoidable (which produces shallow depth of field). Extra video gain may emphasize picture noise.
Interior shots: Day	■ The camera must be balanced to the color temperature of either the daylight or the interior lighting. ■ When strong sunlight enters windows, pull shades or blinds, put filter material over the windows, perhaps adding neutral-density media to reduce sunlight strength. Another option is to avoid shooting windows. Alternatively, filter your lamps to match daylight. ■ A camera light flattens modeling.
Interior shots: Night	■ Either supplement any existing lighting or replace it with more suitably angled and balanced lighting.

REVIEW QUESTIONS

1. What are three of the goals of lighting?
2. What is the advantage of a zebra system?
3. How can soft light be created artificially?
4. How are spotlights used in productions?
5. Describe how to set up three-point lighting.
6. How can a portable reflector be used in lighting a person?
7. What are some of the things you must consider when doing a basic lighting plan?

CHAPTER 13

Backgrounds and Sets

"What we are looking for in a dramatic set is an imaginative substitute. Keep in mind, directors produce illusions. However basic the set materials really are, the end result can appear to the audience as the real thing."

Gerald Millerson, Author

Terms

Chroma-key: Utilizing a production switcher, with this technique, the director can replace a specific color (usually green or blue) with another image source (still image, live video, graphics, prerecorded material, etc.).

Cyclorama (cyc): Serves as a general-purpose detail-less background. Cycloramas generally have a continuous, seamless background that can be projected on or keyed out to create unique backgrounds.

Flat: A panel usually created by building a frame and then either attaching a piece of wood or stretching cloth over it to create a wall for a set in the television studio.

Floor plan (staging plan, set plan): A rough plan of the staging layout usually begins with drawing potential scale outlines of settings, including their main features: windows, doors, stairways. Ensure that there is enough room for cameras, sound booms, and lighting.

Hand properties (props): Any items that are touched and handled by the talent during the production. These could include a pen, dishes, a cell phone, silverware, and so on.

Modular set units: Prebuilt set components that can be compactly stored and then quickly assembled and disassembled.

Stage props: The furniture on the set. These would include news desks, chairs, couches, tables, and the like.

Studio plan: The basis for much of the organization, showing the studio's permanent staging area with such features and facilities as exits, technical supplies, cycloramas, and service and storage areas.

Virtual set: Uses a blue or green seamless background, chroma-keying the computer-generated set into the scene. Most virtual sets employ sophisticated computer software that monitors the camera's movements so that as the camera zooms, tilts, pans, or moves in any other way, the background moves in a corresponding way.

211

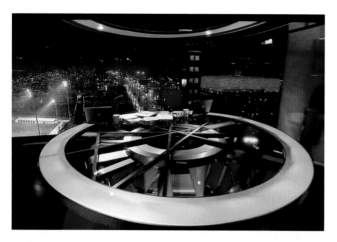

FIGURE 13.1

This television set was designed by the Canadian Broadcasting Corporation (CBC) to show off the context of the Beijing Olympics, with two recognizable buildings in the background (the Olympic stadium and the aquatics center). This background adds credibility to the broadcast, allowing viewers to see where the anchors are located. (Photo by Mike Gilger)

The background is much more than "whatever happens to appear behind the subject." It directly affects the success of the program, and thus it needs to be carefully designed and controlled. Scenery can range in practice from a simple backdrop to extensive construction, but effective design is important to the success of any show (Figure 13.1).

THE INFLUENCE OF THE TELEVISION BACKGROUND

Television shows are shot in a wide range of locations: people's homes, offices, factories, rooms, public buildings, studios, streets, and wide-open spaces. Where we shoot the program may be vital (contextually relevant) to what we want to tell our audience, or it can be merely incidental. To some extent, the importance of the set depends on the director, the way the subject is approached, and the chosen style and form. Effective backgrounds or sets are more a matter of making wise choices than having a big budget.

Surroundings have a considerable influence on how we feel about what we are seeing and hearing. It is not just a matter of choosing a background that looks appropriate or attractive, but determining whether its impact on the audience is right for the specific points being made in the program (Figure 13.2).

The background we choose for our action, and the way we shoot it, can affect how persuasively points are communicated to our audience. It is one thing to see a person standing on a street corner, recommending a type of medicine, and another when we see that same person wearing a white lab coat in a laboratory. The surroundings have swayed our reactions, yet they have nothing to do with the true quality of the product.

FIGURE 13.2

The background of a program significantly influences how the audience responds to the program. Usually sets should make a contribution to the content. (Photo courtesy of UPI/HO/Landov)

The camera cannot avoid being selective. For example, if a video camera is taken to an off-shore oil rig, depending on which parts of the structure are shot, a very different view of life on the rig can be expressed. The final emphasis could be on its huge geometric structure or the isolation of this group of workers in treacherous seas, or it might appear as a scene of endless noise and tense activity. In the end, it is the shot selection and editing that will portray the concept of life on a rig to the audience. The result may be a fair cross-section of life there or it could be overly selective. Much depends on the point of view the director adopts.

BASIC ORGANIZATION

Staging begins with the demands of the script and the aspirations of the director. Much depends on how effectively these can be related to the facilities, time, and budget available. As with all craftsmanship in television, optimum results come from a blend of imaginative perception and practical planning. Television set designers achieve minor miracles in making ingenious use and reuse of materials.

Planning begins with discussions between the director and the set designer. Using sketches, scale plans, and elevations, production concepts are transformed into the practicalities of man-hours, cost, and materials. For larger productions, there is close collaboration with various specialists, who consider shot opportunities for cameras, performer action, and moves, and the various lighting, audio pickup, camera treatment, costumes, makeup, and technical requirements. In such an interdependent venture, teamwork is essential.

The Studio Plan

The basis for much of the organization is the standard printed *studio plan*, which shows the studio's permanent staging area with such features and facilities as exits, technical supplies, cycloramas, service and storage areas, and the like (Figure 13.3).

The Floor Plan

Also known as the *staging plan*, *ground plan*, or *set plan*, the *floor plan* is a rough plan of the staging layout that usually begins with drawing potential scale outlines of settings, including their main features—windows, doors, stairways. Ensure that there is enough room for cameras, sound booms, and lighting (Figure 13.4).

Lighting Plot

The lighting director designs the lighting design, showing the battens, or lighting grid, and each of the lighting instruments on the staging plan.

Design Considerations

Television settings must satisfy several requirements (Figure 13.5):

- Artistically, settings must be appropriate to the occasion, the subject, and the production's purpose.
- The staging must be practical for the production needs: its dimensions, facilities, and the production budget.

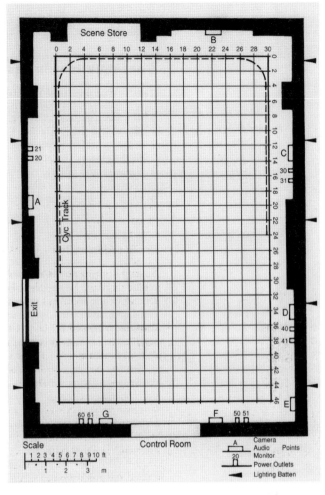

FIGURE 13.3
Sample studio plan.

213

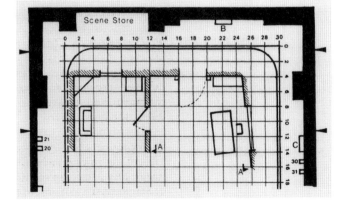

FIGURE 13.4
Sample floor plan.

FIGURE 13.5
The set design must provide ample shot opportunities. (Illustration courtesy of Fifteenhundred/www.fifteenhundred.com)

FIGURE 13.6
Today's sets need to be created with both the 16:9 and the 4:3 formats in mind. (Photo courtesy of FX Group/ www.fxgroup.tv)

- The design should provide suitable shot opportunities: operational freedom for sound, cameras, lighting, and so on.
- The television camera's characteristics will influence the tones, colors, contrasts, and finish of settings.

Set Design for 16:9

HDTV and its 16:9 format are creating more challenges. Sets that were acceptable on SDTV are no longer acceptable due to the high resolution of HDTV. Scratches and dents are much more apparent.

The 16:9 format has also changed the design of sets, and made it more complex, affecting also the locations of the talent. Until the 16:9 format becomes standard, viewers will see more header elements (high sections of the set), because camera operators need to frame for 4:3 as well as 16:9. This is especially true in wide shots. However, once 16:9 framing can be done exclusively, the header elements will be seen much less. It's important to create clean, visually interesting header elements, while not dedicating too much of the budget to elements that may only be seen for a short period (Figures 13.6, 13.7, and 13.8).

Real and Unreal Backgrounds

Most audiences are not concerned about whether the background is real or an illusion. They usually don't care if it is a real location or computer generated. It is the effect that counts. However, it is worth remembering that backgrounds can be derived in a number of ways:

Use of actual place. The action is really shot in the Sahara Desert.
Use of substitute. Shoot the action in a convenient location that looks sufficiently like part of the Sahara Desert.

FIGURE 13.7
On all shots, including ones like this, it is important to remember that 4:3 viewers won't see the areas to the far right and left areas of the screen, so it's important not to put vital scenic elements or graphics in this space. However, 16:9 viewers do expect this area to be filled with visual elements. In this image, the grayed-out areas to the left and right won't be seen by 4:3 viewers, while 16:9 viewers see the entire width, including the gray areas. (Photo courtesy of FX Group/ www.fxgroup.tv)

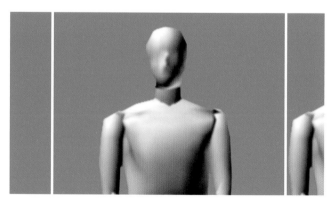

FIGURE 13.8
Whenever two or more talent members appear in one shot, care needs to be taken to make sure that anchors don't appear in each other's shots. In this example of a one-shot, 4:3 viewers, who see only the area between the white lines, will see only the one anchor. However, 16:9 viewers, who see the entire image, see the co-anchor's shoulder to the right. This issue is particularly important with anchor desks—a set needs a desk that seats anchors far enough apart to not encroach on each other's shots, without making anchors seem too far apart. (Photo courtesy of FX Group/www.fxgroup.tv)

Use of a set. Build a set that resembles the real thing in a studio.

Suggested location. The camera shows location shots of the Eiffel Tower (part of a still photo) intercut with shots of someone standing against a brick wall. Thanks to sound effects of traffic and so on, the viewer assumes that this is shot in Paris.

Virtual set. It is possible with various optical and electronic devices to insert the person standing in front of the camera into a separate background picture. With care, it can be done absolutely convincingly.

The Neutral Background

There are times when we want the background to provide totally neutral surroundings for the action. In the extreme, this background could be just a blank white (*limbo*) or black (*cameo*) area, because we are concentrating on the performers. However, we usually want something rather more interesting to look at than a plain area of tone, and TV solved this problem by creating the *neutral setting*: a background that is visually attractive, without actually reminding us of any specific style, period, or place. You will see this sort of setting in broadcast talk programs, studio interviews, and discussions, or, in more elaborate versions, for game shows.

FIGURE 13.9
Economical sets can be created by using just a few elements.

Basically, neutral backgrounds are usually made with scenic units, positioned in front of a *cyclorama* or *cyc*. A cyclorama is a curved wall that is used as a background for a television production. This curved wall suggests unlimited space when seen through the camera.

ECONOMICAL SETS

People working on a tight budget and with limited storage facilities will have little opportunity to build much scenery. But that does not need to be a major limitation, as it is possible to develop very attractive sets, simply and economically, by using just a few multipurpose set units in front of a cyclorama or a background wall (Figure 13.9).

- Lighting alone can significantly change the appearance of a background, whether it is a plain wall or a cyc. The set can be lit evenly, shaded (bottom-lit from a cyc light), have shadows or patterns projected on it, or be used with plain or blended color areas.
- An *open set* can be created by carefully grouping a few pieces of furniture in front of the wall. Even as little as a couch, low table, table lamp, potted plants, screen, chair, and stand lamp can suggest a complete room.

Support frames can be constructed from lengths of aluminum or wood. They can be dismantled or folded, are easily transported, and require little storage space. Various materials can be stretched across these support frames to make *flats*; these are taped, nailed, or stapled on. Many materials can be used, including mesh, trelliswork, scrim, netting, cardboard, wall coverings, translucent plastic sheeting, and so on. (See Figure 13.10.)

Modular units can be constructed out of many different materials, from wood products to plastic sheeting and aluminum. The modules can also be purchased commercially in a variety of configurations. The advantage to modular systems is that they can be assembled and

FIGURE 13.10
A simple flat constructed with 1 × 4-inch wood and a sheet of ¼-inch plywood. This flat is a type of support frame that would require at least one stage weight to keep it from falling down.

215

FIGURE 13.11
Modular units provide a quick and easy way to build a set. They can be constructed or purchased commercially. (Photos courtesy of Uni-Set)

disassembled quickly, are generally designed for minimal storage size, and can look quite professional (Figure 13.11).

Semipermanent Sets

Set design has become more and more complex over the years. Sets incorporate technology, special lighting, monitors, and areas for keying graphics (Figure 13.12). Dramatic sets are being built with such detail that they have become incredibly complex. Most complex sets are installed semipermanently. They are complicated enough that they are not worth installing and uninstalling on a regular basis, at least until they need to be updated or the show is cancelled. This means that they are built into the studio, bolted to the floor, and probably connected to the ceiling (Figure 13.13). When studio space is available, it saves a lot of time to have a set sitting waiting to be used. A regular show can be shot quickly, without all of the setup time.

A permanent or semipermanent set has the advantage that the majority of the set is assembled and ready to be used whenever needed, the set can be dressed and left in place (various props and furnishings), and the lights usually have already been hung and adjusted and then left in position.

When a studio regularly produces a specific program, it may have a permanent set installed, such as a kitchen, a laboratory, an office, a lounge, or a news-desk layout, all designed to fit the production.

FIGURE 13.12
Sets have become more and more complex over the years, loaded with technology and multiple surfaces. (Photos by Jon Greenhoe and Josh Taber)

Pictorial Backgrounds

Because in a 2D television picture it is difficult to distinguish between distant objects that are flat and that are solid, you can simulate 3D effects convincingly using a flat pictorial background. Ideally, it would need to be free from blemishes, evenly lit, and show no shadows; its perspective, proportions, and tones would match the foreground scene; and it would be shot straight on. In practice, you will find that even quite blatant discrepancies can still be very convincing on camera.

PAINTED CLOTHS (BACKDROPS, BACKCLOTHS, SCENIC CLOTHS, CANVAS DROPS)

Ranging from pure vaudeville to near-photographic masterpieces of scenic art, these large painted sheets are used primarily as window backings. Painted cloths are normally hung on battens, pipes, or wooden frames (see Figure 13.9).

PHOTOGRAPHIC ENLARGEMENTS (PHOTOMURALS, PHOTO BLOW-UPS)

Although expensive, enlarged photographs represent the ultimate realism obtainable from studio pictorial backgrounds. Enlargements are made on sections of photosensitized material that are generally backlit on the set (see Figures 13.7 and 13.12).

TELEVISION MONITORS

Television monitors are increasingly being used as pictorial backgrounds, from a single monitor, as shown in Figures 13.9 and 13.12, to a monitor wall that takes up a large part of the set's wall.

217

FIGURE 13.13
A semipermanent dramatic set being built into the studio. The back of the "plaster" walls are wooden flats, shown in Figure 13.20.

FIGURE 13.14
A hard cyclorama.

FIGURE 13.15
This television news station uses a green chroma-key background for its weather reports. Note the final combined image on the monitor behind the talent. The foot pedal in front of the talent is for changing background images. The talent is looking at another monitor (not shown in the photo) to know where to point. (Photo by Josh Taber)

Cyclorama

Even the smallest studio can make full use of a *cyclorama* as a general-purpose background. The cyc (pronounced "sike") serves as a general-purpose detail-free background. Cycloramas generally have a continuous, seamless background that can be used for chroma-key (see next section) or projected on to create unique backgrounds. The cyc provides an extremely useful general-purpose background surface for studios of all sizes. The cyclorama can be the basis of a wide range of program backgrounds from the mundane to the spectacular. It can be built to fit the project and can range from a few feet long to a complete wall around the studio (Figure 13.14).

Cycloramas are usually illuminated by a row of cyc lights. (See Figure 12.24 for an example of a cyc light.) It can be neutral, colored with lights, or include no light (black); also, video can be inserted into a blue cyclorama, providing a virtual set. Note that it curves between the wall and the floor. As corners are difficult to light and still look like corners, its corners are usually rounded so that the cyc can be effectively used as a virtual set.

The cyc is available in two primary forms: soft cyc and hard cyc. A *soft cyc* can be made of cloth, paper, or canvas. A cloth cyc is usually stretched taut by tubular piping along its bottom edge, where a totally wrinkle-free surface is required. Figures 13.16 and 13.18 show soft cycs. Soft cycs are sometimes hung on a straight or curved track (cyc rail), allowing them to be repositioned, changed, and moved out of the way when not required. A *hard cyc* is created out of drywall, metal, or wood to provide a hard, continuous surface (Figure 13.14).

Chroma-Key/Matting

The easiest way to understand the matting processes is to imagine cutting a hole in one video image and inserting an area from another picture that corresponds exactly. Within the area covered by the matte, the studio switcher or postproduction software switches from the main picture channel to a second picture source. The edges of this insert may be sharply defined (hard-edged) or diffused (soft-edged) so that they blend unobtrusively into the composite.

Matting/keying techniques have endless potential as background and as special effects. In television, chroma-keying is used extensively to create backgrounds and is based on a very simple principle. Wherever a chosen *keying color* (usually blue or green) appears in the on-air shot, it is possible to insert a second source (the *background*). Chroma-key replaces the blue or green area (determined by the user) with the corresponding section of the second source (Figure 13.15). This keying technique can be created by using a production switcher in a multicamera production or with a nonlinear editing system equipped with the appropriate software.

Basic one-camera chroma-key techniques have the major disadvantage that unless attached to a computer tracking program, the camera needs to hold a steady shot—it's unable to pan, tilt, zoom, or move, because this would immediately destroy the realism of the scene. However, even simpler chroma-key systems can be extremely effective.

Chroma-key is probably most often used to give the illusion that a person is standing in front of a real location such as a castle, standing in a field, standing out on the seashore, or standing

FIGURE 13.16
The first image shows the set with a section that can be keyed out in blue. The second image is the external video shot and the third image shows what the viewers would see. Any appropriately colored portion of the set can be chroma-keyed. (Photos by Tyler Young)

in a town square—merely at the press of a button. If done well, this technique can be very convincing and effective with an audience.

When utilizing the chroma-key technique, the entire background does not need to be keyed out. Instead, any part of the background or foreground may be chroma-keyed, as long as the appropriate keying color is used. Because the image can be as large as the key color, it offers a very economical method of providing an impressive giant display screen in a shot (Figure 3.16).

Virtual Sets

The use of virtual sets continues to grow. This sophisticated type of chroma-key is changing the way sets are designed in many studios. Although in the beginning the cost of setting up a virtual set system integrated with cameras can be quite significant, the savings of not having to quickly change many different kinds of sets can pay for itself in the long run. Studio space requirements and construction times are reduced with the use of these sets. Virtual sets use a blue or green seamless background, chroma-keying the computer-generated set into the scene. Most virtual sets employ sophisticated tracking computer software that monitors the camera's movements so that as the cameras zoom, tilt, pan, or move in any other way, the background moves in a corresponding way. This system automatically adjusts the background with each shot change, changing the background size and angle to simulate a real set (Figure 13.17).

Outside/Backlot Sets

Building an outdoor backlot set requires quite a bit of financial commitment in terms of both building the set and maintaining it. It is far beyond the means of a small-budget project. However, these sets can be rented and do offer a lot of flexibility. The nice thing about them is that, if designed effectively, they can be reused multiple times. The outdoor set shown in Figure 13.18 was built decades ago and has been used in many different films and television productions. These can be decorated to match the time era; most viewers do not realize that it is the same location that was used for earlier shows.

The Location As a Background

Location backgrounds bring context to the production. They make the production look real and genuine in a way that is hard to imitate in any studio. It usually brings a credibility and urgency to the production. However, any time the production is moved out of the studio, a little control is lost in audio, lighting, camera placement, and so on.

219

FIGURE 13.17
The women sitting on the blue cyc are being shot by a camera that is connected to the virtual set computer located in the foreground of this photo. Notice on the middle monitor that the computer-generated set can be seen. In the monitor on the right, you can see the combined virtual set and keyed talent.

FIGURE 13.18
(Left) The buildings and street are part of a set used in a network television production. (Right) The back of the same set. Notice that the back has been designed so that actors can appear in windows or move in and out of doors.

However, unless it is a very famous place, all the audience knows about the location background is what is shown to them. It is possible to go to an exotic place, and shoot someone leaning against a tree that looks just like one back home. If you're shooting on location, make good use of it. Ensure that there are sufficient visual clues for people to benefit from the specific atmosphere of the place (Figure 13.19).

In the "busyness" of shooting a production, it is so easy to overlook things in the background that can become a distraction in the final image. On the spot, they are just accepted as part of the scene. In the final production, they distract the audience's attention. Even major films often have a microphone sneaking into the shot at the top of the picture, or a shadow of the camera crew, or prominent lighting cables, in spite of all their vigilance.

Sometimes these odd things are puzzling or disturbing to the audience; at other times, they look funny, such as someone standing with a flagpole "growing out of their head," or a circular ceiling light hovering like a halo. Some of these distractions are impossible to avoid, but they are worth looking out for. Following are some reminders of typical things that can spoil the image.

Windows can be an embarrassment when shooting interiors. A large patch of sky in the shot can create problems. Even if the interior is exposed properly, this bright blank area still grabs the audience's attention. Although corrective filters can be used to compensate for the high color temperature of the daylight, its intensity can easily overwhelm the interior illumination and prevent the camera from getting a good tonal balance.

FIGURE 13.19
This ESPN production wanted to show where it was being shot, so the city's skyline was included in the background. (Photo by Dennis Baxter)

In addition to all that, if the audience has a good view of what is going on outside the window, there is always the chance that they will find this more intriguing than the real subject. The simple remedy is to keep the window out of the shot, or close the shades.

Reflective surfaces in the background are difficult to avoid. But glass, plastic, and even highly polished furniture can be very troublesome. These surfaces can even reflect the camera and its crew. So instead of admiring the gleaming new automobile, the audience watches the interesting reflections in its door panel.

Worse still is that shiny surfaces reflect lamps. If a camera light is being used, its beam will bounce straight back into the lens. When the camera is moved, the blob of light will move along with the camera.

Low-intensity reflections give sparkle and life to a surface. Strong light reflections are a pain, both technically and artistically. Apart from avoiding shooting straight-on at these surfaces, or keeping them out of the shot, the quick solutions are to change the camera's location, cover them up (position something or someone so that the highlight is not reflected), or angle the surface.

Any strong lights directly visible in the background of the shot can be similarly troublesome. But unless their intensities can be controlled, or kept out of the shot, the director will probably have to accept the results.

Flashing signs, prominent posters, direction signs, and billboards are among the visual diversions that can easily ruin a shot. They are all part of the scene, but if a dramatic situation is taking place anywhere near an animated advertising sign, do not be surprised if part of the audience's attention is elsewhere.

Even if shooting in a busy spot, it is often possible to find a quiet corner in which there are not too many interruptions. Try to avoid including a door or busy corridor in the background, or similar areas with a continually changing stream of people. People staring at the camera and bystanders watching (particularly the handwaving types) are a regular problem, and there is little one can do, except try as much as possible to keep them out of the shot.

FIGURE 13.20
These flats, or standard set units, are the back of the walls seen in Figure 13.13. This photo reveals how the walls were constructed.

FIGURE 13.21
(Left) This photo shows a cityscape hanging unit (far right of photo) hanging behind the actual set. (Right) This photo was shot from inside the set, showing the cityscape.

FIGURE 13.22
In this situation, a platform is used to bring the talent up to eye level with the camera.

SET COMPONENTS

There are many different types of set components used for production. Here are some of the most common.

Standard set unit: Used instead of interior or exterior walls. A flat is a good example of a standard set unit (Figure 13.20).

Hanging units: Basically, any background that is supported by hanging on a wall, a lighting grid, or another overhead support. These include curtains, rolls of background paper, and canvas (Figures 13.15 and 13.21).

Platforms: Used to elevate the talent or set (Figure 13.22).

Set pieces: Usually three-dimensional objects used on a set. These would include modular set systems, steps, pillars, and so on (Figure 13.11).

Floor treatment: Includes rugs, wood, rubber tiles, paint, and so on.

Stage props: The furniture on the set. These would include news desks (see Figure 13.22), chairs, couches, and tables.

FIGURE 13.23
These set dressings will be used to establish the character of the set.

FIGURE 13.24
Prop room showing the various props available for use in a production.

Set dressings: Set decorations are used to create the character of the set. They can establish the mood and style of the production. The dressings can include fireplaces, lamps, plants, pictures, or draperies (Figures 13.23 and 13.30).

Hand properties (props): Any items that are touched and handled by the talent during the production. These could include a pen, dishes, a cell phone, or silverware (Figures 13.24 and 13.25).

SET CONSIDERATIONS

Camera Height

The camera's height has a significant effect on how much of the scene is visible in the shot. From a lower viewpoint, less of the middle ground is seen, which reduces the feeling of space and distance in the picture. Things nearer the camera become more prominent—perhaps overly so. Even very small foreground objects nearby can obscure the shot. But raise the camera just a little, and not only will it shoot over them, but the audience will not even realize that they are there (Figure 13.26).

As the camera's height is increased, more of the middle ground comes into view, and the audience gets a greater impression of space and distance. However, if the scene is shot from a very high angle, or overhead shots are used, the audience will no longer feel that they are within a location, but will find themselves looking down, inspecting it instead. Of course, the audience is also affected by the speed of the camera move and the content of the shot.

Foreground Pieces

Objects can also be deliberately positioned in the foreground of an image to improve its composition, to increase the impression of distance, or simply to hide something in the scene. Many exterior shots have foliage hanging into the top of the frame. It is almost a visual cliché. But the camera operator has done this because the picture looks more complete, and it gives a better sense of scale, than if there were just a blank open sky. With this "frame," the picture tends to look more balanced and no longer bottom-heavy. When there does not happen to be an overhanging tree to shoot past, a piece of a tree branch can always be held above the lens. If this positively affects the look of the picture, do it—and your audience need never know.

Although the television's picture itself usually has a fixed horizontal aspect ratio (4:3 or 16:9), a foreground window, an arch, or a similar opening can be used to provide a border that alters the apparent shape of the picture.

By carefully framing foreground objects, it is possible to hide things in the background that would be distracting to the audience. They might ruin the shot in some other way. For example, if an historical drama is being re-enacted, it is very convenient (to say the least) if a carefully positioned gatepost, bush, or even a person in the foreground hides the modern signs, power lines, and other elements.

Creating Depth

Foreground pieces can add depth to a limited background. Depth is created by shooting through things, like a bookshelf, a fence, or flowers. Usually the foreground is kept slightly out of focus, so that the attention is drawn to the primary subject. However, the foreground can also help bring context to the image, by using something in the foreground that adds information to the scene (Figure 13.27).

FIGURE 13.25
This prop was used during a production of *The X-Files*. The actor bent the "pipes" and climbed through the "concrete." In reality, the pipes were bendable rubber and the concrete was foam. The "metal" edges and bolts were actually plastic.

223

FIGURE 13.26
By moving the camera to a high angle on a jib, the audience becomes curious, inspecting the scene. (Photo courtesy of Sony)

FIGURE 13.27
Foreground subjects add depth to the images.

Versions of "Reality"

Obviously, the camera does not "tell the truth." It *interprets*. Each aspect of the picture and the sound influences how the audience responds to what they see and hear. A slight change in the camera position can entirely alter the picture's impact. If the sun comes out, what was a drab threatening block of building can become transformed into an attractive, interesting piece of architecture. In the winter, we see a dull-looking street planted with stark, leafless trees. In spring, it becomes a charming avenue, where sidewalks are dappled with shade.

A location can be shot so that the audience envies its inhabitants, or pities them for having to live there. It can appear like a fine place, or an eyesore. It's all a matter of what the director chooses to include, and omit; what is emphasized, and what is suppressed.

As the camera moves around the scene, it can dwell on busy purposeful bustle, as people go to work, or it can linger on those who appear to be lounging around with nothing to do. (In reality, they might be waiting for a bus, but at the moment the camera captures them, they are "aimlessly inactive.") The director can suggest spaciousness by shooting with a wide-angle lens. Use a telephoto (narrow-angle) lens instead, and the same streets can look congested.

In most cities, one can find litter, decay, and graffiti; conversely, there will be signs of prosperity—attractive buildings, green spaces, fountains, wildlife, plus things that are amusing and others that are touching. How the images are selected and related will significantly influence how the viewing audience will interpret the scene.

What Can We Do About the Background?

If the director is shooting in a studio and the background is unsatisfactory for any reason, he or she can usually improve it in some way or other. But what can be done when on location if the background proves to be unworkable?

When a guest in someone's home, the answer may be disappointingly little. So much depends on the people involved, and the director's diplomacy. If the hosts are not accustomed to appearing on camera, they will probably be disturbed when it is suggested that things need to be moved around to any extent.

They may even feel uncomfortable if they are not sitting in their customary chair. There is little point in doing things that will jeopardize the interview. However, there are various little things that can be done unobtrusively to improve matters:

- Natural lighting can be used, rather than introducing lights. The person being interviewed will probably feel more at ease. The problem is that additional lighting cannot be avoided in most interiors in order to get good images.
- Although a room's tones cannot necessarily be changed, it may be possible to shade your lamps off a light-toned surface to prevent them from appearing too bright (using a barn door, flag, or partial diffuser). A little illumination may be able to be added to dark corners.
- If there are reflections in glass-fronted pictures or cabinets, and the lights and camera cannot be moved in order to avoid them, slightly angling the frame or furniture may resolve the dilemma. A wall picture or mirror can often be tilted up or down a bit by wedging something behind it. To avoid seeing the camera in a glass bookcase behind the talent, it may be possible to slightly open its doors.
- Closing or partly closing the room's curtains may help to adjust the lighting balance in a room.

- If shooting in a corridor or hallway, it can help if doors in a side wall are opened enough to let extra light in.
- Even if shooting in daylight, it may provide more interesting images if the table lamps or other lights in the room are turned on.
- It may even be possible to conceal low-powered lamps behind furniture or wall angles in order to illuminate distant parts of the room; but be careful that they do not over-light or even burn nearby surfaces.

Rearranging the Background

Most of the time, the director will be able to alter the background to achieve the best possible scene. Again, this has to be done diplomatically, but if the host's confidence is gained, and the director seems to know what he or she is doing, there should be no difficulties. The simplest changes usually involve moving around what is already there to avoid any unnecessary distractions or unwanted effects (glares) in the picture.

It is important to look at the background of any location to make sure that nothing is apparently growing from the talent's head, or balancing on it, and that no vertical or horizontal lines cut through the center of the head or across the shoulders. These visual "accidents" can make the picture look contrived or comic (Figure 13.28).

Altering the Background

As mentioned earlier, there are times when the background must be altered to improve the appearance of the room for television. There are a number of quick, inexpensive, and simple things that can be done to adjust things for the camera:

- Rearrange the furniture.
- Replace furniture with other pieces from nearby rooms.
- Add or remove rugs.
- Hide a doorway with a folding screen.
- Attach display posters to the walls.
- Position indoor plants (such as ferns) to break up the background.
- Introduce notices and signs on walls, doors, or elsewhere.

When shooting outside, there are relatively few things that can be done cheaply and easily to change the background.

Partial Settings

This is a strategy for convincing your audience that a very modest setting is not only the real thing, but even that it is much more extensive than it actually is. Yet the cost and effort involved are minimal (Figure 13.29).

If the camera does not move, it can only show a limited amount of the scene in a medium or close-up shot. With partial settings, it is important to concentrate on building up a section of the scene, just large enough to fit the camera's shot, and no more. Within the scene, enough features are included to allow the audience to interpret where the action is supposed to be taking place.

FIGURE 13.28
People's homes are designed to be comfortable and to be lived in—they are not designed for television. When going into a home with a camera, it is common to have to move some furniture, things hanging on the wall, rugs, and knick-knacks in order to create an effect that works on television.

225

FIGURE 13.29
By putting the crowd in just the right place, repositioning the camera so that the crowd is directly behind the batter and catcher, and zooming in the lens to a close-up or medium shot, the viewing audience will assume that the baseball stadium was filled with a cheering audience.

Do not underrate this idea. It has been used successfully in film and television for many years. The result does not need to look amateurish. Add the associated sound effects and the combined image can be indistinguishable from the real thing.

Typical Examples of Partial Settings

Creating sets that impact the audience can often be simply designed without building huge complex backgrounds.

- An "instant store" can be created by putting the appropriate type of merchandise on a foreground table (the "counter"), an advertisement or two on the back wall, and a shelf behind the salesperson, holding some more products.
- Sometimes even a single feature in the picture can suggest an environment. A stained-glass window and organ music become a church interior. (The window could even be projected.)
- A convincing "room" can be created in a studio with just a couple of flats or screens and a chair. Add an extra item or two, such as a side table with a potted plant and a picture, and it begins to take on its own character. If a curtain is hung on one of the walls, a window is assumed to be there. Whether it is interpreted as being someone's home, or a waiting room, for instance, largely depends on the way people in the scene behave. If they're lying back casually dressed, reading a paper, it is obviously their home. In outdoor attire, sitting upright and anxious, they are waiting.
- Replace the plant with a computer, and the picture with a framed certificate—magically, the setting becomes an office.

On location, the same concept is still useful: restrict the shot and "doctor" the background. Suppose that a nineteenth-century drama is being shot, in which somebody visits their lawyer. A house exterior of about the right period is found, but the rest of the street is obviously busy and modern. Fortunately, all that is needed is a shot of the house doorway with the appropriate business sign attached to it, and the picture explains itself to the viewing audience. Have the actor go up to the door, or pretend to leave the house, and the audience will immediately accept the location as the lawyer's office. It needs only the sounds of horse-drawn vehicles to replace modern traffic noise, and the period illusion is complete. With a little care and imagination, locations can be created from a minimum of scenery and work.

It is incredible how seemingly trivial techniques can give a totally convincing effect on camera:

- The camera rhythmically tilting up and down sells the illusion of a ship at sea.
- The wafting breeze may really be the result of an assistant waving a piece of board.
- The shuddering camera accompanied by things falling to the ground (pulled by unseen fishing line) implies an explosion or an earthquake. A hanging lamp swings alarmingly—tugged by an out-of-shot line.
- The flickering flames of a nearby fire come from a stick of cloth strips waved in front of a ground lamp.

These are just a few examples of how little ingenuity can apparently achieve the impossible, and create a strong impression in your audience's minds.

Facing Reality

It is one thing to have dreams about creating a program, but it is quite different to turn them into reality. Among the problems facing all directors are the inevitable limitations of budget and facilities. Some of the things that are needed may not even be available.

When faced with such problems, it is tempting to think small: to cut back on the ambitious goals, and to do a simpler version. Do not immediately abandon your ideas! Instead, ask yourself whether there is another way of tackling the situation to get virtually the same effect. How can you get around the difficulty?

What we are looking for are *imaginative substitutes*. Keep in mind that directors produce *illusions*. However basic the materials really are, the end result can appear to be the real thing (Figure 13.30).

As an example, let's look at an actual scene that was used on the air. The scene was the banquet hall of an ancient castle. The king sat on a throne at one end of a long table, eating from golden dishes. That was the illusion.

What was reality? Two small foreground flags on wooden floor stands masked the edges of the shot, so that no one could see the rest of the small studio. The "wooden table" was created from painted boards placed on sawhorses. The far "stone wall" was photographic wallpaper attached to a flat (and was slightly sprayed black in order to "age" it). The "throne" was an old wooden armchair with a red drape thrown over it. The "gold dishes" were sprayed plastic plates. A "window" was painted, black on white, and stuck to the "stone wall." But no one in the audience could recognize all of this in the long shot. Of course the scene would not have worked for close-up shots, but under patchy lighting, it was seen as it was intended to be—the banquet hall of an ancient castle.

FIGURE 13.30
Sometimes ingenuity needs to be used instead of reality. A fireplace was desired for this NBC set, but it was impossible to have a working fireplace in the building in this specific situation, and the heat would have been a problem. So an HD monitor (with a video of fire) was used inside the fireplace as a substitute. (Photo courtesy of LPG/NBC)

227

Set Problems

Here are some of the more common problems that you might have to address when working with sets:

- Check the set for distracting features. This could include things such as bright surfaces or reflections. Check to see whether the lighting can be adjusted to correct the problem. Other options may be using dulling spray, repainting the area with a different color, covering it, or removing that item from the set.
- Colors or tones may be unsuitable (subject merges with background). Modify the background, lighting, or subject (for example, change the clothing).
- Background blemishes (dirty marks, tears, scrapes, wrinkles, etc.). HD is very unforgiving and seems to show every mark. Correcting the problem may require refurbishing the area, covering it, or possibly changing the lighting.
- Distracting shadows may appear on the background. This usually means that the talent or scenery is too close to the background. This often requires moving the scenery/people or relighting the shot.

REVIEW QUESTIONS

1. How do the various format ratios (4:3 and 16.9) affect the set design?
2. What are some of the advantages of a modular set?
3. Why would someone want to use a cyclorama?
4. Explain the relationship between a virtual set and chroma-key.
5. What is a contextual set?
6. What are the various types of props and how are they used?
7. How is depth created on a set?
8. What are some of the set problems that often need to be dealt with?

CHAPTER 14

Makeup and Costumes

"For the makeup artist the soft veil of film has given way to the uncompromising clarity of high definition. Images so sharp that even the most beautiful or handsome talent can have subtle imperfections visible for all to see."

Bradley M. Look, Emmy-winning makeup artist

Terms

Character makeup: The emphasis is on the specific character or type that the actor is playing. By facial reshaping, remodeling, changes in hair, and similar effects, the subject can even be totally transformed.

Corrective makeup: Reduces less-pleasing facial characteristics while enhancing more attractive points.

Straight makeup: A basic compensatory treatment affecting the talent's appearance to a minimum extent.

The television camera is a critical tool and facial characteristics that pass unnoticed in daily life can appear surprisingly exaggerated or distracting on the television screen. Most of us can benefit from the enhancement that a skilled makeup artist provides. Whether this needs to be slight or elaborate depends on the type of production and the role of the talent (Figure 14.1).

FORMS OF MAKEUP
Television makeup treatment follows three general forms: straight, corrective, and character makeup.

Straight Makeup
Straight makeup is a basic compensatory treatment, affecting the talent's appearance to a minimum extent:

Skin-tone adjustment: This provides a good tonal balance in the picture; it involves darkening pale faces and lightening dark complexions.

Routine improvements: These subdue blotchy skin tones, shiny foreheads, strengthen lips and eyebrows, remove beard lines, lighten deep-set eyes, and lighten bags under the eyes.

For many television productions, performers require little or no makeup, with minimum correction and brief last-minute improvements often being sufficient (Figure 14.2). Regular talent may do their own makeup.

229

Corrective Makeup

Corrective makeup seeks to reduce less-pleasing facial characteristics while enhancing more attractive points. Actual treatment can range from slight modifications of lips, eyes, and nose to concealing baldness.

The general aim is to treat the person without them appearing "made up." Skin blemishes and unattractive natural color must normally be covered, preferably by using several thin applications of increased pigmentation, rather than trying to obscure these with heavy mask like coatings. Arms, hands, necks, and ears may need blending to an even tone (with body makeup).

A person's skin quality will modify the makeup materials used. Coarser skin textures provide more definite modeling; finer complexions tend to reveal veining or blotches that the camera may accentuate (Figure 14.3).

FIGURE 14.1
One of the hosts on NBC's *Today* show receives a hair and makeup check before going on the air.

FIGURE 14.2
Straight makeup is the basic type of makeup treatment. (Photo courtesy of Sennheiser)

FIGURE 14.3
Before (left) and after (right) photos of corrective makeup. (Photos courtesy of Jessica Goodall/www.jessicag.tv)

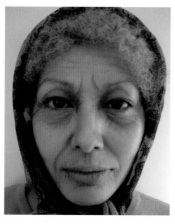

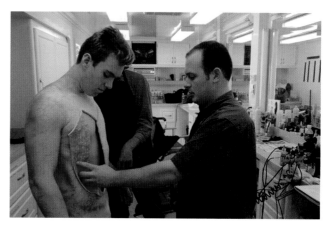

FIGURE 14.4
Character makeup can dramatically age a person. (Photos courtesy of Jessica Goodall/www.jessicag.tv)

FIGURE 14.5
A special effects artist applies character makeup and prosthetics to an actor on the set of the CBS televisaion series *NCIS*. (Photo courtesy of CBS/Landov)

Character Makeup

With character makeup, the emphasis is on the specific character or type that the actor is playing. By facial reshaping, remodeling, changes in hair, and making other such changes, the subject can even be totally transformed; for example, the actor can be aged dramatically. But most character makeup involves less spectacular and more subtle changes (Figures 14.4 and 14.5).

CONDITIONS OF TELEVISION MAKEUP

The principles and practices of television makeup are almost identical with those of motion pictures, except that in television, the continuous performance often prevents the shot-by-shot changes that are possible in film.

A long shot ideally requires more defined, prominent treatment than a close-up. However, such refinements may not be possible under typical television production conditions. You may not even be able to do anything about such distractions as perspiration or disheveled hair when the actor is on-camera for long periods, except to correct them for any retakes, when time permits.

For the very demands of television drama, careful planning and presentation are essential. At a preliminary meeting with the program's director, the makeup artist will discuss such details as character interpretation, hair styling, special treatments, and any transformations during the program (such as aging). Actors who need fitted wigs or trial makeup are then contacted.

Camera Rehearsal

For the camera rehearsal, the most common practice is to apply the makeup to the talent before the rehearsal. Then, while watching the camera rehearsals on a picture monitor, the makeup artist can note the changes that will be required. This process also allows the lighting director to assess tonal balance, contrast, and exposure of the talent while in makeup.

MAKEUP TREATMENT

Generally speaking, a straight makeup for men may take around 3 to 10 minutes; women require 6 to 20 minutes, on average. Elaborate needs can double or even triple these times.

After a few hours, cosmetics tend to become partly absorbed or dispersed through body heat and perspiration. Surface finish, texture, and tones will have lost their original definition, and fresh makeup or refurbishing becomes necessary.

There will always be problematic occasions. Some performers cannot have makeup, due to allergies or other situations. There are also times when the makeup has to be done immediately before airtime, without any opportunity to see the performer on camera beforehand—a situation that the wise director avoids.

PRINCIPLES OF MAKEUP

The broad aims of facial makeup and lighting are actually complementary. Makeup can sometimes compensate for lighting problems, such as lightening eye sockets to anticipate shadowing cast by very high-angled lights. However, whereas the effect of lighting changes as the subject moves, that of makeup remains constant.

Localized highlighting by slight color accents will increase the apparent size and prominence of an area; darkening reduces its effective size and causes it to recede. By selective highlighting and shading, you can vary the impression of proportions considerably. However, you must take care to prevent shading from looking like grime!

You can reduce or emphasize existing modeling or suggest modeling where none exists; remember, though, that the deceit may not withstand close scrutiny.

A base or foundation tone covers any blotchiness in natural skin coloring, blemishes, beard shadows, and the like. This can be extended, where necessary, to block out the normal lips, eyebrows, or hairline before drawing in another different formation.

Selected regions can be treated with media a few tones lighter or darker than the main foundation and worked into adjacent areas with fingertips, a brush, or a sponge. After this highlighting and shading, any detailed drawing is done using special lining pencils and brushes.

HD Makeup
- Makeup artists need to be cautious that they use only enough makeup to conceal a defect, so as to remain undetectable on HDTV.
- Brushes and sponges can easily leave "brush strokes" that are detectable by HD.
- Airbrushed makeup has become very common when shooting on HD.
- Facial hair can be extremely apparent on close-ups with HD.
- Many makeup artists have replaced the traditional opaque crème foundation (which becomes obvious on HD) with a sheer liquid foundation that is available in department stores.

HAIR

Hair may be treated and arranged by the makeup artist or by a separate specialist. Hair work may include changes to the talent's own hair, the addition of supplementary hair pieces, and complete wigs covering existing hair.

Hair Alteration

In television, a certain amount of restyling, resetting, or waving may be carried out on the talent's own hair, but when extensive alterations such as cutting or shaving are needed, complete wigs are more popular. Hair color is readily changed by sprays, rinses, or bleaches. Hair whitener suffices for both localized and overall graying. Overly light hair can be darkened to provide better modeling on-camera; dark hair may need gold or silver dust, or brilliantine, to give it life.

COSTUMES (WARDROBE)

In larger television organizations, the talent's clothing (*costume*, or *wardrobe*) is the responsibility of a specialist (Figures 14.6, 14.7, and 14.8). But for many productions, people wear their own clothing. Diplomatic guidance may be required to ensure that unsuitable attire is avoided.

FIGURE 14.6
A combination of makeup, hair, and costume can radically change the impression that the actor makes on the viewing audience. (Photos courtesy of Jessica Goodall/www.jessicag.tv)

FIGURE 14.7
The costume shop at a production facility.

Be sensitive to the talent's feelings and taste when suggesting changes, particularly when you want them to wear an item from stock (such as an off-white shirt, or a different necktie) to replace their own. Experienced talent may bring along alternative garments for selection on-camera.

A costume that looks attractive in a long shot (full-length) may be less successful when seen as a medium shot (head and shoulders) behind an anchor's desk. Color matching that looks good to the eye can reproduce quite differently under various lights. Some shades of color may look great in the long shot and terrible in the close-up. See Table 14.1.

Costumes are not always available that fit what the director wants. The baseball costumes shown in Figure 13.30 had to be created in order to fit the time period.

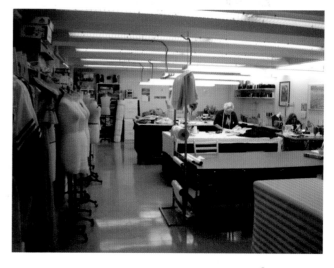

233

FIGURE 14.8
A costume department creates the costumes needed in productions.

Table 14.1	Costume Problems
White shirts, blouses, and so on	White shirts can be so bright that they lose all detail when the camera has to adjust the iris to obtain detail in the talent's face.
Glossy materials, such as satin	High sheen, especially from shoulders, may become too white or even reflect incident light.
Light tones	These emphasize size, but if loosely cut, light garments can appear formless.
Dark tones	These minimize size, but all detail is easily lost in reproduction, particularly with dark velvets.
Strong, vibrant colors	Usually appear over-saturated and can reflect onto the neck and chin.

(continued)

Table 14.1	Costume Problems (*continued*)
Fine stripes, checks, or herringbone patterns on clothing	Patterns can "vibrate," causing a localized flicker. Color detail is liable to be unsharp and lost in longer shots.
Shiny, sequined, or metallic finishes	Incredibly bright highlights can distract the viewers and can reflect onto the face or nearby surfaces.
Noisy jewelry or decorations such as multistring beads	Microphones can pick up extraneous clinks, rattles, or rustles.
Rhinestones and other highly reflective jewelry	Reflects bright spots of light onto chin, neck, and/or face and flashes obtrusively.
Very low necklines	In close shots, can create a topless look.

REVIEW QUESTIONS

1. What is the difference between straight makeup and corrective makeup?
2. How is character makeup used in television production?
3. How is makeup for HDTV different from SDTV?
4. How can costumes be obtained for a character in a television production?

PART 5

Recording and Editing the Production

Audio for Television

"I am not able to tell the story with my music, but I can make the story you are telling more emotional."

Jerry Goldsmith, Oscar-winning composer

Terms

Acoustics: High-frequency sound waves travel in straight paths and are easily deflected and reflected by hard surfaces. They are also easily absorbed by porous fibrous materials. Lower-frequency sound waves (below 100 Hz) spread widely, so they are not impeded by obstacles and are less readily absorbed. As sound waves meet nearby materials, they are selectively absorbed and reflected; the reflected sound's quality is modified according to the surfaces' nature, structures, and shapes.

Audio mixer: The audio mixer is needed whenever there are a number of sound sources to select, blend together, and control (such as microphones, CD, VCR audio output, etc.). The output of this unit is fed to the recorder.

Audio sweetening: The process of working on the program sound after the video portion is completed; also known as a *dubbing session* or *track laying*.

Condenser microphone: This microphone produces very high audio quality and is ideal for musical pickup. A significant advantage to the condenser is that it can be very small, making it the logical choice for a shotgun, lavalier mic, and other miniature microphones.

Directional microphone: The directional (or cardioid) mic pickup pattern. This broad heart-shaped pickup pattern is insensitive on its rear side.

Dynamic microphone: Dynamic microphones are the most rugged, provide good quality sound, and are not easily distorted by loud sounds such as nearby drums.

Dynamic range: The range between the weakest and loudest sounds that can be effectively recorded by a recording device.

Foley: Creating sounds in a studio that can replace the original sounds.

Line level: The audio signal generated by a nonmicrophone device, such as a CD player.

Mic level: The audio level of a signal that is generated by a microphone.

Monaural sound: Also known as *mono*, this single track of audio is limited, because its only clue to distance is loudness, and direction cannot be conveyed at all.

237

Omnidirectional microphone: The omnidirectional pickup pattern is equally sensitive in all directions and cannot distinguish between direct and reflected sounds.

Perambulator: A large microphone boom on wheels.

Super-cardioid microphone: A super-cardioid (or highly directional) pickup pattern is used wherever you want extremely selective pickup, to avoid environmental noises, or for distance sources.

Stereo sound: Two audio tracks create an illusion of space and dimension. Stereo gives the viewer a limited ability to localize the direction of the sound.

Surround sound: Can provide a sense of envelopment when mixed correctly. Instead of the one channel for mono or the two channels for stereo, 5.1 surround has six discrete (distinct, individual) channels.

Wild track: General background noise.

Historically, audio has been slighted in the world of television. Most manufacturers and producers cared more about the image, relegating audio to an inexpensive, poor-sounding little speaker on televisions. However, if you really want to find out how important audio is, just turn off the audio on a video and try to follow the story. You will soon get lost. Look away from the screen, with the audio turned up, and you can still follow the story. Audio is as important to television as the video image. Audio gives images a convincing realism. It helps the audience feel involved in what they are seeing. Dennis Baxter, sound designer for the Olympics, believes that "audio, in partnership with video, delivers a holistic experience with all of the intense emotion and interesting nuances to the viewer."

The valuable contribution that sound makes to television cannot be underestimated. In a good production, sound is never just a casual afterthought. It is an essential part of its appeal.

People often think of television as "pictures accompanied by sound." Yet, when the best television productions are analyzed, people are usually surprised that most of the time it is the sound that is conveying the information and stimulating the audience's imagination, while the image itself may be the accompaniment. Audio has the power to help the audience conjure mental images that enhance what is being seen.

Sounds are very evocative. For example, consider an image of a couple of people leaning against a wall, shown with the open sky as a background. If noises of waves breaking and the shrill cries of birds are heard, we quickly assume that they are near the seashore. Add the sound of children at play, and now we are sure that our subjects are near the beach. Replace all those sounds with the noise of a battle, explosions, and passing tanks, and they are immediately transported to a war situation. They might even appear particularly brave and unfazed as they remain so calm in the middle of this tumult.

In fact, all we really have here is a shot of two people leaning on a wall. The wall itself might have been anywhere—up a mountain, in a desert, or in a studio. The location and the mood of the occasion have been conjured up by the sound and our imagination.

Successful audio is a blend of two things:

- Appropriate *techniques*—the way the equipment is used to capture the audio.
- Appropriate *artistic choices*—how the sounds are selected and mixed.

Both are largely a matter of technical know-how, combined with experience.

"Music cues are the unseen actors in the scene. Music's goal is still the same, to move the story along."
Marc Fantini and Matt Hurwitz

THE AUDIO SYSTEM

The *dynamic range* (volume range) that any audio system can handle is limited. When too loud, sounds will cause overload distortion, producing a deteriorated sound signal. If too quiet, wanted sounds will become merged with background noise of comparable level (volume), such as tape noise, hum, and ventilation. So to avoid exceeding these limits, it is essential that you do not overload the microphone itself (too near a loud source), or over-amplify the signal (overmodulation). Conversely, you must prevent the audio signal from becoming too weak (undermodulation) by placing the microphone close enough and using sufficient amplification. But at the same time, as you will see later, you must not destroy an impression of the dynamics of the original sound source.

ACOUSTICS

You have only to compare sound in an empty room with the difference when that same room is furnished or filled with people to realize how acoustics alter sound quality. If the basics of acoustics are understood, many of the audio problems can be avoided during the production.

A certain amount of reverberation enriches and strengthens sounds, conveying an impression of vitality and spaciousness. Therefore, most television and audio studios have quite carefully chosen the acoustics so that they are neither too live or too dead.

In practice, you will find that the amount of sound absorption or reflection within an environment can change considerably as the conditions alter. Sound quality may be dampened (dull) or brightened (well defined) as furnishings are added or removed. The difference in a theater's acoustics with and without an audience can be quite remarkable. Moving a large scenic flat can alter local sound quality, making it harsh, hollow, or boxy—particularly if there is an extensive ceiling to the setting.

When a sound wave hits a hard surface (plastic, glass, tile, stone walls, metal), little is absorbed, so the reflected sound is almost as loud as the original. In fact, when its higher frequencies have actually been reinforced by this reflection, the sound bouncing off the surface can actually sound brighter and sharper.

When a sound wave hits a soft surface (curtains, couches, rugs), some of its energy is absorbed within the material. Higher notes are the most absorbed, so the sound reflected from this sort of surface is not only quieter than the original sound wave, but lacks the higher frequencies. Its quality is more mellow, less resonant—even dull and muted. Certain soft materials absorb the sound so well that virtually none is reflected (Figure 15.1).

Where there are a lot of hard surfaces around (as in a bathroom, a large hall, or a church), a place can become extremely reverberant, or *live*. Sound waves rebound from one surface to another so easily that the original and the reflected versions completely inter-mixed are heard. This can cause considerable changes in the overall sound quality and significantly degrade its clarity.

When surroundings are very reverberant, reflections are often heard seconds after the sound itself has stopped—in extreme cases, as a repeated echo. Whether reverberations add richness to the original sound or simply confuse is determined by the design of the space, the position of the sound source, the pitch and quality of the sound, and the position of the mic.

FIGURE 15.1

The variety of angles of the set walls, curtains, carpet, furniture, and people help dampen the live sound … but be careful that it is not dampened too much.

DEALING WITH ACOUSTICS

When surroundings are too live, to reduce acoustic reflections:

- Move the microphone closer to the sound source
- Pull curtains if available
- Add thick rugs
- Add cushions
- Use upholstered furniture
- Drape blankets on frames or over chairs
- Add acoustic panels (Figure 15.2)

When surroundings are too dead, to increase acoustic reflections:

- Move the microphone further away
- Open curtains to increase hard surface space
- Remove rugs
- Remove cushions
- Remove upholstered furniture
- Add board or plastic surfaced panels
- Add floor panels (wood, fiberboard)
- Add artificial reverberation

FIGURE 15.2
Acoustic panels were placed on the walls of this audio room in order to reduce the "liveness" of the room.

240

If, on the other hand, the sound is made in a place with many absorbent surfaces, both the original sound and any reflections can be significantly muffled. Under these *dead* conditions, the direct sound can be heard with few reflections from the surroundings. Even a loud noise such as a handclap or a gunshot will not carry very far and dies away quickly. When outside, in an open area, sound can be very dead. This is due to the air quickly absorbing the sound, as there are few reflecting surfaces (Figure 15.3).

We all know how dead sound seems when outside in the open. Open-air sound is very weak and does not travel far, because the air quickly absorbs it and there are few reflecting surfaces. Microphones often have to get much closer to a subject than normal to pick up sufficient sound, especially if a person is speaking quietly.

Open-air sound has a characteristic quality that can be immediately recognized; it has an absence of reflected sounds, combined with a lack of top and bass. This effect can be very difficult to imitate convincingly in the studio, even when the subject is completely surrounded with highly absorbent acoustic panels.

FIGURE 15.3
During the shooting of a dramatic program, the boom operator got the microphone as close as possible, while still being off-camera, because open-air sound does not usually travel far.

Acoustics often influence where the microphone is positioned. To avoid unwanted reflections in live surroundings, the mic needs to be placed relatively close to the subject. If working in dead surroundings, a close mic is necessary, because the sound does not carry well. When the surroundings are noisy, a close mic helps the voice (or other sound) to be heard clearly above the unwanted sounds.

However, there can be problems if a mic is placed too close to the source. Sound quality is generally coarsened and the bass can be over-emphasized. The audience can become very aware of the noise of breathing; sibilants (the letter S); blasting from explosive letters P, B, and T; and even clicks from the subject's teeth striking together. Placed close to an instrument, a mic can reveal various mechanical noises such as key clicks, bow scrapes, and so on.

ROOM ACOUSTICS

Live Surroundings

When a room contains predominantly hard surfaces, the sound is strongly reflected. Many of these reflections are picked up by the microphone, reinforcing and coloring the direct sound pickup.

Dead Surroundings

When surfaces in a room are very sound-absorbent, the direct sound waves strike walls, floor, ceiling, and furnishings and are largely lost. Only a few weak reflections may be picked up by the microphone.

MONO SOUND

In everyday life, the audience is used to listening with two ears. As their brains compare these two separate sound images of the external world, they build a three-dimensional impression from which the direction and distance of sound is estimated (see the next section).

Nonstereo television sound is not as sophisticated as this. It presents a *monaural* (*mono*) representation of sound in space. The only clue to distance is loudness; direction cannot be conveyed at all. Listening to mono reproduction, we are not able to distinguish between direct and reflected sounds, as we can when listening in stereo. Instead, they become intermixed, so that the sound is often "muddy" and less distinct. In mono sound, we become much more aware of the effects of reverberation.

Because the audience cannot easily distinguish direction and distance, the mono microphone needs to be carefully positioned. Audio personnel need to be careful that:

- Too many sound reflections are not picked up.
- Louder sounds do not mask quieter sounds (particularly in an orchestra).
- Extraneous sounds do not interfere with the ones we want to hear.

STEREO SOUND

Stereo sound creates an illusion of space and dimension. It enhances clarity. Stereo gives the viewer the ability to localize the direction of the sound. This localization give the audience a sense of depth—a spatial awareness of the visual image and the sound. However, because the speakers in television receivers are quite close together, the effect can be somewhat limited. Sound quality and realism are enhanced, but our impressions of direction and depth are less obvious.

To simplify sound pickup, many practitioners mix central mono speech, with stereo effects and music. When a stereo microphone is used, care must be taken to maintain direction (such as mic left to camera left), and to hold the mic still; otherwise, the stereo image will move around. In a stereo system, reverberation even appears more pronounced and extraneous noises such as wind, ventilation, and footsteps are more prominent, because they have direction, rather than merging with the overall background.

SURROUND SOUND

Surround sound can provide a sense of envelopment when mixed correctly. Instead of the one channel for mono or the two channels for stereo, 5.1 surround has six discrete (distinct, individual) channels: left front and right front (sometimes called stereo left and

First Surround Sound
Disney introduced surround sound to the cinemas with the movie *Fantasia,* in 1940. Three channels were used behind the theater screen with three additional speakers used on either side and at the rear. However, implementing this system was extremely expensive and the system was only used in two theaters.

241

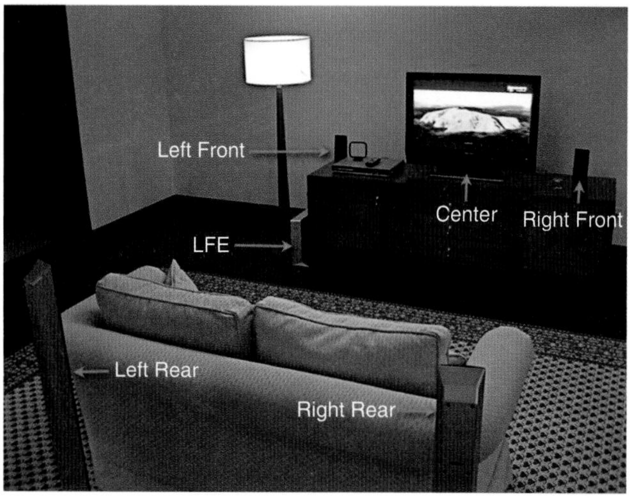

FIGURE 15.4
A home surround-sound setup.

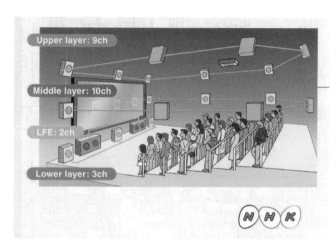

FIGURE 15.5
The NHK network in Japan has designed a 22.2 surround-sound system aimed primarily at theaters. (Illustration courtesy of NHK)

right), center, a subwoofer for low-frequency effects (LFEs), and left rear and right rear speakers (sometimes called surround left and right). The feeling of depth, direction, and realism is obtained by the audio personnel panning between the five main channels and routing effects to the LFE channel (Figure 15.4).

Although 5.1 surround sound is currently the most popular type of surround, it is not the only type available. There are currently 6.1 and 7.1 surround systems and Japan's NHK is currently marketing a 22.2 surround-sound system for theaters (Figure 15.5).

MICROPHONE CHARACTERISTICS

The microphone characteristics and aspects that are most important to you will depend largely on the type of sound pickup involved and operating conditions. For example, ruggedness may be at the expense of fidelity. The main things that you need to know about microphones are:

Physical features. Although size may be unimportant for some situations, it can matter where the microphone is to appear in the shot or to be held by the talent. Appearance also counts. Ruggedness is a consideration where rough or inexperienced usage is likely. Handling noise can also be a distraction for some sensitive microphones. Stability and reliability are features that only time and experience reveal, and most high-grade microphones can be relied on if properly cared for (see the following section on microphone care).

Audio quality. Ideally, a microphone should cover the entire audio spectrum evenly. Its transient response to brief sharp sounds should be impeccable. Audio should be accurately reproduced without coloration or distortion. Fortunately, such parameters are less critical in many situations.

Sensitivity and directionality. A microphone's sensitivity determines how large an audio signal it produces for a given sound volume, although audio amplifiers can compensate for even the least-sensitive microphones. However, excessive amplification can add hiss and hum to the audio signal. All microphones normally have to work closer to quiet sounds than louder ones, but less-sensitive microphones must be positioned even closer. However, they are less liable to be overloaded or damaged by loud sounds, so that in certain applications (percussion) they may be preferable. A sound-boom microphone needs to be pretty sensitive—otherwise, it would have to be placed too close to sources, which may cast shadows or be seen in the shot.

The directional properties of the microphone are determined by its sensitivity pattern in space. Sometimes you will need an omnidirectional response (explained shortly) that picks up sounds equally well in all directions. Other times you will require a very directional response that is able to pick out a selected sound source and ignore or suppress others nearby. Certain microphones even have adjustable directionality.

Choice of microphone/installation suitability. All audio personnel have prejudices about the right microphone for the job and exactly where to place it; no two situations are identical. Listening to a piano performance, we find that the instrument's tone varies considerably with its manufacturer, tuning, and performer and even with temperature, humidity, and acoustics. Although most audio personnel would agree to use a condenser or ribbon microphone, its positioning is influenced by many subtle factors.

On-the-Job Repairs
Audio cables are pulled and walked over so much that they are often the weak link in the audio system. That means that audio personnel must make occasional repairs on microphones. These repairs could mean resoldering cables to the connectors and repairing cables that get severed.

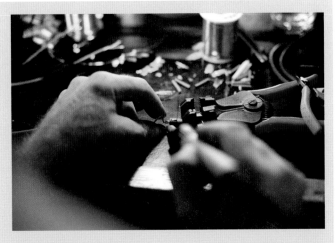

FIGURE 15.6
Repairing cables usually means using wire cutters, a knife, a soldering iron, and possibly a vise grip of some type.

243

Microphone Care

Though most people regard the video camera with a certain apprehension, there are those who tend to dismiss the microphone (or mic) all too casually. They clip it onto a guest's jacket with an air of "that's all we have to do for audio," instead of treating the mic as a delicate tool. The microphone and how it is used is really at the heart of television program sound. If the microphone is inferior, if it is damaged, if it is poorly positioned—the program sound will suffer. No amount of postproduction work with the audio can compensate for doing it right from the beginning. *Program sound all begins with the microphone.*

It is not important to know how various types of microphones work to use them properly. They all convert sound waves in the air into a fluctuating electrical voltage (the audio signal). It does help, though, to be aware of their different characteristics.

Although most microphones are reasonably robust, they do need careful handling if they are to remain reliable and perform up to specification. It is asking for trouble to drop them, knock them, or get liquid on them.

Directional Features of Microphones

Microphones do not all behave in the same way. Some are designed to be *omnidirectional*—they can hear equally well in all directions. Others are *directional* (also known as *cardioid*)—they can hear sounds directly in front of them clearly, but are comparatively deaf to sounds in all other directions.

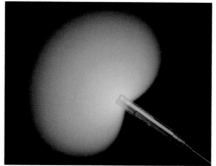

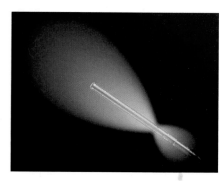

FIGURE 15.7
The omnidirectional pickup pattern is equally sensitive in all directions, generally rugged, and not too susceptible to impact shock. This mic cannot distinguish between direct and reflected sounds, so it must be placed close to the sound source. (Image courtesy of Sennheiser)

FIGURE 15.8
The directional (or cardioid) mic pickup pattern. This broad, heart-shaped pickup pattern (roughly 160 degrees) is insensitive on its rear side. (Image courtesy of Sennheiser)

FIGURE 15.9
A super-cardioid (or highly directional) pickup pattern is used wherever you want extremely selective pickup, to avoid environmental noises, or for distance sources. (Image courtesy of Sennheiser)

244

The advantage of an *omnidirectional* mic (Figure 15.7) is that it can pick up sound equally well over a wide area. It is great when covering a group of people, or someone who is moving around. The disadvantage is that it cannot discriminate between the sound you want to hear and unwanted sounds such as reflections from walls, noises from nearby people or equipment, ventilation noise, footsteps, and so on. The more reverberant the surroundings, the worse the problem. The mic must be positioned so that it is closer to the wanted sounds than to the extraneous noises. This mic is great for picking up ambient or natural (NAT) sounds.

When a directional mic (Figure 15.8) is pointed at the desired sound, it will tend to ignore sounds from other directions, providing a much cleaner result. On the other hand, the directional mic needs to be aimed very carefully. It is also important to make sure that the audio source does not move out of the main pickup zone, otherwise the source will be "off-mic." The off-mic sound becomes weaker, will probably include high-note losses, and may cause the audience to hear what it is being pointed at, instead of the desired source.

There are several different forms of unidirectional pickup patterns. The *cardioid* (see Figure 15.8) or heart-shaped pattern is broad enough for general use, but not overly selective, and the *super-* or *hyper-cardioid* (Figure 15.9) response also has a limited pickup area at its rear to receive reflected sounds.

Microphone Pickup Methods

There are two predominant methods for converting sound energy to an electrical-equivalent signal: electrodynamic and electrostatic, better known, respectively, as *dynamic* and *condenser*.

Dynamic microphones are the most rugged, provide good-quality sound, and are not easily distorted by loud sounds such as nearby drums. These mics need little or no regular maintenance. They can be handheld without causing unwanted "handling noise" and used in all types of microphone mountings. These mics generally cannot be as small as a condenser mic and some are not of as high quality. However, they can be just as high quality as the condenser microphone.

The *condenser* microphone produces very high audio quality and is ideal for musical pickup. A significant advantage to the condenser is that it can be very small, making it the logical choice for a shotgun, lavalier mic, and other miniature microphones. The condenser mic is generally powered by an inboard battery, phantom-powered (power sent from the mixer) audio board, or a special power supply. The electret condenser microphone has a permanent charge applied when it is manufactured, which remains for the life of the microphone and does not need to be externally powered.

TYPES OF MICROPHONES

In most television production situations, any number of a variety of microphones can be used to record the audio. One audio person may select one type of mic and another may choose a radically different mic. Each person is looking for the best mic that will provide the sound that they are looking for. The following microphones are just some of the audio tools that are available. As the audio plan is created, the mic that is right for you must be chosen.

Camera Microphones

If the camera is fitted with a microphone, the theory is that when it is aimed at the subject to capture the video, the mic will also pick up quality audio. However, a lot depends on the situation and the type of sound involved. Nothing beats a separate, high-quality microphone placed in exactly the right place. However, single-camera operators, working by themselves and moving around to various shooting positions, may have to use the camera microphone.

The simplest form of camera microphone is a small built-in mic at the front of the camera. These mics are known to pick up sound from all around the camera, including noise from the camera zoom lens and camera operator sounds. With care, though, this basic microphone is useful for general atmospheric background sounds (traffic, crowds), and is almost good enough for close-up voice. However, it should be used for voice only when better options are unavailable. With most camera mics, trying to pick up a voice more than 4–6 feet away will result in unacceptably high levels of background noise and/or acoustical reflections.

The most popular type of camera microphone is the *shotgun mic*, attached to the top of the camera (Figure 15.10). Plugged into the camera's external mic socket, this mic will give the best-quality long-distance pickup from the subject. As always with directional mics, these must be aimed accurately.

A camera microphone provides the simplest method of picking up program sound:

- The microphone is on the camera and doesn't require a second person to look after the audio.
- Wherever the camera points, the microphone will follow.
- There are no problems with microphone boom shadows.

However, the camera microphone has a number of drawbacks, too:

- Built-in camera microphones seldom provide high-quality sound.
- The microphone is often too far away from the subject for the best sound. Its position is determined by the camera's shot, not by the optimum place for the microphone.
- The microphone's distance is the same for all shots. The camera may zoom in to a close-up shot or take a wide-angle shot, but the sound level remains the same.
- Where there are strong sound reflections from nearby walls, or loud background noises, the microphone really needs to be placed closer to the subject. However, if

FIGURE 15.10
Shotgun mics are the most popular type of camera microphones.

245

the camera is moved nearer to achieve this, the subject may now appear much too close in the video image. Then the only remedy is to widen the lens angle to reduce its apparent size. But close-up shots with a close wide lens angle noticeably distort people and exaggerate space.

- The camera microphone cannot follow somebody if he or she turns away from a frontal position, such as to point to a nearby wall map. The sound's volume and quality will fall off as they move off-mic.

Handheld Microphone

The *handheld mic* (or *stick mic*) is a familiar sight on television, used by interviewers, singers, and commentators. It is a very simple, convenient method of sound pickup, provided that it is used properly. Otherwise, results can be erratic. The handheld mic is best held just below shoulder height, pointed slightly toward the person speaking. Make it as unobtrusive as possible (Figure 15.11).

To reduce the low rumbling noises of wind on the microphone and explosive breath-pops when it is held too close to the mouth, it is advisable to attach a foam windshield to the microphone. Note the yellow foam windshield in the interview photo in Figure 15.11. Whenever possible, talk across the microphone rather than directly into it. This will provide the optimal audio quality.

Some people attempt to hold the mic around waist height to prevent it from being visible in the picture, however, this generally results in weak pickup, poor quality, and more intrusive background noise.

Handheld microphones with cardioid patterns help reduce the amount of extraneous sound overheard, so it can be used about 1–1.5 feet (0.30 m–0.45 m) from the person speaking. If an omnidirectional handheld mic is used, it should normally be held much closer—around 9 inches (22 cm).

When the talent is walking around with a handheld mic, make sure that he or she has plenty of mic cable (or better yet, a wireless mic). The talent should be able to move around easily without the cable limiting movement, as you are making sure that others don't step on it and that no one trips on the cable. It is important to run the cable out of sight of the camera. Gaffer tape (or duct tape) can be used to tape the cable to the floor.

FIGURE 15.11

The handheld microphone is widely used for interviews, commentaries, and stage work. If the mic has a cardioid directional response, extraneous noise pickup is lower. If it is omnidirectional, the mic may need to be held closer to the subject to reduce atmosphere sounds. The mic is normally held just below shoulder height.

"Audio is 70 percent of the visual experience, yet often is relegated to a second thought in field production. This not only weakens the overall production, but also makes a strong statement about the professionalism of the overall production."

Douglas Spotted Eagle, Producer

Shotgun Microphone

The *shotgun microphone* (*hyper-cardioid*) consists of a slotted tube containing an electret microphone at one end. This microphone is designed to pick up sound within quite a narrow angle, while remaining much less sensitive to sounds from other directions. It is great at isolating a subject within a crowd or excluding nearby noises (Figure 15.12).

Unfortunately, the shotgun microphone is not good at maintaining these directional properties throughout the audio range. At lower frequencies, it loses its ability to discriminate. The narrow forward-pointing pickup pattern then becomes increasingly broader.

When shooting in very "live" (reverberant) surroundings, a shotgun microphone has advantages, as it will pick up the subject's sound successfully while reducing unwanted reflections, although how effectively it does so depends on the pitch or coloration of the reflected sounds.

The shotgun microphone is quite adaptable, and is regularly used as:

- A handheld microphone supported by some type of shock mount (see Figure 15.12).
- A mic connected to the end of a boom pole or fishpole (see Figures 15.14, 15.15, and 15.16).
- A mic in the swiveled cradle support of a regular sound boom or perambulator boom (see Figure 15.1).
- As a camera microphone, fitted to the top of the camera head (see Figure 15.10).

Most people working in the field fit a shotgun microphone with some type of a *windshield* (also called a *windjammer* or *wind muffler*). The most effective types at suppressing obtrusive wind noises are a furry overcoat with "hairs" or a plastic/fabric tube (Figure 15.13). An alternative design of the wind filter is a tubular plastic sponge (see Figure 15.12). Although much lighter, this design may prove rather inadequate except in the lightest breeze.

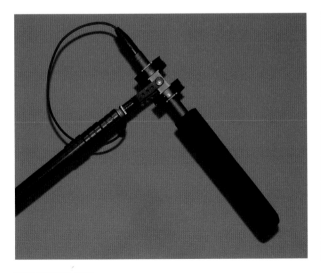 

FIGURE 15.12
Shotgun microphones are one of the most commonly used mics in television. They are very susceptible to handling noise and must be held or connected to a pole or stand with a shock mount.

FIGURE 15.13
Different types of windshields are used to protect a shotgun mic from wind noise.

FIGURE 15.14
A mic boom (or fishpole) is a regular method of mounting the shotgun microphone, particularly in the field. It allows the operator to stand several feet away from the subject, reaching over any foreground obstacles, and to place the microphone at an optimum angle. This position can be tiring if it has to be maintained for a long period of time. However, it may be the only solution when people are standing and/or walking about. (Photo by Dennis Baxter)

FIGURE 15.15
The shotgun microphone is not attached directly to the pole. Instead, a shock mount, such as the one shown here, must be used to prevent the rumbles of handling noise traveling along the pole and being picked up by the microphone. (Photo courtesy of Audio-Technica)

USING THE SHOTGUN MICROPHONE

Selecting the best position for shotgun microphones takes some advance planning. Audio personnel need a clear idea of how the action is going to develop. They may get this from a briefing beforehand or find it out from a camera rehearsal:

- Will the shotgun be used for long takes or for brief shots? It is one thing to stand in a fixed position for someone talking straight to the camera and another to have to follow action around as people and cameras move through a sequence.
- Will audio personnel have an uninterrupted view of the action?
- Is anyone or anything going to get in their way or are they going to get in anyone else's way?

Audio personnel should try to position themselves so that the action moves toward them, instead of away from them. Even talent moves across the action area and it can be embarrassing if the talent is walking away from the microphone. Whenever the mic boom holder or the talent moves around, it is easy for the talent to pass in and out of the microphone's main pickup area. If the talent turns away from the microphone, there is usually no way that the mic boom holder can compensate or move onto the sound axis.

THE SHOTGUN AND THE BOOM POLE (FISHPOLE)

The *boom pole* (or *fishpole*) has become the most popular choice for sound pickup on location and in many smaller studios. This adjustable lightweight aluminum pole is usually about 6–9 feet long, carrying a microphone at its far end. The sound cable is either designed inside the pole or is taped securely along the pole (Figures 15.14 and 15.15).

OPERATING THE FISHPOLE OR BOOM POLE

FIGURE 15.16
Until audio personnel get used to it, the boom pole can be a very unwieldy unbalanced instrument when fully extended, as the weight is all at its far end. There are many different ways that a boom pole can be held (also see Figure 15.3), such as:

- Above the head, with arms fully extended along the pole to balance it.
- Set across the shoulders for added stability, as shown here in the left figure.

The goal is to get the microphone close enough, without showing up at the bottom or top of the camera's shot.

Lavalier (Lapel or Clip-On) Microphone

The *lavalier* microphone, also known as a *lav, lapel, mini-mic,* or a *clip-on mic*, has become the favorite mic in productions where it is unimportant whether the viewer sees a mic attached to someone's clothing. These microphones are compact, unobtrusive, and provide high sound quality. But they do need to be used judiciously if they are to get optimum results. Clip the microphone to outside clothing (such as a tie, lapel, shirt, or blouse) so that noises from rubbing on clothing will be kept to a minimum. If lavalier mics are tucked beneath a heavy sweater or coat, understandably the sound becomes muffled and less distinct (Figure 15.17). The incredibly small lav mics, as shown in one of the photos in Figure 15.17, can also be used as an "earset" or "headworn" mic, as shown in Figure 15.18.

One of the challenges when using a lavalier mic is that the volume and clarity of the sound can change as a wearer turns their head left and right, or toward and away from the microphone.

A lavalier mic can be relied on to effectively pick up only the sound of the person wearing it. When two or three people are speaking, each will need to wear his or her own microphone. However, that does not mean that the mics won't pick up the sound from others—it just won't be the same quality and will not be the same level. When working in noisy surroundings, a small foam windshield over the end of the microphone will reduce the rumble of wind noise. Regular users will conceal the lavalier mic's cable beneath a jacket or shirt.

Lavalier microphones can also be used to record subjects other than people. They are used effectively in sports productions (mounted in places like the nets at a soccer field) and they can be used to pick up the sound of some musical instruments. The clip-on mic in Figure 15.19 is actually a type of lavalier mic.

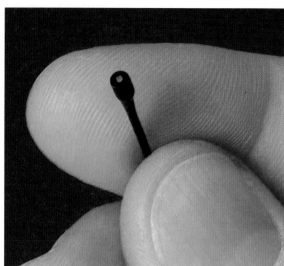

FIGURE 15.17
Lavalier microphones come in many different sizes and shapes. Generally, a lavalier mic is clipped to a necktie, lapel, or shirt. Sometimes a "dual redundancy" pair is used, whenever a standby mic is desired. (Photos courtesy of Audio-Technica and Countryman Associates)

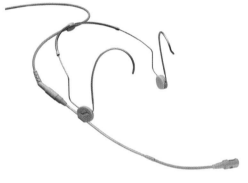

FIGURE 15.18
The talent is using an "earset" or "headworn" microphone that utilizes the lavalier microphone. It is mounted on a tiny mic "boom" and attached to the ear. It is available in a flesh color and is almost invisible to the viewing audience. In this situation, it was used by hosts of ESPN's *X Games*. (Photos courtesy of Dennis Baxter and Sennheiser)

250

FIGURE 15.19
These photos show a variation of lavalier microphones often used to record musical instruments or any other subject that requires close microphones. (Photo courtesy of Audio-Technica)

Boundary or PZM Microphone

The *boundary microphone* and *pressure zone microphone* (*PZM*) are low-profile mics that can be used to capture audio from talent that is 6 or more feet away without the "hollow" sound of a hanging handheld mic. Although the pickup technology is very different, these two mics are used similarly. These microphones are especially good for dramatic productions where microphones should not be seen (they can be attached to the back of set pieces). They are also good for stage performances of large groups. They can be hung from the ceiling, set on a floor, or attached to furniture. The pickup distance can be increased by mounting these mics on a hard surface (Figure 15.20).

Hanging Microphone

Hanging microphones are especially designed for high-quality sound reinforcement of dramatic productions, orchestras, and choirs. The mics are suspended over the performance area. Their small size is ideal since they will probably be visible to the viewing audience (Figure 15.21).

Surround-Sound Microphone

Surround-sound microphones can capture 5.1 to 7.1 channels of discrete (separate) audio with the multidirectional pickup pattern. Using the small microphone shown in Figure 15.22 the audio can be recorded directly on to the camera's internal media along with video images. The small microphone has five microphone elements (left, right, center, left side, right side) and a dedicated LFE (this counts as the ".1" in the channel count) microphone. The higher-end version is much larger and provides 7.1 surround sound. The smaller system, designed specifically for a camcorder, utilizes an internal Dolby® Pro Logic II–encoded line-level stereo output for connection directly to the camera on a single 3.5-mm stereo female miniplug jack. Some of the nonlinear editing systems, like Apple's Final Cut Pro, have a Dolby logic decoder built in, allowing the channels from the stereo input to be split into the five surround channels, which allows a user to record programs in surround sound without having a full-surround mixing board (Figures 15.22 and 15.23).

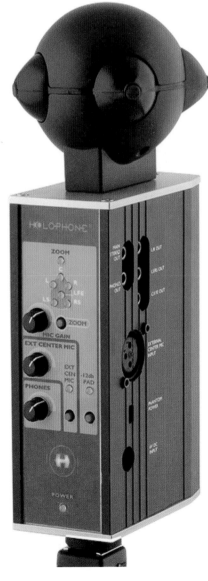

251

FIGURE 15.20
The boundary microphone is a low-profile mic that can pick up accurate sounds from six or more feet away.

FIGURE 15.21
Hanging microphone. (Photo courtesy of Audio-Technica)

FIGURE 15.22
This small surround-sound microphone includes a Dolby® Pro Logic II encoder with a line-level stereo output designed for stereo inputs on camcorders. (Photo courtesy of Holophone)

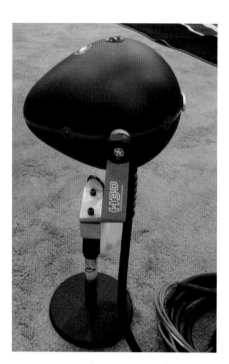

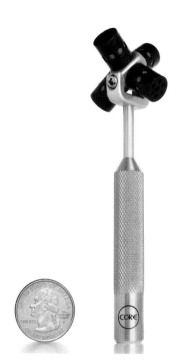

FIGURE 15.23
There are a variety of surround-sound microphones available. Audio personnel must select the one that best fits their specific situation. (Photos courtesy of Holophone and Core Sound)

252

FIGURE 15.24
ABC Television's *Extreme Home Makeover* uses a professional surround-sound microphone, separate from the camera, to capture the audio. (Photo courtesy of Holophone)

Surround-sound microphones must be positioned carefully. They should not just be mounted on top of a camera if the camera will be panning and tilting around quite a bit. Moving the microphone around with the camera can really spatially disorient the audience. Generally these microphones are mounted on a separate stand or clamped to something stationary in order to pick up a quality ambient sound (Figure 15.24).

Suggestions for Using a Surround-Sound Microphone

- Use the surround mic to provide the "base" ambient surround sound for the audio mix.
- For a concert situation with arena-style seating, the sound mic should be placed a little higher than the orchestra, tilting the nose down toward the performers.
- When panning and tilting, mount the mic on a stationary stand.
- In most situations, try to position the surround mic as close to "front row center" as possible, rather than near the back of the room.
- When shooting sports events, it is best to place the surround mic either near the center of the field or near a main camera position. Always keep in mind the perspective of the television viewer. Mounting the surround mic on a side of a field or rink opposite to the main camera angle would seem backwards and unnatural.
- For surround recording of acoustic instruments, including drum kits, pianos, and voice at close range, try placing the mic near or above the instrument that is being recorded. For vocal or choirs, position the singers around the mic and monitor in surround to hear the results.

MICROPHONE STANDS AND MOUNTS

Microphone stands and mics are very useful in situations where the director does not mind the microphone possibly being seen in the shot. It is especially useful for stage announcements, singing groups, and for miking musical instruments. It does have some disadvantages.

If people move around much, they can easily walk out of the mic's range. Directors have to rely on the talent to get to the right place and keep the right distance from the mic. It is a good idea to give talent taped marks on the floor to guide them. And, of course, there is always the danger that he or she will kick the stand or trip over the cable (Figures 15.25 and 15.26).

Wireless Microphones

The most commonly used wireless microphones (or radio microphones) are the lavalier mic and the handheld mics. Both of these types of mics can be purchased with the wireless trans-

mitter built into the mic (or belt pack) and include a matching receiver. Lavalier mics are very popular because they allow the talent to have generally unrestricted movement while moving around the location. They are used in the studio with interview shows, on referees to hear their calls, and hidden on actors to catch their words (Figures 15.27, 15.28, and 15.29).

Wireless microphones generally work on a radio frequency (RF) and many are frequency-programmable, allowing the audio personnel to select the best frequency for a specific location. Care must be taken to make sure that legal frequencies are being used.

There can be a number of challenges when working with wireless microphones:

- These mics work off of batteries. The battery life is roughly 4–6 hours. When working in freezing temperatures, battery life is usually cut in half. New batteries should be placed in the mic before each new session. Do not leave it to chance, assuming that there is enough capacity left from the last time (Figure 15.30).

FIGURE 15.25
An audio person adjusts a microphone stand for an on-location interview project.

FIGURE 15.26
There are many different types of microphone stands and mounts, from bottom-weighted telescopic stands to small versions with thin flexible or curved tubing intended for lavalier or miniature mics. (Photos by Paul Dupree and Dennis Baxter)

FIGURE 15.27
A wireless (radio) belt pack transmitter and receiver. A lavalier microphone can be plugged into the transmitter. (Photo courtesy of Audio-Technica)

FIGURE 15.28
Wireless receivers can be located on a camera. In this situation, the interviewer is using a handheld wireless. (Photo courtesy of Sennheiser)

FIGURE 15.29
Any type of microphone can become a wireless microphone if some type of wireless plug-on transmitter is used. This transmitter converts a dynamic or condenser microphone to wireless, transmitting the signal back to a receiver. (Photo courtesy of Audio-Technica)

FIGURE 15.30
It is important to ensure that the batteries in the transmitter, and possibly the receiver, are at full capacity at the beginning of a program. The transmitters are usually clipped to the back of the talent. (Photo courtesy of Sennheiser)

- If two or more wireless microphones are being used in an area, it is advisable to set them to different RF channels to avoid interference.
- When working near large metal structures, there can be difficulties with RF dead spots, fading, distortion, or interference. Diversity of reception—using multiple antennas—has improved this situation, but it is still cause for some concern.

Hidden Mics

When other methods of sound pickup are difficult, a hidden microphone may be the best solution to the problem. Mics can be concealed among a bunch of flowers on a table, behind props, in a piece of furniture, and so on.

However, hidden mics do have limitations. Although the mic can be hidden, the cable must not be seen and/or the transmitter must be out of sight. Sound quality may also be affected by nearby reflecting or absorbing surfaces. Because the microphone covers a fixed localized area, the talent has to be relied on to play to the mic and not speak off-mic.

CONTROLLING DYNAMICS

Dynamic Range

Everyday sounds can cover a considerable volume range. Fortunately, our ears are able to readjust to an astonishing extent to cope with these variations. But audio systems do not have this ability. If audio signals are larger than the system can accept, they will overload it and become badly distorted. If, on the other hand, sounds are too weak, they get lost in general background noise. In order to reproduce audio clearly, with fidelity, it must be kept within the system's limits.

A lot of sounds pose no problems at all. They don't get particularly soft or loud; that is, they do not have a wide dynamic range. When recording sounds of this type, there is little need to alter the gain (amplification) of the system once it has been set to an appropriate "average" position.

It can be very difficult to capture the wide audio range of audio between a whisper to an ear-shattering blast. Because the blast will exceed the system's handling capacity, the audio person must compensate in some way. The most obvious thing to do is to turn down the system's audio gain so that the loud parts never reach the upper limit. But then the quiet passages may be so faint that they are inaudible. So somehow or other, most of the time, the audio levels need to be controlled.

Automatic Control for Audio

Cameras generally allow the operator to set the camera's audio manually or automatically. To avoid loud sounds overloading the audio system and causing distortion, most audio and video recording equipment includes automatic gain control. When the sound signal exceeds a certain level, the auto gain control automatically reduces the audio input.

A completely automatic gain system amplifies all incoming sounds to a specific preset level. It "irons out" sound dynamics by preventing over- or under-amplification. Quiet sounds are increased in volume and loud sounds are held back. There are no adjustments to make and the camera operator must accept the results.

This can be an effective way of coping with occasional over-loud noises, but if the sounds happen to be so loud that they are continually "hitting the limiter," the results can be very distracting from an unpleasant strangled effect as sound peaks are "pulled back" to moments when quiet background sounds are over-amplified and surge in persistently whenever there is a pause.

Some auto gain systems do have manual adjustments. The idea is to ensure that the gain control is set high enough to amplify the quietest passages without running into over-amplification of the loudest sounds. The auto gain control circuitry limits sound peaks only as an occasional safety measure, and depends on the gain adjustment.

Manual Control

The other method of controlling the audio level is to continuously monitor the program while watching an audio level meter (Figure 15.31). The audio person is responsible for read-justing the audio system's gain (amplification) whenever necessary to obtain a quality audio signal. That does not mean that the dynamics should be "ironed" out by making all the quiet sections loud, and holding back all the loud passages. "Riding the gain" in this way can ruin the sound of the program. Instead, when sounds are going to be weak, anticipate by gradually increasing the gain, and conversely, slowly move the gain back before loud passages. Then the listeners will be unaware that changes are being made to accommodate the audio system's limitations.

FIGURE 15.31
It is the audio person's responsibility to readjust the audio system's gain (amplification) whenever necessary to obtain a quality audio signal. (Photo courtesy of Sennheiser)

How quiet the softest sound is allowed to be will depend on the purpose of the program. If, for example, the recording will be used in noisy surroundings, or shown in the open air, it may be best to keep the gain up to prevent the quietest sounds from falling below −15 or −20 dB. If a piano performance is being shot to be heard indoors, take care not to over-control the music's dynamics, and use the system's full volume range.

Unlike automatic control circuits, audio personnel are able to anticipate and make artistic judgments, which can make the final audio far superior than it would be otherwise. The draw-back to manual control is that the audio personnel need to be vigilant all the time, ready to

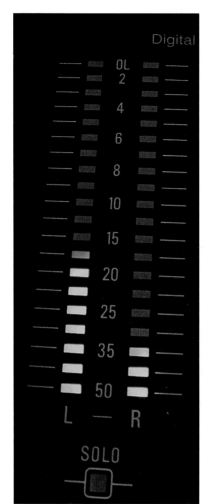

FIGURE 15.32
VU meters and bar graphs are used to monitor the audio signal.

make any necessary readjustments. If they are not careful, the resulting audio may be less satisfactory than the auto circuits would have produced.

There are several types of volume indicators, but the commonest on video equipment take the form of visual displays using bar graphs or some type of VU meter (explained shortly).

A bar graph (Figure 15.32) has a strip made up of tiny segments. This varies in length with the audio signal's strength. Calibrations vary, but it might have a decibel scale from −50 to +10 dB, with an upper working limit of about +2 dB. Adjust the audio gain control so that the sound peaks reach this upper mark. Twin bar graphs are used to monitor the left and right channels. The sound generally distorts if the audio signal goes into the red area of the bar graph.

The VU meter (Figure 15.32) is a widely used volume indicator. It has two scales: a "volume unit" scale marked in decibels, and another showing "percentage modulation." Although accurate for steady tones, the VU meter gives deceptively low readings for brief loud sounds or transients such as percussion. The VU meter can accidentally let the system overload.

The maximum signal coincides with 100% modulation at 0 dB. Above that, in the red area, sounds will distort, although occasional peaks are acceptable. The normal range used is −20 to 0 dB, typically peaking between −2 to 0 dB.

In summary, if the camera operator needs the audio system to look after itself, because he or she is preoccupied with shooting the scene, or is coping with very unpredictable sounds, then the automatic gain control has its merits—it will prevent loud sounds from overloading the system. However, if an assistant is available who can monitor the sound as it is being recorded, and adjust the gain for optimum results, then this has significant artistic advantages.

There are special electronic devices called "limiters" or "compressors" that automatically adjust the dynamic range of the audio signal, but these are found only in more sophisticated systems.

Monitoring the Audio

Monitoring sound for a video program involves:

- *Watching*: checking the volume indicator and watching a video monitor to make sure that the microphone does not pop into the shot inadvertently.
- *Listening*: checking sound quality and balance on high-grade earphones or a loud-speaker to detect any unwanted background noises.

Ideally, the audio level can be adjusted during a rehearsal. However, if a performance is going to be recorded without a rehearsal, such as in an interview, ask the talent to speak a few lines so that the audio level can be accurately adjusted. It is best if the talent can chat with the host in a normal voice for a few minutes or he or she can read from a script or book long enough to adjust the level. Do not have him or her count or say "Test." Both of these can give inaccurate readings, as they do not necessarily reflect normal speaking levels.

It is important to monitor the sound also to get an impression of the dynamic range while watching the volume level. If the results are not satisfactory, the talent may need to be asked to speak a little louder or more quietly, or to reposition the mic.

When shooting a program alone, it is a little more complicated to control the audio manually. Most professional cameras include an audio meter in the eyepiece of the camera, which allows the camera operator to monitor the audio signal. In recent years, camera manufacturers have improved the ability for camera operators to adjust the audio on-the-fly. Usually, if the level is set in advance, it is not difficult to capture good audio levels. However, in difficult situations, the automatic gain control can be used. It is also essential to monitor the audio with an earpiece or the small built-in speaker on the side of some cameras.

The Audio Mixer

An *audio mixer* is needed whenever there are a number of sound sources to select, blend together, and control (such as a couple of microphones, CD, VCR audio output, and so on). The output of this unit is fed to the recorder (Figures 15.33 and 15.34).

On the front panel of the audio mixer are a series of knobs or sliders. Each of these "pots" (*potentiometers*) or faders (Figure 15.35) can adjust its channel's volume from full audio to fade-out (silence). In some designs, the channel can be switched on or off on cue with a "mute" button.

When sources are plugged into the patch panel (connector strip) at the rear of the switcher, the audio person can select the appropriate channel. Some mixers also include channel selector switches that allow the channel to be reselected by utilizing a pot (such as mic-1 or mic-2).

On a large audio mixing panel, there may be group faders (group masters, submasters). Each of these group faders controls the combined outputs of several channels, and it may have its

FIGURE 15.33
The portable audio mixer is used in the field to mix up to three mics; the overall output is controlled by a master fader. A VU meter provides the volume indicator. Some mixers include a limiter to prevent audio overload. (Photo courtesy of Shure Incorporated)

FIGURE 15.34
Some field mixers include a hard drive that can store the audio program directly on the mixer.

FIGURE 15.35
Faders (potentiometers) on a large audio mixer.

FIGURE 15.36
A large surround-sound audio mixer for television productions.

FIGURE 15.37
Some television audio mixers prefer to mix live events, such as a concert, awards show, or similar performance, from inside the performance hall. (Photo courtesy of Dennis Baxter)

own group volume indicator. For instance, one group fader can be used for all the mics on the audience (Figures 15.36 and 15.37).

Finally, there is a master fader that controls the overall audio strength being sent to line (such as on the recorder). This can be used to fade the complete mix in or out. A master volume indicator shows the combined strength of the mixed audio.

Larger audio mixers include a *cue circuit* (also called *audition*) that enables audio personnel to listen "privately" on earphones or a loudspeaker to the output of any individual channel, even when its pot is faded out. That way the source, such as a CD, can be set up at exactly the right spot, ready to be started on cue, without this being overheard on the air.

AUDIO SAFETY

It is always important to take the time to tape down all audio cables (Figure 15.38) that are in pedestrian walkways. This is not only for the safety of other people, but also protects your cables and equipment from excessive damage.

FIGURE 15.38
Taping cables. (Photo courtesy of Dennis Baxter)

MIC LEVEL VERSUS LINE LEVEL

A *line level* is the audio signal generated by a non microphone device such as a CD player, amplifier, video playback unit, MIDI, or line mixer output. The two normal line levels are 0.316 volts and 1.23 volts. A *mic level* is the audio level (or voltage) of a signal that is generated by a microphone. The mic level, typically around 2 millivolts, is much weaker than a line level signal.

Using the Audio Mixer

Located at the audio control console (board, desk, mixer panel), the audio control engineer (sound mixer, sound supervisor) selects and blends the various program sound sources. His or her attention is divided variously between:

- Selecting and controlling the outputs of various audio sources (microphones, discs, tape, etc.).
- Keeping the volume indicators within system limits by adjusting appropriate channel faders (amplifier gains).
- Following the program audio and pictures and the director's intercom.
- Checking the audio quality on high-grade loudspeakers.
- Watching the video monitors showing program and preview shots, to check sound perspective, and warn against microphones or shadows coming into the shot.
- Guiding (and cueing) operators on mic booms, audio disc, and recording playback.
- Possibly operating audio recording equipment.
- Liaison with other production team members.

Whether operating an audio mixer is a matter of "just fading up a microphone or two and controlling the sound levels" or a complex process involving edge-of-seat decisions depends on the type of production. For example:

- A "live" show, which is transmitted or recorded as it happens, involves rapid decisions. There is inevitably a feeling of urgency, tempered with caution. When working on a production that is being taped scene-by-scene, there is time to set up complicated audio treatments. Anything that goes wrong can usually be corrected and improved.
- When there are a number of sound sources that need to be cued in at precisely the right moment, this poses very different problems than a less-complicated program such as an interview.
- Whether the incoming sources have already been prepared, such as when using prerecorded material, or the live incoming sources need to be controlled and continually monitored and adjusted.

These are just a few of the issues that decide how complex the audio mix needs to be. Let's look at typical operations in some detail:

- Sound sources should be faded in just before they begin (to the appropriate pot setting), and faded out when finished.
- Source channels should not be left "open" (live) when not in use. Apart from accidentally recording overheard remarks ("Was that all right?") and other unwanted sounds, it may pick up someone who is on another mic.
- It is important that the right source is selected and faded up/down at the right moment. Individual or group faders can be used. Here is an example:

  Imagine a scene for a drama production is being shot. The audience sees the interior of a home, where the radio (actually from a CD player located near the mixer) plays quietly. An actor is talking (on live mic-1) to another person (on live mic-2) who is not shown in the shot. A nearby telephone rings (a fade-up using a special effects CD of a phone ringing).

259

The actor turns down the radio (we fade down the CD) and picks up the phone (we stop the special effects CD). Continuous background noises of a storm (from another special effects CD) can be heard at a low level throughout the scene. All these fades must be completed on individual channel pots. The different tape and CD machines must be operated by the person at the mixer or by an assistant.

- When combining several sound sources, all of them should not be faded up to their full level. They should be blended for a specific overall effect. For example, if a single microphone were used to pick up the sound of a music group, chances are that the one microphone would pick up certain instruments much better than others. Loud ones would dominate and quiet ones would be lost. The overall balance would be poor. Instead, use several microphones, devoted to different parts of the group. Then the volume of the weaker instruments, such as a flute, could be increased and the volume of the louder ones, such as drums, can be decreased. With care, the result would sound perfectly natural and have a clearer overall balance.
- Sometimes the relative volume of a sound will need to be adjusted in order to create an illusion of distance. If the sound of a telephone ringing is loud, we assume it is nearby; if it is faint, it must be some distance away.
- Sounds may need to be deliberately emphasized. For example, readjust the pot controlling the crowd noise to make it louder at an exciting moment and give it a more dramatic impact.
- The final audio mix needs to fit the mood of the overall production.

Natural Sound

Most video productions are made up of a series of shots, taken in whatever order is most convenient, and edited together later to form the final program. This approach has both advantages and drawbacks. As far as the program sound is concerned, there are several complications.

First of all, although the various shots in a sequence have been taken at different times, it is important that their quality and volume match when they are edited together. Otherwise, there will be sudden jumps whenever the shot changes. If, for instance, a shot is taken of a person walking down a hallway, using a close mic, and then a side view of the same action using a more distant mic, the difference in the sound, when cutting from one shot to the other, could be quite noticeable. The overall effect would draw attention to the editing.

When editing together a sequence of images shot at different times, the background sounds may not match. In the time it takes for shooting one shot, repositioning the camera, adjusting the light, and then retaking the shot, the background noises often have significantly changed. Because the crew members are busy doing their jobs, they may not notice that the background sounds are quite different. Sounds that we become accustomed to while shooting the scene, such as overhead aircraft, farm equipment, hammering, or typing, have a nasty habit of instantly disappearing and reappearing when the shots are edited together.

Anticipation

Anticipation comes with experience. When things go wrong, hopefully you will learn from it and be better prepared next time. There are a number of ways to anticipate audio challenges.

PREPARATION

- Check through the script or preplanning paperwork and then pull together the appropriate equipment so that every audio situation in the production can be covered.
- Prerecorded audio inserts should be checked before the show. Make sure that they are appropriate. Is the duration too long or too short? Is the quality satisfactory? Will an insert require equalization? Is it damaged in any way (for example, surface scratches on

a disc)? Is the insert material arranged in the order in which it is to be used?

- Check all of the equipment to make sure that it is working correctly. Don't rely on the fact that "it was OK yesterday." If additional plug-in equipment is being used, such as a portable audio mixer, have someone fade up each source (microphones or CD) to ensure that each one is working.
- Go to each microphone in turn, scratch its housing (an easy way to test the microphone), and state its location to make sure that the microphone is working and plugged into the correct input (this is "Boom A").
- Have a backup microphone ready in case the main microphone fails. If it is a one-time-only occasion and a lavalier mic is being used, it may be advisable to add a second "dual redundancy" lavalier mic, too (Figure 15.39).
- Is the microphone cable long enough to allow the boom pole to move around freely?

FIGURE 15.39
This lavalier clip is designed to hold two microphones, providing a backup microphone in case one of them fails.

Of course, these suggestions are all a matter of common sense, but it is surprising how often the obvious and the familiar get overlooked. These are just reminders of what should become a regular routine.

ANTICIPATING SOUND EDITING

When shooting a scene, it is important to overcome the challenges of sound editing by anticipating the types of problems that will occur:

Continuity. Try to ensure that the quality and level of successive shots in the same scene match as much as possible.

Natural/atmosphere sounds. Record some general natural sound (atmosphere) and typical background sounds (wild track) in case they are needed during postproduction.

Questions. When shooting an interview, concentrating on the guest, the questions of the interviewer may not be audible. Make sure that the host has his or her own microphone or go back and have them ask the same questions after the interview so that they are recorded.

Filtered Sound

Significant changes can be made to the quality of sound by introducing an *audio filter* into the system. This can be adjusted to increase or decrease the chosen part of the audio spectrum, to exaggerate or suppress the higher notes or the bass or middle register, depending on the type of filter system used and how it is adjusted.

The simplest "tone control" progressively reduces higher notes during reproduction. A more flexible type of audio filter is called an *equalizer*. This filter can boost or reduce any segment(s) of the audio spectrum by changing the slider pots.

Here are typical ways in which filtering can enhance the subjective effect of the sound:

- Cutting low bass can reduce rumble or hum; improve speech clarity; lessen the boomy or hollow sound of some small rooms; and weaken background noise from ventilation, passing traffic, and so on. Overdone, the result sounds thin and lacking body.
- Cutting higher notes can make hiss, whistles, tape noise, sibilant speech, and other high-pitched sounds less prominent. However, if you cut them too much, the sound will lack clarity and intelligibility.

- If the bass and top notes are cut, the sound will have a much more "open-air" quality—a useful cheat when shooting an exterior scene in a studio.
- By slightly increasing bass, the impression of size and grandeur of a large interior can be increased.
- The clarity and "presence" of many sounds can be improved by making them appear closer, by boosting the middle part of the audio spectrum (such as 2–6 kHz).
- Filtering can make the quality of sound recorded in different places more similar (such as shots of someone inside and outside a building). It can help to match the sound quality of different microphones.

Reverberation

As mentioned earlier, most of the everyday sounds we hear are a mixture of direct sound from the source itself, together with "colored" versions reflected from nearby surfaces. The quality of that reflected sound is affected by the nature of those surfaces. Some surfaces will absorb the higher notes (curtains, cushions, carpeting). This reflected sound may even be muffled. Conversely, where surroundings reflect higher notes more readily, these hard reflections will add harshness (also called "edginess") to the final sound.

Where there are few sound-absorbing materials around, there will be noticeable reverberation as sound rebounds from the walls, ceiling, and floor. If the time intervals between these reflections are considerably different, a distinct echo will be heard.

This is a reminder that the room tone will depend on its size, shape, carpeting, drapes, easy chairs, and other furnishings. Where there are no reflections—as in open spaces away from buildings or other hard surfaces—the resulting sound will seem *dead*. The only way we can simulate dead surroundings within a building is to use carefully positioned sound-absorbing materials. On the other hand, if there is too much reverberation, the result is a confused mixture of sound that reduces its clarity.

In practice, the appeal of many sounds can be enhanced by adding a certain amount of real or simulated reverberation to them. Today, the most commonly used method of adding some "liveness" is to use a reverberation unit that digitally stores the sound and is selectively reread over and over to give the impression of reflected sounds.

BUILDING THE SOUNDTRACK

Most television programs contain not only speech but also music and sound effects. These vary with the type of program. A talk show is likely to have music only at the start and end of the production, to give it a "packaged" feel; a dramatic presentation may be strewn with a variety of carefully selected atmospheric sound effects and musical passages (bridges, mood music, etc.).

Some sounds are prominently in the foreground, and others are carefully controlled to provide an appropriate background to the action. Some may creep in, and are barely audible, yet add an atmospheric quality to a scene (such as the quiet tick-tock of a grandfather clock). Others may be deafening, even drowning out the dialogue.

Some sound effects are continuous, and others rely on split-second cueing to exactly match live action.

Types of Program Sound

When a production is running smoothly, it's easy to overlook the complexities that lie behind it. This is particularly true of the sound component of television. The person controlling the program sound often has to work simultaneously with a diversity of sound sources. Some of these are live and therefore liable to vary unpredictably; others may have been prerecorded specifically for the production, or selected from stock libraries.

Contributory sounds can include:

- *Dialogue:* Direct pickup of the voices of people in the picture.
- *Off-camera voices:* The voices of people who are off-camera, such as an unseen bystander, on a radio in the background or a public announcement in a train station.
- *Voiceover (VO):* The voice of a commentator or announcer (with introductory or explanatory information).
- *Sound effects:* Sound coinciding with action in the picture.
- *Background or environmental effects:* General atmospheric sounds, such as the wind, ocean, or traffic.
- *Foreground music:* Someone playing an instrument in the shot.
- *Background music:* Atmospheric mood music (usually recorded).
- *Special effects sounds:* Sounds that enhance the scene.

Program Music

The role of music in television programs is so established that we don't need to dwell on it here. Musical themes often remain in the memory long after the program itself has faded from the mind.

Music can have various purposes. For example:

- *Identifying:* Music associated with a specific show, person, and/or country.
- *Atmospheric:* Melodies intended to induce a certain mood, such as excitement.
- *Associative:* Music reminiscent of, for example, the American West or the Orient.
- *Imitative:* Music that directly imitates, such as a bird song. Music with a rhythm or melody copying the subject's features; for example, the jog-trot accompaniment to a horse and wagon.
- *Environmental:* Music heard at a specific place, such as a ballroom.

Sound Effects

Sound effects add depth and realism to a video production. They significantly affect the audience's experience. Interestingly, if a production is shot in a real location, yet is missing the everyday sounds that occur there, the audience will perceive that it is a contrived location. However, if the same scene is shot in a well-designed television studio setting, but accompanied by the appropriate sound effects, the audience can easily be convinced that it was shot on location. The barely heard sounds of a clock ticking, wind whistling through trees, bird song, passing traffic, the barking of a distant dog (or whatever other noises are appropriate) can bring the scene to life.

Sound effects can come from a number of sources:

The original sounds recorded during a scene: For example, a person's own footsteps accompanying the picture, which may be filtered, have reverberation added, and so on.

Reused original sounds: An example would include the sounds of wind, traffic, or children at play, recorded during a scene, then copied and mixed with that same scene's soundtrack to reinforce the overall effect.

Foley: Creating sounds in a studio that can replace the original sounds. For example, introducing sounds of your own footsteps for the original ones, keeping in time with those in the picture.

Sound effects library: Effects from a commercial audio effects library on CD or DVD.

Digital processing or sound sampling: Computer software offers a plethora of options for creating, manipulating, and sounds. Connected to a keyboard, these effects can be repeated and changed in an endless variety of ways.

Anticipating Sound Editing

When shooting on location, you can make eventual editing and audio sweetening a lot easier if you habitually follow certain practices:

Level continuity: Aim to keep the level and quality of successive shots in the same scene reasonably similar. Particularly in location interiors, you may find that longer shots have lower sound levels and strong reverberation, while closer shots are louder and relatively dead acoustically.

Wild track: It is good practice to make supplementary recordings of general "atmosphere" (background noise) from time to time. This is often referred to as NAT (natural) sound. Even in the studio, there is always a low-level background sound of air conditioning/ventilation (room tone). On location, this atmosphere may include wind in trees, passing traffic, and so on. When editing the program there will be occasions where the soundtrack has been cut, or a sequence is muted, and these cover sounds can be introduced to avoid distracting lapses into silence and to give a feeling of continuity to the edited shots.

When recording on location, keep an alert ear for any potential sound effects that arise when you are not actually shooting, yet might be integrated into the final soundtrack. Even unwelcome intrusive noises, such as a passing fire truck, might prove useful in your sound library for another occasion.

Extra audio recording is useful, too, when shooting interviews on location. Typically, the camera and microphone concentrate on the guest, and separate shots of the interviewer are cut in during editing.

Audio Sweetening

The process of working on the program sound after the production is called *audio sweetening* (or a *dubbing session* or *track laying*). Although it can be a lot cheaper to record a show live to tape and have a complete production ready for use at the end of the session, audio sweetening is both necessary and preferable where extensive video editing is involved.

Audio sweetening can be carried out at various levels:

Additional material: Adding extra material to the finished edited program (playing title music, adding a commentary, etc.).

Corrections: Improving the sound within a scene. One might, for example, readjust varying levels between speakers' voices. Careful filtering could reduce hum, rumble, ventilation noise, and other issues.

Enhancement: Modifying sound quality to improve realism or to achieve a dramatic effect (adding reverberation or changing its equalization). Adjusting the relative strengths of effects and music tracks to suit the dialogue and action.

Continuity: Ensuring that the sound levels, balance, etc. are consistent from one shot to the next when various shots are edited together.

Bridging: Adding bridging effects or music that will run between shots. An overlay track can be played throughout an entire sequence to ensure that the same background sound levels continue without level jumps or changes in quality. It may be kept down behind dialogue and made more prominent during action.

Added effects: When video effects have been introduced into a program after the studio action (laser beams, explosions, disintegrations), suitable sound effects can be added during sound sweetening.

Overdubbing: Replacing unsatisfactory sections of the soundtrack that were spoiled, for instance, by passing aircraft or other extraneous noise.

As you can see, there are very practical reasons to rework the soundtrack after production. Now that television makes increasing use of short takes and sophisticated video editing, it has become a regular part of the production process on complex shows.

Copyright

Whenever material prepared and created by other people is used—a piece of music, a sound recording, video recording, film, a picture in a book, a photograph, and so on—the producer/director are required to pay a fee to the *copyright holders* or an appropriate organization operating on their behalf for copyright clearance.

Copyright law is complex and varies between different countries, but basically, it protects the originators from having their work copied without permission. You cannot, for example, prepare a video program with music dubbed from a commercial recording, with inserts from television programs, magazine photographs, advertisements, and other sources without the permission of the respective copyright owners. The owners will probably require the payment of use fees and these fees will depend on the purpose and use of the program. Some of the exceptions to this policy occur when the program is only to be seen within the home or used in a class assignment that will not be seen by the public. In most cases, the copyright can be traced through the source of the material needed for the production (the publisher of a book or photograph).

Agreements take various forms and may be limited in scope. A license and/or a fee may need to be paid for using the material. For music and sound effects, directors are usually required to pay a royalty fee per use; it may be possible to buy unlimited rights.

The largest organizations concerned with performance rights for music (copyright clearance for use of recorded music or to perform music) include ASCAP (American Society of Composers, Authors, and Publishers), SESAC (Society of European Stage Authors and Composers), and BMI (Broadcast Music, Inc.). When clearing copyright for music, both the record company and the music publishers may need to be involved.

Music in *public domain* is not subject to copyright, but any arrangement or performance may be covered by copyright. Music and lyrics published in 1922 or earlier are in the public domain in the United States. Anyone can use a public domain song in a production—no one can "own" a public domain song. Sound recordings, however, are protected separately from musical compositions. There are no sound recordings in the public domain in the United States. If you need to use an existing sound recording—even a recording of a public domain song—you will either have to record it yourself or license a recording.

REVIEW QUESTIONS

1. How do acoustics affect an audio recording?
2. How are acoustic reflections (or echoes) reduced?
3. How is the speaker setup different between stereo and surround sound (5.1)? How many speakers are involved?
4. What are three microphone characteristics, and how do each of these affect the audio recording process?
5. How is a super-cardioid microphone used for television production?
6. Review the different types of microphones and specify the type that you would use to obtain a quality recording of a piano. Explain your choice.
7. What are some of the different situations where a type of lavalier mic can be used?
8. What are the advantages of a wireless mic?
9. Describe the parts of a sound mixing board.
10. How is a soundtrack designed (built)?
11. When do you need to be concerned about copyright?

CHAPTER 16

Recording and Viewing the Program

"Don't become too emotionally attached to a medium for its own sake—there's no future in it."

Leonard Guercio, Producer, Director, and Educator

Terms

HDTV or HD (high-definition television): Usually any video format between 720 lines and 4000 lines (4K).

Interlaced scanning: The television's electrons scan the odd-numbered lines first and then go back and scan in the remaining even-numbered lines. The "i" in 1080i stands for *interlaced*.

Progressive scanning: Also called sequential scanning; uses an electron beam that scans or paints all lines at once. Note that the "p" in the 720p/1080p stands for *progressive*.

SDTV or SD (standard-definition television): Usually television formats that have 480–576 lines.

An often-asked question—What is the best video recording format?—can be a complicated question to answer. Although there are some 4K HD video cameras available, you may not be able to afford the related camera gear, editing equipment, or the support that is often required. Some formats may have an incredible quality but the cameras are too large for a one-person investigative reporter. The bottom line is that the best format varies for different people and situations. You have to weigh the costs involved, size of the equipment, portability, size of the crew, amount of data storage needed, and the situation that you will be covering, and then go for the highest-quality format that works with your specific requirements and situation. Sometimes, it is not an easy decision to make.

RECORDING THE VIDEO

Fortunately, there is continual development in the design and format of video and audio recording systems. Some are mainly used for acquisition (shooting original material); others are for postproduction editing and archiving (storage) work. Recordings can be done on videotape (the most common professional medium at this moment), hard drives, or flash memory cards. In fact, some cameras can record on DVD, hard disks, and tape—all in one device. Traditionally, videotape has been the most popular medium. However, with the advent of video capabilities in almost all still digital cameras and cell phone cameras, still camera memory sticks are probably being used more by amateurs than videotape. Though professionals are still using tape more than any other medium, digital media has made serious in-roads into tape's territory.

Standard-Definition Television

Standard-definition television (SD or SDTV) is what was used around the world before HD came onto the scene. However, most of the world is now in the process of moving from SDTV to HDTV. SD generally refers to analog and digital broadcasts that scan the image at 480i

Television Standards

Historically, there have been three primary television standards around the world. None of these are compatible with the others. Converters can be used to allow one standard to be viewed on another system:

NTSC: Created by the National Television System Committee (hence the acronym), this analog system utilizes 525 lines and 60 fields. It is used in many countries and regions, including the United States, Japan, Taiwan, South Korea, Mexico, Philippines, South America, Central America, and Canada.

PAL: This system stands for Phase Alternating Line; it is an analog system with 625 lines and 50 fields. The countries and regions that use this standard include Western Europe, China, Hong Kong, Afghanistan, parts of Africa, and Australia.

SECAM: Created in France, SECAM stands for *Séquentiel couleur à mémoire* or Sequential Color with Memory. This analog system uses 525 lines and 50 fields. SECAM countries and regions include Eastern Europe, some of Asia, parts of Africa, the Pacific Islands, and France.

(NTSC) and 576i (PAL). The "i" stands for *"interlaced"* (see the following explanation of this term). Although most SD signals are broadcast in a 4:3 aspect ratio, it is also possible to transmit them with a 16:9 aspect ratio as well.

High-Definition Television

"HD is so much sharper than SD that more attention must be given to the small details. Since the flaws in the background, or even makeup, can hold the audience's attention, directors may not need as many close-up shots . . . which previously was the only way details could be shown."

Brian Douglas, Olympics Producer and Director

The world is rapidly moving to high-definition television (HD or HDTV), which has quite a few more scan lines than SD. The most common HD formats have lines that are 720 or 1080 lines, although there are emerging formats with more lines that are aimed at high-end, high-budget productions. These additional lines, and their scanning strategies, equate to much higher-quality images. For example, a normal consumer cannot see the difference between a 720p and a 1080i image, although a trained eye may be able to. As today's HD has pretty much hit the limits of what normal eyes can discern, going to a higher level of scan lines is not critical for viewers watching at home.

There are two types of HD scanning systems currently being used:

Interlaced: Interlaced television is scanned in the same way SDTV has traditionally been scanned. Interlaced scanning means that the television's electron scans the odd-numbered lines first and then goes back and scans in the remaining even-numbered lines. This methodology can be a little more prone to image degredation and can be less stable than progressive scanning. However, there can be a noticeable flicker on older large screens. As the technology has advanced, the flicker has disappeared. Current CRT television utilizes interlaced scanning, as does the HDTV 1080i standard. The "i" stands for *interlaced*.

FIGURE 16.1
This photo is a single frame from the digital video 4K film Crossing the Line by director Peter Jackson. Note the incredible image clarity. The CMOS sensors in the camera are 12-megapixel. (Photo courtesy of Red Digital Cinema)

Progressive: Also called *sequential scanning*, progressive scanning uses an electron beam that scans or paints all lines at once. The HDTV 720p and 1080p systems use progressive scanning. Note that the "p" in the 720p/1080p stands for *progressive*. The progressive method can be perceived as having less flicker and more stability than the interlaced system. The progressive image displays the total picture. It has a smoother, more precise picture with very limited flicker. However, it also uses more bandwidth.

Although there are a number of different formats within HD (720p, 1080p, 1080i, etc.), it is very difficult for the untrained eye to see the difference between them. There were fairly significant differences when the formats first came out (such as motion blur and flicker), but today the majority of the bugs have been fixed. Most of the HD formats use the progressive scanning method, although one of them (1080i) uses the interlaced scanning method. All of the HD formats include a 16:9 aspect ratio. There are also multiple frame rates to choose from that give a "film look," a "video look," or something in between. Here are the current HD formats with some data that can be used for comparison:

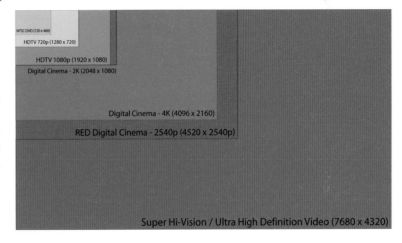

NTSC DVD (720 x 480)
HDTV 720p (1280 x 720)
HDTV 1080p (1920 x 1080)
Digital Cinema - 2K (2048 x 1080)
Digital Cinema - 4K (4096 x 2160)
RED Digital Cinema - 2540p (4520 x 2540p)
Super Hi-Vision / Ultra High Definition Video (7680 x 4320)

269

720p: This is a progressive scanning format that has a pixel aspect ratio of 1280 × 720 and 921,600 pixels per frame. The progressive scanning gives it a little bit of a film look.

1080i: This format utilizes interlaced scanning. It has a pixel aspect ratio of 1920 × 1080 and 1,555,200 pixels per frame. 1080i gives a very high-quality video look.

1080p: This is the newest progressive scanning format and has a pixel aspect ratio of 1920 × 1080 with 2,073,600 pixels per frame. It was designed to compete with film cameras.

FIGURE 16.2
This image quality comparison shows the orange rectangle on the top left as SDTV. The yellow (720 lines) and light-blue (1080 lines) areas are the popular HD consumer formats. As the number of scan lines is increased, the image quality increases proportionally.

There are also 2000-line (2K), 3000-line (3K), and 4000-line (4K) recording formats now available. These high-quality formats are aimed more at theaters and other extremely large-screen productions (Figure 16.1). They are not aimed at viewers watching their televisions in their homes. A comparison of the various recording formats can be found in Figure 16.2.

There are other HD formats under experimentation. One example is being done by Japan's NHK company, which has created an *ultra-high-definition* television system that touts 4320 scanning lines with 7680 × 4320 pixels. Although it is very doubtful that this type of system will ever get into home systems, it may make it into theaters (see Figure 16.2).

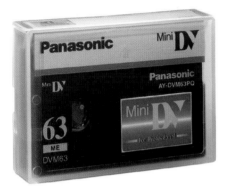

Videotape

As mentioned before, videotape is currently the most popular professional format. Videotape is popular due to:

- The ease of availability (Figure 16.3).
- The large number of tape-based cameras that are still manufactured.
- The sheer number of tape-based systems already owned by companies (Figure 16.4).
- A tape-based infrastructure built by many companies that will take time to move away from.
- The capacity of tapes to record the project and then store the raw and/or finished video.
- The high comfort level of most professionals with videotape.

However, there are many different incompatible videotape formats, and few obsolescent designs are still in use. Although it is not important to worry about design specifics, video producers must realize that there are specific differences between the formats. Tapes can be recorded and reproduced only on equipment that uses identical standards.

Design features can vary considerably between video recorders. Here are some of the differences between formats:

FIGURE 16.3
Videotapes come in many different formats and sizes for professionals and consumers. (Photos courtesy of Panasonic)

- Tapes come in ¼-inch, 8-mm, ⅛-inch, and ½-inch sizes. Cassettes can be different sizes, even within a format, depending on the length of the tape.
- There are two approaches to tape recording: analog (slowly being discontinued) and digital.
- There is a wide range of image quality among the various formats.

With the advent of digital recording, the divisions between consumer and professional formats have significantly blurred. Productions shot on the miniDV tape format are showing up on networks and film festivals and winning top awards; this format was primarily touted as a consumer product.

Analog and Digital

An *analog* system directly records the variations of the video and audio signals. Analog recordings have a tendency to deteriorate when dubbing copies. Analog systems can use only tape to record their signal.

A *digital* system regularly samples the waveforms and converts them into numerical (binary) data. This allows many generations of copies to be made without affecting the quality of the image. Digital systems also allow the data to

FIGURE 16.4
Many companies have heavily invested in a tape-based infrastructure. Moving toward tapeless production will take time. (Photo by Jon Greenhoe)

be recorded on forms of media other than tape, such as hard disks, flash memory, and others (see the following section).

Tape Formats

The following subsections provide a brief summary of some of the most common tape formats that are used in cameras currently produced by manufacturers.

VHS

- Uses ½-inch videotape.
- The VHS deck was the most popular consumer deck ever produced. Until DVDs began to increase in popularity, most video rental stores rented VHS tapes.
- Cameras that utilize VHS tapes are no longer manufactured.
- This format is slowly being phased out.

VHS-C (COMPACT VHS TAPE)

- Uses ½-inch videotape.
- Uses smaller tape than VHS.
- This small tape plays back on a VHS deck, although it usually requires an adapter. Because VHS was the most popular consumer deck, VHS-C gained popularity as a compact camera because its tape could be played on a VHS deck.
- This format is slowly being phased out.

DIGITAL8/HI8

- Uses 8-mm videotape.
- Was highly popular as a subcompact camera format, but is now slowly disappearing from the video market.

MINIDV

- Uses ¼-inch videotape.
- Is the most popular digital format on the market today.
- MiniDV camcorders are compact.
- Uses inexpensive and readily available tapes.
- MiniDV tape will play in the professional DV format DVCPro25/50/HD decks (see later subsection). However, an adapter cassette may be required to fit into the larger decks.

HDV/MINIDV

- A digital HD format that is recorded onto MiniDV tapes.
- JVC and Panasonic utilize 720p; Sony uses 1080i when recording in HDV.
- Many professionals insist that HDV is barely HD, due to color and grayscale issues.
- A MiniDV (non-HDV) tape will play in an HDV deck, but an HDV tape cannot play in a Mini DV deck. In order to play in larger decks, an adapter is usually required.

D-9

- Originally known as D-VHS, this system utilizes ½-inch metal-particle videotape cassettes.
- This system has not been very popular.
- A VHS tape can play in the D-9 deck, but the D-9 tape cannot play in the VHS deck.

DIGITAL BETACAM (DIGIBETA)

- Uses ½-inch videotape.
- This format was created especially for companies that had large Betacam archives. Betacam tapes can be played in the DigiBeta deck, although the DigiBeta tape cannot be played in the Beta deck. The format gave companies, especially news stations, a way to upgrade without having to change their whole archives.

DVCPRO25/50

- Uses ½-inch videotape.
- The DVCPro 50 has lower compression than the DVCPro25, giving a much higher-quality image.
- A DV tape can be played in a DVCPro25/50 deck, but a DVCPro25/50 tape cannot be played in the DV deck.

DVCPROHD

- Uses ½-inch videotape.
- DV and DVCPro25/50 tapes can be played in a DVCProHD deck. However, a DVCProHD tape cannot be played in a DV or DVCPro25/50 deck.

Flash Memory

Flash memory is slowly becoming very popular as a medium to record both SD and HD video. A significant advantage of the flash memory card is that it is very easy to transfer files from the card to a nonlinear editor. The small size of the card allows for very compact camcorders. Cameras using flash memory as their medium generally do not have moving parts and should thus require less maintenance (Figure 16.5).

There are a number of companies who are creating professional cameras using large flash memory cards. One of their advantages is that the larger-card cameras generally have multiple slots, which are "hot-swappable." This means that while one is being recorded onto, an already full card can be removed during the recording process and replaced with a blank card. This feature allows uninterrupted recording. Figures 16.6, 16.7, and 16.8 show professional flash card systems.

272

FIGURE 16.5
There are a number of very small flash memory cards, such as an SD or Pro Duo, that can be used to record video. These cards are currently being used in consumer and semiprofessional cameras.

FIGURE 16.6
The P2 card is a flash memory card used in some professional cameras. The "player" next to it is really a device in which up to five cards can be placed in slots and read by a computer, just like any hard drive or memory stick. (Photos courtesy of Panasonic)

FIGURE 16.7
This P2 player/recorder can be used to record, edit, play back, and play in slow motion anything recorded onto a flash card. Note that there are six slots that are hot-swappable. (Photo courtesy of Panasonic)

Hard Disk Drive/Internal Hard Drive

Hard disk drive (HDD) cameras record directly to a hard drive built into the camera (Figure 16.9). Roughly 4 GB of disk space is required for each hour of video. Some of these compact HDD cameras have as much as 60-GB hard disk storage. Many of the HDD cameras include an SD slot for video recording to a transportable medium, although this feature is not required to transfer footage. It is extremely easy to transfer the data to a nonlinear system. Video footage can be transferred directly to a DVD recorder via the camera manufacturer's transfer device, as seen in Figure 16.10.

External Camera Hard Drives

External camera hard drives can now be attached to most digital cameras, including HD systems. These drives provide extremely long recording times with drives as large as 160 GB. The drives connect directly to nonlinear editing systems, allowing the editor to begin editing the program immediately. Most of these drives attach to the camera via the FireWire port. Audio, timecode, and video and control information are passed directly through the FireWire connector. A 160-GB drive will provide roughly 10 hours of DV recording and 5–6 hours of HD recording (Figure 16.11).

Hard Disk Recorders

Standalone hard disk recorders are now used to record HD video at a very high quality. These real-time recorders/players can be used for SD or HD recording. Frame accuracy is possible. They also usually include smooth fast-motion and slow-motion playback. These recorders can replace standard tape decks (Figures 16.12 and 16.13).

Recordable DVD

DVD cameras have been primarily aimed at the consumer market until now. DVD cameras automatically find a blank section on the disc for recording, so there's no need to rewind or fast-forward. Most of them also use an index screen, which makes it easy to search for a particular scene. When the shooting has been completed, the disc can be taken out of the camcorder and slipped into a DVD player or recorder for immediate playback—there's no need to connect any cables. One of the disadvantages is that discs can be susceptible to scratches (Figure 16.14).

XD Cam Disc

The XD line of optical disc–based camera systems utilizes blue-violet laser technology to achieve extremely high data transfer rates. This professional camera system can record up to four hours of HD on a dual-layer disc that has a large storage capacity of 50 GB. The discs are rewritable. Sony says that it can handle 1000 write-and-rewrite cycles.

Recording Media Care

It is important to care for recording media. Here are some suggestions for prolonging the life of the various types of recording and storage media:

- The optimum storage temperature is around 65 degrees. Above 100 degrees and below 14 degrees can cause problems with some media.

FIGURE 16.8
Some Sony and JVC devices use an S×S memory card. (Photo courtesy of JVC)

273

FIGURE 16.9
This high-end consumer-targeted camcorder includes an internal HDD. (Photo courtesy of JVC)

FIGURE 16.10
The HDD camera has the ability to dock to a DVD recorder in order to transfer all footage to an archival medium. (Photo courtesy of JVC)

FIGURE 16.11
External drives can be attached to most digital video cameras. (Photo courtesy of Firestore)

FIGURE 16.12
Hard disk recorders are gaining popularity in the professional video field. (Photo courtesy of Doremi)

FIGURE 16.13
A slow-motion operator utilizes an EVS hard drive server recording/playback system during a sports event.

FIGURE 16.14
(Left) A full-size recordable DVD. (Right) The camera shown records on a much smaller DVD. (Photo courtesy of JVC)

- Avoid rapid temperature/humidity changes (such as moving from a cold exterior to a warm interior) and allow both media and equipment to become acclimatized before use.
- Before loading a medium, confirm that it isn't protected against recording (that is, reposition the safety switch). Make sure that you're not recording over something that should be retained!
- Store media in their protective boxes to avoid damage and dust (Figure 16.15).
- Make sure that each recorded medium is clearly identified on the label (name, contact information, shot/scene numbers, etc.).

Video Recording Suggestions

Here are some suggestions to consider when recording to video media:

- Record at standard speed rather than at one of the slower speeds on videotape. This approach will provide better sound and video quality.
- Use the highest data rate possible on digital media other than tape. Although this will not allow you to record as many minutes on the medium, it will give you a higher-quality image.

- Watch the elapsed time on the camera to make sure that you know how much memory or tape is left and that you know the state of the battery.
- Reset the tape counter whenever you change the tape.
- Review the end of the takes to check whether the recording is satisfactory.
- When the medium is taken out of the camera, make sure that the protection device is implemented so that someone does not accidentally record over your original footage.
- Clearly label all media as well as the media container.

FIGURE 16.15
The XD disc is protected by a case at all times. (Photo courtesy of Sony)

VIEWING THE VIDEO

Several types of screen are used to display a video signal's picture. The most common are:

CRT (cathode ray tube): This type of monitor has been the standard since it appeared in the 1930s. Historically called "the tube," CRT televisions send an electron beam through a vacuum tube to a phosphor-coated screen. The images are created as the beam hits the screen's surface. Although they have a good-quality image and have become inexpensive, they are large and bulky (Figure 16.16).

Plasma: The plasma television is a high-quality, thin, high-resolution, flat-panel screen that can be viewed from a wide angle. The plasma utilizes a matrix of very small cells that become charged by precise electrical voltages to create an image that has a wide range of color and produces deep blacks. The plasma has a much higher power consumption than the LCD and has a limited lifespan (half of the LCD's, Figure 16.17).

LCD (liquid crystal diode): LCD televisions are flat-screen displays that work by sending variable electrical currents through a liquid crystal solution that crystallizes to form a quality image. At this time, the LCD screens are more expensive than the plasma screens, but seem to have a much longer lifespan and lower power consumption. They work well as smaller televisions and seem to be quickly replacing the CRT technology.

The newest monitors, *LED* (*light-emitting diode*) screens, are more expensive but consume as much as 28% less power.

FIGURE 16.16
Though consumer CRTs are quickly being replaced by LCD televisions, many engineers still prefer and trust the CRT as their quality-control monitor. (Photo courtesy of Sony)

275

How We See Color

Our eyes contain selective "cones," which detect color by analyzing the visible spectrum in terms of three primary color regions: red to orange, green to yellow, and blue to violet.

Most colored surfaces reflect a color mixture of red, green, and blue light in varying proportions. So, for instance, the various shades of "green" we see in foliage are actually color mixtures reflecting quite a wide spread of the visible spectrum. Even yellow can be reproduced by adding suitable proportions of red and green light.

FIGURE 16.17
Plasma screens are considered to be the best at portraying fast motion, such as sports. (Photo courtesy of Panasonic)

How the Camera Sees Color

The color video camera basically relys on the same system as the eyes. The light sensors can only respond to the intensity of light—they cannot directly distinguish *color*. However, by placing red, green, and blue color filters over three light sensors, we can analyze the scene in terms

FIGURE 16.18

A number of companies have developed 3D televisions. (Top) A simulation of a 3D television. (Bottom) A working prototype that requires the viewer to use glasses. (Top photo courtesy of DDD, Inc.)

of its separate color components. If a subject appears to have similar proportions of all three primary colors, we see this mixture as white.

In the color video camera, the lens' image of the scene passes through a special prism, which splits it into three identical versions. Three sensors with their respective red, green, and blue color filters provide three video signals corresponding to the light and shade of these colors in the scene.

Monitors and Receivers

Although both *television receivers* and *picture monitors* are widely used in video production, they have important differences:

Television receivers: These are designed to display off-air pictures of broadcast programs, with accompanying sound. Receivers include a tuner so that they can receive television programming. For technical and economic reasons, picture and sound quality are a bit of a compromise, although the performance of top-grade receivers can be extremely good.

Picture monitors: Monitors were especially designed to provide accurate, stable image quality; their circuit sophistication is reflected in their higher cost. Picture monitors do not include circuitry to receive off-air programming. These video monitors may or may not include audio speakers.

One of the areas that is being experimented with today is 3D television. There are a number of different types of screens available, but a standard has not developed yet. Some screens require 3D glasses; others do not (Figure 16.18).

REVIEW QUESTIONS

1. What is the difference between SD and HD television?
2. What are the advantages of interlaced and progressive scanning?
3. What is the difference between a monitor and a receiver?
4. Compare a tape format with a nontape format and explain the advantages and disadvantages.
5. How do you care for recording media?

CHAPTER 17

Editing the Production

"Being an editor is not for everyone . . . it requires attention to detail, an organizational leaning, the ability to deal with computers but not seem like a 'techie' and there is a need to think qu ickly with others waiting to see your solution. You can make or break a show in post."

Mark West, Emmy-winning Editor

Terms

Clip: A video segment.

Cut/take: An instantaneous switch from one shot to another.

Dissolve: An effect produced by fading out one picture while fading in another.

Fade (a type of dissolve): A gradual change between black and a video image. For example, at the end of a program there is usually a "fade to black" or, if there is a "fade-up," it means that the director is transitioning from black to a video image. A slow fade suggests the peaceful end of action. A fast fade is rather like a "gentle cut," used to conclude a scene.

Linear editing: The copying, or dubbing, of segments from the master tape to another tape in sequential order.

Logging: Loggers view the footage and write down the scene/take numbers, the length of each shot, time code, and descriptions of each shot.

Nonlinear editing: The process where the recorded video is digitized (copied) onto a computer. The footage can then be arranged and rearranged, special effects can be added, and the audio and graphics can be adjusted using editing software.

Postproduction: Taking the video that was previously shot and assembling a program shot by shot, generally with a computer-based editing system.

Timeline: Usually includes multiple tracks of video, audio, and graphics in a nonlinear editing system.

Wipe: A novel transition that can have many different shapes.

Selecting the right image and skillful editing will make a vital contribution to a production's impact. The way the shots are interrelated will not only affect their visual flow but will also directly influence how the audience reacts to what they are seeing: their interpretation and their emotional responses. Poor editing can leave them confused. Proficient editing can create interest and tension or build up excitement that keeps the audience on the edges of their seats. At worst, poor image selection can degenerate into casual switching between shots. At best, editing is a sophisticated persuasive art form.

FIGURE 17.1
Whether directing in a large multicamera control room or cutting a show together in a simple nonlinear editing suite, ultimately, they are both editing suites, and you are editing the program.

EDITING TECHNIQUES IN TELEVISION

There are roughly two broad categories of editing (Figure 17.1):

- Live editing: The director, using live cameras and other video sources, "live edits" (directs) a production using a video switcher.
- Postproduction: Taking the imagery that was previously shot and assembling a program shot by shot, generally with a computer-based editing system.

One style involves a director with cameras and the other style involves a director with prerecorded programming. However you do it, it is still editing—you are deciding which shot the audience will see.

EDITING BASICS

Editing Decisions

During the editing process, a series of decisions need to be made:

Which of the available shots do you want to use? When directing (editing) a live show, choices are irrevocable. You can select only from the shots being presented at each moment by cameras, prerecorded material, graphics, and so on. When you are editing in postproduction, there is time to ponder, to select, and to reconsider.

What is the final shot sequence? The relative durations of shots will affect their visual impact.

At exactly which moment in the action do you want to change from one shot to the next?

How will each shot transition to the next shot? Transitions include cut, dissolve, wipe, fade, and others.

How fast or slow will this transition be?

Is there good continuity between pictures as well as sound that show continuous action? These elements may have actually been shot discontinuously or at different times/places.

Each of these decisions involves you making both a mechanical operation and an artistic choice. Even the simplest treatment (a cut from one image to the next) can create a very different effect, based on the point at which you decide to edit the action. Let's look at an example:

- You can show the entire action, from start to end:

  The intruder reaches into a pocket, pulls out a pistol, and fires it. The victim falls. (The action is obvious.)

- You can interrupt an action, so that we do not know what is going to happen:

  The hand reaches into the pocket/CUT/to the second person's face. (What is the intruder reaching for?) Or the hand reaches into a pocket, and pulls out a pistol/CUT/to the second person's face. (Is the intruder threatening, or actually going to fire it?)

- You can show the entire action, but hold the audience in suspense about its consequences:

  We see the pistol drawn and fired/CUT/but did the shot miss?

Editing Opportunities

As we examine editing techniques, you will see how they significantly contribute to the success of the production:

- You can join together a series of separately recorded takes or sequences to create a continuous smooth-flowing story line—even where none originally existed.
- Through editing, you can omit action that would be irrelevant or distracting.
- You can seamlessly cut in retakes to replace unsatisfactory material—to correct or improve performance; to overcome camera, lighting, or sound faults; or to improve ineffective production treatment.
- You can increase or reduce the overall duration of the program—by adjusting the duration of sequences, introducing cutaway shots, altering playing speed, or repeating strategic parts of an action sequence.
- Library material (stock shots) can be introduced and blended with the program material—to establish location, for effects, or to introduce illustrations.
- When a subject is just about to move out of shot, you can cut to a new viewpoint and show the action continuing, apparently uninterrupted. (Even where it is possible to shoot action in one continuous take, the director may want to change the camera viewpoint or interrupt the flow of the action for dramatic impact.)
- By cutting between shots recorded at quite different times or places, you can imply relationships that did not exist.
- Editing allows you to instantly shift the audience's center of interest, redirecting their attention to another aspect of the subject or the scene.
- You can use editing to emphasize or to conceal/information.
- You can adjust the duration of shots in a sequence to influence its overall pace.
- Editing can change the entire significance of an action in an instant—to create tension, humor, horror, and so on.
- By altering the order in which the audience sees events, you can change how they interpret and react to them.

THE MECHANICS OF EDITING

The actual process you use can have an important influence on the ease and accuracy with which you can edit and on the finesse that is possible. There are several systems, described in the following sections.

Editing In-Camera

It is possible to edit in-camera. To do so, most cameras require that you shoot the action in the final running order, which may not be practicable or convenient. There are even a few cameras that will allow a little bit of in-camera editing, such as trimming a scene or changing the order of the clips. However, cameras have varying abilities and all of them have more limitations than editing on an actual editor.

Production Switcher (Vision Mixer)

The live-edit method of using a production switcher, to combine (cut, dissolve, wipe, fade, etc.) video sources such as cameras, video players, or graphics, is used in many productions. During a production, conditions in most production control rooms are generally a world apart from the relative calm of an editing suite (Figure 17.2).

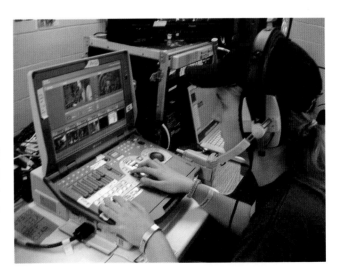

FIGURE 17.2
A small "laptop" video switcher can be used with four-camera productions.

The director needs to watch the monitor wall, which is made up of small monitors showing images from cameras, video feeds, video players, graphics, and any other sources. There are also two larger monitors, a "preview" monitor and a "program" or "on-air" monitor. The director uses the preview monitor to review any video source before going to it. The program monitor shows the final program output. (See Chapter 3 for more details about the control room.)

While all of this is going on, the director's attention is divided between the current shot in the program monitor and upcoming shots—guiding the production crew by instructing, correcting, selecting, and coordinating their work. Of course, this is all done while the director is also checking the talent's performance, keeping production on schedule, and dealing with issues as they arise. It is no surprise that under these conditions, "editing" with a production switcher can degenerate into a mechanical process (Figure 17.3).

Linear Editing

Linear editing involves "dubbing" or copying the master tape to another tape in a sequential order. This process worked well for editors until the director or client wanted significant changes to be made in the middle of a tape. With a linear tape, that usually meant that the whole project had to be entirely re-edited; this was incredibly time consuming and frustrating. Analog linear editing also did not work well if multiple generations (copies of copies) of the tape had to be made, as each generation deteriorated a little more. Linear systems are generally made up of a "player" and a "recorder" along with a control console. The original footage is placed into the player and then is edited to the recorder (Figures 17.4 and 17.5). Although some segments of the television industry are still using linear editing, the majority of programming today is edited on a nonlinear editor.

280

FIGURE 17.3
Directors must be able to select the right image, transition, duration, and make other choices while working with the crew and talent at the same time.

FIGURE 17.4
Linear editing, or copying the contents of one tape to another tape, one clip after another linearly, is still used on a limited basis. Although the use of linear editors has significantly reduced, segments of the industry, such as news, still use them. (Photo by Jon Greenhoe)

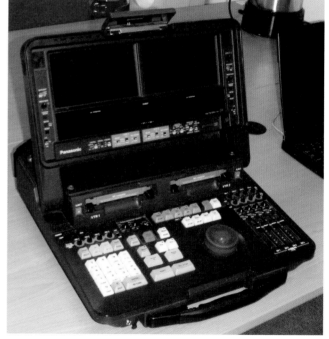

FIGURE 17.5
Digital laptop linear systems have been popular with news and sports crews that are on the road. They also can be used as two separate tape decks when needed.

Nonlinear Editing

Today, almost all video and television programs are edited on a *nonlinear editor*. Nonlinear editing is the process in which the recorded video is digitized (copied) onto a computer. Then the footage can be arranged, rearranged, and have special effects added and the audio and graphics can be adjusted using editing software. Nonlinear editing systems make it very easy to make changes like moving clips around until the director or client is happy. Hard disk and memory card cameras have allowed editors to begin editing much more quickly, as they do not need to digitize all of the footage. Nonlinear systems cost a fraction of what a professional linear editing system does. Once the edited project is complete, it can be output to whatever medium is desired: tape, Internet, iPod, CD, DVD, and others.

AN OVERVIEW OF THE NONLINEAR PROCESS

Step 1: Digitize the footage into the computer. If the footage was recorded onto a hard drive or flash card, it does not have to be digitized. It can be moved directly to the computer (Figure 17.6).

Step 2: Each video segment or *clip* is then *trimmed* (cleaned up), by deleting unwanted video frames.

Step 3: The clips are placed into the *timeline*. The timeline usually includes multiple tracks of video, audio, and graphics. This timeline allows the editor to view the production and arrange the segments to fit the script (Figure 17.7).

Step 4: Video special effects and transitions are added. Nonlinear edit systems allow all kinds of effects, such as ripple, slow/fast motion, color correction, and others. Transitions include dissolves, cuts, and a variety of wipes.

Step 5: Additional audio may or may not be added at this point. Audio effects may be used to "sweeten" the sound. Music and/or voiceovers may be added at different points in the project (Figures 17.8 and 17.9).

Step 6: The final program is output to the distribution medium.

281

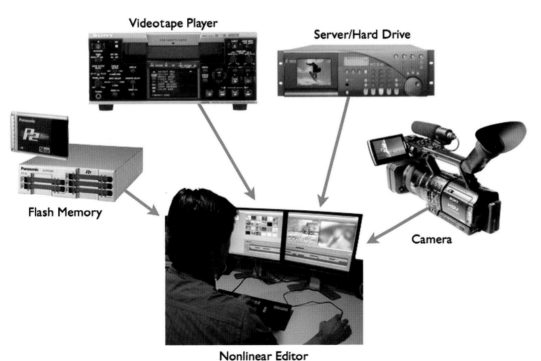

FIGURE 17.6

Many different devices can be used to input video into a nonlinear editor.

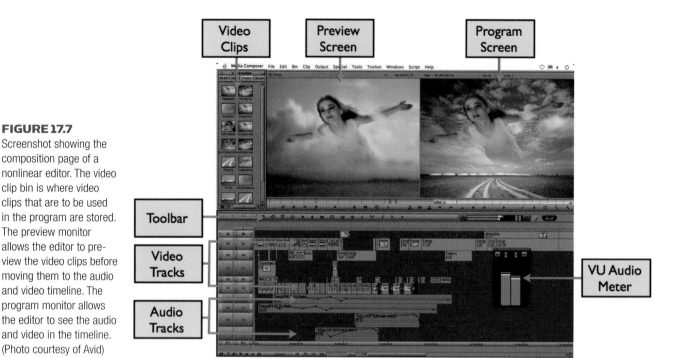

FIGURE 17.7
Screenshot showing the composition page of a nonlinear editor. The video clip bin is where video clips that are to be used in the program are stored. The preview monitor allows the editor to preview the video clips before moving them to the audio and video timeline. The program monitor allows the editor to see the audio and video in the timeline. (Photo courtesy of Avid)

282

FIGURE 17.8
A nonlinear editing suite with an adjoining sound booth for voiceovers.

FIGURE 17.9
The talent is doing a voiceover in an editing suite for a news story at a local news station. (Photo by Jon Greenhoe)

NONLINEAR EDITING EQUIPMENT

Editing equipment has drastically changed over the last decade. Where once a minimal editing system required two editing decks, two monitors, and an edit controller, today the equipment can be as simple as a camcorder and a computer with an editing software package installed.

Higher-leveling edit suites may contain multiple types of input devices using a variety of different connectors to transport the data at a much faster speed. They may also include multiple edit screens, speakers, an audio mixer, and other tools.

Video can be imported into the computer from a camcorder, deck, or a memory storage device. One cable can move large amounts of data, as well as control signals, between the camera and computer.

HABITS OF A HIGHLY EFFECTIVE POSTPRODUCTION EDITOR

1. *Schedule enough time to make a good edit.* Quality editing takes time. Be realistic, and then pad your schedule with a little extra time. It is always better to be done a little early than late. Plus, you can always use a little more time to refine the edit.
2. *Get a little distance from the project occasionally.* It is easy to become emotionally involved with a specific element of a project. Take a break from it; when you come back, your perspective may have changed. Ask others for their opinion—there is a good chance that they will see things that you didn't see.
3. *List the issues before fixing them one by one.* It is good to come up with an organized plan for editing the project. Although it takes time to think it through, it is worth it.
4. *Know the priority of your editing elements.* The most important editing elements are the emotion and story. If you lose those two elements, you lose the production.
5. *Keep a copy of each edited version.* Each time you make changes to the project, keep the original (or previous) version. That way you have something to go back to if you run into problems.
6. *Focus on the shots that you have.* By the time you sit down to edit, it is time to get the best project that you can possibly get from the footage you have recorded. You may even have to forget about the script.

(Adapted from Mark Kerin's *Six Habits of Highly Effective Editors*)

POSTPRODUCTION LOGGING

An often-neglected important aspect of the postproduction process is logging the recorded material. Logging saves time during the actual editing process, as it can be completed before the editing session. After logging the footage, the editor can then just digitize the specific clips that will be used in the program instead of taking time on the editor to search through all of the clips. By digitizing specific clips instead of all of the footage, it also saves hard drive space. Generally, some type of log sheet is used on which notes can be written that include the time code (the address where the footage is located), scene/take numbers, and the length of each shot. The notes may also included a description of the shot and other comments like "very good," "blurry," and so on. Logging can be simple notes on a piece of paper or can done with logging software. An advantage to some of the logging software is that it can work with the editing software, importing the edit decisions automatically into the computer (Figures 17.10 and 17.11).

Shots can be identified for the log a number of different ways:

- Visually ("the one where he gets into the car").
- By shooting a *slate* (*clapboard*) before each shot, which contains the shot number and details (or an inverted board, at the end of shots); see Figure 17.12.
- By *timecode*; a special continuous time-signal throughout the tape, showing the precise moment of recording.

Digital Video Log Sheet

Title:
Overview:
Tape ID#: Location:
Date Shot: Camera/Gear:
Filmed by: Job#:

Page # ______ of Total Pages ______

Scene #	Description	In	Out	Quality A - F	Notes

DV Log Form © Copyright The Avanti Group, Inc. but is FREE to Use and Distribute as is

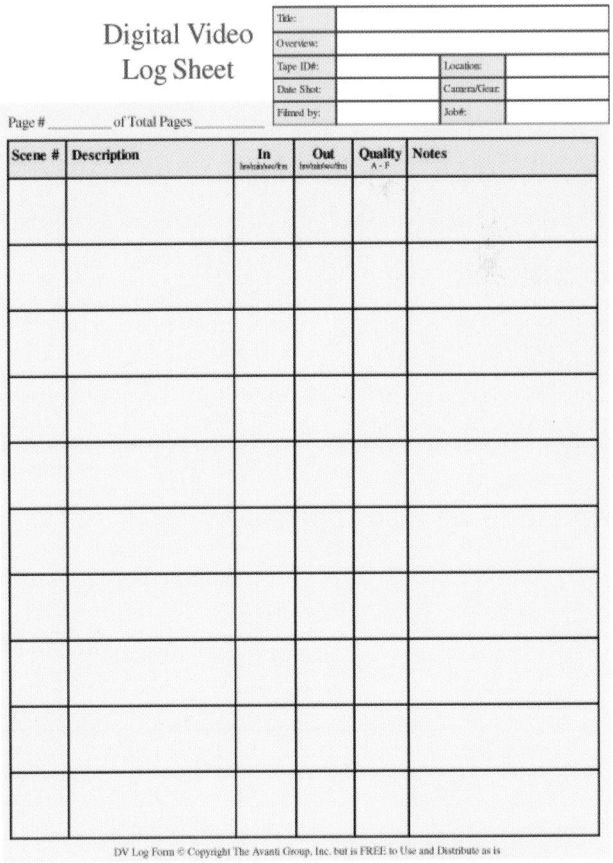

FIGURE 17.10
Sample of a log sheet. (Courtesy of the Avanti Group)

FIGURE 17.11
Logging can be done on paper or via software. Here a camera is connected directly into the computer to capture still frames from each clip and automatically import time code ins and outs. The screenshot shows the stored thumbnail frame, duration, and description. (Photos courtesy of Imagine Products)

FIGURE 17.12
Slates, or clapboards, are often used to identify each shot taken. The numbers on the slate are transferred to the logging sheet.

284

POSTPRODUCTION EDITING PROCESS

Postproduction editing provides ways of correcting and improving the final production:

- Sequences that are uninteresting, irrelevant, or repetitious can be removed or shortened.
- Errors can be corrected by omitting faulty sections and inserting retakes.
- The overall duration can be adjusted.
- Audio sweetening (adding additional sounds to the recording) can be done.
- Graphics can be added.
- Special effects can be added.

The Art and Techniques of Editing: Multiple Cameras and Postproduction

Directors edit by:

1. Selecting the appropriate shots (camera shots or prerecorded video).
2. Deciding on the order and duration of each shot.
3. Deciding on the cutting point (when one shot is to end and the next to begin).
4. Deciding on the type of transition between shots.
5. Creating good continuity.

Let's look at these points in more detail.

SELECTING THE APPROPRIATE SHOTS

Multicamera Editing

The director needs to review the available shots on the monitors and determine which one works best to tell the story (Figure 17.13).

Postproduction Editing

It is a normal practice to shoot much more than can be used on video. As the video can be immediately checked for quality, the director knows when the needed material has been captured. When the shooting is finally complete, it is time to review the footage. Generally, the following shots are found:

- Good shots that can easily be used
- Shots that cannot be used due to defects or errors of various types
- Repeated shots (retakes to achieve the best version)
- Redundant shots (too similar to others to use)

So the first stage of editing is to determine which of the available video (camera shots or recorded video) should be used. Once the shots are chosen, the next step is to decide on the order in which they will be presented.

THE ORDER OF SHOTS

To edit successfully, the editor must imagine being in the position of the audience. He or she is seeing a succession of shots, one after another, for the first time. As each shot appears, the editor must interpret it and relate it to previous shots, progressively building up ideas about what he or she is seeing.

FIGURE 17.13
This sitcom director, sitting out on the set, is deciding which of the cameras best communicates the story.

In most cases, the shots will be shown in chronological order. If the shots jump around in time or place, the result can be extremely confusing. (Even the familiar idea of "flashbacks" works only as long as the audience understands what is going on.)

When a series of brief shots are cut together, the fast pace of the program will be exciting, urgent, and confusing. A slow cutting rhythm using shots of longer duration is more gentle, restful, thoughtful, and/or sad.

In various circumstances, you may find that the order in which the series of shots are presented will influence your audience's interpretation of them. Even a simple example shows the nuances that easily arise: a burning building, a violent explosion, men running toward an automobile. Altering the order of these shots can modify what seems to be happening:

- Fire—automobile—explosion: Men killed while trying to escape from fire.
- Fire—explosion—automobile: Running from fire, men escaped despite explosion.
- Automobile—explosion—fire: Running men caused explosion, burning the building.

Not only is the imagination stimulated more effectively by implication rather than direct statements, but indirect techniques overcome many practical difficulties.

Suppose you join two shots: a boy looking upward, and a tree falling toward the camera. One's impression is that a boy is watching a tree being felled. Reverse the shots and the viewer could assume that the tree is falling toward the boy who, sensing danger, looks up. The actual images might be totally unrelated—they're just a couple of shots from a stock library.

WHERE SHOULD THE EDITS BE MADE?

The *moment* chosen for a cut can affect how smoothly one shot leads to another.

Directors usually transition at the following points:

- At the completion of a sentence, or even a thought
- When the talent takes a breath
- Whenever a reaction or clarifying shot is needed
- About a third of the way into an action such as standing up (this is a rule of thumb that can be broken)

If the first shot shows a man walking up to a door to open it, and the second shot is a close-up of him grasping the handle, the editor usually has to make sure that there is:

285

- No missing time (his arm hasn't moved yet . . . but his hand is on the handle in the close-up)
- No duplicated time (his hand takes hold of the handle in the first shot, then reaches out and grasps it again in the close-up)
- No overextended time (his hand takes the handle in the first shot, and holds it . . . and, in the second shot, is still seen holding it waiting to turn it)

There are occasions when editors deliberately "lose time" by omitting part of the action. For instance, a woman gets out of a car, and a moment later we see her coming into a room. We have not watched her through all the irrelevant action of going into the house and climbing the stairs. This technique tightens up the pace of the production and leaves out potentially boring bits during which audience interest could wane. Provided that the audience knows what to expect, and understands what is going on, this technique is an effective way of getting on with the story without wasting time.

Similarly, it is possible to "extend time," creating a dramatic impact. We see someone light the fuse of a stick of dynamite—cut to people in the next room—cut to the villain's expression—cut to the street outside—cut to him/her looking around—cut to the fuse, and so on, building up tension in a much longer time than it would really have taken for the fuse to burn down and explode the dynamite.

SPECIAL EFFECTS

Most nonlinear editing systems include a number of special effects that can be used to enhance the project. However, directors must be careful to use them appropriately. Overuse of special effects is the sign of an amateur production. Here is a brief list of typical effects:

Freeze frame: Stopping movement in the picture, and holding a still frame.
Strobe: Displaying the action as a series of still images flashed onto the screen at a variable rate.
Reverse action: Running the action in reverse.
Fast or slow motion: Running the action at a faster or slower speed than normal.
Picture in picture: A miniature picture inserted into the main shot.
Mosaic: The picture is reduced to a pattern of small single-colored squares of adjustable size.
Posterizing: Reduces tonal gradation to a few coarse steps.
Mirror: Flipping the picture from left to right, or providing a symmetrical split screen.
Time lapse: Still frames shot at regular intervals. When played back at normal speed, the effect is of greatly speeded-up motion.

WHAT TRANSITION SHOULD BE USED?

Transitions play a significant role in the audience's understanding of what is going on in a scene (Figure 17.14).

Cut

The *cut* or *take* is the most common, general-purpose transition. It is an instantaneous switch from one shot to another—a powerful dynamic transition that is the easiest to make.

Dissolve

The dissolve is an effect produced by fading out one picture while fading in another; a quiet, restful transition. A quick dissolve tends to imply that the action in the two scenes is happening at the same time. A slow dissolve suggests the passing of time or a different location. If a dissolve is stopped halfway, the result is a *superimposition*.

Wipe

The *wipe* is a novel transition that can have many different shapes. While it is occasionally effective, it can be easily overused and quickly become the sign of an amateur.

A

B

C

FIGURE 17.14
A cut portrays something happening in real time, a dissolve and wipe imply a change of time and/or location, and a fade implies the end of a segment or show. (Photos by Josh Taber)

A. *The cut (or take):* An instantaneous switch from one shot to another.
B. *The dissolve:* An effect produced by fading out one picture while fading in another.
C. *Fade:* A fade signifies a dissolve transition to or from black.

Fade

A *fade* is a gradual change (dissolve) between black and a video image. For example, at the end of a program there is usually a "fade to black," or if there is a "fade-up," it means that the director is transitioning from black to a video image. A slow fade suggests the peaceful end of action. A fast fade is rather like a "gentle cut" used to conclude a scene.

GOOD CONTINUITY

Let's say we are watching a dramatic television show. As the director switches from one camera to the next, we notice that in the close-up, the talent's hair is askew, but in the second camera's medium shot, the talent's hair is perfect. Cutting between the two shots in the editing room exposes a *continuity error*. If we see a series of shots that are supposed to show the same action from different angles, we do not expect to see radical changes in the appearance of things in the various images. In other words, we expect *continuity*.

If a glass is full in one shot and empty in the next, we can accept this—if something has happened between the two shots. But if someone in a storm scene appears wet in all the long shots, but dry in the close-ups, something is wrong. If they are standing smiling, with an arm on a chair in one shot but with a hand in a pocket and unsmiling when seen from another angle in the next shot, the sudden change during the cut can be very obvious. The sun may be shining in one shot and not in the next. There may be aircraft noises in one but silence in the next. Somebody may be wearing a blue suit in one shot and a gray one in the next. These are all very obvious—but they happen. In fact, they are liable to happen whenever action that is to appear continuous in the edited program stops and restarts.

There is an opportunity for a continuity error when the crew:

- Stops shooting, moves the camera to another position, and then continues the shoot.
- Repeats part of an action (a retake); it may be slightly different the second time, so you cannot edit unobtrusively with the original sequence.
- Shoots action over a period of time: part of it one day, and the rest of the scene on the next day.
- Alters how they shoot a scene, after part of it was already shot.

The only way to achieve good continuity is to pay attention to detail. Sometimes a continuity error will be much more obvious on the screen than it was during shooting. It is so easy to overlook differences when concentrating on the action, and the 101 other things that arise during production. If there are any doubts, there is a lot be said for reviewing the recording to see previous shots of the scene before continuing shooting.

How To Use Transitions

THE CUT

The cut is the simplest transition. It is dynamic, instantly associating two situations. Sudden change has a more powerful audience impact than a gradual one, and that is the strength of the cut.

Cutting, like all production treatment, should be purposeful. An unmotivated cut interrupts continuity and can create false relationships between shots. Cutting is not the same as repositioning the eyes as we glance around a scene, because we move our eyes with a full knowledge of our surroundings and always remain correctly oriented. On the screen, we know only what the camera shows us, although guesses or previous knowledge may fill out the environment in our minds.

THE FADE

Fade-in

A fade-in provides a quiet introduction to action. A slow fade-in suggests the forming of an idea. A fast fade-in has less vitality and shock value than the cut.

Fade-out

A quick fade-out has rather less finality and suspense than a cut-out. A slow fade-out is a peaceful cessation of action.

Cross-fade or Fade-out/-in

Linking two sequences, the cross-fade introduces a pause in the flow of action. Mood and pace vary with their relative speeds and the pause time between them. This transition can be used to connect slow-tempo sequences in which a change in time or place is involved. Between two fast-moving scenes, it may act as a momentary pause, emphasizing the activity of the second shot.

THE DISSOLVE

As mentioned earlier, a dissolve is produced by fading out one picture while fading in the next. The two images are momentarily superimposed; the first gradually disappears, being replaced by the second.

Dissolving between shots provides a smooth restful transition, with minimum interruption of the visual flow (except when a confusing intermixture is used). A quick dissolve usually implies that their action is concurrent (parallel action). A slow dissolve suggests differences in time or place.

Dissolves are generally comparative:

- Pointing out similarities or differences
- Comparing time (especially time passing)
- Comparing space or position (dissolving a series of shots showing progress)
- Helping to relate areas visually (when transferring attention from the whole subject to a localized part)

Dissolves are widely used as "soft" cuts, to provide an unobtrusive transition for slow-tempo occasions in which the instant nature of a cut would be disruptive. Unfortunately, they are also used to hide an absence of motivation when changing to a new shot!

A very slow dissolve produces sustained intermingled images that can be tediously confusing or boring.

THE WIPE

The wipe is a visual effect, mainly used for decorative transitions. It is primarily produced by a production switcher or on a nonlinear editing system. Wipes were very popular in early movies and are now mainly used in trailers and commercials.

Although the wipe can add a novelty to transitions, it can easily be overused. The audience can easily pay more attention to the wipe effect than the story line that it is intended to be moving forward. The wipe can also draw attention to the flat nature of the screen, destroying the three-dimensional illusion.

The wipe direction can aid or oppose the subject's movement, modifying its vigor accordingly. The wipe's edge may be hard-edged or soft-edged. The soft-edged wipe is much less distracting. Broad soft-edged wipes can be very unobtrusive.

Wipes have many geometric forms with a variety of applications. For example, a rectangular wipe may be used as a transition between close-up detail (entertainers) and an extreme long shot of the venue (Figure 17.15).

The Wipe's Split Screen

If a wipe is stopped before it is complete, the screen remains divided, showing part of both shots. In this way, you can produce an inset, revealing a small part of a second shot or, where the proportions are more comparable, a split screen.

The split screen can show us things simultaneously:

- Events taking place at the same time
- The interaction of events in separate locations (such as a satellite feed)

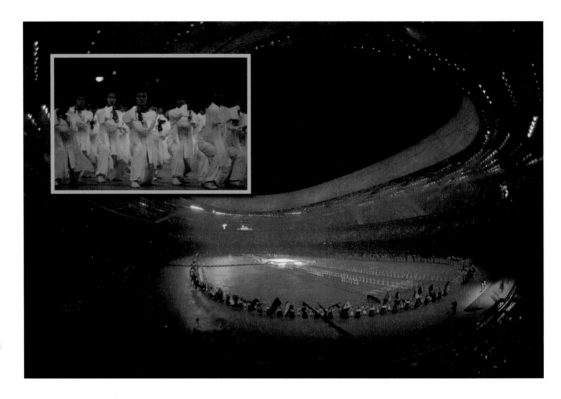

FIGURE 17.15
Wipes can be used in many different situations to enhance the viewing experience.

- A comparison of appearance and/or behavior of two or more subjects
- A before-and-after comparison (developments, growth, etc.)

Cause–Effect Relationships

Sometimes images convey practically the same idea, whichever way they are combined: a woman screaming and a lion leaping. But there is usually some distinction, especially where any cause–effect relationship is suggestible.

Cause–effect or effect–cause relationships are a common link between successive shots. Someone turns his or her head—the director cuts to show the reason. The viewer has become accustomed to this concept. Occasionally, you may deliberately show an unexpected outcome:

1. Two men are walking along a street.
2. Close-up shot of one of the men who is intently telling a story and eventually turns to his companion.
3. Cut to shot of his companion far behind, window-gazing.

The result here is a bit of a surprise and a little amusing. However, sometimes the viewer expects an outcome that does not develop and then feels frustrated or mystified, having jumped to the wrong conclusions:

1. Shot of a lecturer in long shot beside a large wall map.
2. Cut to a close-up of map.
3. Cut back to the lecturer who is now in an entirely different setting.

The director used the close-up of the map to relocate the speaker for the next sequence, but the viewer expected to find the lecturer beside the map, and can become disorientated.

Even more disturbing are situations where there is no visual continuity, although action has implied one:

1. Hearing a knock at the door, long shot of the girl as she turns.
2. Cut to a shot of a train speeding through the night.

The director thought that this would create tension by withholding the identity of the person who was outside the door. However, this inadvertently created a false relationship instead. Even where dialogue or action explains the second shot, this is usually an unsuitable transition. A mix or fade-out/-in would have prevented the confusion.

Montage

In a montage, a series of images are presented that combine to produce an associative effect. These images can be displayed sequentially or as a multiple-image screen (Figure 17.16).

Sequential Montage

One brief shot follows another in rapid succession, usually to convey a relationship or an abstract concept.

Multiple-image Montage

Several images can be shown at the same time by dividing the screen into two or four segments. Although more segments can be used, images become so small that they can lose their impact. These images may be of the same subject, or of several different subjects. They can be stills (showing various stages as an athlete completes a pole vault) or moving pictures (showing different people talking from different locations).

Multiple-image montages can be used for many different purposes—to show steps in a process, to compare, to combine different viewpoints, to show action taking place at different places, to demonstrate different applications of a tool, to show variety, and so on.

I

2

FIGURE 17.16
Montages can be created a number of ways, including: (1) a rapid succession of related images and (2) juxtaposed images, such as this quad split. (Photos in bottom image courtesy of the U.S. Department of Defense)

Duration of Shots

If a shot is too brief, the viewer will have insufficient time to appreciate its intended information; if it's held too long, their attention wanders. Thoughts possibly begin to dwell on the sound and then eventually to channel switching. The limit for most subjects is roughly 15 seconds, depending on the complexity of the shot. A static shot has a much shorter time limit!

The "correct" duration for a shot depends on its purpose. We may show a hand holding a coin for half a minute as its features are described by a lecturer, whereas in a drama, a one-second shot can tell us that the thief has successfully stolen it from the owner's pocket.

Many factors influence how long a shot can be held:

- The amount of information you want the viewer to assimilate (general impression, minute detail)
- How obvious and easily discernable the information is
- Subject familiarity (its appearance, viewpoint, associations, etc.)
- How much action, change, or movement the shot contains
- Picture quality (detail and strong composition hold most interest)

During an exciting scene, for example, when the duration of shots is made shorter and shorter as the tension grows, the audience is conscious only of growing agitation, and fast-moving action (Figure 17.17).

Audience attention is normally keyed to production pace. A short flash of information during a slow-tempo sequence may pass unnoticed, yet in a fast-moving sequence it would have been fully comprehended.

Priority: Video or Sound?

It is worth remembering during the editing phase that either the pictures or the audio may be given *priority*. For example, the dialogue has priority when shooting an important speech. Although the camera should focus on the speaker, a single unchanging shot would become visually boring, even with changes in shot size. To make it more interesting, a number of "cutaway shots" are usually used of the audience, special guests, reactions, and so on. But the dialogue is continuous and unbroken—even when editing the image.

If the speech was too long, it may need to be edited in postproduction in order to hold the audience's attention. Generally the most important passages are then edited together. In this situation, visually it would be easy for the audience to *see* that segments had been removed, therefore shots of the audience may need to be placed over the edits.

There are occasional scenes in which two people are supposed to be speaking to each other, although they were actually shot separately. For instance, all the shots of a boy stranded on a cliff would be taken at the same time (with dialogue). All the shots and comments of his

FIGURE 17.17
Tension can be increased by quicker cutting. Here an increasing cutting rate is combined with closer and closer shots. (Photos by Tyler Young)

rescuer at the top of the cliff would be shot at another time. During editing, the shots with their respective speech would be cut together to provide a continuous conversation.

So there are times when the images have priority, and the sound must be closely related to what we are seeing. Other times, the sound will be the priority, and everything has to be edited to support that sound.

Good Directing/Editing Techniques

If editing is done well, the audience does not notice it, but is absorbed in its *effect*. There are certain established principles in the way one edits, and although like all "rules" they may be occasionally disregarded, they have been created out of experience. Here are a few of the most common:

- Avoid cutting between shots of extremely different sizes of the same subject (close-up to long shot). It is a bit jolting for the audience.
- Do not cut between two shots of the same size (close-up to close-up) of the same subject. It produces a *jump cut*. (See Figure 17.18.)
- If two subjects are going in the same direction (chasing, following), have them both going across the screen in the same direction. If their screen directions are opposite, it suggests that they are meeting or parting.
- Avoid cutting between still (static) shots and moving images (panning, tilting, zooming, etc.), except for a specific purpose.
- If you have to break the continuity of action (deliberately or unavoidably), introduce a cutaway shot. But try to ensure that this relates meaningfully to the main action. During a boxing match, a cutaway to an excited spectator helps the tension. A cutaway to a bored spectator (just because you happen to have the unused shot) would be meaningless, although it can be used as a comment on the main action.
- Avoid cutting to shots that make a person or object jump from one side of the screen to the other.

293

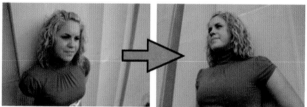
A

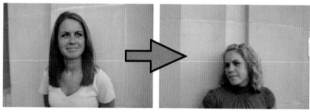
B

C

FIGURE 17.18
Matching cuts: people. (Photos by Josh Taber)
When cutting between images of people, avoid the following distracting effects:
A. Mismatched camera angles.
B. Changes in headroom.
C. Jump cuts: Avoid cutting between shots that are only slightly different in size. The subject suddenly appears to jump, shrink, or grow.

Anticipating Editing

It does not matter how good the video images are; if they are inappropriate, they may not be able to be used. As you plan your shots, keep in mind that the transition from one image to another has to work smoothly. Following are some of the issues to think about when shooting.

MULTICAMERA AND POSTPRODUCTION EDITING

- Edits should be motivated. There should be a reason for the edit.
- Avoid *reverse-angle shots* (shots from the other side of the axis of action) unless needed for a specific reason (such as slow-motion shots of a sports event), or if it is unavoidable (such as when crossing the road to shoot a parade from the other side). Include *head-on shots* (frontal shots) of the same action. These shots can work as transitional shots.
- Keep "cute shots" to a minimum, unless they can really be integrated into the program. These include such subjects like reflections, silhouettes against the sunset, animals or children at play, footsteps in the sand, and so on. They take up valuable time and may have minimal use. However, there are times when beauty shots have their place, such as an establishing shot.
- Where possible, include features in shots that will help provide the audience with the context of the event. This helps them identify the specific location (such as landmarks).
- Always check what is happening in the background behind the talent or subject. Distractions, such as people waving, trash cans, and signs, can take the audience's attention away from the main subject. When shooting multiple takes of a scene, watch the background for significant changes that will make editing the takes together difficult.

POSTPRODUCTION EDITING

- Include *cover shots* (long shots) of action wherever possible to show the overall view of the action.
- Always leave several seconds of *run-in* and *run-out* (sometimes called *heads* and *tails*) at the start and finish of each shot. Do not begin recording just as the action is beginning or the talent is about to speak or stop immediately when action or speech finishes. Spare footage at the beginning and end of each shot will allow more flexible editing.
- Include potential *cutaway shots* that can be used to cover edits when any sequence is shortened or lengthened. These could include crowd shots, longs shots, and people walking by.
- Try to anticipate continuity. If there are only a few shots taken in daylight and others at night, it may not be practical to edit them together to provide a continuous sequence.
- Where there is going to be commentary over the video (voiceover), allow for this in the length and pace of takes. For example, avoid inappropriately choppy editing due to shots being too brief. (Editors sometimes have to slow-motion or still-frame a very short shot to make it usable.)
- Plan to include long shots and close-up shots of action, to provide additional editing options. For example, where the action shows people crossing a bridge, a variety of angles can make a mundane subject visually interesting. For example, an LS—walking away from camera toward bridge; MS—walking on the bridge, looking over; VLS— shooting up at the bridge from the river below; LS—walking from the bridge to the camera on the far side; and so on.
- Remember that environmental noises can provide valuable bridging sound between shots when editing. They can be recorded as a *wild track* (unsynced sound).
- Wherever possible, use an identifying board or slate at the start of each shot. Otherwise, the talent or camera operator can state the shot number so that the editor knows where it goes in the final production.

DIRECTING/EDITING ETHICS

Editing is a powerful tool. And we cannot forget that the way a sequence is directed or edited can strongly influence an audience's interpretations of what is happening. Editing can manipulate—sometimes unwittingly—and, particularly in factual programs (newscasts, documentaries), one needs to be aware of the underlying ethics of certain treatment. A sequence of pictures can be selective, misleading the audience:

- One could deliberately avoid showing significant reactions by cutting out enthusiastic applause or heckling during a speech.
- Omitting important action or dialogue: When a person rises, turns to another, bows reverently, and slowly leaves the room, this action could be edited so that we see the person rise, open the door, and exit—apparently departing abruptly and unceremoniously, and giving a very different impression of events.
- Introduce misleading or ambiguous action: During a speech, cutting between shots of people leaving or of a person in the audience yawning or sleeping.
- Introducing false material: Showing enthusiastic applause that is actually associated with a speech different from the one we have been watching.

REVIEW QUESTIONS

1. Describe the two main types of editing (live and postproduction) and explain how they are alike.
2. How does the act of editing two clips together affect the audience?
3. What is the difference between linear and nonlinear editing?
4. Explain the nonlinear editing process.
5. Why log video footage?
6. How do you determine the order of shots?
7. What are the basic switcher transitions and when are they used?
8. Why is ethics an issue when editing?

PART 6

Production Techniques

CHAPTER 18

Production Practices

"Cutting has sometimes become too frenetic. It is important to let the action in the frame tell the story instead of fast cutting."

John Nienaber, Producer

Terms

Action line/axis of action line/eye line: The imaginary line along the direction of the action in the scene. Cameras should shoot from only one side of this line.

Crash start: Takes us straight into the program, which appears to have begun already: An automobile screams to a stop outside a store, a figure throws a bomb that explodes, an alarm bell shrills, a police siren wails—the show has begun and titles roll over the chasing vehicles.

Cutaway shot: These shots are used to cover edits when any sequence is shortened or lengthened. Generally, it is a shot of something outside of the current frame.

Filmic space: Filmic space intercuts action that is concurrent at different places: As a soldier dies . . . his son is born back home.

Filmic time: Omits intermediate action, condensing time and sharpening the pace. We cut from the automobile stopping to the driver entering an apartment.

Pace: The rate of emotional progression. A slow pace suggests dignity, solemnity, contemplation, and deep emotion; a fast pace conveys energy, excitement, confusion, brashness, and so on.

Teaser: Showing dramatic, provocative, intriguing highlights from the production, before the opening titles. The goal is to convince the audience to stay for the entire production.

Television production companies all over the world follow surprisingly similar practices. This is partially due to the nature of the medium and partially due to the result of sharing knowledge and experience.

PRODUCTION PRESSURES

Preoccupation with the organization and coordination of production mechanics leaves most directors little time to meditate on the medium's aesthetics. Rehearsal time is limited. The camera and sound crews are meeting the director's brainchild for the first time and need to be guided in the interpretation. If the treatment is elaborate and exacting, there is greater opportunity for problems that require immediate solution. If the production is shot out of

299

sequence, it becomes that much more difficult to ensure that each segment is coherent and will provide good continuity when edited together. In such circumstances, there is an understandable temptation to substitute effective known mechanics for creative experiment. However, there has to be a balance.

SHOOTING STYLES

There are a number of different approaches to shooting, ranging from unscripted to fully scripted.

In *unscripted* shooting, the camera tends to record available events, perhaps working from a rough outline (shooting plan). Material is selected during postproduction and compiled into a program format with added commentary. This technique is often used when shooting documentaries and news stories.

Fully scripted productions, on the other hand, are first broken down into their individual shots or scenes, and then the techniques involved for each shot or group of shots are assessed. The staged action is then methodically shot out of story sequence (according to a shooting schedule/plan) for maximum economy and efficiency. For example, if the story line requires a series of intercut shots between the heroine at the cliff top and the hero below, all the sequences involved are shot at one camera setup, then the camera is moved to the other angle for the next shots.

This out-of-sequence shooting prevents having to constantly move the camera back and forth. It saves time (which is money) with fewer camera setups, lighting, and audio, and uses actors more economically.

SINGLE-CAMERA TECHNIQUES

Single-camera shooting is the traditional method of filmmaking. Two or more cameras are used only for situations in which repeat action would be impracticable or costly, or simultaneous angles are required, such as when derailing a train.

Shooting out of sequence often requires the actors to repeat their action for each change in camera viewpoint or shot length, which can introduce continuity problems. Action, gestures, expressions, costume, lighting, and so on must match within the various intercut shots and relate to the story development, although they may have been filmed at different times.

Single-Camera Setups

After a sequence of shots is carefully edited, the continuity can appear so natural that viewers will not think about the fact that it was originally shot as a disjointed series of individual setups.

In a typical sequence, we may find ourselves close to a man as he walks—yet an instant later see him from a distant viewpoint. The camera is often "left behind" as he moves away—yet is at his destination as he arrives (Figure 18.1). The overall effect here is smooth-flowing and provides a variety of angles. To do the obvious and shoot this entire sequence as continuous action would have required several cameras, spread over a significant distance—an approach that might not be practical anyway. Usually, it would not provide the same effect.

Shooting Uncontrolled Action

When using a single camera to shoot broad action over which you have no control, you have the option of:

- Remaining at a fixed viewpoint and relying on the zoom lens to provide a variety of shots.
- Moving the camera to a series of different vantage points, changing the angle and shot size to capture the main features of the occasion.

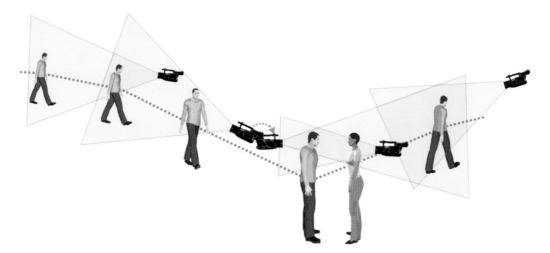

FIGURE 18.1
Single-camera shooting: in order to achieve smooth-flowing action with one camera, a series of camera setups are often necessary.

Clearly, if you are shooting a public event such as a parade with a single camera, the first option would be very limiting. However, if you move around or stop shooting, you will probably lose coverage of some of the action, unless you can time your moves to fit in with a lull in the proceedings (Figure 18.2).

In order to simplify the editing process, it is important to shoot plenty of general material that can be used as cutaway shots. Cutaways tend to be of two types: active and passive. The active cutaway includes subjects that can be edited into the program only at a specific moment, such as shots of a town clock showing that the parade is about to start or the crowd's responses to a specific event. Passive cutaways can be used at almost any time, and might include reflections, flags, sun through branches, and so on.

With news events, you make the most of whatever opportunities are available. You may be able to plan exactly what you are going to do, checking out the route and your angles in advance. You may even be able to influence the events a little, arranging for the beauty queen in the procession to turn and smile in the direction of the camera as she passes. But, on the whole, you have to take things as you find them. There are usually no repeats!

Shooting Controlled Action

When shooting situations that you can control, such as interviews, drama sequences, and the like, the situation is very different from shooting uncontrolled action. Now you can arrange the action, the camera setups, and sometimes the lighting and staging (background and props) to fit each individual shot.

If you want to repeat the same action so that you have long shots, medium shots, and close-up shots of it to ultimately cut together, it is quite practical. Instead of having to select from whatever is happening at the location, you have the option to change things to improve the story line. This could include having the person lean over the bridge to

301

FIGURE 18.2
When shooting with a single camera at a public event, such as this parade, the camera operator needs to decide whether to stay in one place and get whatever comes his way, or move around to different angles to obtain better shots, but possibly miss some of the action.

improve the composition, waiting for the sun to come out, or pausing while a loud aircraft passes overhead.

You generally take the shots in the most convenient, rational order. You can then edit them together afterwards to fit the story line sequence. If, for instance, you have a series of shots of people on either side of a river, it is obviously more sensible, and efficient, to shoot all of the action on one side and then move to the other, rather than moving back and forth, shooting in the script's running order.

When shooting discontinuously, you have to take care that there are no obvious discrepancies that spoil the continuity between the shots when they are cut together. If in our example there happened to be bright sunshine when shooting on one bank of the river but pouring rain when shooting on the other, the intercut shots would look pretty unconvincing (Figure 18.3).

FIGURE 18.3
If the editor wanted to cut between these two shots, continuity would be a problem. Note that the man's shoes are a different color in each shot.

Segmented Shooting

Shooting controlled action with a single camera normally requires the director to break down the action into a series of brief camera setups or action segments. If part of the action adds nothing to the situation, it may be deliberately omitted altogether. At other times, the action may be emphasized. Let's imagine some options with a simple situation:

Someone is walking along the street.

- If we are only really interested in what the person does when he or she reaches a destination, the walk can be omitted completely.
- Perhaps we want to emphasize that the person has hurt a leg, and every step is taken in agony. In that case, we might follow him or her in close detail—the heavy footsteps, the hesitant walking stick, and the uneven sidewalk—in a series of shots taken from different angles.
- Suppose the story's aim is to intrigue us. We wonder what is going to happen . . . is he or she going to be attacked by a robber? In this situation, we would probably shoot the sequence quite differently. The entire walk might be filmed on a stationary camera, using a continuous panning shot. We show the person walking past the camera into the distance—and out of the shot. We hold the empty frame . . . and their pursuer moves into the foreground of the shot.

Clearly, how the action is broken up will depend on the dramatic purpose of the image sequence.

As an exercise, record a long action sequence from a motion picture or documentary. It might be showing someone rock climbing, sailing a boat, or in a car chase. Analyze the shots that make up this action sequence. Time them. Think carefully about the variety of angles.

In a car chase, we might find that at one moment, the camera is in the car beside the driver; in the next, we see a frontal shot of the car showing the driver alone in the car. Cut, and we are behind the driver's shoulder looking through the windshield; and now we are looking down from a high building as the car maneuvers a corner. It moves away into the distance and—cut—we see it coming up toward the camera.

When watching this treatment, we never question the rapidly changing angles, or why the camera is suddenly located on a helicopter. When shooting in the desert, we see the car vanish into the distance—without wondering whether it is going to come back to pick up the camera operator!

Many types of action, in reality, can take too long and become somewhat boring to watch. Shoot them continuously, and the audience's interest will wander. Instead, break sustained action into continually varying angles, and you can create a lively pace and maintain the viewer's interest.

One specific function of editing is that we can create an illusion of continuity between shots or situations where in fact none exists. This is not only a valuable dramatic facility but it enables us to develop action sequences that in reality we could not shoot.

Imagine a scene showing a bird on a branch; a close shot as it dives into the stream, an underwater shot of fish, a fish is caught by the bird, the bird sits beside the river eating its catch. These are probably shots of different birds, and of different fish, shot at different times. The separate shots are edited together to form a complete effective action sequence.

We have looked at these examples in some detail, because they epitomize the thinking and the techniques that underlie single-camera shooting. As you will learn in the next section, they are noticeably different from multicamera treatments.

MULTICAMERA TECHNIQUES

Using two or more cameras gives you additional flexibility to handle any situation. Without missing any of the action, or needing action repeated, you can cut between different shots of the same subject, alter the camera's angle, and move to another area of the set (Figure 18.4).

You can instantly change the significance of a shot. You can provide fresh information, alter emphasis, point out new detail, show reactions, shift the audience's attention, compare relationships, and introduce visual variety. And all while the action continues.

Using several cameras, you can arrange to have one covering the action and another ready to catch the audience's reactions (Figure 18.5). But if you are shooting with a single camera, you are unlikely to turn away from the main event to see whether someone in the crowd is responding. You are more likely to shoot some reaction shots later (probably relating to an entirely different action), and edit them in for effect during postproduction.

Visual Variety

Static shots easily become boring. So audience interest can be encouraged by introducing movement and change—although, if overdone, the pictures can become a strain to watch. Rapid cutting demands continual viewer concentration, which is not easily sustained. Ceaseless action and camera moves lead to images that can wear out the audience. As always, the aim is a well-balanced blend with variations in pace, tempo, and emphasis.

Successful visual variety can be achieved by a number of ways, as described in the following subsections.

PERFORMER MOVEMENT

Most visual variety stems from action within the scene, as people alter positions and regroup. Quite often, more meaningful changes are achieved by talent movement than by camera moves or editing.

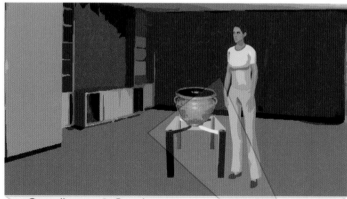

Overall scene & Cam I image

Cam 2 image

Cam 2

Cam I

FIGURE 18.4

Two-camera treatment: shots are divided between two cameras. Cam 1 concentrates on long shots and Cam 2 takes close-ups that provide detailed information.

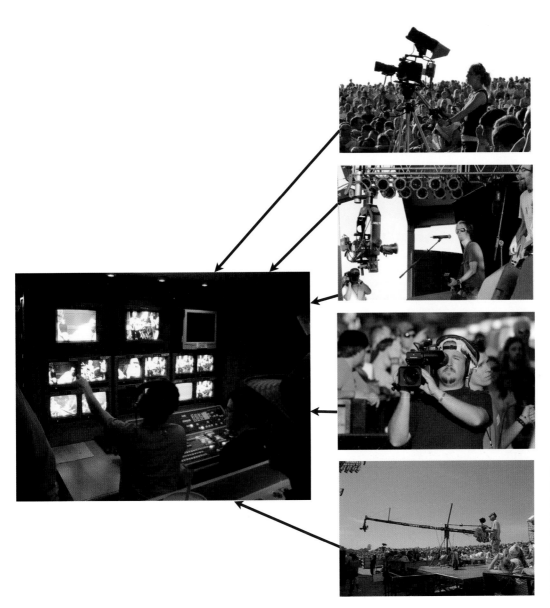

FIGURE 18.5
Shooting with multiple cameras allows the director to show a variety of angles, assisting in maintaining the audience's attention. (Photos by Josh Taber and Paul Dupree)

In a close shot, the talent dominates. As he or she moves away from the camera, the audience becomes more aware of their relationship to the surroundings. In long shots, these surroundings may dominate. So by changing the length of the shot, you change emphasis and create visual variation.

CHANGES BY GROUPING

Where people are seated (panels, talk shows), you can achieve visual variety by isolation, selectively shooting individuals, two-shots, and subgroups (Figure 18.6).

SHOOTING STATIC SUBJECTS

Visual variety can be introduced into your treatment of nonmoving subjects (statuary, pottery, paintings, flowers) by the way you shoot and light them. Variety can be created with viewpoint-altering camera movements: selectively panning over the subject, interrelating its various parts; changing to lighting isolate or emphasize sections or alter the subject's appearance; or handling smaller objects, turning them to show the different features.

FIGURE 18.6
Shooting groups: static groups can be broken into a series of smaller individual shots. For single-camera shooting, this involves repositioning the camera (or repeated action). With multicamera shooting, the director can cut between the various angles.

FIGURE 18.7
The décor, background, or lighting can add variety to a production.

VARIETY BY DÉCOR

The presentation of certain subjects may be restricted (piano playing, singers). They can be relatively static and meaningful shot variations can be limited. You can prevent sameness between productions by introducing variations in the décor. This can happen with background or scenic changes or by lighting. The pictures can look significantly different, even if the shots and angles follow a recognizable format (Figure 18.7).

Crossing the Axis of Action Line

Camera viewpoints can easily confuse the audience's sense of direction and their impression of spatial relationships if care is not taken when selecting camera positions. For example, during a basketball game, if cameras are placed on both sides of the court, it is confusing to see a player running toward the left side of the screen and then, when the director cuts to the camera on the other side of the court, seeing the same player running toward the right side of the court if he hasn't actually changed direction.

To avoid this, draw an imaginary line along the direction of the action (*action line, axis of action, eye line,* or *center line*). Then be careful that cameras shoot from only one side of this line—generally, it is not crossed. It is possible to dolly across the line, or shoot along it, or change its direction by regrouping people, but cutting between cameras on both sides of this imaginary line produces a *reverse cut* or *jump cut* (Figures 18.8, 18.9, and 18.10).

307

FIGURE 18.8
Crossing the axis of action line: By moving the camera across the line of action, the direction of the walk appears to change, confusing the audience. (Photos by Josh Taber)

FIGURE 18.9
The red line represents the axis of action at a sporting event. All "live" cameras must stay on one side of that line. The yellow area represents where the cameras can be placed on one side of the field of play. Sometimes additional cameras are placed on the other side for slow-motion replay, but not live.

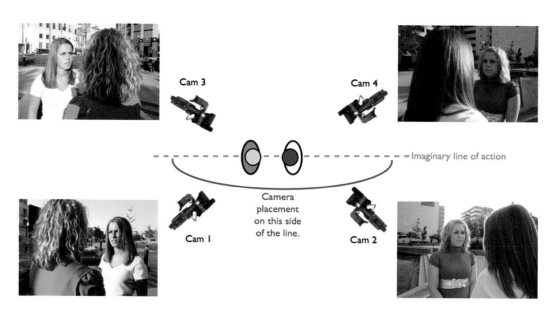

FIGURE 18.10
The line of action: Shots can be cut between cameras located on the same side of the imaginary line of action: between 1 and 2, or 3 and 4. Cutting between cameras on opposite sides of this line could cause a jump cut (1 and 3, 1 and 4, 2 and 3, 2 and 4). (Photos by Josh Taber)

FIGURE 18.11
Directors create an organized approach to covering the story, selecting camera positions that provide angles that are effective in showing the subject.

Organizing the Angles

It is important for directors to create an organized approach to covering the story. Obviously, you could just distribute the cameras around a location and just use the images that happen to be captured. However, even if the cameras captured some great images, there would usually be little relationship between these images, there would probably be some nearly identical shots and some useless shots, and the coverage would be erratic. Shots must be appropriately chosen and interrelated according to a coordinated plan, and only the director is in a position to do this (Figure 18.11).

Using this technique, you begin by analyzing where the action will take place (where people move, what they do there, and so on) and arrange strategic camera angles from which to shoot it.

Each camera position provides a series of shot opportunities; you select from these available shots as required (Figures 18.12 and 18.13).

At sports events, large concerts, and other large-scale public occasions, this is the only practical approach. Cameras are often widely dispersed, camera movement is often restricted, and the director sometimes has to rely on camera operators to use their initiative to find appropriate shots. The director's knowledge of actual shot opportunities is mostly derived from what the cameras reveal and on-the-spot assistants. He or she guides selection, adjusts shot sizes, suggests desirable shots, and chooses from the available material.

You can use a similar strategy in studio production for certain types of shows with a regular format. For example, you can assign specific shots to each camera:

Camera 1: Long shots and extreme long shots
Camera 2: Primarily close-up shots
Camera 3: Medium shots and close-ups

This approach is especially useful for unscripted "live" productions. However, it is also valuable for talent that knows which camera to look at for close-ups at any time.

309

FIGURE 18.12
Each camera position provides a limited number of shot opportunities on a news set. The director selects from the available shots as required. Note that the second camera moves from the main set to the chroma-key set. (Photos courtesy of KOMU-TV, WLEX, and Josh Taber)

Cam 1

Cam 3

Cam 2

FIGURE 18.13
In a formal interview, there are relatively few effective shots, although more than are available on a news set.

310

CAMERA MOVES

FIGURE 18.14
When shooting talent sitting down, be prepared to either follow him or her with the camera or have a second camera ready that is already zoomed out for when he or she stands. Otherwise, his or her head will be cut off. Similarly, be ready for the talent to sit, if he or she is standing.

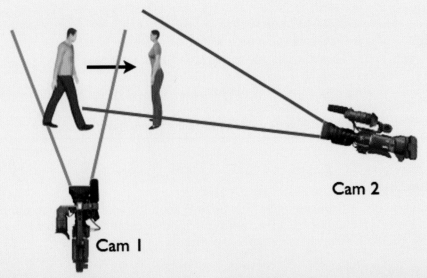

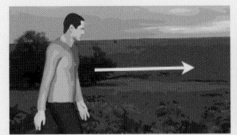

Shot from Cam 1

Shot from Cam 2

FIGURE 18.15
Widely spaced moves: if two people are quite a distance apart, you can cut between them, pan between them, or just shoot the action from a different angle.

311

Table 18.1	Arranging the Shot
Broad objectives	In arranging a shot, you should be able to answer such questions as: ■ What is the purpose of the shot? What is it aiming to show? ■ Is the shot to emphasize a specific point or feature? ■ Which is the main subject? ■ Are we primarily concerned with the subject or its relationship to another or to its background/environment?
The actual image	■ Is the shot too close or distant for its purpose? ■ Is the attention reasonably localized—or split or diffused? ■ Is the composition arrangement appropriate? ■ Is the subject suitably framed headroom, offset, edge cut off, overcrowded frame? ■ Are subjects clearly seen sharp, not obscured, good background contrast? ■ Is there any ambiguity or distraction in the shot?
The action	■ Are we aiming to show what a person is doing—clearly, forcefully, incidentally, not at all? ■ Does action (movement, gestures) pass outside the frame? ■ Are any important features or action accidentally excluded?

Continued

Table 18.1	Arranging the Shot (*Continued*)
Specific objectives	■ Is the presentation to be straightforward or dramatic? ■ Do we want to indicate subject strength or weakness? ■ Do we aim to reveal, conceal, mislead, puzzle? ■ What effect, mood, atmosphere are we seeking: businesslike, clinical, romantic, sinister? ■ Does the shot relate successfully to the previous and subsequent shots?

Program Opening

Establishing shots, usually a long or extreme long shot, introduce the scene and the action, setting the mood and influencing the audience's frame of mind toward what you have to say and show. There are many different types of openings.

THE FORMAL START

A "Good evening" or "Hello" introduces the show and moves into the content. Whether the presenter appears casual, reverent, indifferent, or enthusiastic can create an ambience directly influencing the audience's attitude.

THE TEASER

We are shown dramatic, provocative, intriguing highlights from the production before the opening titles. The goal is to convince the audience to stay for the entire production.

THE CRASH START

We are taken straight into the program, which appears to have begun already. An automobile screams to a stop outside a store, a figure throws a bomb that explodes, an alarm bell shrills, a police siren wails—the show has begun and titles roll over the chasing vehicles.

THE CHARACTER INTRODUCTION

A montage of symbols or shots of the hero in various predicaments provides an introduction to the characters that we are to meet.

THE EAVESDROPPING START

The camera peers through a house window, sees a group of people sitting around a table talking quietly, and moves in to join them.

THE SURPRISE WELCOME

The camera dollies in to someone who is supposedly preoccupied. Realizing that the audience has arrived, his welcome of "Oh, there you are!" provides informality—or nauseating artifice.

THE SLOW BUILD UP

The camera pans slowly round, arousing curiosity or suspense until we reach a climax point (the bloodstained dagger!). It is essential to avoid diminishing interest or anticlimax.

THE ATMOSPHERE INTRODUCTION

A series of strongly associative symbols establish the place, period, mood, or personality. On a shelf: a brass telescope, a ship in a bottle, and a well-worn uniform cap—the old sea captain is introduced long before we see him.

Focusing Audience Attention

Directors can hold the audience's attention by taking care with how they arrange and present subjects.

Audience concentration easily lapses, so you need to continually direct and redirect their attention to hold interest along specific lines. Such redirection implies change. But excess or uncontrolled change can lead to confusion or irritation. Pictorial change must be clearly motivated, to allow the viewer to readjust easily to each new situation.

Some of the most common ways of focusing the audience's attention on a specific area are (see Table 18.2):

Brightness: Eyes are always drawn to the brightest areas on the screen. This could include lighting, set design, or costumes (Figure 18.16).

Focus: Eyes are attracted to the sharpest areas of the image (Figure 18.17).

Motion: Movement can attract attention, such as having a person stand up within a seated group or moving the camera around the subject (Figure 18.18).

Dominant figure: Placing the dominant person or subject in a position that makes them stand out (Figure 18.19).

Table 18.2	Methods of Focusing Attention
Exclusion	Taking close-up shots. Excluding unwanted subjects. Using neutral backgrounds.
Visual indication	Indication with a finger or graphic of some type (arrow, circle).
Aural indication	A verbal clue or instruction: "Look at the black box."
Color	Using prominent contrasting hues against neutrals or muted (pastel) colors. The area of interest might have the lightest tones or maximum contrast in the picture.
Camera viewpoint	Avoid weak angles (side or rear shots) or weakening angles (high or long shots).
Composition	Use convergent lines or patterns, picture balance, isolation, and prominence through scale.
Contrasting the subject with its surroundings	Through differences in relative size, shape, proportions, scale, type of line, movement, or association.
By movement	Movement attracts according to its speed, strength, and direction. Change direction during motion, or interrupt and resume, rather than maintaining sustained action. According to how it is introduced, a movement can attract attention to itself (a moving hand), the subject (person whose hand it is), or the purpose of the movement (what the hand is pointing at). Remember, when the camera moves (or zooms), it can virtually create the illusion of the subject movement. Synchronizing a movement with dialogue, music, or effects (especially the subject's own) gives it strength and draws attention to it. Having a person move on his or her own dialogue emphasizes both action and speech.
By subject attitude	Having performers use strong movements—upward or diagonal, stand up, play to camera, move in front of others, or scenic elements.

FIGURE 18.16
Attention can be drawn by lighting or even clothing. Eyes are always drawn to the brightest area of the screen. (Photos by Lee Peters and David Clement)

FIGURE 18.17
Eyes are always drawn to the sharpest parts of the image.

FIGURE 18.18
Movement can draw attention. This includes talent movement as well as camera movement (such as a moving dolly as shown here).

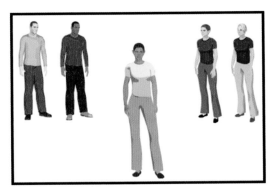 

FIGURE 18.19
By placing a person or an object in a dominant position, viewers know where to look.

Shifting Visual Interest

It is just as necessary to be able to shift the viewer's attention to another aspect of the picture as it is to localize their attention originally. You can do this by readjusting any of the influences that we use to originally direct their attention. Here are a few of the alternatives:

- Transfer the original emphasis (contrast, isolation, etc.) to the new subject.
- Use linking action; first person looks to camera right—cut to new subject on screen right.
- Weaken the original subjects by reducing their size within the picture or alter the camera height when shooting.
- Adjust the focus, pulling it from the old subject to the new.
- Change the sound source; a new person speaks instead.

Table 18.3 Selecting Camera Treatment

	Mechanical Purpose	Artistic Purpose
Why pan or tilt?	■ To follow action ■ To exclude unwanted subjects ■ To show an area that is too large to be contained in a static shot	■ To join separate items ■ To show spatial relationships ■ To show cause/effect ■ To transfer attention ■ To build up anticipation or suspense ■ As an introductory move
Why elevate the camera (camera up)?	■ To see over foreground objects ■ To see overall action	■ To reduce prominence of foreground ■ To look down onto objects ■ To reduce subject strength
Why drop the camera down (ped down)?	■ To frame picture with foreground objects ■ To obscure distant action ■ To obtain level shots of low subjects	■ To increase their prominence ■ To emphasize subject strength
Why dolly in?	■ To see or emphasize detail or action ■ To exclude nearby subjects ■ To recompose a shot after one of the subjects has been repositioned or exited	■ To underline an action or reaction ■ To emphasize subject importance ■ To localize attention ■ To reveal new information

Continued

Table 18.3	Selecting Camera Treatment *(Continued)*	
	Mechanical Purpose	**Artistic Purpose**
Why dolly in? (continued)	■ To change emphasis to another subject ■ To emphasize an advancing subject	■ To follow a receding subject ■ To provide spatial awareness ■ To increase tension ■ To create a subjective effect
Why dolly back (out)?	■ To extend field of view ■ To include more of subject(s) ■ To include widespread action ■ To reveal new information ■ To include entry of a new subject ■ To accommodate advancing action ■ To withdraw from action	■ To reduce emphasis ■ To show relationship or scale of previous shot to the wider view (whole of subject, other subjects) ■ To increase tension, as more significance is gradually revealed ■ To create surprise (e.g., reveal unsuspected onlooker) ■ To provide spatial awareness ■ To create a subjective effect
Why truck (also referred to as a crab or track)?	■ To follow subject moving across the scene ■ To reveal the extent of a subject/ scene, section by section ■ To examine a long subject or series of subjects	■ To emphasize depth
Why arc?	■ To see subject from another viewpoint, without transitions ■ To exclude/include a foreground/ background subject ■ To realign or recompose subject(s) when it moves ■ To reveal new information or a new (extra) subject ■ To correct for inaccurate subject positions (actor off marks)	■ To change visual emphasis
Why follow a moving subject?	■ In close shots—to keep it in frame while showing reactions or detail information ■ In long shots—to show subject progress through an environment, or its relationship to other subjects	■ To spatially interrelate subjects ■ To avoid transitions or viewpoint changes; to maintain continuity

Creating Tension

Tension in a dramatic situation derives partly from the dialogue, story line, and interaction between characters, but it can also be considerably influenced by the way in which the subject is presented:

- Using progressively more powerful shots (cutting to closer and closer shots; lower viewpoints, gradual canting).
- Using suspenseful music and effects.

- Presenting ambiguous information—is the nocturnal shadow a bush … or a prowler?
- Presenting insufficient information—the audience sees the figure in the doorway—is it the bad guy (Figure 18.20)?
- The audience knows something a character does not—the victim runs to escape, but we know the route is blocked.
- A character is suddenly confronted with an insurmountable problem—the stairway collapses up on reaching it.

FIGURE 18.20
Tension is often created by presenting insufficient information. The audience sees the man watching from a shadowy area and wonders: bad guy or good guy?

The borderline between creating tension and creating a ludicrous situation can be narrow. An intended climax too easily becomes an anticlimax. So you have to take care not to emphasize the trivial, or unintentionally to permit an emotional let-down after an emotional peak.

Pace

We might define *pace* as the rate of emotional progression. A *slow pace* suggests dignity, solemnity, contemplation, and deep emotion; a *fast pace* conveys energy, excitement, confusion, and brashness.

A well-balanced show continually readjusts its pace. A constant rapid tempo is exhausting; a slow sustained one becomes dull. Pace comes from an accumulation of factors:

The script: Scene length, speech durations, phrasing, word lengths. Sharp witty exchanges produce a faster pace than lengthy monologue.

The delivery: Fast, high-pitched, interrupted sounds provide a rapid pace compared with slow, low-pitched ones.

Production treatment: The rate of camera movement, switching, performer movements.

The eye can maintain a quicker pace than the ear. The eye can assess, classify, and evaluate almost immediately, but the ear has to piece together consecutive sounds to interpret their overall meaning.

Although a fast visual pace is readily assimilated, it is usually at the expense of less attention to the accompanying sound—unless visual changes are so rapid that the viewer ignores the information and just listens! When emphasis is to be on the sound, visual pace generally needs to be relaxed.

Timing

There are two different kinds of timing in television. One kind deals with a clock or stopwatch. This type of timing refers to keeping a television program on schedule—when to play commercials, how long a story can be on the news, and so on. Because television is run on a very specific time schedule, the clock is an important piece of production equipment.

The second type of timing is artistic timing. Artistic timing is choosing the right moment and duration for an action—exactly when to cut, the speed of a transition, the pause duration between a comment and a response.

Inept timing may mistakenly communicate the wrong emphasis and can disrupt continuity.

VISUAL CLARITY

If an image is to effectively communicate its message quickly and unambiguously, the audience must be able to see relevant details easily and clearly. The goal is to avoid confusion, ambiguity, obscured information, restricted visibility, distractions, and similar visual confusion.

Viewing Angle

A poor viewing angle can make even the commonest subjects look unfamiliar. Occasionally, this may be done deliberately. However, the goal is to provide a clear, unambiguous presentation, even if, for instance, it becomes necessary for a demonstrator to handle or place items in an unaccustomed way to improve shot clarity.

Distractions

Poor lighting treatment can distract and confuse the audience, hide the subject's contours, and cast misleading or unmotivated shadows (especially from unseen people). It can also unnecessarily create hot spots, lens flares, and specular reflections.

Strong tonal contrasts can distract, as can strongly marked detail. When someone stands in front of a very busy background, the audience may begin to look at the background instead of the subject (Figure 18.21).

Slightly defocused details, particularly lettering that we cannot read easily, can sidetrack the audience's attention. Directors should also be careful about including strongly colored defocused objects in the background. These objects should be excluded from shots whenever possible because they become distractions.

Confusing and Frustrating Subject Treatment

How often, when watching regular television productions, do you experience total frustration or antagonism at the way the show is being handled? It is important for directors to be very sensitive to these situations. Here is a list of frequent annoyances:

- Someone points to a detail—but it is too small or fuzzy for the audience to see.
- Titling or graphics are shown—but too briefly for us to read or examine.
- A demonstrator shows us how to prune a tree—but the camera gets a close-up shot at the end, depriving the viewer of the "big picture."
- We can hear the events taking place off-camera—but the camera is still on the talent.
- The interviewer who asks questions (quoting from notes)—but is not really listening to the guest's replies.
- The interviewer who asks the guest questions that require only "Yes" or "No" replies.

FIGURE 18.21
Background contrast is often difficult to deal with. Although strong tonal contrasts can be too distracting, similar tones can often prove distracting as well.

- A too-brief glimpse of a subject—followed by a shot of the commentator talking about it instead.
- The shot that leaves us wondering what we are supposed to be looking at or where we are now.
- Too much information, such as statistics, is covered, resulting in the audience being overwhelmed.

The Visual Problem

Directors often have to deal with subjects in their programs for which directly appropriate visuals are not obvious. These may include:

- Abstract subjects—philosophical, spiritual, social concepts
- Imaginary events—hypothetical, fantasy
- Historical events—before photography, or unphotographed events
- Events that will be occurring in the future
- Shooting is not possible—prohibited or subject inaccessible
- Shooting is impracticable—too dangerous, meaningful shots impossible
- Appropriate visuals are too costly—would involve distant travel, copyright problems

POSSIBLE SOLUTIONS

When directors cannot show the actual subject being discussed, they often have to provide suitable alternative images—a kind of visual padding or screen filler (also known as "wallpaper shots").

The most economical solution, and the least compelling, is to introduce a commentator, who tells us about what we cannot see, as he or she stands at the now-empty location (historical battlefield, site of the crime, or outside the conference hall). Inserts in the form of photographs, video clips, paintings, or drawings (typically used for courtroom reports) can all provide illustrative material. Occasionally, a dramatic re-enactment may work.

When discussing future events, stills or stock library shots of a previous occasion may be used to suggest the atmosphere or to show what the event may look like (celebration days, processions); see Figure 18.22. A substitute subject (not the animal that escaped but one just like it) may also be used, letting the audience know that they are not seeing the actual subject.

FIGURE 18.22
Often stock footage can be used when discussing abstract ideas. For example, this stock airport could be shown when discussing future growth of the airport.

Occasionally, the camera can even show the absence of the subject: the frame of the stolen painting or where the castle once stood.

Associated subjects are frequently used. We visit the poet's birthplace, often using stock tourist location shots. However, they may not be strictly applicable (wrong period), or irrelevant (not architecture, but social conditions influenced his poetry). But apart from family album snapshots or newspaper cuttings, nothing else may be available!

When using library (stock) shots or stills, there is always the danger that available shots will become overly familiar through repeated use. This issue is particularly likely with historic material, or unexpected tragedy (assassination, air crash).

Some forms of visual padding suit a variety of occasions. The same waving wheat field can epitomize food crops, daily bread, prosperity, agriculture, the war on insect pests, and so on.

Abstracts can be pressed into service at almost any time. Atmospheric shots of rippling water, shadows, light reflections, into-the-sun flares, and defocused images are all used regularly (Figure 18.23).

FIGURE 18.23

320

Abstract subjects can be difficult to visualize. This type of photo is often used by people attempting to visualize the concept of "heaven."

The Illusion of Time

Motion-picture editing has long accustomed us to the concepts of filmic space and time:

Filmic space intercuts action that is concurrent at different places: As a soldier dies, his son is born back home.
Filmic time omits intermediate action, condensing time and sharpening the pace: We cut from the automobile stopping to the driver entering an apartment.

When all the intervening action has no plot relevance, the viewer can often get frustrated with a slow pace just to state the obvious.

Time Lapses

There are a number of techniques that can be used to indicate the passage of time. Explanatory titles are direct and unambiguous, but other and subtler techniques are generally preferable. For short time lapses:

- Slow fade-out, new scene slowly fades in.
- Cutting away from a scene, we assume that time has elapsed when returning to it.
- A time indicator (clock, sundial, burning candle) shows passage of time.
- Lighting changes with passing time (a sunlit room gradually darkens).
- Dissolve or wipe between before/after shots of a meal, fireplace, and similar images.
- Transition between sounds with time association—nocturnal frogs and owls to early-morning roosters and birdsong.
- Defocus shot, cut, dissolve, or wipe to another defocused shot and then refocus.

For longer time lapses:

- A calendar changes pages or changes date.
- Seasonal changes—from winter snow to spring flowers.

- Changes in personal appearance—beard growth, aging, fashion changes.
- New to old—dissolving from a fresh newspaper to a yellow, crumpled, discarded version.

Flashbacks

A familiar device, the flashback turns back time to see events before the present action as a reminder or an explanation, or for comparison purposes. Typical methods include reversing the previously discussed time-lapse techniques (such as the old becoming new again), a special effect wipe, a defocus, or even a brief flash cut-in ($\frac{1}{2}$–2 seconds long) can convey recognition or moments of memory recall.

Cutaway Shots

By cutting from the main action to a secondary activity or associated subjects (such as spectator reactions), you can:

- Join shots that are unmatched in continuity or action.
- Remove unwanted, unsuccessful, dull, or excess material.
- Suggest a time lapse to compress or expand time.
- Show additional explanatory information (detail shots).
- Reveal the action's environment.
- Show who a person is speaking to; how another person is responding (reaction shots).
- Show what the speaker is seeing, talking about, or thinking about.
- Create tension to give dramatic emphasis.
- Make comment on a situation (cutting from a diner to a pig at trough).

Interviews can be shot using a continuous multicamera setup or as a one-camera treatment. A separate series of cutaway shots (cutaways, nod shots) are often recorded afterwards, in which the interviewer and interviewee are seen in singles or over-the-shoulder shots, smiling, nodding, reacting, or looking interested. When edited in (to disguise cuts, continuity breaks, or to add visual variety), the added shots appear quite natural. Without these cutaways, any continuously held shot would jump frames when edited (although dissolves may improve the disruption).

Cut-ins or inserts may also be used when reshooting parts of the action from another camera setup (different shot size or angle).

Reaction Shots/Partials/Cut-In Shots

By skillfully concealing information, you can prime the audience's imagination and arouse their curiosity. Instead of showing the event, you can demonstrate its effect:

Reaction shot: The door opens—but we see the victim's horror-stricken face, not the intruder.

Partial shot: A switchblade opens, is moved out of frame; we hear the victim's cry, then silence.

Cut-in shot: We watch the victim's cat drinking milk to sounds of a fight and a body falling; the victim's hand comes into frame, upsetting the milk dish.

This technique can provide maximum impact with minimum facilities, conveying information by implication rather than direct statement. It aims to intrigue and tantalize.

The Recorded Insert

Occasionally, during a studio production, we may cut away from studio cameras' pictures to show prerecorded material. There are several reasons why we might want to do this:

- To illustrate a lecture, demonstration, or talk, such as footage of a trip down the Amazon.
- To imply that the studio setting is in a specific location, showing stock shots of the outside of a building or cityscapes.

- To authenticate a setting. We see a small boarded room in the studio. A stock shot of a ship is inserted so that we accept that this is a ship's cabin.
- To show environments that could not be recreated effectively in the studio, like a typhoon.
- To extend action. You can have a person walk through a door in the studio set (an apartment) and then out into the street (prerecorded).
- Once-only action. Prerecording is essential when action might prove unsuccessful in the studio (for example, involving animals) or take too much time during the recording period (an elaborate makeup change), or is too dangerous (fire) or unrepeatable (an explosion) or very critical (an accurately thrown knife).
- Visual effects. To produce time-lapse effects, reversed action, transformations, and the like.
- Animation sequences. These may be cartoon or animated still-life.
- To include performers otherwise unavailable—filming persons who could not attend the taping session, such as overseas guests.

Stock Shots (Library Shots)

These are short film, still, or video sequences of illustrative material, held in an organization's archives or rented from specialist libraries. Stock shots are inserted into a program where it would be impracticable or uneconomic to shoot new material. These short clips cover a very wide field, including news events, location shots, manufacturing processes, natural history, personalities, and stunts. They are widely used to illustrate talks, demonstrations, and newscasts and to provide atmospheric and environmental shots for drama (see Figure 18.22).

REVIEW QUESTIONS

1. How do you determine whether to shoot with a single camera or multiple cameras?
2. Describe a continuity error and explain how it could occur.
3. What are the advantages and disadvantages to multicamera production?
4. How is visual variety created when shooting groups of people?
5. Why do cameras need to stay on one side of the axis of action?
6. What are some of the issues that you need to think about as you arrange a shot?
7. How do you focus the audience's attention on a specific subject on the screen?
8. How does pacing affect a production?

CHAPTER 19

The Studio Production

There is a sense of exhilaration that I feel every time I step into a TV studio that has not lessened over the years. For me, the studio is like my very own giant sandbox, where I can build castles and get dirt under my fingernails.

Doug Smart, Director

Terms

Camera blocking (stumble-through): The initial camera rehearsal, coordinating all technical operations and discovering and correcting problems.

Cue card: Large card-stock can be used by a floor crew member to show brief notes, an outline, or other information.

Dress rehearsal (dress run): The goal of the dress rehearsal is to time the wardrobe and makeup changes.

Dry blocking (walk-through): Actors perform, familiarizing themselves with the studio settings and surroundings while the studio crew watch, learning the format, action, and production treatment.

ISO (isolated camera): A camera of which the signal is not only being sent to a switcher but is being recorded on its own recorder or camcorder.

Teleprompter: Shows the script on a two-way mirror that is positioned directly over the camera's lens.

323

Although there are many well-established methods of preparing and recording television productions, the method that you should choose depends not only on the type of show, but whether it is to be live or recorded, the facilities, and the amount of time and the size of the budget available for the production. There are differences between the way local productions and network productions work in the studio. However, in this chapter, the information is condense to provide an overview of the subject.

UNREHEARSED FORMATS

Every production benefits from a rehearsal before being recorded or going out live. But what do you do when the talent is going to arrive at the last minute, or even while you are live? If it is a live show with long prerecorded and edited packages, such as a magazine program, it may be possible to quickly review what will be happening. Otherwise, you must accept that the action will have to be live or recorded "raw."

Fortunately, many television productions fit into familiar routine formats. Consequently, even when it is not possible to rehearse the action beforehand, you can still prepare a setup that will work successfully when the talent does arrive. Interviews, for example, have regular plans so that you can quickly line up the appropriate chair positions and move the cameras into their positions. Crew members can be used as stand-ins while the lighting and sound arrangements are being checked. When the talent appears, you can quickly review the camera shots and adjust voice levels, makeup, and lighting.

When the unrehearsed action is less defined—such as a late-arriving band—you have to rely on cameras arranged strategically in front and cross-shooting positions. Instead of cameras grabbing shots of whatever is near them, you can allocate cover shots (long shots) to one camera, and have another concentrate on close-ups of the instruments, while another shoots close-ups of individuals or small groups. Before the production begins, always explain to the performers the floor area limits within which they must work or their action may uncontrollably spread into areas that cannot be covered by the lighting or cameras. Production treatment is largely a matter of recognizing effective shots as they are offered by the cameras—taking care to dwell on any special features, such as action detail of hands playing a piano or grouping shots of a chorus.

ADVANCE REHEARSALS

If you are renting cameras and/or even a studio, time is expensive, leaving few opportunities to experiment, try out variations, or work out half-formed ideas. It is imperative that you practice as many elements of the production as possible before the actual camera rehearsal. The director and talent can discuss the various production options, making sure that the ideas work. This can be done in any room that has enough space to work through the material.

Certainly, when it comes to the complexities of larger productions, preparatory work needs to be completed long before the camera rehearsals. It is essential to practice dialogue and action, coordinate performances, and discuss the camera angles. Drama and comedy shows are often rehearsed a week or two before the shoot date. Another rehearsal may even take place hours before the actual shoot time. This practice reduces the cost of the production by avoiding the need for a rental space.

A prerehearsal for a typical drama production usually begins with a read-through (also known as a *briefing* or *line rehearsal*). The director goes over the script, indicating specific points about style and presentation that will help familiarize the cast with their parts. They read their lines from the script, becoming more accustomed to the dialogue, the other actors, and their characterizations.

The rehearsal room's floor is often tape-outlined with a full-size layout of the studio set. Doors, windows, stairways, and so on are usually outlined. Stock rehearsal furniture substitutes for the actual studio items, and action props (telephone, tableware, etc.) are usually provided. Rehearsing in this mockup, actors become accustomed to the scale and features of their surroundings, with vertical poles or chairs marking the main limits of each setting.

The director arranges the action, the actors' positions, and their groupings to suit the camera production plan. Rehearsing a scene at a time, the cast is able to learn their lines and practice their performance until it flows naturally and the show runs smoothly, finally ready for the actual camera rehearsal. The durations of segments are checked and adjusted. (In calculating the overall timing, allowances are made for the time taken by later inserts such as prerecorded sequences.)

Studio Rehearsal

Before the studio rehearsal, the stage crew, supervised by the set designer, erects and dresses the set. Lamps are rigged and adjusted under the guidance of the lighting director. Camera and sound equipment are then positioned. The performers arrive, seeing the set possibly for the first time. The studio rehearsal is ready to begin (Table 19.1 and Figure 19.1).

Table 19.1	The Effective Studio Rehearsal
Unrehearsed or briefly rehearsed studio production	■ The director's assistant confirms that available production information is distributed (breakdown sheet/running order) and that contributory graphics or prerecorded inserts are correct. The assistant has details of all word cues for inserts, announcements, and their timings.
	■ The director, with the floor manager, technical director, lighting director, cameras, and sound crew, arranges basic talent/performer and camera positions (usually the floor is marked). Even a basic plan needs coordination. The director outlines action or moves and shoots coverage. Lighting is set.
	■ If the talent is available, line up the shots and explain to them any shot restrictions or special care needed in demonstrating items and so on. (Otherwise use stand-ins for shot line-up and then brief talent on arrival.)
	■ Check that performers and crew, including the teleprompter operator, are ready to start.
	■ If a full rehearsal is impractical, carry out the basic production checks: rehearse beginnings (open) and ends (close) of each segment; check any complicated action. Fix any errors or problems.
Intercom and the director	■ Remember that the production team has to depend on each other in order to do a good job. A quiet, methodical, patient approach is best with the crew. Be firm but friendly. Avoid critical comments on the intercom.
	■ Generally cameras are called by their numbers (such as "Cam 1" or "Cam 2"), guiding all camera moves (and zooms) during the rehearsal, warning the crew of upcoming action and movements. However, it is not uncommon for a director who works with a regular crew to call them by name instead of their camera number.
	■ Examine each shot. As necessary, modify positions, action, movement, and composition.
	■ Consider shot continuity. It is important to remember that altering shots may affect earlier shots.
	■ Remember, the crew and performers are learning what you want them to do from your production paperwork and your intercom reminders/instructions.
	■ Do not be vague; be concise. Make sure that your intentions are understood. In correcting errors, explain what was wrong and what you want. Not "Move him left a bit," but "He is shadowing the desk." Do not assume that performers will see and correct problems.
	■ Keep in mind that there is a difference between stage directions ("Actors, move stage left") and camera directions ("Cam 1, truck left").
	■ If a camera operator offers alternative shots (to overcome a problem), briefly indicate whether you accept or disagree. If you have time, explain why.
	■ Where practicable, at the end of each sequence, ask whether there are any problems, and whether anyone needs to rehearse that section again.
	■ Remember that various staging and lighting defects may be unavoidable in early rehearsals. Certain details (set dressing, light effects) take time to complete. Some aspects need to be seen on camera before they can be corrected or get final adjustment (overly bright lights, lens flares, etc.). Shot readjustments during rehearsal often necessitate lighting changes.

325

Continued

Table 19.1	The Effective Studio Rehearsal (*Continued*)
	■ At the end of the rehearsal, check timings, let the performers and crew know if there are any errors to be corrected, changes needed, or problems to be solved. Check whether they had difficulties that need your attention.
	■ At least one complete uninterrupted rehearsal is essential for reliable recording/transmission.

FIGURE 19.1
The set of CBS's *The King of Queens* sitcom is shown here, ready for the next rehearsal. The set has been put in place and the lights have been rigged. (Photo courtesy of CBS/Robert Voets/Landov)

FIGURE 19.2
Photographs are used as stand-ins for the cameras to rehearse with at the Academy of Country Music Awards. The photos allow the camera operators to learn where each nominee or performer will be sitting during the show. This helps the operators know where to point their cameras when an award is announced. (Photo courtesy of Monty Brinton/CBS/Landov)

Directors organize their studio rehearsals in several ways, according to the complexity of the production, available time, and the performer's experience. Following are some of the options (Table 19.2.)

DRY BLOCKING (WALK-THROUGH)

Actors perform, familiarizing themselves with the studio settings, and so on, while the studio crew watch, learning the format, action, and production treatment. The director is usually in the studio. The camera crew usually leaves their cameras alone and just looks at their script.

CAMERA BLOCKING (STUMBLE-THROUGH)

This is the initial camera rehearsal, coordinating all technical operations, discovering and correcting problems. The goal is to make sure that the corrections worked and that the timing is appropriate (Figure 19.2).

DRESS REHEARSAL (DRESS RUN)

The goal of the dress rehearsal is to time the wardrobe and makeup changes. Notes about issues are taken and then shared with everyone at the end of the rehearsal.

Table 19.2	The Director's Instructions During Rehearsals and Productions

To cameras

	Opening shots please	■ Cameras to provide initial shots in the show (or scene).
	Stand by 2	■ Stand by cue for Cam 2.
	Give me a single: two-shot; three-shot/group shot	■ Isolate in the shot the single, two, or three persons specified. A group shot includes the whole group of people.
	Zoom in (or out)	■ Narrow (or widen) the zoom lens angle.
	Tighten your shot	■ Slightly closer shot (slight zoom in).
	Get a wider shot	■ Get the next wider standard shot, such as from a CU to an MS.
	More (or less) headroom	■ Adjust space between top of head and top of frame.
	Center (frame-up)	■ Arrange subject in the center of the image.
	Pan left (or right)	■ Horizontal pivoting of camera head.
	Tilt up (or down)	■ Vertical pivoting of camera head.
	Dolly back/out	■ Pull camera mounting away from the subject.
	Dolly in	■ Push camera mounting toward the subject.
	Truck left (or right)/crab left (or right)	■ Move camera and mount to the left (or right).
	Arc left (or right)	■ Move camera and mount around the subject in an arc.
	Ped up (or down)	■ Raise (or lower) the column of the pedestal mount.
	Crane up (or down)/ boom up (or down)	■ Raise (or lower) crane arm or boom.
	Lose focus on the building	■ Defocus the building, remain sharp on other subject(s).
	Follow focus on the horse	■ Maintain focus on the moving horse.
	Focus 2/two, you're soft	■ Criticism that Cam 2's shot is not sharply focused.

To the floor manager

	Opening positions please	■ Talent (and equipment) in position for start of show (or scene).
	Standby	■ Alert host to get ready to start the show.
	Cue action/cue	■ Give sign for action to begin (perhaps name person or character).

Continued

Table 19.2	The Director's Instructions During Rehearsals and Productions (*Continued*)	
	Back to the top/take it from the top	▪ Begin again at the start of the scene; repeat the rehearsal.
	Pick it up from shot 20	▪ Start rehearsal again from script shot 20.
	Clear 2's shot	▪ Something or someone is obscuring Cam 2's shot.
	Tighten them up	▪ Move them closer together.
	Show Maria 3/she's on 3	▪ Indicate to her Cam 3, which is shooting her.
	Tell host to stretch/keep talking	▪ Tell host to improvise until the next item is ready.
	Give host 2 minutes . . . 1 minute . . . 30 seconds	▪ The host has 2 minutes left (followed by countdown on fingers).
	Kill it/cut it	▪ Stop immediately.
	He is clear	▪ We have left him. He is free to move away (or relax).
To audio (sound mixer)		
	Fade up sound	▪ Fade up from zero to full audio.
	Stand by music	▪ Warning before music cue.
	Cue music/go music	▪ Start music.
	Fade in music	▪ Begin very quietly, gradually increasing the sound.
	Fade out music	▪ Reduce volume (level) of audio.
	Music under/music to background	▪ Keep music volume low, relative to other audio sources.
	Start music	▪ Begin music, at full volume.
	Sound up (or down)	▪ General instruction to increase (or decrease) overall volume.
	Kill (cut) the music	▪ Stop the music.
	Cross-fade; mix	▪ Fade out present source(s), while fading in the next.

Rehearsal Procedures

In many types of productions, directors prepare and rehearse the entire action and treatment until it really works, then record the polished performance. In other productions, each small section is rehearsed and recorded before going on to the next segment.

CAMERA BLOCKING/STUMBLE-THROUGH/FIRST RUN/STOPPING RUN

Camera blocking—also known as the *first run* or *stumble-through*—is usually when the director controls the production from the production control room, only "going to the floor" when on-the-spot discussion is essential (Table 19.3). Otherwise, his or her eyes and ears are focused on the camera monitors and the speakers. All communication with the crew is through the intercom system, with the floor manager cueing and instructing the talent through intercom guidance.

Many directors use the *whole method*, going continuously through a segment (sequence, scene) until a problem arises that requires stopping and correction. The director discusses problems, solutions, and revisions, then reruns the segment with corrections. This method gives a good idea of continuity, timing, transitions, and operational difficulties. But by skimming over the various shortcomings before the breakdown point, quite a list of necessary minor corrections may develop. The cast and crew usually prefers the whole method.

Other directors, using the *stopping method*, stop action and correct faults as they arise—almost shot by shot. This precludes error adding to error, ensuring that everyone knows exactly what is required throughout. For certain situations (chroma-key treatment), this may be the only rational approach. However, this piecemeal method gives the impression of slow progress, and can feel tedious for everyone involved (crews usually dislike this style). The continual stopping makes checks on continuity and timing much more difficult. Later corrections are given as notes after the run-through.

Table 19.3 Prerehearsal Blocking Suggestions	
Timing	■ A preliminary read-through gives only a rough timing estimate. Time needs to be allowed for prerecorded video or graphic inserts. Anticipate potential script cuts if an overrun is evident. Many productions include sequences that can be dropped, reduced, or expanded to obtain the correct timing. At this point, only the dialogue and blocking moves are times (not laughter).
Briefing the talent	■ Ensure that all performers have a clear idea of the program format, their part in it, and their relationships with others.
	■ Ensure that performers have a good understanding of the setting: what it represents, where things are.
Props	■ Provide reasonable substitutes when the real props are not available. Sometimes only the actual item will suffice.
Directing performers	■ Maintain a serious attitude toward punctuality, inattention, and background chatter during rehearsals in order to avoid frustration and wasting time.
	■ Avoid excessive revisions—of action, grouping, line cuts, and so on. Wrong versions can get remembered and new ones forgotten.
Shot arrangement	■ A portable viewfinder may be helpful to arrange shots.
	■ Always think in terms of shots, not of theatrical-styled groupings, entrances, and exits.
	■ When setting up shots in a rehearsal hall, do not overlook the scenic background that will be present in the studio. Check shot coverage with plans and elevations.
	■ Consider depth of field limitations in close shots or deep shots (close and distant people framed together).
	■ Think in terms of practical camera operations. Although you may be able to rapidly reposition your handheld viewfinder, the move may be impossible for a studio camera.
Audio and lighting	■ Be sensitive to audio and lighting problems when arranging talent positions and action. For example, when people are widely spaced, a mic boom may need time to swing between them, or have to be supplemented.

FIGURE 19.3

Floor blocking allows the director to sit in the studio, reviewing the camera shots from a monitor. Note the quad-split monitor in the lower-right corner of the photo. The director can see the shots from all four cameras being used on this production.

FLOOR BLOCKING

Using this method, the director works out on the studio floor, viewing the camera shots on studio monitors. Guiding and correcting performers and crew from within the studio, the director uses the intercom to give instructions to the AD or technical director for the switcher (Figure 19.3). During the actual recording, the show may be shot as segments, scenes, or continuous action.

THE FLOOR MANAGER

The floor manager (FM) plays a major role in studio production and is usually brought into the project from the beginning of production.

During the studio preparations for the rehearsal, the FM checks to make sure that the studio and crew are ready to go at the scheduled time. Progress checks ensure that there are no staging hang-ups. This may include making sure that all action props work, the scenery and furniture are in the planned positions, the doors do not stick, and similar checks.

As the performers arrive, the FM welcomes them and makes sure that they are taken care of. This usually includes telling the talent when and where they are required. The goal is to ensure punctuality, which is an important aspect of the FM's duties, whether for rehearsal starts, turnarounds at the end of a rehearsal (returning equipment, props, sets to opening positions), or studio breaks (meals).

Rehearsal

When the director is in the control room, the FM is the director's contact on the studio floor. Wearing a headset, the FM listens to the director's instructions on the intercom system and then passes this information on to the talent. The FM anticipates problems, rearranges action and grouping, adjusts furniture positions, and performs other tasks as instructed by the director, marking the floor where necessary and supervising staging and prop changes.

Normally, the FM is the only person in the studio who will cue and stop all action based on the director's instructions. Most directors rarely use the studio loudspeaker system to talk directly to the talent, as this can be quite disrupting. The FM talks back to the director over the intercom. Being on the spot, the FM can often correct problems not evident to the director in the control room (Figure 19.4).

A good FM combines calmness, discipline, and firmness with diplomacy and friendliness—making sure to put talent at ease, and always available, yet never in the shot. The FM maintains a quiet studio, yet understands that various last-minute corrective actions may be needed.

FIGURE 19.4

The floor manager, or stage manager, is the director's representative in the studio. The floor manager is the person in the middle of the bottom of the photo.

Recording/Transmission

When the director is ready to record or transmit the program, it is the FM's responsibility to confirm that all studio access doors are shut, talent and crew are standing by in their opening positions, and the studio monitors are showing the correct images. The FM will cue the announcer (Figure 19.5).

FIGURE 19.5
The announcer is responsible for getting the audience fired up for the CBS game show *The Price Is Right*. (Photo courtesy of CBS/Robert Voets/Landov)

FIGURE 19.6
During a production, the floor manager is responsible for cueing the talent. In this photo, a floor manager is cueing the talent on NBC's *Today Show* set.

During the show, the FM is cueing talent, keeping a wary eye all about, listening to intercom guidance, anticipating hazards, and generally smoothing proceedings (Figure 19.6). At the end of taping, the FM holds talent and crew until results have been checked, announcing and preparing any necessary retakes, and finally "releasing the studio" (performers and crew). The FM checks on safe storage of any valuable or special props or equipment and ends duties with a logged account of the production.

Guiding the Talent

How much guidance the talent needs varies with their experience and the complexity of the production. However, you must always ensure that the talent understands exactly what you want them to do and where to do it. A preliminary word may be enough, or a painstaking rehearsal may be essential.

INEXPERIENCED TALENT

Having welcomed talent, put them at ease and explain what is needed of them. They are best supported by an experienced host who guides and reassures them. Have them talk to the host rather than the camera, as the host can steer the guest by questions. Unfamiliar conditions make most people uncomfortable. However, it is important that the talent feels self-confident—that confidence is essential for a good performance. Keep problems to a minimum, with only essential instructions to the talent. Avoid elaborate action, discourage improvisation, and have minimal rearrangements. Even slight distractions can worry inexperienced talent. Sometimes a small cue card or a list of points held beside the camera may strengthen their confidence. However, few inexperienced people can read a script or teleprompter naturally—they usually give a stilted, uncomfortable delivery.

The balance between insufficient and excessive rehearsal is more crucial with inexperienced talent. Uncertainty or over-familiarity can lead them to omit sections during the final program. Sometimes the solution lies in either taping the production in sections or compiling from several takes.

PROFESSIONAL TALENT

You will meet a very wide range of experienced professional performers in television production—actors, presenters, hosts, commentators, demonstrators, and anchors. Each has a specific part to play in a production. Familiar with the studio process, they can respond

FIGURE 19.7
Familiar with the studio process, professional talent like Brad Pitt and Conan O'Brien can respond to the most complicated instructions from the floor manager. (Photo courtesy of NBC-TV/The Kobal Collection)

332

to the most complicated instructions from the FM, or an earpiece intercom without the blink of an eye, even under the most difficult conditions—and yet maintain cool command of the situation. Comments, timing and continuity changes, item cuts, and ad-libbing and padding are taken in stride.

The professional can usually make full use of a teleprompter displaying the script—this requires that cameras must be within reading distance. The talent can play to specific cameras for specific shots, making allowances for lighting problems (e.g., shadowing) or camera moves (Figure 19.7).

CUEING

To ensure that action begins and ends at the instant it is required, precise cueing is essential. If you cut to performers and then cue them, you will see them waiting to begin or watch action spring into life. Cue them too early before cutting and action has already begun. Wrong cueing leaves talent bewildered. If they have finished their contribution and you have not cut away to the next shot, they may stand there with egg on their face, so to speak, wondering whether to ad lib or just grin!

Methods of Cueing

HAND CUES

Given by the FM, these are the standard methods of cueing action to start or stop. Remember, some stations have their own variations on the signals and it is advisable to use whatever is given to you by your supervisor. However, make sure that your signals can be understood by the talent. Explain the basic cues to them if necessary. Do not assume that they know what you are doing—especially with inexperienced talent (Figure 19.8).

WORD CUES

An agreed-upon word or phrase during a dialogue, commentary, or discussion may be used to cue action or to switch to a prerecorded package (insert). It is also important to note out-cues (the last spoken words) at the end of a preproduced television package to ensure that the talent knows when to begin again.

MONITOR CUES

Commentators and demonstrators often watch the preproduced package on a nearby television monitor, taking their cues from seeing the package end.

TALLY LIGHT CUES

Performers can take a cue from the camera's tally (cue) light that lights up when the switcher selects a specific camera. Announce booths sometimes use a small portable cue light to signal the commentators to begin (Figure 19.9).

INTERCOM CUES

These cues are given directly to a performer (newscaster, commentator) wearing an earpiece—it is usually called an IFB, which stands for interrupted (interruptible) feedback. It can also be called a *program interrupt* (Figure 19.10).

CLOCK CUES

The talent may be told to begin at an exact time.

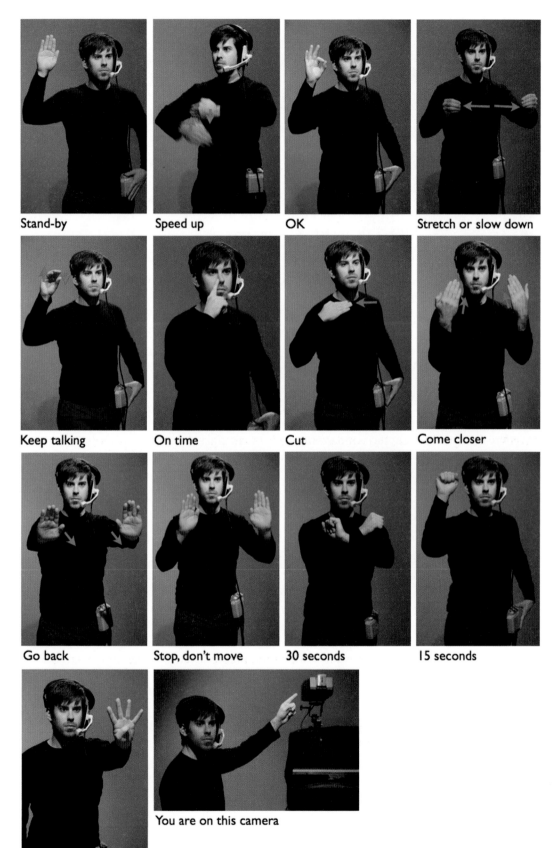

Stand-by

Speed up

OK

Stretch or slow down

Keep talking

On time

Cut

Come closer

Go back

Stop, don't move

30 seconds

15 seconds

4-minute countdown

You are on this camera

333

FIGURE 19.8
Floor manager signals or cues. (Photos by Austin Brooks)

FIGURE 19.9
Camera tally lights—note the red light on the studio viewfinder—are often used to cue the talent when to begin their presentation.

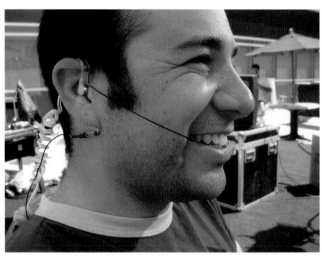

FIGURE 19.10
This ESPN talent uses an IFB (intercom) earpiece to hear cues from the producer. He also has a small boom microphone attached to his ear. (Photo by Dennis Baxter)

334

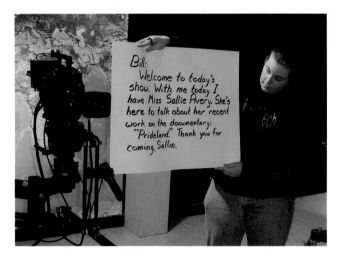

Bill:
Welcome to today's show. With me today I have Miss Sallie Avery. She's here to talk about her recent work on the documentary: "Prideland." Thank you for coming, Sallie.

FIGURE 19.11
Cue cards should be held so that the crew member holding the card can see the wording. This allows him or her to move the card up, adjusting the card so that the line being read is even with the lens.

Prompting the Talent

Rarely can talent be expected to memorize a script accurately and deliver it easily. Even the most experienced performers are liable to deviate from the written script and forget or drop lines. Although this is not a big issue with some types of shows that are spontaneous, it can be serious with programs such as news shows.

There are a number of different ways that the talent can get help with delivery:

Notes: 4 × 6-inch index cards are probably the most common note size. They are also popular, because the card-stock does not crinkle. Most talent prefer not to use standard sheets of paper on an interview show, because they can distract the audience and can crinkle, making unwanted noises. Standard-sized paper is usually used for news scripts on a news desk or table.

Cue card: Large card-stock can be used by a floor crew member to show brief notes, an outline, or other information. These cards are usually held so that the line being read is even with the lens (Figure 19.11).

Teleprompter: Teleprompters generally show the script on a two-way mirror that is positioned directly over the camera's lens. A teleprompter operator can vary the speed of the text on the screen so that it is comfortable for the talent. Cameras equipped with a teleprompter must be close enough to the talent for comfortable reading (Figure 19.12).

Production Timing

Broadcast television productions run by the clock. They start and stop at specific times, because they must fit their allocated time slot *exactly*. If a live show goes over the time limit, it may just be cut off or will cause problems with other programs. Shows that are live-on-tape will get edited so that they are the appropriate length.

FIGURE 19.12
(Left) The camera is equipped with a teleprompter. (Right) What the text looks like from the talent's point of view. (Left photo courtesy of JVC)

Scripts may be roughly timed by reading aloud and allowing time for any mute action, commercials, or preproduced material. Most scripts run at roughly a minute per full page. During the rehearsal each segment or scene is timed, then adjusted to fit into the allocated time slot.

RECORDING THE PRODUCTION

Although "live" productions were how television began, most television programs today are prerecorded. Recording a program allows the directors more freedom. They can edit out the mistakes and enhance the show with special effects that may not have been possible in a "live" situation. So it is not surprising that today most shows are recorded whenever possible. Let's take a look at the variety of recording methods that are used, including their advantages and limitations (see also Table 19.4).

The most common recording methods are:

- Live-on-tape
- Basic retakes
- Discontinuous recording
- Isolated camera (ISO)—each camera has its own recorder

Live-on-Tape

Here the program is recorded continuously in its entirety, as if it were live. Most editing is completed on the production switcher during the performance and the show is usually ready for transmission at the conclusion of the recording session. However, there are times when additional editing is needed.

Basic Retakes

Here the production is recorded continuously, the same as for a live production. However, any errors (performers, production, technical) are rerecorded and the corrected sections substituted. Duration trimming may require some editing cuts—often covered by introducing cutaways/reaction shots.

Table 19.4 Methods of Recording Productions	
Live-on-tape: *Tonight Show* *David Letterman* *Conan O'Brien*	■ Utilizes a single camera or multiple cameras.
Advantages	■ Program is ready for transmission immediately after taping. ■ No lengthy postproduction editing is needed (saves cost, equipment, staff, time). ■ Recording period needed is only slightly longer than the length of the show. ■ No loss of pace or interaction, which can occur when action is continually interrupted. ■ Performers and team are all pumped up to give their best performances.
Disadvantages	■ Most shots and transitions are normally unchangeable. ■ There are no opportunities for second thoughts or alternative treatment. ■ The production may include some errors in performance and treatment (camera work, sound, lighting). ■ All costume, makeup changes, scene changes, and other changes have to be made in real time during the show. ■ Any editing is usually nominal, unless insert shots are recorded afterward (cutaway shots or brief retakes inserted).
Shooting in segments/ scenes/sections: Daytime dramas, *All My Children* *The Young & the Restless*	■ Utilizes a single camera or multiple cameras
Advantages	■ Opportunities for corrective retakes and alternative treatments are available. ■ Editing within the sequence can be made with the switcher. When necessary, further editing decisions can be left to editing. ■ The talent and crew can concentrate on each segment and get it right before going on to the next. ■ Recording breaks can be arranged to allow costume, makeup changes, scene changes, and so on. ■ Scenes can be shot in the most convenient time-saving order: in sequence or out of sequence. ■ Performers who are not required for later scenes can be released (actors, extras, musicians). This can save costs and reduce congestion in the studio. ■ If a setting is used at various times throughout a show (e.g., a classroom), all scenes with action there may be shot consecutively, and the scenery struck to make room for a new set. This technique virtually extends the size of the studio, and makes optimum use of available space. ■ Where a set appears in several episodes of a series, all sequences there can be shot in succession to avoid the need to store and rebuild the set over and over. ■ Similarly, when a program consists of a series of brief episodes (a story told in daily parts), these can all be recorded consecutively during the same session.

Continued

Table 19.4	Methods of Recording Productions (*Continued*)
Disadvantages	■ Much more time is needed to record the show. Time lost during breaks can become greater than anticipated. ■ Retakes and revisions can take so much time that the session falls behind schedule (an overrun). This can result in economic and administrative problems. There is a continuing pressure to save time and to press on. ■ Extensive postproduction editing is essential. At the end of the recording session, you have no show until the separate segments are sorted and edited together. ■ All extended transitions between segments (mixes, wipes, video effects) must wait until postproduction. Similarly, music/effects/dialogue carrying over between segments must be added during audio sweetening. ■ In a complicated production, recording out of sequence can lead to confusion and to continuity errors in a fast-moving taping session.
Multicamera with ISO camera: *NFL Football* *MLB Baseball*	■ All cameras are fed to the switcher and then recorded by a master recorder. The director may choose one camera of which the video signal will be recorded by an ISO recorder.
Advantages	■ The ISO recorder can be used to continuously record the output of any chosen camera. ■ Provides slow-motion replay for inserts into the program. ■ Provides extra shots for postproduction editing.
Disadvantages	■ The arrangement ties up a second recorder. ■ Most of the material on the ISO recording is not used.
Multicamera with dedicated recorders/camcorders: Sitcoms *Big Bang Theory* *Two and a Half Men*	■ Action is shot live-on-tape or in segments/scenes/sections.
Advantages	■ Every camera has its own recorder. ■ No shots are missed. ■ Alternative shots are available throughout the show. ■ No irrevocable editing is carried out during the performance. ■ Unexpected action or unrehearsed action is recorded and available. ■ Postproduction editing can be adjusted to suit the final performance. ■ Camera treatment needs little planning. ■ Most nonlinear editors allow multiple recordings to be synced for switching.
Disadvantages	■ The entire show requires total postproduction editing. ■ There is a separate recording for each camera, creating a large amount of material. ■ The arrangement can lead to poor production treatment; off-the-cuff shooting. Concentration on action rather than visual development. ■ When camcorders are used, an effective program requires the director to give advance instructions to each camera operator.

Continued

Table 19.4	Methods of Recording Productions (*Continued*)
Single camera: Prime time dramas Some sitcoms *My name is Earl* *CSI*	■ Single camcorder taking brief shots or continuous sequences.
Advantages	■ An extremely flexible, mobile method. ■ One camera is easier to direct than a multicamera crew. ■ There are advantages in working with a small unit. ■ The director can concentrate on the action and treatment. ■ No switching is involved. ■ No cueing of preproduced inserts.
Disadvantages	■ All the strain of camera work falls on one operator. ■ The production process is much slower than multicamera treatment. ■ There is a temptation to shoot retakes for better performance, or extra "just-in-case" shots that might be used. These extra shots can absorb allotted shooting time. ■ All material requires sorting and detailed editing. ■ Production flow is continually interrupted (unlike multicamera treatment). ■ All preproduced inserts in the program must be introduced during postproduction.

Shooting Out of Order (By Set)

Many productions are shot out of order, stopping and starting as needed. For example, if one set is needed both for the beginning and the end of a production, both segments can be shot one after another. This method allows the set to be removed and another brought in for the next scene, which saves lighting and set building time.

Block and Shoot

There are a number of variations of shooting out of order. However, the most common style is to rehearse each segment or scene. As soon as the director determines that everyone is ready to shoot, that segment is recorded. The crew and talent then move on to the next segment.

Using this method, the director goes through the entire production during the camera rehearsal period, rehearsing each sequence or scene in turn. Any problems or revisions needed to correct or improve the action, camera work, sound, or lighting are noted, and, if necessary, that section will be rehearsed again. The individual segments are then edited together using the appropriate transitions and audio.

In addition, various postproduction work may still be needed, such as audio sweetening (adding music and effects, sound quality adjustments, and so on), video effects, graphics, and any other necessary work.

Isolated Camera (ISO)

In this approach, each camera's output is separately recorded on its own dedicated recorder or camcorder. Images from the ISO camera can be selected on the switcher whenever they are needed, but all its shots (on-air and off-air) are taped on the isolated recorder. This arrangement provides several useful opportunities.

INSTANT-REPLAY INSERTS

The ISO recorder can be used to provide instant replay in slow motion during a live or live-on-tape production. At any chosen moment (such as after a goal has been scored in a game), the ISO recorder is used to play its recorded footage into the program. (This recorder may also be used for later videotape editing.)

COVER SHOTS

If the ISO camera concentrates on one specific aspect of the scene (such as the goal area), there is no danger of important action there being missed while the director is using other cameras' shots.

STANDBY SHOTS

When a production switcher is used on a multicamera shoot, the resulting program tape contains all the shots of the event that are available. So if you subsequently need to modify the final tape, the ISO camera recording can be edited into the program tape wherever necessary as cutaways, to allow changes or corrections to be made.

Single-Camera Recording

In this situation, a single portable camcorder shoots the action. As the main production camera, the material is recorded in any convenient order. Because no switching is involved, the director has the opportunity to concentrate on the action on the set.

REVIEW QUESTIONS

1. What are some of the situations that can happen when an unrehearsed studio production occurs?
2. What are the goals of a prerehearsal?
3. What are the differences between dry blocking and camera blocking?
4. Describe the role of the floor manager in the studio.
5. What are some of the cueing methods in the studio?
6. What are some of the devices used to prompt the talent?
7. How could paid professional talent actually save you money over friends who work for free?
8. Why ISO a camera?

CHAPTER 20

Production Style

"The look of the show is achieved by striving to be as minimalistic as possible. We shoot entirely with handheld cameras in real locations rather than constructed sets. We don't tell the actors where to go or what to do; we just sort of follow them around."

Jeff Reiner, Executive Producer, *Friday Night Lights*

Terms

Actuality: A type of production that is very transparent, even willing to deliberately reveal all of the production equipment and crew to help at "authenticity."

Ambience: Production ambience influences the audience's perception of the show. Some of the ambience factors may include music, graphics, and the set.

Display: An unrealistic, decorative way of presenting the subject to your audience. Game shows would be an example of a display type of production.

Treatment: The production method used to encourage the interest of the audience. There are many different styles or treatments than can be chosen such as narrative, comedy, news, documentary, etc.

341

There is no "correct method" of presenting any subject. Directors have tried a variety of approaches over the years. Some of these have become standard; others were just a passing trend. Techniques that have been used adroitly by some (such as background music) have been overdone by others, and become distractingly intrusive. Certainly, if you choose an inappropriate technique, you are likely to find your audience becoming confused, distracted, or simply losing interest.

VISUAL STYLE

Appropriateness

So what is appropriateness? In reality, it is largely a matter of custom, fashion, and tradition:

Informal presentations usually take the form of "natural" situations. We chat with the craftsperson in his or her workshop, at a fireside, or while on a country walk.

Formal presentations often follow a very stylized artificial format. We see people in carefully positioned chairs, sitting on a raised area in front of a specially designed set.

Display is an unrealistic, decorative way of presenting your subject. Emphasis is on effect. We see it in game shows, open-area treatment (music groups, dance), and in children's programs (Figure 20.1).

Simulated environments aim to create a completely realistic illusion. Anything breaking that illusion, such as a camera coming into shot in a period drama, would destroy the effect.

FIGURE 20.1

A display treatment is an unrealistic, decorative way of presenting the subject with the emphasis on effect. (Photo courtesy of CBS/John Paul Filo/Landov)

342

FIGURE 20.2

Newscasts have become very routine in their presentations, freeing the audience to concentrate on the subject. (Photo courtesy of KOMU-TV)

Actuality is a more transparent style. We make it very clear to the audience that we are in a studio by deliberately revealing all of the production equipment and crew. On location, the unsteady hand-held camera and microphone dipping into shots supposedly give an authenticity to the occasion.

Routines

Some production techniques have become so familiar that it would seem strange if we presented them in any other way—such as a newscaster presenting an entire newscast in shorts or on a set with flashing lights.

Certain approaches have become so stereotyped that they enter the realms of cliché—routine methods for routine situations. A number of standard production formats have emerged for productions, such as newscasts, studio interviews, game shows, chat shows, and others. If we analyze these productions, we usually find that styles have evolved and become the most effective, economical, and reliable ways of handling their specific type of subjects (Figure 20.2).

If we regard these formats as "a container for the content," these routine treatments can free the audience to concentrate on the show. However, if we consider the treatment as an opportunity to encourage interest and heighten enjoyment, then any "routine" becomes unacceptable.

Clearly, a dramatic treatment would not work for many types of television productions. Instead, it is best to aim for a variety of camera shots, coupled with clear, unambiguous visual statements that direct and concentrate the audience's attention, rather than introduce any imposed style. How many sensible meaningful shot variations can you take of people speaking to each other, or driving an automobile, or playing an instrument, or demonstrating an item? The range is small.

For certain subjects, the picture is virtually irrelevant. What a person has to say may be extremely important; what the talent looks like is immaterial to the message. It may even prove a distraction or create prejudicial bias. "Talking heads" appear in most television shows. However, unless the speaker is particularly animated and interesting, the viewers' visual interest is seldom sustained. Changing the shot viewpoint can help, but may be a distraction.

Ambience

From the moment a show begins, we are influencing our audience's attitude to the production itself. Introductory music and graphic style can immediately convey a serious or casual feeling toward what is to come. We have only to recall how the hushed voice, quiet organ notes, and slow visual pace can provide a reverential air to proceedings, or the difference between a regal and a "showbiz"-type opening fanfare to realize how our expectancy changes.

Surroundings can also directly affect how convincingly we convey information. Certain environments, for example, provide a context of authority or scholarship: classroom, laboratory,

> "Dialogue should simply be a sound among other sounds, just something that comes out of the mouths of people whose eyes tell the story in visual terms."
>
> **Alfred Hitchcock**

museum, or other setting. A plow shown at work on the farm is better understood than if it were just shown standing alone in a studio with someone trying to explain what it does.

The Illusion of Truth

As you've seen, even when trying to present events "exactly as they are," the camera's angles, lens angles, image composition, the choice and sequence of shots, and other factors will all influence how our audience interprets what they are seeing. Keep in mind that the way a program is directed and shot has a significant impact on the final show. Where we lay emphasis, what we leave out, even the weather conditions (gloomy, stormy, or sunlight) will all modify the production's impact.

In a documentary program, the audience usually assumes that they are seeing a fair and informative story. However, that will always depend on how the director tackles the subject:

- There is the hopeful approach—an "adventure" in which the director points the camera around, giving a "tourist's view" of the events. This invariably results in a set of disjointed and unrelated shots. Sometimes, by adding commentary, graphics, music, and effects, it is possible to develop a coherent program theme. However, it can also be a disaster.
- Usually the director begins by researching the subject and then making a plan of approach. As discussed earlier, there are great advantages in anticipating and advance planning. By finding out about potential locations and local experts, the director can develop a schedule, arrange transport and accommodations, obtains permits, and so on. However, there is also the danger that preconceived ideas will dominate, so that you develop a concept before you arrive on location, and then reject whatever does not seem to fit in with the concept when you actually get there.
- Occasionally, we encounter the contrived approach, in which the director has staged what we are seeing—arranged the action and edited selectively. Dressed in their best, the participants put on a show for the camera, yet the television audience assumes that they are looking at reality.

Leaving aside ethics, even these brief (but real) examples are a reminder of the power of the image, and the director's responsibilities regarding the way in which it is used.

Pictorial Function

Most television images are factual, showing subjects in a familiar way. However, by carefully arranging these same subjects, with careful composition and a selective viewpoint, you can modify the subject's entire impact and give it a quite different implied significance. You can interpret the scene for the audience. You can deliberately distort and select reality so that your presentation bears little direct relationship to the actual situation—and you might do this to create a dramatic illusion, or to produce an influential force (advertising, propaganda).

Abstracting further, you can stimulate emotions and ideas simply by the use of movement, line, and form, which the viewer personally interprets. There are occasions when we seek to stimulate the audience's imagination—to evoke ideas that are not conveyed directly by the camera and microphone. In this chapter, we will examine these concepts and how they can be used.

Picture Applications

Because so much television program material is explicit, it is easy to forget how powerful it can be. Images can be used for a number of different purposes:

- To convey information directly (normal conversation).
- To provide context (establishing the location), such as Big Ben, to imply that the location is London (Figure 20.3).
- To interpret a situation, conveying abstract concepts (ideas, thoughts, feelings) through associative visuals, such as plodding feet suggesting the weariness of a trail of refugees.
- To symbolize—we associate certain images with specific people, places, and events.

FIGURE 20.3
Providing context for the audience helps them understand what is being said by the speaker. (Photo courtesy of the U.S. Navy)

- To imitate—pictures appear to imitate a condition (the camera staggers as a drunk reels, defocusing to convey loss of consciousness).
- To identify, showing features such as icons, logos, or trademarks associated with specific organizations or events.
- To couple ideas—using pictures to link events or themes (panning from a boy's toy boat to a ship at sea, on which he becomes the captain).
- To create a visual montage—a succession of images interplay to convey an overall impression (epitomizing war).

Production Rhetoric

Rhetoric is the art of persuasive or impressive speech and writing. Unlike everyday conversation, it stimulates our imagination through style and technique, by inference and allusion, instead of just direct pronouncement. The rhetoric of the screen has similar roots that directors such as Alfred Hitchcock have explored over the years to great effect.

It is amazing what the camera can communicate: without a word of dialogue, it can convey the whole gamut of human responses. For example: a veteran performer ends his brave but pathetic vaudeville act amid heckling from the crowd. He bows, defeated. We hear hands clapping; the camera turns from the sad lone figure, past derisive faces, to where his aged wife sits applauding.

AUDIO STYLE

Imaginative Sound

The ear is generally more imaginative than the eye. We are more perceptive and discriminating toward what we see. Consequently, our ears accept the unfamiliar and unrealistic more readily than our eyes, and are more tolerant of repetition. A sound effects recording can be reused many times, but a costume or curtain quickly becomes too familiar after being seen just a couple of times.

In many television shows, the audio is taken for granted, while attention is concentrated on the visual treatment. Yet without audio, the presentations can become meaningless (talks, discussions, interviews, newscasts, music, game shows), whereas without video, the production can still communicate.

Audio can explain or support the image, enriching its impact or appeal. Music or effects can suggest locale (seashore sounds), or a situation (pursuing police siren heard), or conjure a mood (excitement, foreboding, comedy, horror).

A nonspecific picture can be given a definite significance through associated sound. Depending on accompanying music, a display of flowers may suggest springtime, a funeral, a wedding, or a ballroom.

Sound Elements

VOICE

The most obvious sound element, the human voice, can be introduced into the production in several different ways:

- A single person addressing the camera, formally or informally.
- An off-screen commentator (voiceover) providing a narrative (documentary), or the spontaneous commentary used for a televised sports event.
- We may "hear the thoughts" of a character (reminiscent or explanatory narration) while watching the talent's silent face, or watching the subject of the thoughts.
- Dialogue—the informal natural talk between people, with all its hesitance, interruptions, breaking off, overlapping, and the more regulated exchanges of formal discussion.

EFFECTS

The characteristic sound image that conjures a specific place or atmosphere comes from a blend of stimuli: from action sounds (footsteps, gunfire), from environmental noises (wind, crowd, traffic), and from the subtle ways in which sound quality is modified by its surroundings (reverberation, distortion).

MUSIC

Background music has become "required" for many programs. It can range from purely melodic accompaniment to music that imitates, or gives evocative or abstract support.

SILENCE

The powerful dramatic value of silence should never be underestimated. However, silence must be used with care, as the audience could easily perceive it to just be a loss of audio. Continued silence can suggest such diverse concepts as: desolation, despair, stillness, hope, peace, extreme tension (we listen intently to hear whether pursuing footsteps can still be heard).

- Sudden silence after noise can be almost unbearable: A festival in an Alpine village, happy laughter and music, the tumultuous noise of an unexpected avalanche engulfing the holiday makers . . . then silence.
- Sudden noise during silence creates an immediate peak of tension: The silently escaping prisoner knocks over a chair and awakens the guards—or did they hear him after all?
- Silent streets at night . . . then a sudden scream.
- The explosive charge has been set, the detonator is switched—nothing happens . . . silence.

Sound Emphasis

You can manipulate the volumes of sounds for dramatic effect: emphasizing specific sources, cheating loudness to suit the situation. A whisper may be amplified to make it clearly audible, a loud sound held in check.

You may establish the background noise of a vehicle and then gradually reduce it, taking it under to improve audibility of conversation. Or you could deliberately increase its loudness so that the noise drowns the voices. Occasionally, you might take out all environmental sounds to provide a silent background, perhaps for a thought sequence.

You can modify the aesthetic appeal and significance of sound in a number of ways. For factual sound, you can use:

- Random natural sound pickup (overheard street conversations)
- Selective pickup of specific audio sources

For atmospheric sound:

- By choosing certain natural associated sounds, you can develop a realistic illusion. (A rooster crowing suggests that it is dawn.)
- By deliberately distorting reality, you create fantasy to stimulate the imagination. (A flute's sound can suggest the flight of a butterfly.)

Sound Applications

As with visual images, sound can be used for a number of different purposes:

To convey information directly: Normal conversation.

To establish a location: Traffic noises that imply a busy street scene nearby.

To interpret a situation: Conveying abstract concepts (ideas, thoughts, feelings) through associative sounds; a slurred trombone note as a derisive comment.

To symbolize: Sounds that we associate with specific places, events, moods (such as a fire truck's siren).

To identify: Sounds associated with specific people or events (such as signature tunes).

To couple ideas: Using music or sound effects to link events and themes, such as a musical bridge between scenes, or aircraft noise carried over between a series of images showing the plane's various stops along the route.

To create a sound montage: A succession or mixture of sounds arranged for comic or dramatic effect. For example, separate sound effects of explosions, gunfire, aircraft, sirens, and whistles create the illusion of a battle scene.

Off-Screen Sound

When someone speaks or something makes a sound, it might seem logical to show the source. But it can be singularly dull if we do this repeatedly: She starts talking, so we cut and watch her.

You can use off-screen sound in many ways to enhance a program's impact:

- Once you have established a shot of someone talking, you might cut to see the person he or she is speaking to and watch their reactions, or cut to show what they are talking about. The original dialogue continues, even though we no longer see the speaker. As you can see, you can establish relationships, even where the two subjects have not been seen together in the same shot.
- Background sounds can help to establish location. Although a mid-shot of two people might occupy the screen, if the background sounds have been used appropriately, the audience will interpret whether they are near the seashore, a highway, or a sawmill.
- Off-screen sounds may be chosen to intrigue us, or to arouse our curiosity.
- A background sound may introduce us to a subject before we actually see it, informing us about what is going on nearby or what is going to appear (the approaching sound of a diesel truck).
- The background sound may create audio continuity, although the shots switch rapidly. Two people walk through buildings, down a street—but their voices are heard clearly throughout at a constant level.

Substituted Sound

It is often difficult to find a source for a specific sound, requiring us to create a substitute. There are several possible reasons for this approach:

- No sound exists, as with sculpture, painting, architecture, inaudible insects, and prehistoric monsters.
- Sometimes the actual sounds are not available, not recorded (mute shooting), or not suitable. For example: the absence of bird sounds when shooting a country scene; location sounds were obtrusive, unimpressive, or inappropriate to use; or the camera used a telephoto lens to capture a close-up shot of a subject that is too distant for effective sound pickup.
- The sounds you introduce may be just replacements (using another lion's voice instead of the missing roar), or artificial substitutes in the form of effects or music.

Background music and effects should be added cautiously. They can easily become:

- Disproportionate (too loud or soft)
- Too familiar
- Obtrusive (distracting)
- Inappropriate (have wrong or misleading associations)

Controlling Sound Treatment

Various working principles are generally accepted in sound treatment:

- The scale and quality of audio should match the picture (appropriate volumes, balance, audio perspective, acoustics, etc.).
- Where audio directly relates to picture action, it should be synchronized (like movements, footsteps, hammering, other transient sounds).
- Video and audio should normally be switched together. No audio advance or hangover should occur on a cut.
- Video cutting should be on the beat of the music, rather than against it, and preferably at the end of a phrase. Continual cutting in time with music becomes tedious.
- Video and audio should usually begin together at the start of a show, finishing together at its conclusion, fading out as a musical phrase ends.

The Effect of Combining Sounds

When we hear two or more sounds together, we often find that they interrelate to provide an emotional effect that changes according to their relative loudness, speed, complexity, and so on:

- Overall harmony conveys unity, beauty, organization.
- Overall discord conveys imbalance, uncertainty, incompletion, unrest, ugliness, irritation.
- Marked differences in relative volume and rhythm create variety or complication.
- Marked similarities result in sameness, homogeneity, mass, or strength of effect.

Focusing Attention

Audience attention is seldom divided equally between picture and sound. One aspect usually dominates. However, you can transfer concentration between ear and eye. For example, a movement will emphasize a remark made immediately afterwards. Dialogue before a move gives it emphasis.

We can transfer aural attention to another subject by:

- Giving the original subject's sound pattern (rhythm, movement, etc.) to the new source.
- Weakening the original subject's attraction and strengthening the new source.

- Linking action, such as having the pattern of the original sound change to that of the new subject, before stopping it.
- Cutting to a shot of the new source alone.
- Dialogue attracting attention either to its source or to its subject.

Selective Sound

In recreating the atmosphere of a specific environment, the trick is to use sound selectively if you want the scene to carry authenticity, rather than try to include all typical background noises. You may deliberately emphasize, reduce, modify, or omit sounds that would normally be present, or introduce others to convey a convincing sense of location.

The selection and blend of environmental sounds can strongly influence the interpretation of a scene. Imagine, for example, the slow, even toll of a cathedral bell accompanied by the rapid footsteps of approaching churchgoers. In developing this scene, you could reproduce random typical sounds. Or, more persuasively, you might deliberately use audio emphasis:

- Loud busy footsteps with a quiet insignificant bell in the background.
- The bell's slow dignity contrasted with restless footsteps.
- The booming bell overwhelming all other sounds.

So you can use the same sounds to suggest hope, dignity, community, or domination—simply through selection, balance, and quality adjustment.

Instead of modifying a scene's natural sounds, you might augment them or replace them by entirely fresh ones.

AUDIO/VIDEO RELATIONSHIPS

The picture and its audio can interrelate in several distinct ways:

- The picture's impact may be due to its accompanying audio. A close shot of a man crossing a busy highway:
  - Cheerful music suggests that he is in a lighthearted mood.
  - But automobile horns and squealing tires suggest that he is jaywalking dangerously.
- The audio impact may be due to the picture:
  - A long shot of a wagon bumping over a rough road; the accompanying sound is accepted as a natural audio effect.
  - But take continuous close-ups of a wheel, and every jolt suggests impending breakdown!
- The effect of picture and audio may be cumulative: A wave crashes against rocks along with a loud crescendo in the music.
- Sound and picture together may imply a further idea: Wind-blown daffodils along with birds singing and lambs bleating can suggest spring.

REVIEW QUESTIONS

1. How is "appropriateness" determined with visual style?
2. What are some of the applications that video images can be used for in a program?
3. Describe three of the various sound elements.
4. What are some of the effects of combining sounds?
5. How can audio make the video more powerful?

CHAPTER 21

Remote Production

"Live remote events are the core of television. They are the one thing television can do that no other medium can match. There are things movies can do better, there are things radio can do better, but no other medium can bring you a visual report of an event as it's happening."

Tony Verna, Director

Terms

Coordination meetings: These meetings provide a forum for all parties involved in the production to share ideas, communicate issues that may affect other areas, and ensure that all details are ready for the production.

Remote survey (recce): This site survey assesses the venue and determines how, where, how many, who, what, and how much.

Today's television production equipment is highly mobile, and able to access any location. There are times when the only way a show will be authentic is to get out to the event. Most remotes are live productions, with the director having little or no control over it, requiring the crew to cover whatever happens. However, other remote productions, such as dramas, have scripted (controlled) productions. Remote productions, other than news, usually utilize multiple cameras. As mentioned in earlier chapters, single-camera remote productions are generally referred to as ENG (electronic news production) or EFP (electronic field production) productions. In this chapter, we will use remote productions to refer to both multicamera and single-camera productions.

WHAT IS A REMOTE PRODUCTION?

Any production that occurs outside of the studio is considered to be a remote production or an outside broadcast (OB). Remote productions include all kinds of events:

- News events
- Sports events
- Parades
- Concerts
- Award shows
- Telethons
- Talk or variety shows that are "on the road"

Remote Production versus Studio Production

Both of these types of productions have pros and cons. Studio productions provide the maximum amount of control over the subject. The lighting and audio can be minutely controlled, providing the perfect levels for the production. Studios provide a clean location that is usually impervious to weather conditions and has full climate control.

However, there are times when the crew has to be on location. Remote locations can provide context and an exciting atmosphere (cheering crowds); see Figure 21.1. While weather can disrupt or even cancel a remote production, when the weather is nice, natural lighting and outdoor scenery can provide stunning images. There are also times when it is actually less expensive to shoot in the field than to rent and schedule studio time.

FIGURE 21.1
NBC decided to interview Michael Phelps after he had won his eight Olympic gold medals, outside and with a crowd as the backdrop to provide an exciting atmosphere.

Shooting on Location

Remote productions require anticipating what may happen. It is essential to assemble a team that can anticipate what is going to happen and know how to deal with it. The crew must be able to work well together and plan for contingencies in case something goes wrong.

The more familiar the crew is with an event—especially a news or sports event—the better they can cover it. Understanding the intricacies of the event allows the director and talent to clearly communicate what is happening.

350

FIGURE 21.2
ENG camera crews cover a press conference with a government official. (Photo courtesy of the U.S. Department of Defense, by Cherie A. Thurlby)

THE SINGLE CAMERA ON LOCATION

The single-camera production has some important advantages. It is extremely mobile, and thus easily relocated. It can be surprisingly unobtrusive. It is largely independent of its surroundings, and it is economical (Figure 21.2).

Typical Setups

Single-camera crews come in all different sizes, depending on the goals and the size of the production budget:

- One-person single-camera crews are increasingly being used by many news stations, sports shows, and documentaries. These operators run the camera, a microphone, and even an on-camera light. Some may even act as the reporter (Figure 21.3).
- Two-person single-camera crews are often made up of a camera operator who is responsible for the camera and a second person who is the reporter/director and may be responsible for the audio.
- Three-person single-camera crews are usually made up of a camera operator, an audio person, and a director/reporter (Figure 21.4).

Power Supplies

Professional video cameras normally require a DC power supply, which can be obtained by using an AC power adapter or batteries, or even by plugging into a car's cigarette lighter or DC outlet. Batteries come in all different configurations. Some batteries fit on the camera, others

FIGURE 21.3

This one-person ENG crew writes the stories, does the reporting, and runs the camera, microphone, and on-camera light.

FIGURE 21.4

This three-person single-camera crew is made up of a camera operator, a boom mic operator/audio person, and a reporter/director. (Photo courtesy of Andy Peters)

FIGURE 21.5

(Left) Most professional cameras use a battery that attaches to the back of the camera. (Right) The news photographer is using a battery belt to power his camera. Belts help distribute the weight of the battery around the body. (Photos courtesy of Matt Giblin and Thom Moynahan)

fit in a compartment under the camera, and some are designed to be worn on a belt in order to spread the weight around (Figure 21.5).

Batteries cannot be taken for granted. Carelessly used, they can become unreliable. Correctly used, they will give excellent service. Always carry spare batteries with you. How many depends on the nature and duration of your project and your opportunities to recharge exhausted cells.

Battery Care

There are a lot of dos and don'ts here, but remember: When batteries fail, the shooting may come to a halt:

■ Batteries power your camera viewfinder, the recorder, on-camera lights, and anything else attached to the camera. So switch off (or use the standby mode) and conserve power whenever possible. If you are not careful, time taken reviewing tapes and lighting can leave you with low power for the take.
■ Handle batteries carefully. Dropping can cause a battery breakdown.
■ Always check a battery's voltage while it is actually working.
■ Recharge batteries as soon as possible.
■ Stored batteries tend to discharge themselves to a noticeable extent.
■ In addition to the main battery that powers the camera, there may be "keep-alive" batteries for memory circuits within the camera that should be checked regularly.

SINGLE-CAMERA SHOOTING

Handling the Camera

If you are using the camera shoulder-mounted, make sure that it is comfortably balanced before you begin shooting. Try to use the camera as an extension of your body: turning with a pan, bending with a tilt. With your legs comfortably braced apart, turn to follow movement—preferably from a midway position between the start and end of the pan. Learn to shoot with one eye looking through the viewfinder and the other *open*, seeing the general scene. (With practice, it's not as difficult as it sounds.) You stand a better chance of walking around without an accident this way than if your attention is glued to your viewfinder's picture alone.

Even though its image is magnified, you must look carefully at the viewfinder picture to detect exact exposure adjustments. You can overlook something intruding into the frame that will be very obvious on a large-screen television monitor. Distracting, brightly colored items can easily pass unnoticed in a black-and-white viewfinder.

Walking should be kept to a minimum while shooting. If you must move, slightly bent legs produce smoother results than normal walking. (Practice to see what you find comfortable and effective—and critically examine the results.)

Lens Angles

Generally speaking, avoid extreme lens angles. A wide-angle lens makes camera work easier, and slight jolts are much less noticeable. However, everything looks so far away. Moving an extreme wide-angle lens closer may seriously distort the subject, which might actually be okay unless the subject is a person. With an extremely wide angle, you imagine that you have much more space to maneuver than you actually have, and are liable to trip or walk into things in the foreground.

Long telephoto lenses produce unsteady shots, and focusing can be difficult. On handheld cameras, they are often suitable only for brief stationary shots while holding your breath. A little wider than normal is probably the best compromise.

If you have a camera assistant, while walking around and shooting you can be guided by a hand on your shoulder, particularly when moving backwards. Walking backwards unguided is at best hazardous, and at worst foolish, unless you are on an open flat area without any obstructions. People can move toward you a lot faster than you can hope to walk backwards.

Table 21.1	Be Prepared: System Checklist
	As with the studio camera, preliminary checks before shooting can help you anticipate and prevent problems later. If you do not have access to a color television monitor as you shoot, you may have to rely on a small black-and-white viewfinder for all image checks. So if, for example, you forget to white-balance the camera, it will not be apparent until the picture is reviewed at base!
The camera	■ *Viewfinder*. Check the controls and adjust for a good tonal range.
	■ *Lens*. Lens clean? Lens firmly attached?
	■ *Focus*. Check both manual and autofocus systems.
	■ *Aperture (f-stop)*. Manually adjust the range of the aperture ring, checking the results in the viewfinder. Check auto-iris movements while panning over different tones.
	■ *Zoom*. Operate manual zoom over full range, checking focus tracking. Operate power zoom in and out over full range.
	■ *Microphone*. Test both camera microphone and hand microphone.
	■ Check the audio output through an earpiece/headset. Record and then replay the recording to confirm that the audio recording was accurate.
	■ *Subsidiary controls*. Looking at a color monitor, check filter-wheel positions, white balance, black adjust video gain, and other controls.
Recorder	■ If possible, examine playback in viewfinder and on a color monitor.
Power supplies	■ Check all batteries. Confirm that all spare batteries are fully charged. Are AC cords (main cables), AC adapters, car battery adapters, and other accessories all set?
Cables	■ Don't leave cables attached to equipment during storage. Never be casual about cables; they have a will of their own, and tangle easily. Coil them neatly, and secure them with a quick-release fastener or tie.
Spares	■ Examine all recording media to make sure that you have the type you need—as well as extras.
	■ Spare fuses may be needed for certain pieces of equipment.
	■ Take a spare microphone.
	■ Avoid field maintenance and cleaning unless you are experienced and the equipment is in need. Protective camera covers prevent problems (Figure 21.6).
Tools	■ Small and medium screwdrivers and pliers; electrical insulating tape; masking tape; gaffer tape; cord.
	■ Head-cleaning fluid (isopropyl alcohol), cotton-tipped cleaning sticks.
	■ Compressed-air can.
Accessories	■ Flashlight (with spare bulb and batteries).
	■ White material (or card) for checking white balance.
	■ Small reflectors (white, silver foil).
	■ Another matter for personal preferences. There are circumstances in which mosquito repellant, sunscreen preparations, or waterproofing material can be more essential than a comprehensive toolkit! Much depends on where you are working.

353

FIGURE 21.6
Camera covers can protect the cameras from dust, rain, and snow. (Photo by Josh Taber)

Automatic Controls

Automatic controls such as autofocus and auto-iris provide a safety net when you do not have the opportunity to control your camera accurately by hand adjustments. But remember that automatic controls are far from foolproof and should be used only in certain situations.

Audio

You can adjust the audio system manually, or switch it to *AGC* (*automatic gain control*). In the *manual mode*, watch the volume indicator for sound peaks. If they are far below the upper level (100 percent modulation/0 VU), increase the audio gain until the peaks reach this limit. But remember, if anything louder comes along, it will probably distort. Switching to AGC instead will protect against unexpected overloads, but may bring up background sounds and smooth out the audio dynamics.

Storing the Gear

Before putting the camera away at the end of a shoot, camera care should be a priority:

1. Cover the lens using a lens cap or filter wheel or just close the iris.
2. Make sure that all equipment is switched off.
3. Remove all camera accessories (light, mic, cables, etc.).
4. Remove all recording media and replace with fresh ones if appropriate.
5. Clean and check all items before storing.
6. Make sure that the camera is safely stored in its case.
7. Replace any worn or damaged items.
8. Check and recharge batteries.

MULTICAMERA REMOTE PRODUCTION

Although a single-camera production has its advantages, there are many production situations in which a single camera has little hope of capturing much more than a glimpse of the event, and multicamera coverage is the only answer:

- Coverage from different viewpoints is to be continuous and comprehensive.
- Action is spread over a large area (a golf course).
- At an event where there is no time or opportunity to move cameras around to different viewpoints.
- There is to be a "one-time-only" event (demolition of a bridge).
- The location of action continually changes (sports field of play).
- Cameras could not move to new angles or locations (because of obstructions).
- Cameras must be concealed, or located in fixed places.
- You cannot accurately anticipate where the action is to take place.

Multicamera Planning and Preparation

Multicamera productions have a number of aspects that make them quite different from studio productions or single-camera productions. Because they are larger productions, requiring more equipment and personnel, they need much more planning and preparation regarding the basics, like whether there is power, how long the cables need to be, whether there is enough light—things you don't need to think about in the studio. Following are discussions of some of these unique issues.

COORDINATION MEETINGS

Coordination meetings are essential to the planning phase of the production. These meetings provide a forum for all parties involved in the production to share ideas, communicate issues that may affect other areas, and ensure that all details are ready for the production. Coordination meetings usually include event officials, venue management, and production personnel.

REMOTE SURVEY (RECCE)

Once the production team has a good general idea of how the event will be covered, a survey team should visit the shoot location. This visit must assess the venue and determine how, where, how many, who, what, and how much. The answers to these questions will provide the foundation for the production's planning. The purposes of the remote survey are to:

- Determine the location for the production.
- Determine where all production equipment and personnel will be positioned.
- Determine whether all of the production's needs and requirements can be handled at the location.

Areas that must be determined and assessed include: contacts, location access, electrical power, location costs, catering/food, security, telephones/Internet access, parking, and lodging. Figure 21.7 shows a sample remote survey form.

CAMERAS

There are many decisions that have to be made when it comes to cameras in remote locations. These can include:

- How many cameras are required to cover the event?
- What type of camera should be used (dolly, jib, handheld, POV)?
- Where are the best locations to place the cameras? Does anything obscure a camera's viewpoint?
- Are special camera mounts required (scaffolding, jibs, etc.)?
- Are special lenses required (such as long telephoto lenses)?
- Where can camera cables be run?

AUDIO

Although audio may be one of the least-appreciated aspects of a television production, it is one of the most important areas of a production. Some of the issues for consideration include:

- What does the audience need to hear? How many mics are needed to cover the event?
- What type of microphone works best in each situation (handheld, lapel mic, shotgun, etc.)?
- Stereo or surround sound?
- Can microphones appear in the shot?
- Wired or wireless microphones?
- Is the natural sound of the location a problem (traffic, crowds, airplanes)?

Additional information about the remote survey is covered in Chapter 5.

REMOTE PRODUCTION VEHICLES

The facilities needed to cover a remote production will depend partly on the scale of coverage and partly on the nature of the event. Production trucks vary in size from very small to very large. Other vehicles could include cars, motorcycles, golf carts, boats, and helicopters. For example, marathon coverage might include a few stationary cameras, a couple of handheld

Remote Survey Form

Client: _____ Date of Survey _____
Shoot Date _____ Time of Shooting _____
Program Name _____ Air Date(s) _____
Location _____
Director _____ Producer _____ TD _____

Location Contacts:
Primary Contact _____ Phone _____
Secondary Contact _____ Phone _____
Permits Needed _____ Phone _____
Truck Location _____
Other Parking _____
Credentials Contact _____

Cameras: (add sketch of camera locations at event)

	Camera	Position/locations	Lens	Cable run
1				
2				
3				
4				
5				
6				

Audio: (add sketch of microphone locations at event)

	Mic Type	Location		Mic Type	Location
1			6		
2			7		
3			8		
4			9		
5			10		

Lighting: (add lighting plot if needed)
Available Light _____
Talent Light _____
Special Instructions _____
_____

Power:
Location Electrician Contact _____
Program Requirements _____
AC Outlets

	Location	Voltage	Connect. Type		Location	Voltage	Connect. Type
1				4			
2				5			
3				6			

Communications:

	Type/Style	Location(s)
Camera Headsets		
Intercoms (PL)		
Business Phone		
Wireless		

Location Sketch: (should include important dimensions, location of props and building, truck, power source and sun during time of telecast)

FIGURE 21.7
Sample of a small event remote survey form.

cameras, a motorcycle with a camera to stay with the lead runner, and a helicopter or two to get the long-shot/"big picture" images that establish the scene. It always come down to the event and what you want to accomplish.

Remote Production Truck/OB Van

The most common unit for remote productions is the remote production truck, otherwise known as an outside broadcast (OB) truck or van. These units vary in size from a small van with two or three cameras to a large truck with more than 20 cameras (Figures 21.8 and 21.9). They provide a full broadcast standard production control center with complete video and audio facilities. The trucks include everything needed to produce a television program: monitor wall, video production switcher, audio, recording and playback decks, graphics, intercom, and anything else you might need for a remote production. See Chapter 3 for more details about remote production trucks.

The unit may be used in several ways:

- Parked within the action area (in a public square or at a sports venue) with cables extending to cameras at various vantage points.
- As a drive-in control room parked outside a permanent or temporary studio. This could include a public hall, a theater, or even a soundstage (usually used for film).
- The program may be recorded (and edited) on board the remote truck, or it may be relayed back to their base by a microwave link, data line, or some other transmission path.

FIGURE 21.8
Small production trucks are easier to drive into some locations but usually offer limited facilities.

FIGURE 21.9
Large remote trucks offer more space and additional facilities but are difficult to maneuver within some venues.

FIGURE 21.10
Transmission trucks come in all sizes, depending on what is needed. This unit is a combination satellite uplink and microwave van.

LIVE TRANSMISSION

If an event is being produced for a live audience, the production's signal must be sent back to a location in order to be broadcast, cablecast, or cybercast. There are a variety of transmission methods: uplink trucks and microwave trucks, fiber optics, and the Internet.

Transmission trucks provide units that can be quickly relocated and provide broadcast-quality images and sound. Most systems provide a two-way communication link between the unit and base or studio (Figure 21.10).

Event Coverage

As in every other type of event, directors shooting remote productions must keep the axis of action in mind, placing all cameras on one side of that line (see Figures 18.8, 18.9, and 21.10).

Sports Action

Sports productions are a bit unique, because the participants can be going all over the venue. Some venues are large (a car racetrack or golf); other venues are very small (a wrestling match). Events here are categorized by different types of action: horizontal, vertical, and round.

HORIZONTAL ACTION

Horizontal sports include basketball, soccer, American football, among others. The cameras are placed on a long side of the venue, panning right to left to capture the athletes' action (Figure 21.11).

VERTICAL ACTION

One vertical sport is tennis. Although it is a sport that takes place on a rectangular venue, like basketball and soccer, the action is difficult to follow by the audience with two players hitting a small ball back and forth. Instead, the cameras are placed behind one of the

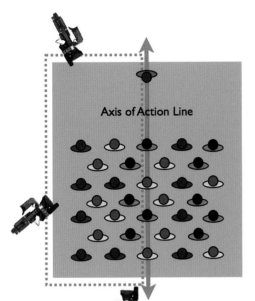

FIGURE 21.11

In a meeting in which a speaker is speaking to a group of people, the axis of action is between the two. That means that all of the cameras must be on one side of the line.

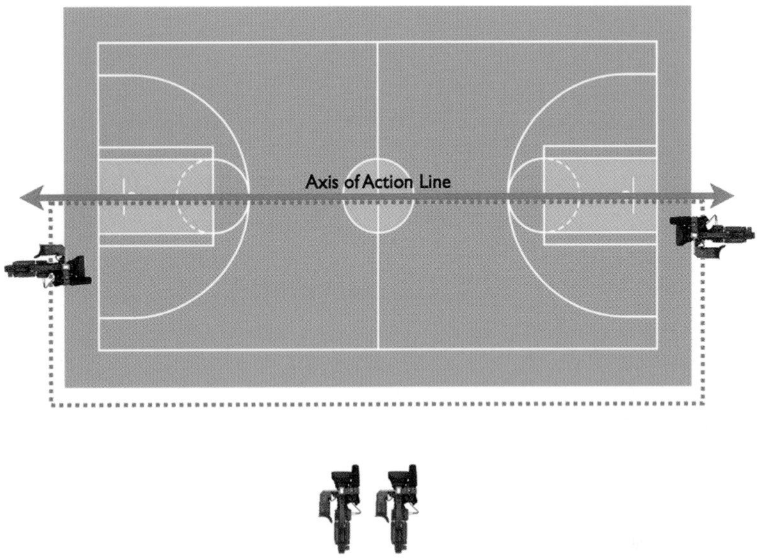

FIGURE 21.12

Basketball is a horizontal sport, one that is directed by placing all of the cameras on one side of the horizontal axis of action (blue area) on the field of play.

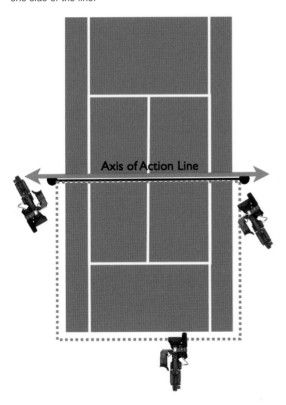

FIGURE 21.13

Tennis is a vertical sport. In order to make the shots more interesting, the axis of action line runs across the court vertically. Keep all of the cameras on one side in the blue area.

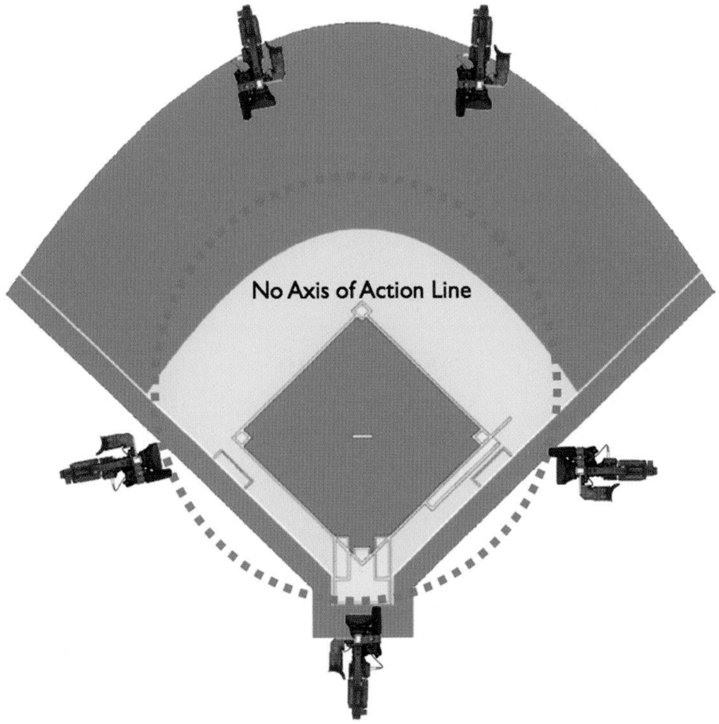

FIGURE 21.14

Baseball is a round action sport. There is no axis of action line, allowing the cameras to be placed anywhere. However, the director often needs to go to a long shot, re-establishing the location for the audience.

athletes, looking over his or her shoulder at the other athlete. So the axis of action is located at the net (Figure 21.13).

ROUND ACTION

Round sports include auto racing and baseball. Because cameras are needed to cover the action the whole way around the circle or oval, an axis of action is not chosen. Instead, the director has to constantly re-establish the scene in order to avoid confusing the viewers. This means that if a camera has a close-up shot of a car as it drives around the track, every once in while a long shot must be shown to establish the current location of the car and where it is in relation to the other cars (Figure 21.14).

REVIEW QUESTIONS

1. Define a remote production.
2. What are the advantages and disadvantages of studio productions and remote productions?
3. What are some of the suggestions for handling a single camera?
4. What are some of the challenges with extreme wide-angle and telephoto lenses?
5. What are some of the situations in which multicamera productions are essential?
6. Describe the three primary types of sports action and give examples of each type.

PART 7

Engineering

CHAPTER 22

Basic Video Engineering

"Having some technical knowledge will enhance your ability to get the most out of the tools at your disposal in order to more effectively communicate."

Adam Wilson, Engineer

Terms

Black level: The intensity of black in the video image.

Camera setup: Adjusting the controls within the camera's circuitry.

Color bars: A chart used as a reference source to correctly adjust the camera's colors.

Frame sync: Used to match the timing of a real-time incoming video source (such as a camera or satellite feed) to the timing of an existing video system.

Gamma: Adjusts the tone and contrast of a video image.

Genlock: Adjusting the timing of the local sync pulses to get them into step with a remote (non sync) source.

Time-base corrector (TBC): Equipment that provides automatic compensation for synchronizing inaccuracies on replay or imperfect sync pulses from mobile cameras.

Vectorscope: An oscilloscope that is used to check the color accuracy of each part of the video system (cameras, switcher, recorder, etc.).

Video gain: The amplification of the camera's video signal, usually resulting in some video noise.

Waveform monitor: The waveform monitor is an oscilloscope that is designed to monitor the video signal.

White balance: The most common technique used to color balance a camera. It is the process of calibrating a camera so that the light source will be reproduced accurately as white.

Understandably, most people involved with producing television production programs are content to leave the technical aspects to the *engineers*—those who install the equipment and keep it working. However, it is important to know the basics, because you never know when you are going to need this information.

BEHIND THE SCENES

The work of television engineers generally falls into three categories:

- Maintenance/servicing
- Setup
- Shading/vision control (adjusting picture quality)

Maintenance/Servicing

This is usually a standard routine in which the video and audio equipment is checked to ensure that everything is working to specifications. When necessary, units are repaired or replaced.

Camera Setup

If you want consistently high-quality images, it is necessary to keep cameras adjusted to within very close technical limits. Even high-end systems drift to some extent, whether sitting in a case or during use. It is advisable to make periodic adjustments before rehearsals begin and before recording. Drifting picture quality may not be obvious when working with a single camera (until cutting between various shots during editing!), but in a multicamera production, differences can be very evident.

Setup involves adjusting the controls within the camera's circuitry. Each camera is linked to its CCU (camera control unit), where most of the circuitry involved in generating and processing the video and its associated sync pulses is centralized. The CCU's main electronic adjustments are usually made manually, using precision test equipment to confirm what is being seen in a monitor (Figure 22.1). Color bars (used as a reference source) and a series of charts are used and measured on waveform monitors and vectorscopes to ensure quality (Figure 22.2). The CCU's circuits are adjusted to

364

FIGURE 22.1
CCUs are used to set up the camera during the preparation phase of the production. They are also used during production in order to maintain image quality.

FIGURE 22.2
A series of charts and color bars are used and measured on waveform monitors and vector-scopes to ensure image quality.

conform to established standards. These checks range from engineering specifics (precise timing, amplitudes, phasing of signals) to very subjective judgments (such as the color balance of monitor pictures). This setup or *line-up* process is time consuming, and results may depend on individual skills.

TEST EQUIPMENT

The most common test equipment used by engineering are the waveform monitor and the vectorscope. Manufacturers are now making models that combine the waveform and vectorscope in one unit (Figure 22.3).

WAVEFORM MONITOR

The waveform monitor is an oscilloscope that is designed to monitor the video signal. It is used to check for exposure errors, ensuring that the video signal does not exceed the system's limits and checking the accuracy of sync pulses.

VECTORSCOPE

An oscilloscope that is used to check the color accuracy of each part of the video system (cameras, switcher, recorder). Ideally, the color responses of all equipment should match. Color bars are used with the vectorscope in order to check color accuracy.

Adjusting Picture Quality

VISION CONTROL/SHADING

Although scenery and lighting can build an atmospheric effect, how successfully this is conveyed by the camera will depend on the video equipment and how it is adjusted.

Producing images that are consistently attractive and persuasive requires forethought, skill, and patience. To obtain optimum picture quality, you must do more than just point a camera at a scene. Appropriate camera control is necessary; otherwise, shadows can lose their detail, the lightest tones can merge, and some shots can look washed out while others are overly contrasty.

In the studio, good image quality is ensured by carefully selecting tones, lighting, wardrobe, and so on. But on location, where the situation is less easily adjusted, it may be necessary to avoid shots that produce unacceptable results, such as an over-exposed exterior seen outside the window of a room. Alternatively, you may be able to introduce a window gel (filter) or compensatory lighting.

365

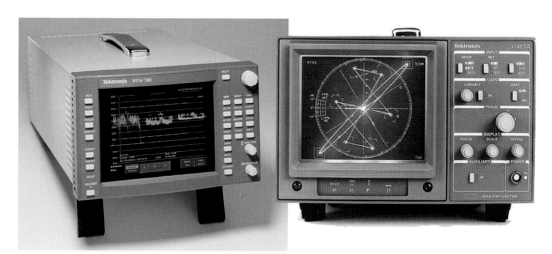

FIGURE 22.3
Waveform monitors and vectorscopes are used when adjusting camera settings. (Photo courtesy of Tektronix)

"Image processing" in the form of video control (shading) is necessary for a quality video signal from the equipment (cameras, video players, and other devices). Ideally, all video sources should be continuously monitored and their images appropriately adjusted. Three basic approaches to the control of the television picture quality have evolved, as follows.

Preset Adjustments

Here the system is adjusted and left, as one hopes that no significant lighting problems arise.

Automatic Control

With this method, we rely on automatic adjustments. The problem with automatic control is that it is not always successful at creating a quality image—it can be fooled by different areas of the image (or someone walking in front of the camera).

Manual Control

An operator monitors pictures and adjusts picture quality. This is by far the ideal situation. Each piece of equipment can be individually monitored, providing the best image quality. Video operators, or video engineers, sit at the CCU and adjust equipment to suit each shot. Adjustments include: lens aperture/f-stop, black level, video gain, color balance, and gamma (Figure 22.4).

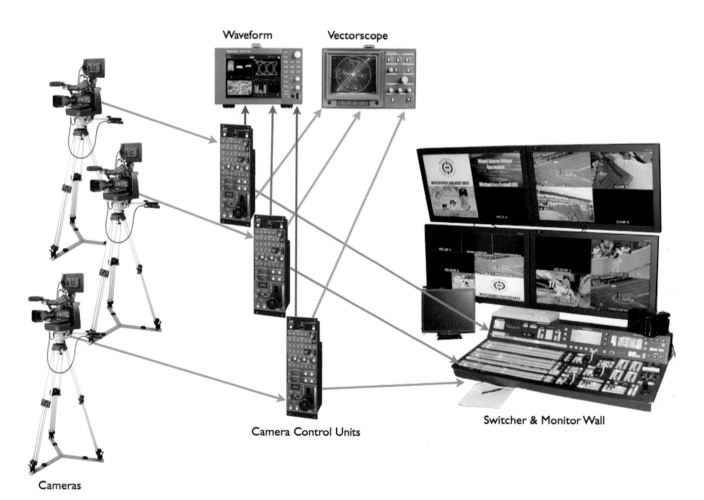

FIGURE 22.4

Video signals travel to the CCU, which adjusts the incoming image with the help of the waveform monitor and vectorscope. Once adjusted, the signal travels from the CCU to the video switcher. (Photos courtesy of JVC, Tektronics, and Russ Jenisch)

Video Operator Terminology

- *Black level:* The intensity of black in the video image. If set incorrectly, picture detail quality will be poor in dimly lit areas. Lowering the picture's black level moves all image tones toward black and crushes the lowest tones. Raising the black level lightens picture tones but does not reveal detail in the blackest tones.
- *Color balance:* Balancing (matching) the color between all of the video sources is accomplished by using color bars (see Figure 22.2), a vectorscope (see Figure 22.3), and a CCU (see Figure 22.1).
- *White balance:* The most common technique used to color-balance a camera. It is the process of calibrating a camera so that the light source will be reproduced accurately as white. In order to balance the color, the camera is aimed at a white subject, usually a white card lit by the scene's light source, and the white balance button is pushed, adjusting the color (Figure 22.5). By capping the camera or closing the iris, *black balance* can also be used to provide a reference for black after white balancing.
- *Lens aperture:* The opening in the lens (iris) that lets light into the camera. It allows the operator to darken or brighten the video image, depending on the light in the scene.
- *Gamma:* Adjusts the tone and contrast of a video image. High gamma settings produce a coarser, exaggerated contrast; lower settings result in thin and reduced tonal contrast.
- *Video gain:* The amplification of the camera's video signal, usually resulting in some video noise. Boosting the gain allows the camera to shoot in lower light situations than normal. However, it also provides a lower-quality image.

FIGURE 22.5
Cameras are zoomed in on the white card, allowing accurate white balance. (Photo by Luke Wertz)

EXPOSURE AND COLOR CONTROL

"Correct exposure" can be very subjective. The exposure suitable for one camera position will not necessarily be appropriate for another. Subtle changes in the lens aperture or iris can readjust all picture tones.

- Unless a surface is rough, its brightness can alter significantly as we shoot it from various angles.
- Flat lighting (overall bright with no shadows or texture) produces uninteresting images, so skilled lighting directors avoid it. Light and shade create depth and texture in a scene.

- Similarly, when scenic tones exceed the camera system's limits, by carefully adjusting exposure, gamma, and black level, they can often be accommodated. It is a lot easier (and cheaper) to adjust the system than to change the staging.
- Where we want to see detail or tonal gradation in very light-toned or very dark-toned subjects, appropriate video adjustments can show them more clearly. When taking a close-up of a page in a book, for instance, a combination of reduced exposure and lower black level can improve clarity. Otherwise the page would probably appear blank.
- Deliberately under-exposing an image will help to suggest a dull overcast day or improve a dingy scene. Controlled over-exposure, on the other hand, can simulate dazzling sunlight.
- Slight changes in a camera's color balance can help to compensate for unwanted subjective color effects (faces can appear warmed); see Figure 22.6.

Sometimes a slight color bias will enhance an atmospheric effect: a warmer cast for fireside or sunset scenes; a colder bluish cast for moonlight, or gaslight effects. This coloration can take place a number of ways: by using the light-blue cards (Figure 22.6), adjusting the RGB channel gains, or using filters (used to match the camera to different lighting color temperatures).

SYNCHRONIZING SOURCES

To match two independent video sources' synchronization, several ingenious electronic systems have evolved. The earliest and simplest was *genlock*, which adjusts the timing of the local pulses to get them into step with the remote (non sync) source. This system of slaving works well as long as the remote's syncs are not interrupted or distorted, because then *all* local equipment being run from these genlocked pulses would "lose sync."

Recorder sources present another problem. Although the original sync pulses are recorded along with the picture, upon replay these syncs become irregular and distorted. Although pictures will appear quite satisfactory on a video monitor (which adjusts itself to varying sync pulses), if we tried to use such an unstable source with a precisely synchronized television system, this would cause color loss and image break-up. Particularly when editing, some form of synchronizer is needed that will accept these randomly changing syncs and adjust them to match local pulses.

The most common tools used to sync video signals are *time-base correctors* (TBCs) and *frame syncs*. Although this equipment has merged in function over the years, the TBC is primarily used for syncing prerecorded material from video playback units, and the frame sync is primarily used with real-time video signals, such as those coming from a camera or satellite.

FIGURE 22.6

Instead of using a white card to white balance the camera, light-blue cards can be used for the color balance process, resulting in a warmer image. Keep in mind that it is always best to use a waveform/vectorscope and a monitor when color correcting in the field. (Photos courtesy of Vortex)

This equipment provides automatic compensation for synchronizing inaccuracies on replay or imperfect sync pulses from cameras. They store the video information and then clock it out at precisely timed intervals in perfect synchronism with the master sync-pulse rate. These units often offer additional facilities, such as freeze frame, digital enhancement, noise reduction, and color correction.

REVIEW QUESTIONS

1. What are the three areas that engineers are responsible for?
2. What are some of the types of equipment used to test the quality of the video signal?
3. How does "shading" enhance the quality of the video signal?
4. Why does a camera need to be white-balanced?
5. Why is it important to synchronize video signals?

720p This HDTV format has 720 scan lines and uses progressive scanning. The 720p format is best for fast-moving motion scenes.

1080i This HDTV format has 1080 scan lines and uses an interlaced scanning system. The 1080i format has a sharper image than the 720p format.

1080p This HDTV format has 1080 scan lines and uses a progressive scanning system. It is often referred to as *full HD*.

Acoustics Higher-frequency sound waves travel in straight paths and are easily deflected and reflected by hard surfaces. They are also easily absorbed by porous fibrous materials. Lower-frequency sound waves (below 100 Hz) spread widely, so they are not impeded by obstacles and are less readily absorbed. As sound waves meet nearby materials, they are selectively absorbed and reflected; the reflected sound's quality is modified according to the surfaces' nature, structures, and shapes.

Action line (line/eye line) The imaginary line along the direction of the action in the scene. Cameras should shoot from only one side of this line.

Ambient sound The background sounds that are present when shooting a production.

Analog (analogue) recording Analog systems directly record the variations of the video and audio signals. They have a tendency to deteriorate when dubbing copies and can be recorded only on tape.

Animation (image composition) Refers to when video images give the audience the same emotional response that you had while shooting.

Aperture The opening in the lens that lets light into the camera.

Arc A camera move that moves around the subject in a circle, arc, or horseshoe path.

Aspect ratio The ratio of the width to the height of a television screen. For example, television screens are either 4:3 or 16:9.

Audio filters Audio filters may be used to reduce background noises (traffic, air conditioners, wind), or compensate for boomy surroundings.

Audio mixer A unit used to select, control, and intermix audio sources. It may include filter circuits and reverberation control. It is usually operated by the audio mixer (it's a job title as well as the name of the board), also known as *A-1*.

Audio sweetening The process of working on the program sound after the video portion is completed; also called a *dubbing session* or *track laying*.

Autofocus A process by which some lenses automatically focus on the subject.

Axis of action line Often also called the *action line* or *eye line*, this is an imaginary line along the direction of the action in the scene. Cameras should shoot from only one side of this line.

Backlight control When there is more light in the background than on the subject, some cameras use a backlight control button that opens up the iris an arbitrary stop or so above the auto-iris setting in order to improve the subject's exposure.

Barn doors These metal flaps are usually attached to the top, bottom, and sides of the light in order to shape the beam.

Baselight The minimal amount of light that allows the camera to see the subject.

371

Batten The bar to which studio lights are connected.

Bidirectional microphone This microphone can hear equally well both in front and back but is deaf on either side of it.

Black level The intensity of black in the video image.

Black stretch control Camera circuitry that makes shadow detail clearer and improves tonal gradation in darker tones.

Boom pole A pole that is used to hold a microphone close to a subject. Often referred to as a *mic boom*.

Breakdown sheet An analysis of a script, listing all of the production elements in order of the schedule.

Camcorder A camera with a built-in video recorder.

Camera blocking (stumble-through) The initial camera rehearsal, coordinating all technical operations, and discovering and correcting problems.

Camera control unit (CCU) Equipment that controls the camera from a remote position. The CCU is part of the setup and adjustments of the camera: luminance, color correction, aperture.

Camera script The camera script adds full details of the production treatment to the left side of the "rehearsal script" and usually also includes the shot numbers, cameras used, positions of camera, basic shot details, camera moves, and switcher instructions (if used).

Camera setup Adjusting the controls within the camera's circuitry.

Cathode ray tube (CRT) CRT televisions send an electron beam through a vacuum tube to a phosphor-coated screen. These "tube" televisions are large and bulky.

Character generator (CG) A generic name for any type of television graphic creation equipment.

Character makeup The *makeup* emphasis is on the specific character or type that the actor is playing. By facial reshaping, remodeling, and changes in hair, the subject may even be totally transformed.

Charge-coupled device (CCD) An image sensor used in most video cameras.

Chroma-key Using a production switcher and this technique, the director can replace a specific color (usually blue or green) with another image source (still image, live video, prerecorded material).

Clapboard (clapper or slate) Shot at the beginning of each take to provide information such as film title, names of director and director of photography, scene, take, date, and time. Primarily used in dramatic productions.

Clip A video segment.

Close-up shot (CU) The CU shot encourages the viewer to concentrate on a specific feature. When shooting people, it is used to emphasize emotion.

CMOS See *Complementary metal-oxide semiconductor*.

Color bar generator Color bars provide a consistent reference pattern that is used for matching the video output of multiple cameras. They are also used to obtain the best-quality image on a video monitor. This test signal is composed of a series of vertical bars of standard colors (white, yellow, cyan [blue-green], green, magenta [red-purple], red, blue, black). A color bar generator actually creates the pattern electronically. However, it is possible to use a printed color chart, as long as it has been cared for and is not faded.

Complementary metal-oxide semiconductor (CMOS) An image sensor that consumes less power, saving energy for longer shooting times.

Composition The goal of composition is to create an image that is attractive or that captures and keeps the audience's attention and effectively communicates the production's message.

Compressor/expander Deliberately used to reduce or emphasize the audio dynamic range (i.e., the difference between the quietest and loudest sounds).

Condenser microphone A high-quality microphone that can be very small and is generally powered by an in-board battery, phantom power, or a power supply.

Context (image composition) The content of the image should allow the viewer to understand the subject better. Compose the shot in such a way that it includes a background, or foreground, that adds additional information or context to the image.

Continuity Making sure that there is consistency from one shot to the next in a scene and from scene to scene. This continuity includes the talent, objects, and sets. An example of a continuity error in a production would be when one shot shows the talent's hair combed one way and the next shot shows it another way.

Contrast The difference between the relative brightness of the lightest and darkest areas in the shot.

Control room Sometimes known as a *gallery*, an area in a studio where the director controls the television production. Although the control room equipment may vary, they all include video and audio monitors, intercoms, and a switcher.

Convertible camera This type of camera generally starts out as a camera "head." A variety of attachments can then be added onto the camera head, including different kinds of lenses, viewfinders, and recorders, to suit a specific production requirement.

Coordination meetings A forum for all parties involved in the production to share ideas, communicate issues that may affect other areas, and ensure that all details are ready for the production.

Corrective makeup Reduces less-pleasing facial characteristics while enhancing more attractive points.

Cover shot A video clip that is used to cover an edit so that the viewers do not know that the edit occurred.

Crab See *Truck*.

Crash start Takes us straight into the program, which appears to have begun already.

Crawl The movement of text horizontally across the television screen.

Credit roll Continuous information moving vertically into the frame, and passing out at the top.

Credits The text that lists and acknowledges those appearing in and contributing to the program.

CU See *Close-up shot*.

Cue card The talent may read questions or specific points from this card, which is positioned near the camera. Generally, it is held next to the camera lens.

Cut The "cut" or "take" is the most common transition when editing. It is an instantaneous switch from one shot to the next.

Cutaway shot These shots are used to cover edits when any sequence is shortened or lengthened. Generally, it is a shot of something outside of the current frame.

Cyclorama (cyc) The cyclorama (or *cyc*, pronounced "sike") serves as a general-purpose detail-free background. It can be neutral, colored with lights, or have no light (black).

Dead surroundings When area surfaces are very sound absorbent, the direct sound waves strike walls, floor, ceiling, and furnishings and are largely lost. Only a few weak reflections may be picked up by the microphone.

Deep focus Deep focus, or large depth of field, is when everything in the shot is clearly in focus.

Depth of field (DoF) The distance between the nearest and farthest objects in focus.

Dichroic filters These filters produce three color-filtered images corresponding to the red, green, and blue proportions in the scene.

Diffusion material Can be attached to the front of a light in order to reduce the intensity of the light beam.

Digital recording A digital system regularly samples the waveforms and converts them into numerical (binary) data. This allows many generations of copies to be made without affecting the quality of the image. Digital systems also allow the data to be recorded on forms of media other than tape, such as hard disks and flash memory.

Digital zoom Zooming is achieved by progressively reading out a smaller and smaller area of the same digitally constructed image. The image progressively deteriorates as the digital zoom is zoomed in.

Digital video effect (DVE) Digital video effect equipment, working with the switcher, is used to create special effects between video images. A DVE could also refer to the actual effect.

Digitizing Converting the audio and video signals into data files. This term is used when transferring video footage from a camera (or other video source) to a computer.

Directional microphone This type of microphone can hear sounds directly in front of it.

Dissolve A gradual transition between two images. A dissolve usually signifies a change in time or location.

Dolly (track) (1) The action of moving the whole camera and mount slowly toward or away from the subject. (2) A platform with wheels that is used to smoothly move a camera during a shot.

Drag The variable friction controls located on a tripod head that steady the camera's movements.

Dress rehearsal (dress run) The goal of the dress rehearsal is to time the wardrobe and makeup changes.

Dry blocking (walk-through) Actors perform, familiarizing themselves with the studio settings while the studio crew watch, learning the format, action, and production treatment.

Dutch Tilting the camera is called a "dutch" or a "canted" shot. This movement increases the dynamics of the shot.

DVE See *Digital video effect*.

Dynamic range The range between the weakest and loudest sounds that can be effectively recorded by a recording device.

Dynamic microphone A rugged, low-maintenance microphone that is not easily distorted.

ECU or XCU See *extreme close-up shot*.

Electronic field production (EFP) EFP cameras are used for non-news productions such as program inserts, documentaries, magazine features, and commercials. EFPs can also be used for multicamera production.

Electronic news gathering (ENG) Camcorders generally used for news gathering. Many times, they are the cameras that are equipped with a microphone and camera light and are used to shoot interviews and breaking news.

ELS Extreme long shot.

Ellipsoidal A sharply focused/defined spotlight.

Empirical production method The empirical method is where instinct and opportunity are the guides.

Equalizer An audio filter that can boost or reduce any segment of the audio spectrum.

EXT The abbreviation used to signify an external location on a script.

Eye-level shots Provide an image that is roughly at the eye level of the talent (in a studio show) or the average viewing audience.

Eye line (line) Where people appear to be looking, or line of sight.

Fact sheet/run down sheet Summarizes information about a product or item for a demonstration program; or, details of a guest for an interviewer.

Fade A gradual change (dissolve) between black and a video image. Usually defines the beginning or end of a segment or program.

Filmic space Intercuts action that is concurrent at different places.

Filmic time Editing technique that tightens up the pace of a production by leaving out potentially boring portions of the scene when the audience interest could wane.

Filter wheel Filters wheels are often fitted inside the video camera, just behind the lens. The typical wheel is fitted with a number of different correction filters and may include a 5600 K (daylight), 3200 K, and neutral-density filters.

FireWire Also known as IEEE 1394 or iLink; a method for connecting different pieces of equipment, such as cameras, drives, and computers, so that they can transfer large amounts of data, such as video, quickly and easily.

Fishpole See *Boom pole*.

Flash memory Flash cards can store large amounts of digital data but have no moving parts. This makes them durable and able to work in a variety of temperatures, and allows data to be easily transferred into a nonlinear editor.

Flats Free-standing background set panels.

Flood lighting Scatters in all directions, providing a broad, nondirectional light.

Floor plan (staging plan or set plan) A rough plan of the staging layout that usually begins with drawing potential scale outlines of settings, including their main features—windows, doors, stairways. Ensure that there is enough room for cameras, sound booms, and lighting.

Focal length An optical measurement: the distance between the optical center of the lens and the image sensor, when you are focused at a great distance such as infinity. It is measured in millimeters (mm) or inches.

Focus puller The person responsible for keeping the camera in focus using a follow-focus device.

Focus zone See *Depth of field*.

Foley Creating sound effects that can be used to replace the original sounds such as hoof beats or footsteps.

Follow focus This technique requires the camera operator to continually change the focus as the camera follows the action.

Format The show format lists the items or program segments in a show in the order in which they are to be shot. The format generally shows the durations of each segment and possibly the camera assignments.

Fresnel light An unfocused spotlight. It is lightweight, less expensive than an ellipsoidal, and has an adjustable beam.

***f*-stop** A setting that regulates how much light is allowed to pass through the camera lens by varying the size of the hole the light comes through.

FU FU is the abbreviation used on scripts for a fade-up (from black to a video signal).

Full script Includes detailed information on all aspects of the production. This includes the precise words that the talent/actors are to use in the production.

Gain (1) (video) Amplification of the camera video signal, usually resulting in some video noise. (2) (audio) Amplification of the audio signal.

Gamma Adjusts the tone and contrast of a video image.

Gel Colored flexible plastic filters used to adjust the color of the lights.

Genlock Adjusting the timing of the local sync pulses to get them into step with remote (nonsync) source.

Goals Broad concepts of what you want to accomplish with the program.

Graphic equalizer (shaping filter) Device with a series of slider controls; allows selected parts of the audio spectrum to be boosted or reduced.

Grip clamps Clamps designed to allow a light to be attached to almost anything.

Group shot (GS) A director's command to frame the entire group into the shot.

GS See *Group shot.*

Handheld camera (HH) A camera that is held by a person and not supported by any type of camera mount.

Handheld microphone Generally refers to any microphone held in the hand, used to pick up human speech.

Hand properties (props) Any items that are touched and handled by the talent during the production. These could include a pen, dishes, a cell phone, or silverware.

Hard disk drive (HDD) Used for recording digital video images; can be built into the camera or attached to the outside of the camera.

Headroom The space from the top of the head to the upper frame.

High angle When the camera is positioned higher than the subject.

High-definition television (HDTV, HD) Video formats that currently use a range from 720 to 1080 lines of resolution are considered to be high definition.

Hue Refers to the predominant color: for example, blue, green, or yellow.

Image magnification (I-mag) Video on large television screens next to a stage in order to help the viewers see the stage action.

Incident light (direct lighting) The measurement of the amount of light falling on a subject.

INT The abbreviation used on a script to signify an internal location.

Intercom A wired or wireless communication link between members of the production crew.

Interlaced scanning The television's electron scans the odd-numbered lines first and then goes back and "paints" in the remaining even-numbered lines.

Iris The adjustable diaphragm of the lens. This diaphragm is adjusted to be open or closed based on the amount of light needed to capture a quality image.

Isolated (ISO) When all the cameras are connected to the switcher as before, the ISO (or isolated) camera is also continuously recorded on a separate recorder.

Jib A counterbalanced arm that fits onto a tripod that allows the camera to move up, down, and around.

Jog Playing the video on a recorder/player frame by frame.

Jump cut Created when the editor cuts between two similar shots (two close-ups) of the same subject.

Lavalier microphone These small microphones clip on the clothing of the talent and provide fairly consistent, hands-free audio pickup of the talent's voice.

LCD See *Liquid-crystal display.*

LED The abbreviation for a light-emitting diode lightbulb.

LED light panel A camera or studio light that is made from a series of small LED bulbs.

Lighting plot A lighting plot shows where each light will be placed on the set.

Limiter A device for preventing loud audio from exceeding the system's upper limit (causing overload distortion), by progressively reducing circuit amplification for louder sounds.

Linear editing The copying, or dubbing, of segments from the master tape to another tape in sequential order.

Line level The audio signal generated by a nonmicrophone device such as a CD player.

Liquid-crystal display (LCD) These flat-screen displays work by sending variable electrical currents through a liquid crystal solution that crystallizes to form a quality image.

Live surroundings Signifies an area, usually a room, that contains predominantly hard surfaces, which strongly reflect sound, creating an echo.

Logging Loggers view the footage and write down the scene/take numbers, the length of each shot, time code, and descriptions of each shot.

Long shot (LS or wide-angle shot) The long shot is used to help establish a scene for the viewer.

Low angle When the camera is positioned lower than the subject.

Lower third (L/3rd) A graphic that appears in lower third of the television screen. Traditionally, this contains biographical information.

LS See *Long shot*.

Luminance The brightness of the image—how dark or light it appears.

Macro Some lenses include a macro setting, which is designed to provide a sharp image almost up to the actual lens surface.

Medium shot (MS) A shot close enough to show the emotion of the scene but far enough away to show some of the relevant context of the event.

Mic level The audio level of a signal that is generated by a microphone.

Minimum focused distance (MFD) The closest distance a lens can get to the subject. With some telephoto lenses, the MFD may be a few yards. Other lenses may be {¼} inch.

Modular set Designed in a number of components, these sets can be easily assembled, dissassembled, and stored.

Monaural (mono) This single track of audio is limited; its only clue to distance is loudness, and direction cannot be conveyed at all.

Monitors Monitors were designed to provide accurate, stable image quality. They do not include tuners and may not include audio speakers.

Monopod A one-legged camera support.

MS See *Medium shot*.

Multicamera production Signifies that two or more cameras were used to create a television production. Usually the cameras are switched by a production switcher.

Narrow-angle lens See *Telephoto lens*.

Natural sound (NAT) The recording of ambient or environmental sounds on location.

Nonlinear editing The process whereby the recorded video is digitized (copied) onto a computer. Then the footage can be arranged, rearranged, and special effects added, and the audio and graphics can be adjusted using editing software.

Normal lens The type of lens that portrays the scene approximately the same way a human eye might see it.

Notch filter (parametric amplifier) A filter that produces a very steep peak or dip in a selected part of the audio spectrum, such as to suppress unavoidable hum, whistle, or rumble.

NTSC (National Television System Committee) The television system traditionally used by the United States and Japan. It has 525 scan lines.

Objective camera This role is that of an onlooker, watching the action from the best possible position at each moment.

Objectives Measurable goals; something that can be tested for to confirm that the audience did understand and remember the key points of the program.

Omnidirectional microphone This type of microphone can pick up audio equally well in all directions.

Opening titles Introduce the show to the audience.

Open set Can be created by carefully grouping a few pieces of furniture in front of the wall. Even as little as a couch, low table, table lamp, potted plants, a screen, chair, and stand lamp can suggest a complete room.

Optical zoom Uses a lens to maintain a high-quality image throughout its zoom range.

Outline script Usually provides the prepared dialogue for the opening and closing and then lists the order of topics that should be covered. The talent will use the list as they improvise throughout the production.

Outside broadcast (OB) Also known as a *remote production*, an OB takes place outside of the studio.

Pace The rate of emotional progression. A slow pace suggests dignity, solemnity, contemplation, and deep emotion; a fast pace conveys energy, excitement, confusion, and brashness.

PAL (Phase-alternating line) The color television system widely used in Europe and throughout the world. It was derived from the NTSC system but avoids the hue shift caused by phase errors in the transmission path by reversing the phase of the reference color burst on alternate lines. It has 625 lines of resolution.

Pan head (tripod head) Enables the camera to tilt and pan smoothly. Variable friction controls (drag) steady these movements. The head can also be locked off in a fixed position. Tilt balance adjustments position the camera horizontally to assist in balancing the camera on the mount.

Pan shot When the camera pivots to the left or right with the camera pivoting on a camera mount.

Patch panel/jackfield Rows of sockets to which the inputs and outputs of a variety of audio units are permanently wired. Units may be interconnected with a series of plugged cables (patch cords).

Photographic lighting See *Three-point lighting*.

Pickup shot If an error is made during the shooting of a scene, this is created by changing the camera angle (or shot size) and retaking the action from just before the error was made.

Planned production method Organizes and builds a program in carefully arranged steps.

Plasma A high-quality, thin, flat-panel screen that can be viewed from a wide angle.

Point-of-view (POV) camera These small, sometimes robotic cameras can be placed in positions that give the audience a unique viewpoint.

Postproduction Editing, additional treatment, and duplication of the project.

Preamplifier An amplifier used to adjust the strength of audio from one or more audio sources to a standard level (intensity). It may include source switching and basic filtering.

Preliminary script/writer's script Initial submitted full-page script (dialogue and action) before script editing.

Preview monitor This video monitor, located in the control room's monitor wall, is used by the director to preview video before it goes on air.

Prime lens (primary lens) A fixed coverage, field of view, or focal length.

Program monitor (on-air monitor) Shows the actual program that is being broadcast or recorded.

Progressive scanning This sequential scanning system uses an electron beam that scans or paints all lines at once, displaying the total picture.

Prosumer equipment Sometimes known as *industrial equipment*; a little heavier-duty, sometimes employs a few professional features (such as interchangeable lenses on a camera), but may still have many of the automatic features that are included on the consumer equipment.

Public domain Music and lyrics published in 1922 or earlier are in the public domain in the United States. No one can claim ownership of a song in the public domain; therefore, public domain songs may be used by anyone. Sound recordings, however, are protected separately from musical compositions. There are no sound recordings in the public domain in the United States.

Quick-release mount Attached to the camera and fits into a corresponding recessed plate attached to the tripod/pan head. Allows the camera operator to quickly remove or attach the camera to the camera mount.

Reflected light metering The light bouncing off of the subject. A handheld light meter or a camera's built-in meter is used to measure by aiming directly at the subject.

Rehearsal script Usually includes the cast/character list, production team details, and rehearsal arrangements. There is generally a synopsis of the plot or story line, location, time of day, stage/location instructions, the action, dialogue, effects cues, and audio instructions.

Remote survey (recce) A preliminary visit to a shooting location.

Remote truck (OB van) A mobile television control room that is used when away from the studio.

Reverberation Device for increasing or adjusting the amount of echo accompanying a sound.

RGB (red, green, blue) The three primary colors used in video processing.

Roll The movement of text up or down the video screen.

Running order The order that the scenes or shots will be shown in the final project, which may differ greatly from the shooting order.

Safe title area The center 80 percent of the screen where it is safe to place graphics.

Sampling rate Measures how often the values of the analog video signal are converted into a digital code.

Saturation The chroma, purity, and intensity. It effects its richness or paleness.

Scene Covers a complete continuous action sequence.

Scoop A simple floodlight. It is inexpensive, usually not adjustable, lightweight; does not have a sharp outline.

SECAM (*Séquentiel couleur à mémoire*, Sequential Color with Memory) Video system used by France and many countries of the former USSR.

Shooting order The order that the scenes or shots may be shot using the video camera, which may differ greatly from the running order.

Shot sheet (shot card) A list, created by the director, of each shot needed from each individual camera operator. The shots are listed in order so that the camera operator can move from shot to shot with little direction from the director.

Show format The show format lists the items or program segments in a show, in the order they are to be shot. It may show durations, who is participating, or shot numbers.

Single-camera production One camera is used to shoot the entire segment or show.

Site survey A meeting of the key production personnel at the proposed shooting location. A survey allows them to make sure that the location will meet their production needs.

Situation comedy (sitcom) A television program that has a story line plot (situation) and is a humerous drama.

Shotgun microphone A highly directional microphone used to pick up sound from a distance.

Soft light Provides a large amount of diffused light.

Spotlight A highly directional light.

Stage props The furniture on the set: news desks, chairs, couches, tables.

Standard-definition television (SDTV, SD) Standard definition signifies television formats that have 480–576 lines.

Standby Alerting the talent to stand by for a cue.

Stereo sound Uses two audio tracks to create an illusion of space and dimension.

Stick mic See *Handheld microphone*.

Storyboard A series of rough sketches that help visualize and organize your camera treatment.

Straight makeup A basic compensatory makeup treatment, affecting the talent's appearance to a minimum extent.

Stretch Telling the talent to go more slowly (meaning that there is time to spare).

Studio Indoor locations designed to handle a variety of productions, with a wide-open space equipped with lights, sound control, and protection from the impact of weather.

Studio plan The basis for much of the organization, showing the studio's permanent staging area with such features and facilities as exits, technical supplies, cycloramas, and service and storage areas.

Subjective camera See *Point-of-view (POV) camera*.

Subtitles Identify people and places.

Super-cardioid microphone A super-cardioid (or highly directional) pickup pattern that is used for extremely selective pickup, to avoid environmental noises, or for distance sources.

Surround sound Instead of the one channel for mono or the two channels for stereo, 5.1 surround has six discrete (distinct, individual) channels. Can provide a sense of envelopment when mixed correctly.

Switcher (vision mixer) A device used to switch between video inputs (cameras, graphics, video players).

Symbolism (image composition) Using images that have hidden or representational meaning to the viewer.

Synopsis An outline of the characters, action, and plot; helps everyone involved in the production understand what is going on.

Take See *Cut*.

Tally light A light usually found on the front of the camera and in the viewfinder. The front tally light is to let the talent know that the camera is recording. The back tally light lets the camera operator know when his or her camera has been chosen to be recorded by the director.

Teaser Showing dramatic, provocative, intriguing highlights from the production before the opening titles. The goal is to convince the audience to stay for the entire production.

Telephoto lens A narrow-angle lens that is used to give a magnified view of the scene, making it appear closer. The lens magnifies the scene.

Teleprompter A device that projects computer-generated text on a piece of reflective glass over the lens of the camera. It is designed to allow talent to read a script while looking directly at the camera.

Television receivers Monitors that include a tuner so that they can display broadcast programs with their accompanying sound.

Three-point lighting A lighting technique that utilizes three lights (key, fill, and back lights) to illuminate the subject.

Tightening a shot Zooming the lens in a little bit.

Tilt balance Adjustments located on the pan head of a tripod to position the camera horizontally and assist in balancing the camera on the mount.

Tilt shot The camera moves up or down, pivoting on a camera mount.

Time-base corrector (TBC) Equipment that provides automatic compensation for synchronizing inaccuracies on replay or imperfect sync pulses from mobile cameras.

Time code (TC) A continuous time-signal throughout the tape, showing the precise moment of recording.

Timeline Includes multiple tracks of video, audio, and graphics in a nonlinear editing system.

Triangle lighting See *Three-point lighting*.

Trimming Cutting frames off of a shot to make it shorter.

Tripod A camera mount that is a three-legged stand with independently extendable legs.

Tripod arms (pan bars) These handles attach to the pan head on a tripod or other camera mount to accurately pan, tilt, and control the camera.

Truck (crab, track) The truck, trucking, or tracking shot is when the camera and mount move sideways (left or right) with the subject.

Vectorscope An oscilloscope that is used to check the color accuracy of each part of the video system (cameras, switcher, recorder). Incorrect adjustments can create serious problems with the color quality. Ideally, the color responses of all equipment should match. Color bars are usually recorded at the beginning of each videotape to check color accuracy.

Video gain The amplification of the camera's video signal, usually resulting in some video noise.

Videotape Tape has been the traditional means of recording video images. However, it is slowly being replaced by hard drives and flash cards.

Viewfinder Monitors the camera's picture; allows the camera operator to focus, zoom, and frame the image.

Virtual set Set that uses a blue or green seamless background, chroma-keying the computer-generated set into the scene. Most virtual sets employ sophisticated tracking software that monitors the camera's movements so that as the cameras zoom, tilt, pan, or move in any other way, the background moves in a corresponding way.

Voiceover (VO) Commentary over video.

Waveform monitor An oscilloscope that is designed to monitor the video signal.

White balance The process of calibrating a camera so that the light source will be reproduced accurately as white; the most common technique of color-balancing a camera.

Wide-angle lens Shows us a greater area of the scene than is normal. The subject looks unusually distant.

Wide shot (WS) See *Long shot (LS or wide-angle shot)*.

Wild track General background noise.

Wild track interviews A wild track interview usually means that while images are being shown of a person doing something (sawing wood, for example), the voice of the person shown in the images is heard being interviewed, like a voiceover.

Wipe A special effect transition between two images. Usually shows a change of time, location, or subject. The wipe adds a bit of novelty to the transition but can easily be overused.

XCU Extreme close-up.

XLS Extreme long shot.

Zebra An indicator included on some video cameras in the viewfinder. Allows camera operators to evaluate the exposure of the image in the viewfinder by showing all over-exposed segments of the scene with stripes.

Zone focus Camera operators are focused on a portion of the scene. When the subject comes into that area, the camera has been prefocused to make sure that the action is sharp.

Zoom lens A lens that has a variable focal length.

383

396

Also by Jim Owens:

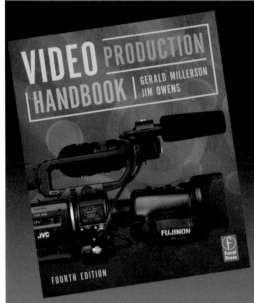

Video Production Handbook, Fourth Edition

The **Video Production Handbook** shows the full production process, from inception of idea to final distribution. The book focuses especially on why each step occurs as it does and provides guidance in choosing the simplest methods of creating the shots your students want in their video projects.

Concentrating on the techniques and concepts behind the latest equipment, this book demonstrates the fundamental principles needed to create good video content on any kind of budget.

Television Sports Production, Fourth Edition

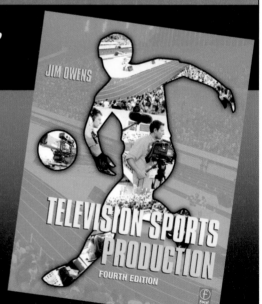

Television Sports Production walks you through the planning, set-up, directing, announcing, and editing involved with producing a sports event. Detailed descriptions of mobile units/OB vans, cameras, audio equipment and lighting requirements enable you to produce live or taped coverage of sporting events like an expert.

Available from www.focalpress.com